# Republics, Kingdoms, Towns and Cities
# in
# Ancient India

## Reconstructing Indian History & Culture
(ISSN 0971-3824)

1. Society in Ancient India by Sures Chandra Banerji (ISBN 81-246-0000-7)
2. Political Thought in Ancient India by G.P. Singh (ISBN 81-246-0001-5)
3. Early Indian Historical Tradition and Archaeology by G.P. Singh (ISBN 81-246-0005-8)
4. Vasantotsava: The Spring Festivals of India by Leona M. Anderson (ISBN 81-246-0011-2)
5. Ecological Readings in the Veda by M. Vannucci (ISBN 81-246-0009-0)
6. Vṛndāvana in Vaiṣṇava Literature by Maura Corcoran (ISBN 81-246-0024-4)
7. Social History of the Tamils (1707-1947) by P. Subramanian (ISBN 81-246-0045-7)
8. Ancient Indian Coinage by Rekha Jain (ISBN 81-246-0051-1)
9. Buddhism and Socio-Economic Life of Eastern India by Bimal Chandra Mohapatra (ISBN 81-246-0055-4)
10. Chandragupta Maurya by P.L. Bhargava (ISBN 81-246-0056-2)
11. Mṛtyu: Concept of Death in Indian Traditions by Gian Giuseppe Filippi (ISBN 81-246-0072-4)
12. Yama: The Glorious Lord of the Other World by Kusum P. Merh (ISBN 81-246-0066-X)
13. Sacred Complex of Ujjain by D.K Samanta (ISBN 81-246-0078-3)
14. Vedic View of the Earth by S.R.N. Murthy (ISBN 81-246-0091-0)
15. Society in the Atharvaveda by B.S. Kharade (ISBN 81-246-0093-7)
16. Orissan History, Culture and Archaeology by S. Pradhan (ISBN 81-246-0117-8)
17. Education in Ancient India by Mitali Chatterjee (ISBN 81-246-0113-5)
18. Surā: the Liquor and the Vedic Sacrifice by M.B. Kolhatkar (ISBN 81-246-0114-3)
19. Human Ecology in the Vedas by Marta Vannucci (ISBN 81-246-0115-1)
20. Governance in Ancient India by Anup Chandra Pandey (ISBN 81-246-0135-6)
21. The Cultural Glory of Ancient India: A Literary Overview by Sures Chandra Banerji (ISBN 81-246-0137-2)
22. Kauṭilya's Arthaśāstra in the light of Modern Science & Technology; by Sunil Sen Sarma (ISBN 81-246-0187-9)
23. History of Jainism — with Special Reference to Mathura by V.K. Sharma (ISBN 81-246-0195-X)
24. Cultural Tourism in India: Museums, Monuments & Arts — Theory and Practice; by S. P. Gupta; Krishna Lal; Mahua Bhattacharyya (ISBN 81-246-0215-8)
25. Ancient Indian Historiography — Sources and Interpretations by G.P. Singh (ISBN 81-246-0228-X)

Reconstructing Indian History & Culture, no. 26

# Republics, Kingdoms, Towns and Cities in Ancient India

*by*

**G.P. Singh**

**D.K. Printworld (P) Ltd.**
New Delhi

**Cataloging in Publication Data — DK**

**Singh, G. P. (Girish Prasad), 1942 –**

Republics, kingdoms, towns and cities in ancient India.
(Reconstructing Indian history & culture, no. 26).
Includes bibliographical references (p. )
Includes index.

1. Cities and towns, Ancient — India. 2. India — Politics and government — To 997. 3. India — History — To 324 BC 4. India — History — 324 BC-1000 AD
I. Title. II. Series : Reconstructing Indian history & culture, no. 26.

**ISBN 81-246-0237-9**

*First published in India in 2003*



**D. K. Printworld (P) Ltd.**
*Regd. office* : '*Sri Kunj*', F-52, Bali Nagar
New Delhi - 110 015
*Phones* : (011) 2545-3975; 2546-6019
*Fax* : (011) 2546-5926
*E-mail*: dkprintworld@vsnl.net
*Web*: www.dkprint.com

# Preface

This volume contains the histories of republics, kingdoms, towns and cities in ancient India.

The present work, I hope, will be of some use to students and scholars and historians and archaeologists. The work will be useful especially for those who intend to take up a fresh study of urban history of ancient India.

I am grateful to all those scholars whose works I have utilized in the volume.

I take the opportunity of expressing my grateful thanks to Shri S.K. Mittal, D.K. Printworld (P) Ltd., New Delhi, for all the sincerity and seriousness he has shown in the publication of this volume as well as my other works.

The present writer craves the indulgence of readers for all omission and commission and mistakes and misprints which may be discernible to their eyes.

**G.P. Singh**

# Contents

# Abbreviations

| | |
|---|---|
| *AAR* | *Annals and Antiquities of Rajasthan.* |
| *ABORI* | *Annals of the Bhandarkar Oriental Resarch Institute,* Poona. |
| *Agn.* | *Agni Purāṇa.* |
| *AI* | *Ancient India — Bulletin of the Archaeological Survey of India,* New Delhi. |
| *AICL* | *Ancient India as Described in Classical Literature*, by J.W. McCrindle. |
| *AIHA* | *Aspects of Indian History and Archaeology.* |
| *AIHT* | *Ancient Indian Historical Tradition.* |
| *AII* | *Ancient India Its Invasion by Alexander the Great*, by J.W. McCrindle. |
| *AIIC* | *Ancient India and Indian Civilization,* by P. Masson-Oursel & C. |
| *AIKK* | *Ancient India as Described by Ktesias the Knidian*, by J.W. McCrindle. |
| *AIMA* | *Ancient India as Described by Megasthenes and Arrian*, by J.W. McCrindle. |
| *AIN* | *Ancient Indian Numismatics.* |
| *AIT* | *Ancient India as Described by Ptolemy*, by J.W. McCrindle. |
| *Ait.Br.* | *Aitareya Brāhmaṇa.* |
| AN | *Aṅguttara Nikāya.* |
| *Anab.* | *Anabasis (History of Alexander's Expedition)*, by Arrian. |
| *An.Ind Tr.* | *Ancient Indian Tribes.* |
| *Antiquity* | *A Quarterly Review of Archaeology,* Cambridge, England. |
| *APP* | *Ancient Peoples of the Punjab* (Eng. trans of two articles of J. |

| | |
|---|---|
| | Przyluski, originally pub in French in the *Journal Asiatique*, Paris, in 1926 and 1929), by C. Sen. |
| *Ar.Ant.* | *Ariana Antiqua,* by H.H. Wilson. |
| *ARNWI* | *Archaeological Reconnaissances in North-Western India and South-Eastern Iran,* by M.A. Stein. |
| *Arth.* | *Arthaśāstra of Kauṭilya.* |
| ASB | Asiatic Society of Bengal, Calcutta. |
| *ASIAR* | *Archaeological Survey of India, Annual Reports.* |
| *A.S.Res.* | *Asiatic Researches (Comprising History and Antiquities, the Arts, Sciences, Ethnology and Literature of Asia).* |
| *ASWI* (or *Arch.SWI*) | *Archaeological Survey of Western India, Reports.* |
| *AV* | *Atharvaveda.* |
| *BGP* | Bhāratiya Jñānapīṭha, Kāśī. |
| *Bhāg.* | *Bhāgavata Purāṇa.* |
| *Bh.Sāv.* (or *Bh.Sv*) | *Bhārata Sāvitri (An in-depth historical study of the Mahābhārata),* by V.S. Agrawala. |
| *Bhv.* | *Bhaviṣya Purāṇa.* |
| *BI* | *Buddhist India.* |
| *Bib.Hist* | *Bibliotheca Historica* (*Universal History*) of Diodoros Siculus |
| *BIS* | *Bibliotheca Indica Series* (a Collection of Oriental Works), Asiatic Society, Calcutta. |
| *Bmd.* | *Brahmāṇḍa Purāṇa.* |
| *Bmv.* | *Brahmavaivartta Purāṇa.* |
| BORI | Bhandarkar Oriental Research Institute, Poona. |
| *Br.* (or *Brh*) | *Brahma Purāṇa.* |
| *Br. Sam* | *Bṛhat (Vārāhī) Saṁhitā.* |
| *BRWW* | *Buddhist Records of the Western World* (Eng. trans of the Chinese *Si-Yu-Ki* of Hiuen Tsang), by Samuel Beal. |

| | |
|---|---|
| *BSOAS* | *Bulletin of the School of Oriental and African Studies,* London. |
| *CAGI* | Cunningham's *Ancient Geography of India*. |
| *CAI* | *Classical Accounts of India* (a compilation of the English translations of the Early Greek and Roman Writers' accounts of India), by R.C. Majumdar. |
| *CASR* | Cunningham's *Archaeological Survey of India, Reports.* |
| *CCBM* | *Catalogue of the Indian Coins in the British Museum, Ancient India,* by John Allan. |
| *CCGBM* (*or CCBMG*) | *Catalogue of the Coins of Greek and Scythic Kings of Bactria and India in the British Museum*, by Gardner. |
| *CCIM* | *Catalogue of the Coins in the Indian Museum,* Calcutta, *Coins of Ancient India*, vol. 1, by V.A. Smith. |
| *CCPM* | *Catalogue of the Coins in the Punjab Museum*, I, by R.B. Whitehead. |
| CHI | *Cambridge History of India*, vol. I, *Ancient India*. |
| *CII* (or *Corp. Ins. Ind.*) | *Corpus Inscriptionum Indicarum.* |
| *CISSK* (*or CSSK*) | *Coins of Indo-Scythians, (Śakas) and Kuṣāṇas*, by A. Cunningham. |
| *CMI* | *Coins of Medieval India,* by A. Cunningham. |
| *CNES* | *Commerce and Navigation of the Erythraean Sea*, by J.W. McCrindle. |
| *Co.An.Ind.* | *Coins of Ancient India from the Earliest times down to the Seventh Century* AD, by A. Cunningham. |
| *Com.Hist.Ind.* | *Comprehensive History of India*. |
| *DIP* | *Dipavaṁsa* (An Ancient Buddhist Historical Record). |
| *DN* | *Dīgha Nikāya.* |
| *DPI* (or *Pent. Ind*) | *De Pentapotamia Indica* or *Pentapotamia Indica* (Ancient Geography and History of North-Western India based on Greek and Latin Sources), by C. Lassen. |
| *DPPN* | *Dictionary of Pālī Proper Names*, by G.P. Malalasekera. |
| *EAI* | *Ethnography of Ancient India*. |

| | |
|---|---|
| *EB* (or *En. Br.*) | *Encyclopaedia Britannica.* |
| *EHI* | *Early History of India*, by V.A. Smith, rev. by S.M. Edwards, 4th edn. |
| *EHIDS* | *Early Hindu India : A Dynastic Study.* |
| *EIA* | *Essays on Indian Antiquities.* |
| *EIC* | *Encyclopaedia of Indian Culture.* |
| *EIHTA* | *Early Indian Historical Tradition and Archaeology.* |
| *EIP* | *Early India and Pakistan to Ashoka,* by M. Wheeler. |
| *EP.Ind.* | *Epigraphia Indica,* Delhi. |
| *ESAI* | *Ethnic Settlements in Ancient India,* by S.B. Choudhuri. |
| *E'tude.* | *E'tude Sur la Geographie Grecque et Latine de l'Inde* (Geography of India as Derived from the Greek and Latin Sources), by M.V. de St. Martin. |
| fn. | footnote. |
| *GBI* | *Greeks in Bactria and India,* by W.W. Tarn. |
| *GDAMI* | *Geographical Dictionary of Ancient and Medieval India,* by N.L. Dey. |
| *GDEP* | *A Critical Study of the Geographical Data in the Early Pirāṇas.* |
| *GEB* | *Geography of Early Buddhism*, by B.C. Law. |
| *GEI* | *Great Epic of India.* |
| *GEM* (or *GESM*) | *Geographical & Economic Studies in the Mahābhārata, Upāyana Parva*, by Motichandara. |
| *Geographical Essays* | *Geographical Essays Relating to Ancient Geography of India, by* B. C. Law. |
| *Geog.Jour* | *Geographical Journal,* London. |
| *GNAII* | *Geographical Names in Ancient Indian Inscriptions* (up to AD 650). |
| *Grd.* (or *Gar.*) | *Garuḍa Purāṇa.* |
| *GSH* | *Geographical System of Herodotus.* |
| *GTCP* | *Glossary of the Tribes and Castes of the Punjab and North-West* |

| | |
|---|---|
| | *Frontier Province*, by H.A. Rose. |
| *HA* | *History of Antiquity*, trans. from the German of Max Duncker by E. Abbott. |
| *HAG* | *History of Ancient Geography Among the Greeks and Romans from the Earliest Ages till the Fall of the Roman Empire*, by E.H. Bunbury. |
| *HAI* | *History of Ancient India.* |
| *HASA* | *Historical Atlas of South Asia.* |
| *HDAI* | *Historical Disquisition Concerning Ancient India.* |
| *HGAI* | *Historical Geography of Ancient India,* by B.C. Law. |
| *HHK* | *Hindu History of Kashmir.* |
| *HIL* | *History of Indian Literature.* |
| *Hiouen Thsang.* | *Hiouen Thsang's Life and Travels,* trans by M. Julien with an Apendix by St. Martin. |
| *HISI* | *Historical Inscriptions of South India*, Madras University Historical Series, No. V, 1932. |
| *Hist. Alex.* | *History of Alexander the Great,* by Q. Curtius Rufus. |
| *Hist Eccles.* | *History Ecclesiastical.* |
| *Hist. Phil* | *Historiae Philippicae of Justin.* |
| *Historical Researches* | *Historical Researches into the Politics, Intercourse and Trade of the Principal Nations of Antiquity.* |
| HOS | Harvard Oriental Series. |
| *HPL* | *History of Pāli Literature*, by B.C. Law. |
| *HSL* | *History of Sanskrit Literature.* |
| *Hv.* | *Harivaṁśa Purāṇa.* |
| *IAR* | *Indian Archaeology — A Review*, Delhi. |
| *IC* | *Indian Culture — Journal of the Indian Resarch Institute*, Calcutta. |
| *IETBJ* | *India as Described in Early Texts of Buddhism and Jainism.* |
| *IGI* (or *Imp. Gaz. Ind*) | *Imperial Gazetteer of India.* |

| | |
|---|---|
| IHC | Indian History Congress. |
| *IHQ* | *Indian Historical Quarterly*, Calcutta, new rpt., Delhi. |
| *IHR* | *Indian Historical Review*. Journal of the Indian Council of Historical Research, Delhi. |
| *IIA* | *Invasion of India by Alexander the Great as Described* by Arrian, Q. Curtius, Diodoros, Plutarch and Justin, by J.W. McCrindle. |
| *INC* | *Indian Numismatic Chronicle,* Patna. |
| *Ind.Alt.* | *Indische Alterthumskunde* (A German work on the History and Antiquities of India), by C. Lassen. |
| *Ind. Ant.* | *Indian Antiquary* (*Journal of Oriental Research in Archaeology, History, Literature, Language, Folklor, etc.*), Bombay. |
| *Ind. Co.* | *Indian Coins.* |
| *Ind.Stud.* | *Indische Studien.* |
| *IP* | *India as Known to Pāṇini* (A Study of the Cultural Material in the *Aṣṭādhyāyī*), by V.S. Agarwala. |
| *IPPH* | *India Through the Ages : A Popular and Picturesque History of Hindustan.* |
| *Itin. Alex.* | *Itinerary of Alexander the Great,* by Julius Valerius. |
| *ITP* | *India in the time of Patañjali.* |
| *JA* | *Journal Asiatique*, Paris. |
| *JAOS* | *Journal of the American Oriental Society.* |
| *JAS* | *Journal of the Asiatic Society,* Calcutta. |
| *JASB* | *Journal of the Asiatic Society of Bengal,* Calcutta. |
| *Jāt.* | *Jātaka.* |
| *JBBRAS* | *Journal of the Bombay Branch of the Royal Asiatic Society,* Bombay. |
| *JBIAS* | *Journal of the Bhāratīya Itihāsa Adhyayan Saṁsthān*, Allahabad. |
| *JBORS* | *Journal of the Bihar and Orissa Research Society*, Patna. |
| *JGRI* | *Journal of the Ganganath Jha Research Institute,* Allahabad. |
| *JGRS* | *Journal of the Gujarat Research Society.* |
| *JHR* | *Journal of Historical Research*, Jaipur. |

| | |
|---|---|
| *JIH* | *Journal of Indian History*, Trivandrum. |
| *Jinist Studies* (or *JS*) | *Jinist Studies* by Otto Stem, ed. by Jin Vijaya Muni, Ahmedabad, 1948. |
| *JNSI* | *Journal of the Numismatic Society of India*, Vārāṇasī . |
| *JPASB* | *Journal and Proceedings of the Asiatic Society of Bengal,* Calcutta. |
| *JPTS* | *Journal of the Pāli Text Society,* London. |
| *JRAS* | *Journal of the Royal Asiatic Society of Great Britain and Ireland,* London. |
| *JRASB* | *Journal of the Royal Asiatic Society of Bengal*, Calcutta. |
| *JRASB(L)* | *Journal of the Royal Asiatic Society of Bengal, Letters,* Calcutta. |
| *JRGS* | *Journal of the Royal Geographical Society*, London. |
| *JUPHS* | *Journal of the UP Historical Society*, Lucknow. |
| *Kāl. Ko.* | *Kalidāsa-Kośa,* by S.C. Banerji. |
| *Km*. (or *Krm*) | *Kūrma Purāṇa*. |
| *LAIJC* | *Life in Ancient India as Depicted in the Jaina Canon and Commentaries.* |
| *Lg*. | *Liṅga Purāna.* |
| *Lif. Alex.* | *Life of Alexander* (as told by himself in his epistles or letters), by Plutarch. |
| *MAGK* | *Memoir on Maps Illustrating the Ancient Geography of Kashmir.* |
| *MAHA* | *Manual of Ancient History*: *The Constitutions, the Commerce and the Colonies of the States of Antiquity.* |
| *Mahā.* | *Mahāpurāṇa.* |
| *MAICL* | McCrindle's *Ancient India as Described in Classical Literature.* |
| *MAIMA* | McCrindle's *Ancient India as Described by Megasthenes and Arrian.* |
| *MAINW* | *Monumental Antiquities and Inscriptions of North-Western Provinces and Oudh.* |
| *MAIT* | McCrindle's *Ancient India as Described by Ptolemy.* |
| *Manu.* | *Manu-Smṛti.* |
| *MASI* | *Memoirs of the Archaeological Survey of India*, Calcutta. |

| | |
|---|---|
| Mass. | Massachusetts, USA. |
| *Mat* (or *Mts.*) | *Matsya Purāṇa.* |
| *Mbh.* | *Mahābhārata.* |
| *Mbh.Ko.* | *Mahābhārata Kośa* (*A Descriptive Index to the Names and Subjects in the Mahābhārata*), by R.K. Rai. |
| *MDJG* | Manikchand Digambara Jaina Granthamālā Series, Bombay. |
| *Mhv.* | *Mahāvaṁsa.* |
| *Mhv.Comm.* | *Mahāvaṁsa Commentary.* |
| *Mkd.* | *Mārkaṇḍeya Purāṇa.* |
| *MMH* | *Memoir of a Map of Hindoostan* (based on M. D'Anville's Maps of Asia and India published in 1751-52), by James Rennell. |
| *MN* | *Majjhima Nikāya.* |
| *MRI* | *Martial Races of India.* |
| *NAB* | *Notes on Afghanistan and part of Baluchistan*, by G.H. Raverty. |
| *Nat.Hist.* (or Hist. Nat.) | *Naturalis Historia* (*Natural History*) *or Historia Naturalis* (*History Natural*), by Pliny. |
| *Nu. Chr.* (or *N. Chr.*) | *Numismatic Chronicle.* |
| *OIB* | *Original Inhabitants of Bhāratavarṣa.* |
| OUP | Oxford University Press. |
| *PAHI* | *Prehistoric Ancient and Hindu India.* |
| *PAPDI* | *Pre-Aryan and Pre-Dravidian in India* (Eng. trans. of Original French articles by Sylvain Levi, Przyluski & c), by P.C. Bagchi. |
| *PASB* | *Proceedings of the Asiatic Society of Bengal,* Calcutta. |
| *PDKA* | *Purāṇa Text of the Dynasties of the Kali Age.* |
| *Pdm.* | *Padma Purāṇa.* |
| *Periplus* | *Periplus of the Erythraean Sea*, trans from the Greek and annotated by W.H. Schoff. |
| *PHAI* | *Political History of Ancient India*, by H.C. Raychaudhuri, 6th edn. |
| *PIHC* | *Proceedings of the Indian History Congress.* |

| | |
|---|---|
| *PIOC* | *Proceedings (or Transactions) of the International Oriental Congress.* |
| *PK* | *Paurāṇic Kośa*, by R.P. Sharma. |
| *PNEIHA* | *Proceedings of North-East India History Association.* |
| *POC* | *Proceedings of the All India Oriental Conference.* |
| *PPIP* | *Prehistory and Protohistory of India and Pakistan.* |
| PTS | Pāli Text Society, London. |
| *Purāṇa* | Half yearly Bulletin of the Purāṇa Department, All India Kāśīrāj Trust, Rāmnagar, Vārāṇasī. |
| *RANIT* | *Racial Affinities of Early North Indian Tribes.* |
| *RBK* | *Record of the Buddhist Kingdoms* (an account of Fa-hien's Travels, AD 399-414). |
| *RBR* | *Record of the Buddhist Religion as Practised in India and the Malaya Archipelago*, trans from the Chinese of I-tsing (AD 671-95) by J. Takakusu. |
| *RTGEA* | *Researches on Ptolemy's Geography of Eastern Asia.* |
| *R̥V* | *R̥gveda.* |
| *Śat. Br.* | *Śatapatha Brāhmaṇa.* |
| *SBA* | *Sacred Books of the Aryan Series,* Delhi. |
| *SBB* | *Secred Books of the Buddhists.* |
| *SBE* | *Secred Books of the East*, Oxford. |
| *SBLN* | *Sanskrit Buddhist Literature of Nepal,* by R.L. Mitra. |
| *SEHHW* | *Social and Economic History of the Hellenistic World.* |
| *SGAMI* | *Studies in the Geography of Ancient and Medieval India.* |
| *SHC* | *Studies in History and Culture* (Journal of the Post-Graduate Department of History, Berhampur University). |
| *SI* | *Select Inscriptions Bearing on Indian History and Civilization.* |
| *Skd.* | *Skanda Purāṇa.* |
| *SN* | *Saṁyutta Nikāya.* |
| *TAI* | *Tribes in Ancient India.* |

| | |
|---|---|
| *Tai. Aran.* | *Taittirīya Āraṇyaka.* |
| *Taitt. Saṁ* | *Taittiriya Saṁhitā.* |
| v | Verse. |
| *Vāl. Rām.* | *Vālmīki-Rāmāyaṇa.* |
| *Vāl. Rām.Ko.* | *Vālmīki-Rāmāyaṇa Kośa* (Descriptive Index to the Names and Subjects of *Rāmāyaṇa*), by R.K. Rai. |
| *VE* | Vikrama Era. |
| *VI* | *Vedic Index of Names and Subjects*, by A.A. Macdonell and A.B. Keith. |
| *Vmn.* | *Vāmana Purāṇa.* |
| *Vrh.* | *Varāha Purāṇa.* |
| *VS* | Vikrama Samvat. |
| *Vṣṇ* | *Viṣṇu Purāṇa.* |
| *Vṣṇ. Dh.* (or *VSh.Dh.*) | *Viṣṇudharmottara Mahāpurāṇa.* |
| vv. | verses. |
| *Vy* | *Vāyu Purāṇa.* |
| *YCTI* | *Yuan Chwang's Travels in India* (AD 629-45), by Thomas Watters. |

# Introduction

REPUBLICS, kingdoms, towns and cities form very important parts of ancient Indian history. In the present volume, an attempt has been made as far as possible to provide a comprehensive, systematic and graphic picture of the republics that flourished and declined during the period falling in between the epic age (the age of the *Mahābhārata*) and the fourth century AD, the kingdoms that existed in the age of the Buddha (sixth and fifth centuries BC), and the towns and cities that grew up and decayed in different parts of India between *c.* 1000 BC and AD 550.

The two prevailing forms of government in Ancient India were monarchy and republic. The latter in the true sense of the word emerged in post-Vedic times. Its history can be traced back to the epic age. The ardent desire of the tribal communities to have their own political organization based on the principle of self-government led to the formation of republics. A number of tribal republics came into existence and some of them continued to survive down to the fourth century AD.

One of the characteristic features of ancient Indian polity was the transition from monarchy to republic. The most vital factor for change from one form of government to the other was the transformation of the political system. Ancient Indian political system was vibrant because of its flexibility.

The earliest description of the republics can be found in the *Mahābhārata*. The period extending from the sixth century BC to the fourth century AD saw the rise and fall of various republics in various parts of India. The details of all the republics that existed in the times of the Buddha (*c.* 563-483 BC), Pāṇini (fifth century BC), Kauṭilya (fourth century BC), Alexander (*c.* 327-325 BC), the Mauryas (*c.* 321-184 BC), Śuṅgas (*c.* 184-72 BC) and Samudragupta (*c.* AD 335-75) have been provided in this volume on the basis of available evidences. All possible attempts have been made to harmonize all the available data about a particular republic of a particular time so as to present a clear and accurate picture of the subject. The literary and archaeological (epigraphic and numismatic) evidence have been found in many cases supplementary to each other. The details of the republics of north-west India (Afghanistan, the Punjab and Sindh) have been furnished on the combined testimony of Pāṇini, classical (Greek and Roman) writers and Archaeology. It is significant to note that Pāṇini, being a native of Gāndhāra region had first-hand knowledge of history and geography of greater part of north-western India. His *Aṣṭādhyāyī* is repository of information about the republics of this part of the country. A great many republics were in the flourishing state in his time. The Punjab and Sindh were the two important centres of republics in the times of Pāṇini and Alexander. The latter in the course of his invasion of north-west India personally met many republican communities and witnessed with his own eyes the functioning of their government. He presented an eye-witness account of the political system prevailing there in his time in his letters along with other details which was later utilized by Plutarch, one of the five historio-graphers of Alexander (the other four being Arrian, Curtius, Diodorus and Justin), for writing his biography. These five classical writers have provided very reliable accounts of the monarchies, and republics/oligarchies/democracies in north-west India in their respective works. The functioning of republics has been critically assessed, and the factors responsible for their decline and disappearance have been explained in detail.

The territorial expansion of the state, in fact, began from the sixth century BC onwards. With the expansion of its territory and the increase in its population the state became fairly extensive and large. There were sixteen such state in northern India in the age of the Buddha which include fourteen kingdoms and two republics. The details of all sixteen *mahājanapada*s have been provided in the volume. The history of their rise as territorial states has been dwelt upon at length. Of all the sixteen states, Magadha was the largest. The rise of kingdoms proved to be stumbling block in the way of the growth of republics. Both republics and kingdoms form parts of political history of ancient India.

The factors leading to urbanization, patterns of urban settlement, town-planning, and growth and decline of post-Harappan towns and cities in different parts of India have been dealt with within a wide canvas. There were two urban revolutions, one in the Indus Valley and other in the Gaṅgā Valley. The first half of the first millennium BC (PGW or Painted Grey Ware period) was the first phase in the history of second urbanization in the Gaṅgā Valley. The second half of the first millennium BC (NBPW or Northern Black Polished Ware period) was very important phase for the growth and development of towns and cities in the Gangetic Valley. An attempt has been made to correlate the literary evidence and archaeological data so as to present a cohesive picture of the subject. The period, first to third century AD, proved to be blooming one for the growth of towns and cities in different parts of India including the Gaṅgā Valley. The process of decay actually started from the early fourth century AD in most of the cases.

By the end of the fifth or sixth century AD most of the towns and cities had declined and decayed. However, some towns continued to exist further. Some towns were found in existence even in post-Gupta times.

Dvārakā was one of the largest city of ancient India about which we have both literary and archaeological evidence. The entire credit goes to Shri S.R. Rao, a distinguished marine archaeologist, for his archaeological rediscovery of this city. In the course of archaeological exploration, the seals were also discovered by him some of which are exactly similar to those discovered by me in the *Mahābhārata* and Purāṇas. Some of the seals described therein do not figure in his archaeological findings. The literary discovery of the seals of Dvārakā in the epic age constitutes a supplement to archaeological discovery by Shri Rao. The details of the subject have been provided highlighting the political significance and economic value of the seals used in Dvārakā city in the time of Lord Kṛṣṇa.

The details of the emergence, growth and decay of urban centres in north-west India in the pre- and post-Maurya period provided in the volume are primarily based on the information supplied by classical geographers and historians of pre- and post-Christian era. It is noteworthy that some big or developed villages and semi-urban areas also figure in the lists of towns and cities provided in the classics. The classical concept of a town or city was totally different from that of ours. The statements of classical writers are contradictory with regard to number of towns and cities in north-west India. The Greek historians in particular have exaggerated their statements in this regard just to magnify the exploits and glorify the achievements of Alexander. However, it is a fact to reckon with that Afghanistan, the Punjab and Sindh were studded with towns and cities many of which were conquered and destroyed in the course of military operation of Alexander. Some of them have passed into oblivion but some are still in existence. There are some remains and ruins of towns and cities which constitute the mute evidence of urban culture and past glory of north-west India. The classical accounts of the subject have been corroborated and supplemented wherever necessary and possible by non-classical sources. The facts brought to light will be of some help for those who wish to make a fresh historical disquisition into the history of urbanization in north-west India.

One can get some idea about the socio-economic, political, religious and cultural life of the people having settlements in towns, cities or urban centres. The study of towns and cities is important also from the point of view of having some idea about culture and civilization of India in ancient times.

# 1

# The Post-Vedic Republics

## Introductory Remarks

ANCIENT India had a very rich republican tradition. The Vedic age, no doubt, marked the beginning of this tradition. But the republics actually flourished in post-Vedic times. That is why they are generally regarded as the "post-Vedic institutions".[1] The political consciousness of the tribal commmunities to stand as a corporate body and to have self-government went a long way in the formation of republics. Most of the non-monarchical states can be placed under the category of either tribal republics or tribal oligarchies. The period extending from the age of the *Mahābhārata* to the fourth century AD saw the rise and fall of several republics in northern India.

It is undeniable that some scholars have already dealt with the subject partly or fully, but some republican communities are still shrouded in obscurity and they have not yet attracted their serious attention. Some mistakes in respect of identification of some republican or oligarchical tribes and determination of their locations are yet to be rectified. The different factors responsible for their disappearance have also not yet been properly analysed. We, therefore, find an ample scope to recast the subject in a correct historical perspective. The subject as a whole needs a fair treatment at our hands.

There were different types of republic. In some republican states, the supreme power was vested in certain privileged members of the political community representing the nobility or aristocracy. The sovereign power was vested not in the populace in general but in the aristocratic leaders who were, of course, numerous. The members of the aristocratic class were undoubtedly very powerful, but they always worked together for the welfare of the state paying due regard to the general will of the people. The chiefs or heads of the kṣatriya families bearing the title of the *rājā* or their descendants called

1. K.P. Jayaswal, *Hindu Polity*, Pt. I, p. 21.

*rājanyas* were generally vested with the highest power or authority. They constituted the ruling class and met together in the General or Central Assembly. Some states were governed by a body or class of nobles or members led by chiefs, kings or *rājās*. Such republics (as described above) may collectively be called either as aristocratic republics or aristocrartic oligarchies or aristocratic democracies or oligarchical republics. The line of difference between them is so thin that one can hardly be distinguished from the other. They are all interchangeable terms. They represent more or less the same political system. In the ancient Indian context, aristocracies, oligarchies or democracies may be, unhesitatingly, taken as republics. A.S. Altekar[2] also subscribes to the same view. However, a state which was governed by a small class or body may exclusively be placed under the category of an oligarchy. There were some states where the sovereignty was vested in the whole body of the citizens or whole community and their elected representatives, thus varying from the most exclusive oligarchy to a pure democracy. They had no king or monarch but some councillors. They were democratic or autonomous clans. It is significant to note that in the republican system of government the kings or rulers were generally elected by the people. However, as exception there were some hereditary kings particularly in north-western India. In fact, they were more chiefs than the kings or *rājās*. Some powerful independent tribes formed leagues or confederacies which did not last long for various reasons which need not be explained immediately here. We shall do it later. But it is worthwhile to note that the representatives of the confederate state jointly shared the political power.

After having made a thorough investigation into the subject as a whole we gather an impression that the internal organisation, constitutions and administrative procedures of the republican states were not uniform. The pattern of administration was, of course, different but the guiding principle was almost the same, i.e., the rule of many and not one.

The popular terms, *gaṇa* and *saṁgha*, appearing in some Sanskrit, Jain and Buddhist texts are two different manifestations of ancient Indian republics. The *Mahābhārata* furnishes us with valuable information in this regard. The disquisition in the text makes it clear that *gaṇa* stands for the whole body politic, the entire political community, or a large number of people who managed the affairs of the state.[3] The leaders of the *gaṇas* vested with power have also been referred to therein.[4] The *gaṇas* generally formed

2. *State and Government in Ancient India*, pp. 109, 111-12.
3. *Mbh*., Śānti Parva, 108, 8, 24.
4. *Ibid*., 108, 23, 25.

*saṁghas* or confederacies.[5] It is categorically stated that the safety of the *gaṇas* usually depended on a confederacy.[6]

The *Aṣṭādhyāyī* of Pāṇini (who flourished in the fifth century BC)[7] is repository of information about the republics. He has used *gaṇa* and *saṁgha* as synonymous words (*sūtra*, III, 3, 86)[8] for a republic. He speaks of the Yaudheyas as a *saṁgha*, "whereas they refer to themselves as a *gaṇa* on their coins, albeit in the post-Pāṇinian period".[9] Pāṇini not only refers to *gaṇa* or *saṁgha*, but also to *avayavas* (IV, 1, 71) or "member states of a Union, Leagues or confederacies as in the case of *Trigarta-ṣaṣṭha* (V, 3, 116)".[10] He has used the term *saṁgha* also in the sense of "a multitude of human beings". "*Saṁgha* was a term for a Nikāya, which is defined by Pāṇini as a corporate body where the distinction of upper and lower does not exist (III, 3, 42)".[11] Kātyāyana (ascribed to the fourth century BC), while commenting on Pāṇini's *sūtra* (IV, 1, 168), informs that the ruling kṣatriya tribes were governed by two-fold constitutions. Some were monarchies and others were *saṁghas* or republics. He takes *saṁgha* as a from of government distinct from *ekarāja*, where sovereignty was vested in one (*ekādhīna*) and not in the many as in the *saṁgha* (*gaṇādhīna*).[12] The republics functioned under the behest of oligarchic assemblies. According to Pāṇini, the heads of the kṣatriya families were called the *rājās* and their descendants the *rājanyas*, while the others were known as *rājans* (IV, 1, 137).[13] The *rājanyas* also represent the ruling class in a *gaṇa*. He specifically makes a mention of *rājanyas* (VI, 2, 34). Kātyāyana also speaks of *rājanyas* (IV, 1, 168, 3) more or less in the same sense. The privilege of political sovereignty was handed down in the families of the descendants of the kṣatriya kings from generation to generation. The *Kāśikā* (an authoritative commentary on the *Aṣṭādhyāyī*)[14] makes clear that the *rājanyas* or leaders of the kṣatriya families were consecrated to rulership. It appears that all the members

5. *Mbh.*, 108, 13-15.
6. *Ibid.*, 108, 32.
7. The date assigned to Pāṇini by different Indian and foreign scholars on the whole ranges from the seventh century BC to the fourth century BC. But in all probability he flourished in the middle of the fifth century BC or a hundred years before the rise of Mauryan imperialism.
8. V.S. Agrawala, *IP*, p. 428.
9. *Ibid.*
10. *Ibid.*, p. 484.
11. *Ibid.*, p. 428.
12. *Vārttika*, IV, I, 168, I cf. *ibid.*, pp. 427-28.
13. *IP*, p. 430.
14. See *Kāśikā* by Paṇḍita Vāmana and Jayāditya, ed. by Bāla Śāstrī (Vārāṇasī, 1898).

of a *saṁgha* were not entitled to exercise political power which was the privilege of only the governing class. The head of each kṣatriya family bearing the title *rājā* represented his *kula* in the *saṁgha* assembly. The republics consisted of other castes also besides the ruling kṣatriya caste, but the political sovereignty was in the hands of the dominant kṣatriya clan, and only in exceptional cases of others (brāhmaṇas and other castes). According to Patañjali (*Mahābhāṣya*, V, 1, 59),[15] the term *gaṇa* signified the form of government, and *saṁgha* the state. The latter term has been referred to also in the sense of a united body. The different systems of government that existed in ancient India thus find reflection in Pāṇini's work as well as in the commentaries on it.

From the Jain canon also it transpires that ancient Indian states had different forms of republican government. The state without a king (*arāyaṇi* or *vai-rajjāni*), the state ruled by a crown prince (*yuva-rāyaṇi*), states ruled by two rulers (*do-rajjāni*) or the state governed by the *gaṇa*s (*gaṇa-rāyāṇi*) find mention in the *Ācārāṅga-sūtra* (I, 3, 160; II, 3, 1, 10).[16]

In one of the Pāli canonical texts, the terms *saṁgha* and *gaṇa* have been used synonymously by citing the examples of the *vajji*s and *malla*s of the time of the Buddha.[17] Both the terms signified *par-excellence* the republics. In the *Jātaka*s, an assembly or association of the republican communities find expression in the form of a *gaṇa*.[18] There are some Sanskrit Buddhist texts which also contain relevant information in this regard. In one of the texts, the body of ministers has been referred to as the *gaṇa* of ministers.[19] There is a positive evidence to prove that in the time of the Buddha in northern India some states were under the rule of the *gaṇa*s and some under the rule of kings.[20]

Amarasiṁha (who flourished sometime between the fifth and sixth century AD) in his lexicon has distinguished between two types of the kṣatriya republic: in one republic the power was vested in *rājanyaka-gaṇa* or the descendants of the original founder-families enjoying the title of the *rājā* and in the other the power was vested in all the kṣatriya families called *rājaka-gaṇa* whether descended from the original founders or

15. See *Mahābhāṣya*, ed. F. Kielhorn, vol. II, p. 356.
16. See trans. H. Jacobi, SBE, XXII (Oxford, 1884).
17. *MN*, I, 4, 5, 35.
18. *Jāt.*, 1, 422; II, 45.
19. *Divyāvadāna*, ed. E.B. Cowell and R.A. Neil, pp. 404, 429.
20. *Avadānaśataka*, ed. J.S. Speyer, II, p. 103.

not.[21] The equality of the members of a republic in respect of their caste and family status has been highlighted in the *Mahābhārata*.[22]

The two terms, *gaṇa* and *saṁgha*, appear to have wide connotation. However, one cannot be blindly equated with the other. In fact, they denote two different types of the republican state with two different forms of government.[23] The state ruled by the *gaṇas* or a group of people was called *gaṇa-rājya*. The noted *gaṇa* states were that of the Licchavis, the Śākyas, the Mallas, the Yaudheyas and the Mālavas. The states which joined a confederation or *saṁgha* were called *saṁgha-rājya*. In fact, the *saṁgha* stands for confederation of the tribes as well as states. The league of Andhaka-Vṛṣṇīs of the *Mahābhārata* period, the confederation of the Licchavis of Vaiśālī and the Videhas of Mithilā of the Buddha's time, the union of Trigarta-Ṣaṣṭhas of Pāṇinian period and the confederacy of the Kṣudrakas and Mālavas of Alexandrian period are the noted examples of this category of republics. Some of the republican states jointed together and formed federations and confederations for better security, greater military strength and all-round prosperity. Sometimes they formed leagues for a short period to avert an imminent danger. But they maintained sovereignty of the constituent parts.

K.P. Jayaswal has justifiably taken *gaṇa-rājya* as a "government by assembly or Parliament".[24]

Ksuṭilya (*c*. 330-300 BC) has divided *saṁgha* into two classes : *rājaśabdopajīvin saṁghas* and *śastropajīvin saṁghas*. He has placed under the former class the Licchavikas, the Vṛjika, the Mallakas, the Madrakas, the Kukuras, the Kurus and the Pāñcālas whose elected leaders or chiefs were entitled to be called *rājās*. The *śastropajīvins* (who did not bear the title of the *rājā*) lived not only by the military profession but also by the profession of the trade and agriculture. It appears that both the military and trading classes shared the political power. He has put the Kāmbojas, the Surāṣṭras, the kṣatriyas, the Śreṇīs and others under the latter class of republics.[25] His classification of the *saṁghas* is based on the two different characteristics of the republic. Kauṭilya's *śastropajīvin saṁghas* corresponds exactly to the *āyudhajīvin saṁghas* of Pāṇini. The *śastropajīvins* of the

---

21. *Amarakoṣa* with 'Maṇiprabhā Hindi Commentary' by Commentater Pt. H.G. Śāstrī, II, 8, 3-4.
22. Śānti Parva, 108, 30.
23. See G.P. Singh, *Political Thought in Ancient India*, pp. 137, 145.
24. *Op. cit.*, p. 23.
25. *Arth.*, XI, I.

former is absolutely identical with *āyudhajīvins* of the latter (V, 3, 91).[26] These free or independent communities were the most famous for their military skill. The Punjab and the Indus Valley were the two noted centres of the *āyudhajīvin saṁghas*. Only the brāhmaṇas and kṣatriyas belonged to this *saṁgha* and not any other social class. Pāṇini mentions the brāhmaṇas and *rājanyas* of the Vāhika region (Punjab and Sindh) as members of the *āyudhajīvī saṁghas* (*sūtra*, V, 3, 114).[27] This region is said to have been "the cradle-land of martial tribes who cultivated military art as a way of life".[28] The military art constituted the vital part of the constitutions of the republican states falling under the category of *āyudhajīvī saṁghas*. Pāṇini includes in the list of the members of this *saṁghas* the Vṛka, Dāmanī, Trigarta-Ṣaṣṭha, Yaudheyas, Pārśava, etc. (*sūtras*, V, 3, 115-17).[29] The *Kāśikā* (on *sūtra*, V, 3, 114) had added the Kṣudrakas and the Mālavas to the list concerned. The *āyudhajīvī saṁghas* mentioned in the *gaṇa-pāṭha* include "Dāmanyādi, Pārśvādi and Yaudheyādi groups".[30] The Kathaians (Skt. Kaṭhas), Oxydrakai (Kṣudrakas), Malloi (Mālavas), Agalassians (Agra-Śreṇīs), Siboi (Śibi), Ossadioi (Yaudheyas) and Abastanoi (Ambaṣṭhas) of Punjab and Xathroi (kṣatriyas) and Brachmans (brāhmaṇas) of Sindh as mentioned by the Greek historians of Alexander (the details of which follow later) also fall under the *āyudhajīvī saṁghas*. They were well-equipped with arms and weapons. Some of them had well-organised armedforces, which faced Alexander and his army. The military training in their states was compulsory for both men and women. They took up the arms to defend their states against the external danger. The numerous *āyudhajīvī saṁghas* in north-west India continued to exist down to *c.* 300 BC.

The tradition recorded by Megasthenes in the fourth century BC reflects the truth that monarchies were replaced by demorcacies in various places.[31] A few instances may be cited here to prove it. The Videhas, the Mallas, the Śibis, the Kurus, the Pāñcālas and the Kāmbojas before adopting the republican form of government followed the monarchical constitution. The former two turned into republican communities in the sixth century BC, and the latter four towards the end of the fifth century BC or the beginning of the fourth century BC or after the Buddha and before Kauṭilya (i.e., sometime

26. IP, p. 484.
27. *Ibid.*, p. 445.
28. *Ibid.*
29. *Ibid.*, pp. 445-47.
30. *Ibid.*, pp. 448-53.
31. J.W. McCrindle, *AIMA*, 1st edn., pp. 38, 40.

between *c*. 483 and 430 BC). Their dynastic genealogies preseved in the epics, Purāṇas and Buddhist literature also bear witness to the fact that they were originally under the monarchical governments. The transition from monarchy to republic was a significant political development in ancient Indian History of the period falling in between the sixth century BC and the fourth century BC. Each state was free to choose its own form of government. Each was sovereign and independent so long as its freedom was respected by the neighbouring states. It is said that they followed both "Oligarchical and republican constitution".[32]

The subject offers a scape for comparative study of the republics of ancient India, on the one hand, and that of ancient Greece and Rome, on the other, to a certain extent. In the city-states of Athens and Sparta in Greece power was not vested in the whole body of the citizens but in a small class of full-fledged citizens. Their assemblies or councils like that of some ancient Indian republican states were also not represented by the whole population. The Roman Senate was also represented only by some privileged members of the society or a small aristocratic class like the aristocratic republics of ancient India. In both Greece and Rome, the franchise was confined to a small minority who governed a vast majority. None of them possessed full democratic character. They stand in sharp contrast to the well developed democracies of the modern type. Nevertheless, their city-states concerned are described as seats of democracies. Greece is even considered as the birth-place of democracy. In contradistinction to the monarchies, in all ancient republics the powers were after all not centralised in the hands of one individual but in a group of persons. This constitutes the common feature of all the republics. The decentralisation of powers constituted the back-bone of these republics.

The existence of republican states in different parts of northern and north-western India can be irrefutably proved by the evidences recorded in the Sanskrit, Jain, Buddhist and classical (Greek and Latin) literature. There are some epigraphic and numismatic evidence to confirm and supplement the literary account of the subject. Here we shall provide the details of the republics together with their internal functioning and causes of thier decline maintaining a chronological sequence, as far as possible.

---

32. See J.E. Schwartzberg (ed.), *HASA*, p. 169f.

One of the salient features of ancient Indian political system was transition from monarchy to republic. Romila Thapar (*A History of India*, I, p. 53) has also pointed out that "The two systems, republican and monarchical, were not mutually exclusive and a change from one to the other was not unheard of."

## Andhaka-Vṛṣṇī Saṁgha

We shall begin with one of the oldest republics popularly known as the Andhaka-Vṛṣṇī *saṁgha*, which belonged to the Yādava clan. There are copious references to this republic in ancient Indian literature. Some of the confederate clans also figure in the coins and inscriptions.

According to the Purāṇic evidenc, Andhaka and Vṛṣṇī were the offspiring of Sātvata.[33] Their descendants known as the Andhakas and Vṛṣṇīs, accroding to the *Mahābhārata*, formed a *saṁgha* or confederacy whose two other constituent units were the Kukuras (the descendants of Kukura in the one of Andhaka) and the Bhojas (who descended from Mahābhoja). They reposed their full confidence in the leadership of Śrī Kṛṣṇa.[34] This was more or less a type of federal republic. Its antiquity can be traced back to a period preceding the outbreak of the Great Bhārata battle. It did not flourish in the sixth or fifth century BC, as held by some scholars. Its high antiquity is beyond dispute. The original seat of this republic was Mathurā (Pāli = Uttara Madhurā), the capital of Śūrasena. The Andhaka-Vṛṣṇīs "had contracted a political marriage between their families".[35] The Purāṇas contain numerous allusions to them.[36] The "Andhaka-Vṛṣṇī *saṁgha*" also finds mention in Pāṇini's *Aṣṭādhyāyī* (IV, 1, 114; VI, 2, 34).[37] Kauṭilya has mentioned both the Vṛṣṇī *saṁgha*[38] and the Kukura's *saṁgha*[39] (i.e., a republican corporation). Some of the Jain texts refer to the rulers of "Andhagavahni" (Andhaka-Vṛṣṇī) families of Mathurā, and to Vasudeva (father of Kṛṣṇa), Akura (Akrūra), Uggasena (Ugrasena), etc.[40] The

---

33. *Vy.*, 96, 1-2; *Bmd*; III, 71, 1-2, *Br.*, 15, 30-31; *Mat.*, 44, 45-48; *Bhāg.*, IX, 24, 6-10; *Agn.*, 275, 24-28; *Pdm.*, V, 13, 31-32; *Lg.*, 1, 69, 1-2, *Vṣṇ.*, IV, 13, 1-6.

34. Śānti Parva, 82, 8-18, 25-27, 29; see also Sabhā Parva, 13, 3-9, 24-25, 29-34, 49-51, 58; 14, 4; 48, 15 (for only the Kukkuras), 42 (for Andhaka-Vṛṣṇī *gaṇa*); Ādi Parva, 1, 138; 210, 15-19; 211, 2; 212, 12; 213, 1, 23-29, 34-35, 52-53; Bhīṣma Parva, 10, 37-42 (only for the Kukkuras and Bhojas); Āraṇyaka Parva, 13, 1; Udyoga Parva, 28, 11-12; *Bh. Sav*, vol. 3, pp. 259-60, *Mbh. KO.*, p. 34.

    There were 98 leading *kula*s or families of the Andhaka-Vṛṣṇīs. There were 18 *kula*s of the Bhojas.

35. Jayaswal, *op.* cit., Pt. II, App. A, p. 355.

36. *Vy.* 96, 1-90, *Bmd.*, III, 71, 1-85; *Mat.*, 44, 45-85; *Vṣn.*, IV, 13, 1-10, 19-20, 35-70; *Br.*, 14, 14-25; 16, 9-49; *Bhāg.*, 1, 3, 23; 1, 8, 41; IX. 23, 30; IX, 24, 6-45; X, 90, 46, etc.

37. *IP*, pp. 430, 454; also Von Otto Bohtlingk, *Pāṇini's Grammatik* (Sanskrit text with German Trans), Leipzig, 1887.

38. *Arth.*, tr. V. Gairola, 1, 5, 3 (In the original text ed. by R. Sharma Sastry it is 1, 6, 3).

39. *Ibid.*, XI, I.

40. *Vasudevahiṇḍī* (Bhavanagar, 1930-31), pp. 77ff, 110f, 357f; *Uttarādhyayna Ṭikā*, 22, 1ff, 2, pp. 37, 39, 45; *Kalpasūtra Ṭikā*, 6 pp. 172-78 cf. J.C. Jain, *LAIJC*, pp. 448, 459-60.

"Andhakavenhu" (Andhaka-Vṛṣṇī), Vasudeva, Kānha (Kṛṣṇa), Vasudeva's descendants, Ankura (Akrura) of the Vṛṣṇī *kula* and others who ruled over Uttara-Madhurā and Dvāravatī or Dvārakā find mention in the Pāli texts.[41]

In the Andhaka-Vṛṣṇī *saṁgha* the descendants of Śvaphalaka, Caitraka, Śini and and Vāsudeva (all of the Vṛṣṇī clan) bore the title *rājanya*, whereas other members of the *saṁgha* did not have that status (Pāṇini, VI, 2, 34).[42] The *rājanyas* or leaders of families of the Andhakas and Vṛṣṇīs were elected to rule over the state.

In the Śānti Parva of the *Mahābhārata* Śrī Kṛṣṇa has been mentioned as *saṁgha-mukhya* (the president of the Andhaka-Vṛṣṇī *saṁgha*).[43] Śrī Kṛṣṇa on behalf of the Vṛṣṇīs and Ugrasena on behalf of the Andhakas were elected or nominated by all the members of the Assembly as Chiefs or Presidents of the *saṁgha* in their respective times. Patañjali also in his *Mahābhāṣya* (IV, I, 114) mentions Ugrasena, who belonged to the Andhaka family. Ahuka and Akrūra were the leaders of two different politcal parties in the *saṁgha-sabhā* (or Federal Assembly). They were a source of trouble. Each party tried to gain the upper hand in political matters.[44] In the Purāṇic genealogies of Sātvata's descendants Ahuka clearly figures as a progeny of Andhaka and Akrūra as that of Vṛṣṇī. But sometimes they are put in reverse order. In some of the Purāṇas Akrūra has been connected also with the Andhaka *kula*[45] which is source of confusion. It is said that "Ahuka on the side of the Vṛṣṇīs and Akrūra on the side of the Andhakas led" the members of their respective groups in the "Joint *saṁgha*" or "Federal Parliament".[46]

One of the chief features of the Andhaka-Vṛṣṇī constitution appears to be a full-fledged party sytem. According to the established practice, parties were usually named after their leaders. The members of the party (*varga*) of Vāsudeva or Kṛṣṇa and that of Akrūra were known as *vāsudeva-vargya* or *kṛṣṇa-vargya* and *akrūra-vargya* respectively. Patañjali (II, 295) refers to them as *vāsudeva-vargya*, *vāsudeva-vargina* and *akrūra-*

---

41. See *Jāt.*, IV (*Ghaṭa Jātaka*), pp. 79-89; B.C. Law *IETBJ*, pp. 99-103.

42. *IP*, p. 430.

43. Śānti Parva, 82, 25.

44. *Ibid.*, 82, 10.

45. For details see *Vy.*, 96, 1-60; *Vṣn.*, IV, 13, 1-6, 8-10, 19-20, 35-70, 108-61; IV, 14, 1-45; IV, 15, 11f; *Mat.*, 44, 45-85; 45, 1-34; 46, 1-29; *Bhāg.*, IX, 24, 6-45; *Br.*,14, 14-25; 15, 30-45; 16, 9-49, *Agn.*, 275, 24-49; *Bmd.*, III, 71, 1-44; *Pdm.*, V, 13, 31-117; *Lg.*, 1, 69, 1-45; *Hv.* (Harivaṁśa Parva), Ch. 34; *Krm.*, 1, 24, 35-70, *Gar.*, 1, 139, 36-55; *PK*, pp. 5, 113, 393, 476, 496 & 499; F.E. Pargiter, *AIHT*, pp. 103-7; G.P. Singh, *EIHTA*, 1994) pp. 60-61.

46. Jayaswal, *op. cit.*, p. 355.

*vargya*, *akrura-vargina*, which shows that "the followers of each leader were designated in accordance with their respeictive party leaders".[47] Kātyāyana (on Pāṇini, IV, 2, 104) also refers to these two parties. At one time there were two froups, one of Vāsudeva and other of Ugrasena and then of Vāsudeva and Akrūra. The information supplied by the *Kāśikā* (on Pāṇini)[48] in this regard is also of considerable importance. Whatever may be their party affiliation, it is almost certain that the Andhakas and the Vṛṣṇīs were divided into two different groups, and they were bitterly opposed to each other.

In the Andhaka-Vṛṣṇī republic the head of all the parties was known as the *parama vargya* (*Kāṣikā*, VI, 2, 131). Members of the parties sat in separate groups (*Kāśikā*, VIII, 1, 15), as we find in modern parliaments. The formation of groups under different leaders gave birth to group rivalry, which prived to be detrimental to the growth of this republic. Śrī Kṛṣṇa as the President of a republican state of the Andhakas, Vṛṣṇīs, etc., complains to Nārada that "he is not the master but the slave (of the Central Assembly), as he has to listen patiently to the bitter criticisms of the different parties. He is entitled only to the half of the executive powers".[49] The Head or President of the *saṁgha* was the highest executive officer, and all the members of the executive assisted him in the execution of policies and programmes. It was well-nigh impossible for Kṛṣṇa to oust the member-followers of the party of Ugrasena from the *saṁgha* for fear of disunion with a relative, etc.[50] It has been remarked that in the *Mahābhārata* period a new tendency grew up among the people to place themselves under the protection of individual leaders for better defence against external aggression.[51]

The group-rivalry, party-politics or party-functions proved to be major hurdles in the way of the smooth functioning of the Andhaka-Vṛṣṇī republic. There were several other impediments to the growth of this republic. The interference of various groups in the internal functioning of the republic and disunity and discord led to its gradual decline. The internal dissension was the root cause of its downfall. In the context of this republic it has been categorically stated in the Śānti Parva of the *Mahābhārata* that destruction of a *saṁgha* lies in disunion. Nārada exhorting Kṛṣṇa says that you are its leader. You

---

47. *IP*, p. 454.
48. See V.S. Agrawala, *ABORI*, vol. 37, Pts. 1-4, pp. 19ff.
49. Śānti Parva, 82, 5.
50. *Ibid.*, 82, 16-18.
51. U.N. Ghoshal, *A History of Indian Political Ideas*, Ch. 13, pp. 239-40.

act in the manner that it should not decline.[52] "Act in a way that destruction may not befall the relatives".[53] It has been repeatedly mentioned in the text concerned that the internal danger is more disastrous than the external one for the republics (whether *gaṇas* or *saṁghas*). The Andhaka-Vr̥ṣṇī *saṁgha* fell an easy prey to the internal dissensions.[54] In the game of power-politics the opposite parties oppress one another through spies, intrigues, military force, the policy of conciliation, subsidy and division, and by applying other means of decay, waste and dangers.[55]

The Andhakas, Vr̥ṣṇīs, Bhojas, Kukuras and other associate tribes conducted the republican experiment first at Mathurā in the north and then at Dvārakā in Gujarat in the west, where the capital was shifted from the former place in the pre-Bhārata war period itself. They had actually settled in Saurāṣṭra with Dvārakā as their headquarters. Here they somehow remained united for about thirty-six years after the war. Thereafter a fratricidal strife ensued in Prabhāsatīrtha, which led to their destruction but not extinction. Some sections of them continued to settle in Saurāṣṭra and some of the surviving population diffused in different parts of northern India.[56] Their life in the republican state under the presidentship of Kr̥ṣṇa was on the whole very prosperous.[57] But after his death in Prabhāsatīrtha the confederacy of the Yādavas naturally got dissolved. However, some of its constituent clans continued to survive and further carried on their age-old republican tradition.

The Vr̥ṣṇī *gaṇarājya* continued to flourish down to the first century BC, which can be confirmed by the numismatic evidence. An inscribed silver coin of the Vr̥ṣṇīs (now in the British Museum) was discovered by A. Cunningham. But he has not adduced any evidence of its find spot. However, the coin on its obverse side bears the legend in Brāhmī : *vr̥ṣṇī-*

---

52. Śānti Parva, 82, 25; also 108, 8, 13-14,
53. *Ibid.*, 82, 27.
54. *Ibid.*, 82, 13-15; 108, 28-29; also *Bh. Sāv.*, vol. 3, pp. 89-95.
55. *Ibid.*, 108, 12-13.
56. For details see *Mbh.* Maūsala Parva, 2, 1-20, 3, 1-22; 4, 33, 36, 41; Ch. 5; 6, 1-15; 7, 9-22; 8, 4-11, 32-47, 58-74; Āśvamedhika Parva. 84, 13-16; Āraṇyaka Parva, 16, 5-18; *Bh. Sāv.*, vol. I, pp. 143-44; vol. 3, pp. 221-23; *Mbh. ko*, p. 100; *Vy.*, 96, 46, 57-66, 83-93, 111-42, see up to 258; *Bmd.*, III, 61, 18-23, III, 71, 48, 62, 85; *Br.*, 14, 53-56; 17, 5ff; 195, 1-12; 196, 5-15; 210, 56-58; 212, 9; *Vṣn.*, IV, 1, 62-65, 91-94; IV, 13, 35-70; V, 23, 9-15; V, 24, 5-7; V, 37, 22-39, 42-63; V, 38, 34-35; *Bhāg.*, IX, 3, 1-2, 27-36; X, 50, 1-23, 34-57; X, 53, 5-22; X, 58, 12; X, 80, 8-12; XI, 30, 4-48; XI, 31, 23-25, 46-48, *Hv.* (Viṣṇu Parva), 34, 1-22; 35, 1-111; 36, 1-40; 39, 10-32; 56, 7-35; 58, 3-56, *Bmv.*, 107, 7-33, 80; *Pdm.*, VI, 200, 66, 246, 40-45; *PK*, pp. 121, 242, 393; G.P. Singh, *op. cit.* pp. 66-67.
57. *Mbh.*, Udyoga Parva, 28, 12.

*rājaññya* (*rājanya*)-*gaṇasya-tratarasya* (*trātasya*) and on its reverse in Kharoṣṭhi : *vṛṣṇī-rājañña-gaṇasya-tr.* . . . The symbol depicted on the reverse side stands for *sudarśana-chakra* (discus) or *rājanya* Kṛṣṇa.[58] The legneds of the coin are in the scripts of the first century BC. On the basis of this discovery we may affirm that the Vṛṣṇīs carried on their republican system of government in the form of a *gaṇa* till the end of the first century BC. And the power was vested in *rājanyas* or the leaders of their families. They probably lost their independence to the Śaka-Kṣatrapas after the first century AD.

## THE KUKURAS

They find mention in inscriptions of western India ascribed to a period extending from the first century BC to the second century AD.[59] They clearly figure in Jūnāgarh Rock Inscritption (Brāhmī script) of Rudradāman I (*c.* AD 150),[60] the Śaka ruler of Saurāṣṭra region (Kāṭhiāwāḍ in Gujarat). They might have lost their independence during his ascendancy or after *c.* AD 150.

Motichandra has identified the ancient Kukuras with Khokharain in Dasuya Tahsil in Hośiārpur district of the Punjab. He has located also the Vṛṣṇīs in the same district of the Punjab.[61] But in absence of any positive evidence we can neither confirm nor deny it. The Vṛṣṇīs might have settled in the eastern part of the Punjab between the upper courses of the Rāvī and the Vyāsa at much later period. In the Sabhā Parva (47, 19) of the *Mahābhārata*, the Vṛṣṇīs, of course, has been placed in the mountainous region of northern India.

## THE BHOJAS

They were originally associated with the Andhaka-Vṛṣṇī confederation in the peninsula of Kāṭhiāwaḍ in western India. They appear to have followed the republican constitution for a considerable period of time. The Bhojakas found in Cutch (or Kacch) are believed to be their descendants.[62]

---

58. *Co. An. Ind.*, p. 70, pl. IV; J. Allan, *CCBM*, pp. clvi-clvii, 281. See also *JRAS*, 1900, pp. 416, 420, 424; P.L. Gupta, *IHQ*, vol. XXVII, p. 203; *Bh. Sāv.*, vol. 3, pp. 259-60; R.C. Majmudar, *Corporate Life in Ancient India*, p. 119.
59. *Ep. Ind.*, vol. VIII, pp. 42f, 44, 52, 60.
60. D.C. Sircar, ed., *SI*, vol. I, Line-12, pp. 178-79.
61. *GESM*, p. 64.
62. *Ind. Ant.*, vol. LXII, pp. 127-29.

THE SURĀṢṬRAS

The *saṁgha-rājya* of the "Surāṣṭras" (in Kāṭhiāwāḍ) alluded to by Kauṭilya in his *Arthaśāstra* (XI, 1) also deserves our notice here. They revived the old republican tradition of the Andhaka-Vṛṣṇīs in the fourth century BC or in the time of Kauṭilya. They seem to have sruvived the Mauryan imperialism, as they figure in the inscriptions of Bala-Śrī or Balabhī (about 58 BC) and in Jūnāgarh Rock Inscriptions of Rudradāman I (second century AD).[63] The importance of their *saṁgha* began to decline after the dawn of the second century AD, and about the same time they probably lost heir independent political status.

## Republics in the Time of the Buddha (*c.* 563-483 BC)

The republics of the time of the Buddha (sixth and fifth centuries BC) deserve our special attention. In his time, both small and big republics belongning to the kṣaṭriya clans existed side by side with the monarchies, as evidenced by Buddhist sources (Pāli canon, chronicles and commentaries, and some Sanskrit Buddhist texts). There were a number of democratic or autonomous kṣatriya clans. They were located in eastern Uttar Pradesh, which corresponds to modern districts of Gorakhpur, Deoriā and Bastī, in the Tarāi or Nepal, to the east of the kingdoms of Kośala and Kauśāmbī, to the north of Magadha (or in north Bihar) and to the south of the Himālayas. A list of republican or oligrachical communities of his time with their respective capitals or headquarters as inserted in one of the Pāli canonical texts[64] is furnished below :

The Licchavis of Vesāli (Vaiśālī)
The Videhas of Mithilā } = conjointly called the Vajjians

The Śākyas of Kapilavatthu or Kapilavastu

The Koliyas of Rāmagāma

The Moriyas of Pipphalīvana

The Mallas of Kuśinārā

The Mallas of Pāvā

---

63. See *Ep. Ind.*, VIII, pp. 44, 60 (for both inscriptions) : *SI.* vol. I, Line-12, pp. 178-79 (only for Jūnāgarh inscription) : Also K.P. Jayaswal, *JBORS*, 1 (1914), 101.

64. *Mahāparinibbāna Suttaṁ* DN, ed. T.W. Rhys Davids and J.E. Carpenter, vol. II, pp. 166-67; *Mahāparinibbāna Suttaṁ*, Ch. VI, 21-27 cf. T.W. Rhys Davids and C.A.F. Rhys Davids (tr.), *The Dialogues of the Buddha*, Pt. 2, pp. 179-90, see also T.W. Rhys Davids, *BI*, p. 22.

The Kālāmas of Kesaputta

The Bulis of Allakappa and

The Bhaggas (Bhargas) of Suṁsumāragirinagara or Suṁsumāra Hill

THE LICCHAVIS OF VAIŚĀLĪ AND THE VIDEHAS OF MITHILĀ

The republic of the Licchavis[65] came into existence probably after the decline and fall of the Videhan monarchy in the latter half of the sixth century BC. They were the most powerful of the eight constituent clans (*aṭṭhakulas* or *aṭṭha-kulakā*[66]) of the Vṛji *saṁgha* or Vajjian confederacy. The other seven clans who jointed the confederacy included the Vajjīs themselves and the Videhans. The Licchavis, of course, constituted the largest group — a group of oligarchs. Their representatives, one each from 7,707 families entitled to the called the *rājā*, were vested with power to govern the state (which lay north of Pāṭaliputra, situated on the bank of the Ganges, and extended as far as the Nepal Hills) with its capital at Vaiśālī (identical with modern Basāḍh, about twenty miles north of Hājīpur in Bihar). The commentaries on the *Ekapaṇṇa Jātaka*[67] and the *Cullakāliṅga Jātaka*[68] speak of 7,707 Licchavi *rājās* of Vaiśālī. In fact, they were chiefs or heads of

65. Some scholars have attempted in vain to prove that the Licchavis were of foreign origin. V.A. Smith (*Ind. Ant.*, vol. XXXII, 1903, pp. 233-36) considers them Tibetans in origin. S.C. Vidhyābhūṣaṇa (*Ind. Ant.*, vol. XXXVII, 1908, pp. 78-80; 'Licchavi race of ancient India', *JASB*, vol. LXXI, pt. I, 1902, pp. 143ff) holds that they were originally Persians, and they migrated from their original home at Nisibi and settled in India and Tibet. Mr. Hodgson (*Collected Essays* by Hodgson, Trubner's edn., p. 17) takes them as a branch of the Scythian race. But neither of these theories will stand the test of a thorough critical examination. We do not have anything at our disposal to support their views. Taking their views as purely fanciful we can dispose them of. As a matter of fact, they belonged to the kṣatriya tribes of Indian origin. They are the original inhabitants of Vaiśālī in north Bihar. Early Indian tradition is unanimous in representing them as kṣatriyas. Manu (X, 22) places them under the category of Vrātya kṣatriyas. According to him, the Nicchivis (Licchavis), Mallas and others sprang from the *rājanya vrātya* (see also V.S. Agrawala, *India as described by Manu*, p. 18), That the Licchavis were kṣatriyas by origin can be proved by evidence recorded in a celebrated canonical Pāli work, the *Mahāparinibbāna Suttaṁ* of the *Dīgha Nikāya* (DN, vol. II, p. 164) and in the Tibetan text, the *Dulva* (quoted in W.W. Rockhill 's *The Life of the Buddha*, p. 97, note). This is also corroborated by the Jain account given in the *Kalpasūtra* (verse 128, p. 266; see trans. H. Jacobi; SBE, vol. XXII, Oxford, 1884, pp. xii, 227). In support of their kṣatriya origin see B.C. Law, 'The Licchavis in Ancient India' in his *Historical Gleanings*, pp. 66-68: Some *Kṣatriya tribes of ancient India*, p. 26f.

66. *Sumaṅgalavilāsinī* (*aṭṭhakathā* or commentary of the *Dīgha Nikāya*) ed. Rhys Davids, vol. II, p. 519.

67. *Jāt.*, I, p. 504.

68. *Jāt.*, III, p. 1.

their respective families and not the *rājās* or kings as such. They were chosen by the citizens of Vaiśālī. Their total population (residing within the city of Vaiśālī) was much larger which is stated to be double of 84,000 (i.e., 1,68,000 in number).[69] But only 7,707 families belonged to ruling class. There is a reference in the *Bhaddasāla Jātaka* to the Licchavi *gaṇa* or Licchavi rulers of *rājakula* or family of the *rājās* consecrated rulership by sprinkling sacred water on them (*vesāli-nagare gaṇa-rājakulānām abhiṣeka-maṅgala-pokkharaṇi*).[70] This practice was followed in accordance with an established tradition. In a commentary on the *Vinaya Piṭaka* we are told of the kings of the Licchavi *gaṇa*.[71] According to testimony of another Pāli commentary, the *rājās* ruled by turns.[72] A statement recorded in one of the Sanskrit Buddhist text that "amongst them (the Vaiśālians) the rule of having respect for the high, the middle ones, the oldest, the elders, is not observed; everyone considers himself to be the rājā; I am the rājā; I am the rājā and no one becomes a follower of another"[73] castes an aspersion on their constitutional tradition. Some other Sanskrit Buddhist texts also contain valuable information about them. In one of the texts there is an allusion to the *gaṇa*s of the Vaiśālikas (the inhabitants of Vaiśālī),[74] while in the other the Licchavis and the Vaiśālikas are mentioned as two different confederate clans.[75] Pāṇini mentions only the Vṛji clan (IV, 2, 131).[76] But Kauṭilya mentions both the Licchavikas and the Vṛjikas, and includes them in those *saṁgha*s whose chiefs or leaders bore the title *rājā*.[77] He, however, distinguishes one from the other. It appears that those who joined the group of the Licchavi and the Vṛji having allegiance to them were known as the Licchavikas and the Vṛjikas respectively. Patañjali has also given more or less the same interpretation of the two in his *Mahābhāṣya* (IV, 2, 45, V, 3, 52).

E.J. Rapson has correctly observed that "In the sixth century BC Vaiśālī was the seat

---

69. *Mahāvastu*, ed. E. Senart, vol. I, pp. 256, 271; *Jāt.*, I, p. 271.
70. *Jāt.*, IV, p. 148; see also *IP*, p. 431; V.S. Agrawala, 'Gaṇarājya ki Samanīti' in *Itihāsa-Darśana* (collection of his papers), ed. by P.K. Agrawala, p. 71.
71. *Sāmantapāsādikā*, eds. J. Takakusu and M. Nagai, vol. I, p. 212.
72. *Dhammapada-Aṭṭhakathā* (Hos, 30), p. 168.
73. *Lalitavistara*, ed. R.L. Mitra, Ch. III, p. 21.
74. *Bodhisattvāvadāna Kalpalatā*, 20th Pallava, p. 38.
75. *Divyāvadāna*, pp. 55-56, 136.
76. *IP*, pp. 61, 453.
77. *Arth.*, XI, I.

of a small but powerful aristocratic oligarchy of nobles belonging to the Licchavi clan which seems to have been a branch of the Vr̥ji tribe".[78] James Legge has also stated that ". . . the chiefs of Vaiśālī city had an oligarchical constitution".[79]

It is striking to note that 431 BC out of 42,000 citizens of Athens in Greece generally 2,000 or 3,000 citizens attended the Assembly. And certain resoultions were supposed to be taken by the "entire people", but in actual practice only 6,000 votes constituted a quorum. Likewise, out of the total population of the Licchavis of Vaiśālī, only 7,707 chiefs were vested with power to rule the state.

It is quite apparent that the governing body of the republic consisted of the heads of the families of the Licchavi clan. The administration of the state was largely carried on by the Licchavi *gaṇa* who elected their members. According to the *Aṭṭhakathā* (a commentary on the *Mahāparinibbāna Suttaṁ* by Buddhaghoṣa), when the citizens of Vaiśalī (Vaiśālians) came to their "House of Law" (Assembly or Parliament) the too sin was sounded.[80] Actually, by beat of drum the meeting was announced and everyone tried to attend the meeting and having done their work they dispersed at the same time. They used to hold frequent meetings. They discussed both political and non-political matters in the Assembly. Matters relating to various parts of the state were heard and discussed. It has been rightly pointed out that the Licchavis of Vaiśālī transacted the business on behalf of the whole people — Vajjians.[81] The Licchavi *gaṇa* in session used to appoint one of the distinguished members as the envoy (*mahattaka*) to deliver message on behalf of the Licchavis of Vaiśālī. According to the *Mahāparinibbāna Suttaṁ* of the *Dīgha Nikāya*, meetings were characterised by concord and harmony, and the opinions of the elders and not the vote of the majority decided the issue. This was the usual practice among the Licchavis during the golden period of their republican constitution.[82] The elders of the Licchavi clan are mentioned in the Pāli texts as *Mahallakas*.[83] The minutes of the meetings held in the Assembly Hall were recorded and kept by the four great kings.[84]

---

78. *Ancient India (from the earliest times to the first century* AD), p. 85.
79. *The Travels of Fa-Hien* or RBK, pp. 70-71.
80. Turnour, *JASB*, vol. VII (1838), pp. 994-95.
81. *Mahāvastu*, vol. 1, p. 254.
82. Rhys Davids, *The Dialogues of the Buddha*, pt. II, p. 80.
83. *Mahāparinibbāna Suttaṁ* (Pāli text with parallel Hindī trans.) ed. Sthavira G. Prajñānand, pp. 5-6; *DN*, vol. II, p. 74; *AN*, ed. R. Morris and E. Mardy, vol. IV, p. 19.
84. *The Dialogues of the Buddha*, p. 263.

The chief authority was no doubt exercised by a whole body of the Licchavi chiefs. But it can hardly be denied that the representatives of ther clans had also their say in the general administration of the state. Their's was a Federal Assembly (*saṁgha sabhā*) which was composed of the representatives of as many as eight allied clans. The Licchavi chiefs and the representatives of other seven confederate clans residing in Vaiśalī and its suburbs and neighbouring villages and towns met together in General Assembly at Vaiśālī and worked together. This constitutes the distinguishing feature of *saṁgha* polity. They had a common Assembly Hall in which all important matters relating to administration were discussed and decided.[85] The city of Vaiśalī was not only the capital of the Licchavi clan but also the metropolis of the entire confederacy.[86] It is said that "the union of the Vajjian states consisted of a confederation of chiefs".[87] Theirs was an oligarchical republic. It became more popularly known as the Licchavi republic. The corporate aspect of government was held to be the major strength of the republic.

The four top-ranking administrative officials called *rājā* (chief or president), *upa-rājā* (deputy chief or vice-president), *senāpati* (generalissimo) and *bhaṇḍāgārikā* (treasurer or the chancellor of the exchequer)[88] were members of the Executive of the State. They were elected by the ruling clans. According to the constitution of the Licchavis, the whole state was divided into a number of small administrative units for carrying on efficient administration. The head (*rājā*) of each unit in Buddhist period was probably a member of Supreme Assembly of the state. Each head of the administrative unit was assisted by other three officials or functionaries mentioned above. According to a Buddhist tradition, as quoted by Rockhill "the city of Vaiśālī proper consisted of three districts — the seats of three different clans, the Licchavis, the Videhas and the Vajjis".[89] We notice a striking resemblance between the constitution of the Licchavis of Vaiśālī and Cleisthenian Constitution of ancient Athens.

D.R. Bhandarkar's view that the Licchavi state was a confederation of 7,707 principalities each having full authority under its *rājā*, *upa-rājā*, etc.,[90] does not appear to be tenable.

---

85. Lae, *Some Kṣatriya Tribes of Ancient India*, Ch. V; *DPPN*, vol. II, p. 814.
86. *MN*, vol. II, p. 101.
87. Turnour, *JASB*, VII, p. 992, and note.
88. *Ibid.*, p. 993; *Jāt.*, I, p. 504.
89. *The Life of the Buddha*, p. 62.
90. Carmichael Lectures on Ancient History of India (Calcutta, 1918), p. 135; for further interpretation see Majumdar, *op. cit.*, pp. 53-54.

The Licchavi republic was noted for its unique judicial system. The judiciary formed very important part of state administration. Justice was administered carefully, promptly and imparitally. Law and order was well-maintained in the republican state. Every possible care was taken to safeguard the liberty of the people. The judicial procedure followed in the Licchavi state was extremely elaborate. Cases were tried by a hierarchy of judicial officials in seven successive courts, which are the following : 1. The court of Justices (*viniccaya mahāmāttas*) — a court of preliminary enquiry. It was also called a lower court. 2. The Court of Lawyers and Judges (*vohārikas* and *antokārikas* respectively). It was a court of appeal. 3. The High Court had its judges called *sūtra-dharas* (Doctors of law or rehearsers of the law-maxims). 4. A Council or Jury consisting of representatives of eight confederate clans (*aṭṭhakulakā*). Besides these four Courts, the three members of the executive of the State known as the General (*senāpati*), the Vice-Consul (*upa-rājā*) and the Consul (*rājā*) examined the case separately. The *rājā* was the highest Court of appeal. Any of these successive courts could acquit and accused person in case he was found innocent after trial. But when the accused was adjudged guilty unanimously by all the courts, the Consul or *rājā* finally awarded punishments according to the Book of precedents called *paveṇi potthaka* (which contained the particulars of the crimes and punishments awarded to the citizens found guilty). This was one of the sources of law. The *rājā* exercised his judicial authority with the aid of a law minister. Regular records were maintained of the cases decided by the courts.[91] A book of legal precedents and tables of the law both find mention in the *Jātakas*.[92] A system the Licchavis followed as regards the administration of justice has no parallel in the history of judicial administration.

From the time of Janaka until the appearance of the Buddha on the scene, Videha corresponding to ancient Tirabhukti or modern Tirhut (northern Bihar) with its capital at Mithilā (Janakapur, now within the border of Nepal, about 35 miles north-west from Vaiśālī) had been a kingdom. But sometime in the latter half of the sixth century BC it turned into a republic. In the Brāhmaṇical age the Videhans quite naturally were the followers of monarchical constitution but in the age of the Buddha they adopted the

---

91. For details see *Mahāparinibbāna Suttaṁ*, ed. Prajñānand, p. 5, fn, *Aṭṭhakathā*; Turnour, *ASB*, VII, pp. 993-95, *BI*, p. 22, *Sumaṅgalavilāsinī* (Sinhalese edn.) vol. I, p. 356 cf. Law, *Historical Gleanings*, p. 74, Law, *Kṣatriya Clans in Buddhist India*, pp. 120-21.

92. *Jāt.*, III, p. 292; V, p. 125.

republican form of government, which marks a radical transformation of their political system. The Videha clan, of course, had its seat at Mithilā. But a section of them might have settled at Vaiśālī and joined the confederate clans as a republican community. The Videhas attained eminence as one of the eight confederate clans included in the Vajjis. The Tibetan text *Dulva* bears and eloquent testimony to the settlement of some people of Videha at Vaiśālī. From Csoma de Koros' analysis of the work it appears that "Dumbu, a minister of the king of Videcha state escaped to Vaiśālī and settled there. He first declined to give his advice in the assembly of the people there, but afterwards rendered them great service by his prudent counsel. . . . He was made chief tribune there and after his death his second son. . . ."[93]

At the time of the Buddha the large adjoining realm of Videha with its capital at Mithilā was one of the eight constituent principalities of the Vajjian confederacy. And Mithilā became the seat of republic. In the lifetime of the Buddha and Mahāvīra the Licchavis of Vaiśālī had entered into a league with the Videhas of Mithilā and thereafter they were together called the Samvajji (United Vajjis). Patañjali in his *Mahābhāṣya* mentions the Vṛji (VI, 2, 42) and the Videhas (IV, 1, 168) separately "although in earlier times the two were politically knit together".[94] It is Kielhorn who has made it clear that "the Videhas are treated as a republic by Patañjali also. . . ."[95]

Csoma de Koros deriving his authority from the text *Dulva* has observed that "There is evidence sufficient to the fact of the existence of republics in India in early times, though but few distinct details are extant as to their exact forms of constitution. The republic of which most frequent mention is made is that of Vaiśālī, which is repeatedly referred to in the *Dulva*, and casual indications are afforded of the powers possessed by the citizens in the time of Sakya (Buddha)".[96]

The Licchavis had a separate Executive Council of nine members headed by a Chief called the *rājā*. The real power of administration in regard to foreign and military affairs seems to have been vested in this smaller body. The Federal Council consisted of eighteen members, nine Licchavis and nine Mallakis (Mallas), who were designated as *gaṇarājā*s. Each of the confederating state elected its respective members.

---

93. *As. Res.*, vol. XX, p. 69.
94. B.N. Puri, *India in the time of Patañjali*, p. 76.
95. *Op. cit.*, pp. 368-69.
96. *As. Res.*, XX, pp. 66, 72.

The Licchavis had formed a confederation once with the Videhas and once with their neighbour, the Mallas. We learn from a Jain source that Cetaka, a Videhan prince, was the most influential leader of the confederacy which the Licchavis had formed with the Videhas.[97] According to a Jain tradition recorded in one of the canonical texts, there was a league of the nine Licchavis, nine Mallakis and the eighteen *gaṇarājās* (chieftains) of Kāśī and Kośala.[98] The details of said eighteen *gaṇarājās* are not available in this source concerned. This evidence has received different interpretations from different scholars.[99] However, there are some positive indications to prove that a league of the Licchavis, the Videhas, the Mallas and eighteen confederate kings of Kāśī-Kośala was formed under the leadership of Cetaka against Ajātaśatru (*c*. 491-459 BC), the most powerful monarch of Magadha, who was firmly determined to subdue the Vajjians (the Licchavis and Videhas).

The Pāli text makes mention fo the Vajjis and the Mallas as forming *saṁghas* and *gaṇas*[100] which implies that the clans were governed by organised corportaions.

Ajātaśatru took the Vajjians as stumbling-block in the way of the expansion of the kingdom of Magadha, for they were in the habit of making frequent attacks on Pāṭaligrāma on the bank of the Ganges which later developed into the capital of the kingdom and became popularly known as Pāṭaliputra. He, therefore, made up his mind to destroy the Vajjian power. But he found them too powerful to crush. However, in order to achieve his goal he chalked out a strategy ingeniously and dexterously. He sent his chief minister Vassakāra to Vaiśālī to seek advice of the Buddha as to the feasibility of invading and subduing them.[101] The Buddha addressing one of his foremost disciples, Ānanda, passed seven remarks about them to be heard by Vassakāra which may be summed up as follows: the Vijjians hold frequent meetings. So long as they meet together in concord and live in peace and harmony, act in accordance with the ancient institutions of the Vajjians, support the Elders, they may be expected not to decline but to prosper. So long

97. *Niryāvaliyā Suttaṁ* (Sūtra), trans. S. Warren (Oxford, 1879), sec. 26.

98. Bhadrabāhu's *Kalpasūtra* (sec. 128), cf. *LAIJC*, p. 464; trans. H. Jacobi, SBE, XXII (Oxford, 1884), p. 266; see also Law, *Some Kṣatriya Tribes of Ancient India*, Ch. IV.

99. See H.C. Raychaudhuri, *PHAI*, p. 125, note 3.

100. *MN*, vol. I, p. 231.

101. *Mahāparinibbāna Suttaṁ*, ed. Prajñānand, pp. 1, and fn, *Aṭṭhakathā*, 2, 32, and fn, *Aṭṭhakathā*, 33-34, *DN*, vol. II, pp. 72ff.

as they maintain unity they would be invincible. The Licchavis were strenuous and diligent, zealous and active. If they would be given to luxury and indolence, they were sure to be conquered by the Magadhan king Ajātasattu.[102] Vassakāra felt that only possible way to conquer them was to sow the seed of dissensions among the Licchavis and to break their unity. He took three years (483-480 BC) to accomplish his objective. Ajātaśatru like Philip of Macedon was bent upon conquering the territories of his neighbouring republican communities. He swooped down upon the Vajjians with an overwhelming army and completely destroyed them in 480 BC or three years after the demise of the Buddha. He conquered Vaiśālī and annexed it to his kingdom. Thus Vaiśālī formed part of the Magadhan empire. "The whole Vajjian confederacy, which remained independent of Magadha up to the end of the Buddha's life"[103] was utterly destroyed after his death in 483 BC.[104] It is stated in the Tibetan text, the *Dulva*, that when Moggallāna entered Vaiśālī in search of alms, the Licchavis were coming out of the city of subdue Ajātaśatru.[105] The Licchavis were defeated but not broken up by Ajātaśatru. They, however, maintained their internal autonomy for sometime. They migrated to Nepal sometime after AD 355. Thus, the Licchavi republic disappeared sometime in the fourth century AD. As a sequel to it the Videhan republic also came to an end.

## THE ŚĀKYAS OF KAPILAVASTU

The Śākyas were settled in the territory bordered on the north by the Himālayas, on the east by the river Rohiṇī, and on the west and south by the Rāptī. Their territory on the whole included the north-western part of Gorakhpur, the north-eastern part of Bastī and the southern part of Nepal. The majority of the clan were residing in the long and level alluvial plain stretching about 50 miles from east to west and 30 or 40 miles to the southward from the foot of Himālaya Hills. According to an old Buddhist tradition preserved by Buddhaghoṣa in his commentary of the *Dīgha Nikāya*, there were more

---

102.. For details see the *Mahāparinibbāna Suttaṁ* of the *Dīgha Nikāya*, trans. in *Dialogues of the Buddha* Pt. II, pp. 79-85; *Mahāparinibbāna Suttaṁ*, ed. Prajñānand, pp. 3-4, 8-13; *Aṭṭhakathā Sūtta* 66, pp. 52, Rāhula Sānkṛtyāyana, *Pāli Sāhitya Kā Itihāsa*, pp. 37-38; SBE, vol. XI (Buddhist Sūttas), pp. 3-6; *SN*, ed. M.L. Feer and Mrs. Rhys Davids, vol. II, pp. 267-68; see also *Mhv.*, trans. by E.M. Coomaraswamy from the German of W. Geiger, Ch. XCIX; *Mahāvastu*, vol. I, pp. 253, 262.

103. *Dialogues of the Buddha*, Pt. II, 78-80.

104. *DPPN*, vol II, pp. 781-82.

105. Rockhill, *The Life of the Buddha*, p. 97.

106. *Dialogues of the Buddha*. pt. I, p. 147, note.

than 80,000 families of the Śākya clan[106] to which the Buddha himself belonged.[107] Their territory was no doubt very extensive and populous.[108] Their old capital, Kapilavastu, which stood close to the western bank of the Rohiṇī some 8 miles to the west of Lumbinī (of hallowed memory being the birth-place of the Buddha), can be identified with Tilaura Koṭ and neighbouring ruins in the Tarāi of Nepal. This city is famous in the history of Buddhist India as the home of the Śākyas. The Pāli text[109] as well as the Sanskrit Buddhist texts[110] throw some light on this aspect of the subject.

> "The administrative and judicial business of the clan was carried out in public assembly, at which young and old were alike present, in their common Mote-Hall (*Santhāgāra*) at Kapilavastu. It was . . . a parliament or palaver. . . ."[111]

In one of the Pāli *suttas* we are told that when Ambaṭṭha went to Kapilavastu on business, he went to the Mote-Hall where the Śākyas were then in session.[112] one of the Sanskrit Buddhist texts mention similar sessions of the Śākya *gaṇa* in *santhāgāra*.[113] The Mote-Hall (or an open Assembly Hall), where the meetings were held, was covered with a roof supported by pillars, but with no walls. It is said that a technical term, *santhāgāra*, is "never used of the council chamber of kings".[114] Actually, it was House of the people.

> "A Single Chief — how, and for what period chosen, we do not know — was elected a soffice-holder, presiding over the sessions, and, if no sessions were sitting, over the state. He bore the title of *rāja*, which must have meant something like the Roman Consul, or the Greek archon".[115]

---

107. Law, *HPL*, vol. I, p. 248.
108. *Sutta Nipāta*, ed. Rahul Sānkṛtyāyana (Rangoon, 1937) and trans. V. Fausboll, SBE, vol. X (2nd edn. Oxford, 1898), Verse 1012.
109. *MN*, vol. I, p. 353.
110. *Mahāvastu*, vol. I, pp. 350 ff, vol. II, p. 75f, Law, *A Study of the Mahāvastu*, pp. 58 ff; *Divyāvadāna*, p. 548; *Lalitavistara*, pp. 58, 77, 98, 101-2, 113, 123, 234; *Buddhacarita Kāvya*, Bk I, vv. 2 and 4; *Saundarānanda Kāvya* by Aśvaghoṣa, trans. Law, Ch. I, cf. Law, *Geographical Essays Relating to Ancient Georgraphy of India*, pp. 33-35.
111. *BI*, p. 19; also *DN*, vol. I, p. 91.
112. *Ambaṭṭha Suttaṁ*, trans. in *Dialogues of the Buddha*, Pt. I, 113; also *DN*, vol. I, pp. 87ff.
113. *Lalitavistara* (BIS), Ch. XII, p. 115.
114. *JPTS*, 1909, p. 65 cf. *CHI*, vol. I, p. 156.
115. *BI*, p. 19.

At one time Bhaddiya, a young cousin of the Buddha, was the *rājā*,[116] and at another Śuddhodana, the Buddha's father, held that rank.[117] As a matter of fact, the office of the chief bearing the title *rājā* was not hereditary but elective. He neither enjoyed the absolute power nor ruled over the whole state. The real power to rule the state was vested in the Śākya *gaṇa* or their elected representatives. The chief of the *gaṇa-rājya* of the Buddha's time was also known as *gaṇapati*, *gaṇarāja*, *gaṇajyeṣṭha* or *gaṇa-mukhya* like the *saṁgha-mukhya* of the *saṁgha-rājya* of the *Mahābhārata* period.

The most important political institution of the republican state of the Śākyas was a Council called *pariṣā* or *pariṣat* (*pariṣada*). Their governing council seems to have been consisted of 500 members.[118] The number of members of a Council at Athens was exactly the same. The Council was generally constituted to assist the assembly in running the administration of the state. In this respect we find striking similarity between the ancient Indian and Greek democracies.

Besides the principal city (Kapilavastu), there were some small towns and villages in the Śākya state which had also Mote-Halls or Assembly-Halls to conduct their administrative business. Names of such townships mentioned in the most ancient texts are Cātumā, Sāmagāma, Khomadussa, Silāvati, Metalupa, Ulumpa, Sakkara and Devadaha. The Assembly Hall of particularly Cātumā is expressly mentioned in one of the Pāli texts.[119] The ruins of their capital city and some small towns have been discovered in the vicinity of Lumbinī on the river Rohiṇī. A curious information is supplied by Hiuen Tsang regarding the administration of the small towns. He observes: "The country was without a sovereign each city having its own chief. . . ."[120] In course of his visit to the land of the Śākyas he found besides the royal city more than ten deserted cities all in utter ruin.

One of the distinctive features of the Śākyan republic is that both the towns and villages adopted the republican system of government. The local affairs of each village were carried on in open assembly of the householders held in the groves. Each of the villages which was the smallest administrative unit of the state fabric also followed the republican trends. Each of them was a tiny self-governed republic. The village was ruled

116. *Vinaya* ed. H. Oldenberg, vol. II, p. 181.

117. *DN*, vol. II, p. 52.

118. *Lalitavistara*, pp. 136-37.

119. *MN*, vol. I, p. 457.

120. *YCTI*, vol.. II, p. 1.

by the headman (*grāmaṇī*) chosen by the villages together with a number of other members to assist him. All the political and non-political matters were freely discussed and decided in an open assembly. In the Buddhist period traders and craftsmen formed their own professional guilds or corporations, which were autonomous corporate bodies exercising full authority. These were organised on the model of a republican state. These were known as *saṁgha*, *nikāya*, *nigama* or *śreṇī*. Their own president called *jyeṭṭhaka*, *jyeṣṭhaka* or *seṭṭhi* played very important role in the field of administration. They had borrowed many elements of republican government. They kept high democratic ideals. The functioning of their *saṁgha* or *nikāya*, a non-political body, was based on the vote of majority like that of *gaṇa*, a political body.

The Pāli texts throw a good deal of light on the constitution and administrative procedures of the Śākyas. It appears that there were certain rules regarding their meetings, deliberations and decisions. The whole proceedings were conducted in their *santhāgāra* or Mote-Halls at Kapilavastu and other towns. The meetings were held therein with proper seating arrangements made by a special officer called *āsana-prajñāpaka*. The presence of the requisite number of members was essential to make a quorum for the purpose of holding a meeting. It was the duty of the chief-whip (*gaṇapūraka*) to secure the quorum by requisitioning the presence of members. The business began with the formal presentation (*sthāpanaṁ*) of the motion (*ñatti* or *jñapti*) by the president or chairman (*vinayadhara*). The motion before the House was debated thoroughly in a true democratic spirit. A resolution (*pratijñā*) was moved and read normally once, but sometimes if necessary thrice. If no objection was raised to it, the same was considered as passed. But in case of difference of opinion or disputation (*saṁvāda*), the matter was referred to a Committee of arbitrators with a view to arriving at a unanimous decision (which finds expression in a technical term *ubbāhikā*). After all hopes of reaching such a decision belied or if there was no chance of having a consensus opinion the matter concerned was put to vote (*chanda*). The members exercised their franchise quite freely. The practice of casting votes by ballot seems to have been in vogue. The voting was carried on by tickets or *śalākās* (slips of wood or small piece of thin sticks) of various colours to indicate different views. These voting tickets were used as ballot-papers. These votes were collected by an officer called *śalākāgāhāpaka* (*śalākāgrāhaka*) and counted by the president. And ultimately the majority view (*yebhuyyasikaṁ*) prevailed. A question once decided was noted allowed to be re-opened. A resolution apporved by the House by voice-vote usually took the form of an act (*saṁghakarma* or *karma*). The entire proceedings were recorded, and preserved by clerks.

The religious *saṁgha* of *bhikkhus* (or the Buddhist *saṁgha*) was modelled on the republican assemblies or political *saṁghas*. The former was the prototype of the latter.[121] The democratic procedures of the Śākyas are very much similar to that of followed in modern state Assemblies and Central Parliament.

The evidence Buddhist literature shows that in Central Assemblies of the rupublics, besides other issues, the momentous issues of peace, war and alliance were decided.

The Śākyas were a peaceful community. The cases of theft and other crimes were rare. However, a regular police force was maintained. The offenders caught by them wer produced before a court of justice for trial. The punishments were inflicted on them according to the nature of crimes the details of which are not available in any source.

The Śākyas after acknowledging the suzerainty of king Pasenadi (Prasenajit) of Kośala became his vassals and claimed to be Kośalans. In the north of the kingdom of Kośala included within its frontier (in the hills in what is now Nepal) the region occupied them. Their political subjection to the king of Kośala is clear from the evidence of Pāli records.[122] It was Viḍūḍabha (Virūddhaka), son of Pasenadi, who crushed them during the lifetime of the Buddha.

The king Pasenadi wante to marry a girl from the Śākyan community. But his hope soon turned into despair. He was actually deceived by the Śākyas. One of their leading chiefs gave a slave girl named Vāsabha Khattiyā in marriage to him. When Viḍūḍabha came to know that he was the son of a slave girl, his anger know no bound. And he immediately decided to wreak his vengeance on them. But it appears to have been merely a pretext. His real motive like that of Ajātaśatru of Magadha was to destroy their autonomy. He invaded them, destroyed their capital city, Kapilavastu, brutally massacred a large number of them without distinction of age and sex and conquered their territories in the last year of the Buddha's career. He perpetrated terrible atrocities on them.[123] This proved to be fatal blow to the Śākyan republic. However, they were not

121. For details see *Mahā-Govinda Suttaṁ* of the *Dīgha Nikāya DN*. vol. II, p. 220f; *Dialogues of the Buddha*, pt. II, pp. 259-64; *Vinaya Texts*, trans. T.W. Rhys Davids and H. Oldenberg, *Mahāvagga*, SBE, vol. XIII (Oxford, 1881) pp. 269, 307; vol. XVII, pt. II (Oxford, 1882), p. 265f; *Cullavagga*, SBE, vol. XX, pp. 25, 44f, 49f, also 408 (for an account of the Congress of Vesāli), Rockhill, *The Life of the Buddha*, pp. 118-19; Law, *Kṣatriya clans in Buddhist India*, pp. 110-19.

122. *Aggañña Suttaṁ* of the *Dīgha Nikāya*, *DN*. vol. III, p. 83; *Dialogues of the Buddha*, pt. III, p. 80; *Sutta Nipāta* (verse 422) cf. trans. V. Fausboll, SBE, vol. X, pt. II, pp. 67-69, *MN*, vol. II, p. 124.

123. *Jāt*., IV, pp. 144-45; *Dhammapada-Aṭṭhakathā* (Commentary), ed. H.C. Norman, vol. I, p. 359; *Mhv*., VIII, 18 and the *Ṭīkā* on it; also Motichandra *Sārthavāha*, p. 50.

uprooted or exterminated. Because we find that a section of the community claimed and received a share of the Buddha's bodily remains.

It is recorded that when the capital of the Śākyas was besieged by the king of Kośala, they assembled to discuss whether they should open the gates or not. Some supported the proposal while others opposed it. Votes were taken to ascertain the majority view which favoured capitulation.[124] Thus, they surrendered at the feet of the Kośalan king without offering any resistance to him.

The Śākyas built a new capital at Piparahwā in the north of the Bastī district at a distance of about 10 miles from their original capital at Tilaura Koṭ in Nepal. According to Fleet, the village of Piparahwā at a distance of 9 km from Birdpur marks the site of Kapilavastu.[125] The archaeological discovery of some clay seals bearing the inscriptions "... Kapilavastu Bhikku Saṁghas" in the Brāhmī script of first and second century AD in course of excavations carried out at Piparahwā by K.M. Srivastava and his associates during 1973-74, of course, confirms their settlements at this place. But Srivastava's identification of the place with original Kapilavastu is questionable. In defence of his view he has stated that the Śākyas had originally settled here in the eighth century BC and continued to be there up to the second or third century AD. There has been some controversy among historians and archaeologists since 1858 over the location of Kapilavastu. However, the fact remains that there were two capital cities built at two different places at two different periods of history. Actually, it was the destruction of their old capital at the hands of the Kośalan king shortly before the Buddha's death which compelled them to build a new capital. The Śākyan republic seems to have disappeared from history before the dawn of the fourth century AD.

Fa-hien (AD 399-414) in course of his visit to Kapilavastu near Lumbinī found that there was neither king nor people. He found the city desolate and barren, and the inhabitants few and far between.[126]

## THE KOLIYAS OF RĀMAGĀMA

They were one of the independent political communities. "They were to the east of the

124. Rockhill, *op. cit.*, pp. 118-19.
125. *JRAS* (1906), p. 180.
126. H.A. Giles, *The Travels of Fa-hsien*, pp. 37-39; James Legge, *op. cit.*, pp. 64-65.

Śākyas, and the river Rohiṇī formed the dividing line between the two territories".[127] The Koliyans were one of the subordinate subdivisions or a branch of the Śākya clan. The neighbouring clan, the Koliyas, are traditionally believed to have been closely related by descent with the Śākyas.[128] The Śākyas appear to have once formed a confederacy with the Koliyas.[129]

The Koliyas had two settlements, one at Rāmagāma (Rāmagrāma) and the other at Devadaha. Their capital, Rāmagāma, which stood close to the eastern bank of the Rohiṇī at a distance of 5 *yojana* (about 40 miles), according to Fa-hien,[130] or more than 200 *li*, according to Hiuen Tsang,[131] eastward from Kapilavastu, is identified with modern Rāmagarhtāla near Gorakhpur.[132] B.C. Law, however, identifies it with "Rāmpur Deoriyā" in the district of Bastī.[133] The former identification is generally accepted in preference to the latter. From Fa-hien's account of the subject it appears that their chiefs were also styled as kings, Devadaha on the other side of the Rohiṇī was the seat of government of the first Koliyan territory. The prince Dvadaha after whom the town was so named was a Koliyan chief. This town fell under the joint occupation of both the republican clans. There were five other towns in the possession of the Koliyas.[134] The Koliyan central authorities were served by a special body of police.[135]

## THE MORIYAS OF PIPPHALIVANA

There is positive evidence to show that the so-called Moriyas were of Śākyan origin. In the commentary on the Pāli chronicle, the *Mahāvaṁsa*, they are spoken of as an offshoot of the Śākyas.[136] In fact, one section of the Śākyas of Kapilavastu after having escaped the attack of the Kośalan king, Viḍūḍabha, as stated before, occupied the territory to the south-east of Gorakhpur and founded their city in the locality which always resounded

127. *Jāt.*, V, p. 412; *Paramatthajotikā* (Aṭṭhakathā or commy. on *Suttanipāta*), ed. H. Smith, vol. II, p. 358.
128. *Sumaṅgalavilāsinī*, vol. I, pp. 258-62.
129. *Jāt.*, V, p. 412.
130. H.A. Giles, *op. cit.*, pp. 38-39; James Legge, *op. cit.*, p. 70.
131. *YCTI*, vol. II, p. 20.
132. Raja Bali Pandey, *Bhāratīya Itihāsa kā Paricaya*, p. 41.
133. Law, *GEB*, p. 32.
134. See *CHI*, vol. I, p. 158.
135. *SN*, Vol. IV, p. 341, see also *DPPN*, I, pp. 689-90.
136. '*Mahāwanso*' (*Mahāvaṁśa*) — *Ṭīkā*, ed. Turnour, Introd., pp. XXXVIII-XLII.

with the cries of peacocks. The city called Pipphalivana (or Mayūrnagar) became famous as their capital, which lay, according to Fa-hien, 4 *yojana* (about 30 miles) to the east of the river Anomā, and 7 *yojana* (about 54 miles) to the west of Kuśinārā. Raja Bali Pandey has located it near the modern village named Rājadhāni in the immediate vicinity of Kusumhi Rly. station to the east of the Koliyan capital Rāmagrāma.[137] They became gradually popular as one of the republican clans of the Buddha's time.[138] They also seem to have been close neighbours of the Koliyas beyond the river Anomā an the Mallas of Anupiya on the banks of that river. The *Mahāvaṁsa* commentary traces the origin of the Maurya dynasty of Magadha to the Moriyas of Pipphalivana. We are told that Candagutta (Candragupta) belonged to the Moriya clan.[139] The Moriyas are, therefore, absolutely identical with the Mauryas or "Morieis" of the Greeks.[140]

## THE MALLAS OF KUŚINĀRĀ AND PĀVĀ

The Mallas were to the east of the Śākyas. The river Anomā obviously formed a boundary between the two territories. According to Pāli records, the river was 30 leagues to the east of Kapilavastu.[141] The distance of the river from the Śākya capital was perhaps 6 leagues only. It appears that there were two branches of the Mallas. Those whose territory touched the realm of the Uttara Kośala have been distinguished from the Dakṣiṇa Mallas[142] who were probably not very far from the Videhas. Their territory no doubt touched the northern border of the Vajji state. In the *Mahāparinibbāna Suttaṁ* (5, 19) Licchavis neighbour has been mentioned as Vāśiṣṭha Malla.

It is worth nothing that the territory of the Mallas originally or before the time of the Buddha formed a part of the Kośalan empire.

The Mallas like the Videhas had at first a monarchical form of government. But later on, in the time of the Buddha, they adopted a republican constitution. The state was divided basically into two autonomous parts with their respective capitals known as Kuśinārā (Kuśāvatī of the pre-Buddhan time or mod. Kuśinagar) and Pāvā. The former is identical with Kasiā (in the present Deoriā district), about 35 miles to the east of

137. *Op. cit.*, p. 41.
138. *DN*, vol. II, p. 167; *Petavatthu*, ed. Minayef, p. 57.
139. *Mahāvaṁśa-Ṭīkā*, Sinhalese ed. (Colombo, 1895), pp. 119-21; also Law *Some Kṣatriya Tribes of Ancient India*, pp. 211-13.
140. See Lassen, *Ind. Alt*, vol. II, p. 205, note 4.
141. *Jāt.*, I, p. 64f, *Paramatthajotikā*, II, p. 382, *DPPN*, I, p. 102.
142. *Mbh.*, Sabhā Parva, 27, 3, 12.

Gorakhpur, and the latter with Papa-Ura near Padaraona, 12 miles to the north-east of Kasiā, or with Fāziḷpur, 10 miles south-east of Kasiā. "The river Kakuṭṭhā formed the dividing line between the two capital cities".[143] The two cities frequently appear in Buddhist literature as capitals of two different republican states of the Mallas.[144] Besides these two chief cities, they had other important cities namely, Bhoganagara, Anupiyā and Uruvelakappa.[145]

One of the Jain sources mentions the *gaṇa* of the Mallas,[146] which denotes their political assembly or corporate assembly. One of the Pāli canonical texts refers to *saṁgha*s and *gaṇa*s of both the Vajjis and the Mallas.[147] From a passage in the same Pāli text it is apparent that the Mallas were a typical example of a *saṁgha-rājya*.[148] Kauṭilya (*Arth*., XI, 1) also refers to their *saṁgha*. According to him, their chiefs were entitled to be called *rājā*s. In actual practice the whole body including the elected chiefs were vested with authority to rule the state.

The Mallas too had a common Mote-Hall or *santhāgāra* for discussing all important matters pertaining to administration of the state and for transacting other administrative business. According to the *Mahāparinibbāna Suttaṁ* (6, 23) when Ānanda went to inform the Mallas about the death of the Buddha they were having their session in the Mote-Hall to consider that very matter.

The Mallas like the Licchavis had also an Executive Council of nine members, who were elected by the ruling clan. They were entrusted with the responsibilities of dealing with external affairs. In the *Mahāparinibbāna Suttaṁ* mention is made of a set of officers called *puriṣa*s about whose duties and functions very little is known. However, there is clear evidence to show that they too had a special body of police to maintain law and order in general and to check the occurrences of crime in particular.[149]

143. *DN*, II, pp. 129, 134; *Udāna*, trans. D.M. Strong, VIII, 5.

144. *Mahāparinibbāna Suttaṁ*, ed. Prajñānand, pp. 78, 96, 102-3; *DN*, II, pp. 137, 170 f (*Mahāparinibbāna Suttaṁ* and *Mahāsudassana Suttaṁ* respectively); *Dialogues of the Buddha*, II, pp. 179-96; *Vinaya Texts*, III, p. 370; SBE, XVII, II, p. 135; *Sāmantapāsādikā*, I, p. 4; see also *Dip*. and *Mhv*. cf. Law, *HPL* II, pp. 555-56; *Divyāvadāna*, pp. 208-9; *Dvāviṁśāvadāna*, cf. R.L. Mitra, *SBLN*, p. 86; R. Shafer, *EAI* (Wiesbaden, 1954), p. 143.

145. *AN*, V, p. 228; *SN*, IV, p. 438; also Law, *Some Kṣatriya Tribes of Ancient India*, p. 149; *Mahāvastu*, II, p 164.

146. *Abhidhāna-rājendra* — Jain Prākṛta Encyclopaedia, III, pp. 812-14.

147. *MN* (1. 4. 5. 35), cf. vol. I, p. 231.

148. *Ibid*.

149. *DN*, II, pp. 159, 161.

The Mallas and the Licchavis, the two neighbouring republican clans, formed a confederacy and thereby established friendly relations between them at least for their self-defence, as noted before. The two of the most important oligarchical powers were the confederacies of the Vajjis or Licchavis of Vaiśālī and of the Mallas of Kuśinārā and Pāvā. These are the two notable examples of *saṁgha-rājya*, federal republics or oligarchical republics of the Buddha's time.

It is recorded that both the main sections of the Mallas appeared among the claimants for shares of the bodily remains of the Buddha.[150] However, this evidence cannot lead us to come to conclusion that they retained their independence till the demise of the Buddhas or only up to the end of the fifth century BC.

The rising powers of the Kośala and Magadha adversely affected the democratic way of life of the Mallas and eventually proved to be disastrous for them. They were temporarily under the sway of Kośala. Their territory was finally annexed to the kingdom of Magadha. It certainly formed a part of the Maurya empire in the third century BC, and by this time or little later their republican system of government came to an end. However, they continued to exist as a non-republican community. Fa-hien refers to desolation of only Kuśinārā. In the city he found only few inhabitants who were scattered.[151]

## THE KĀLĀMAS OF KESAPUTTA

They were one of the small republican clans. They were settled in the north-east of Kośala. It is well-nigh impossible to locate their capital, Kesaputta, with absoulte certainty. However, we have definite information about its annexation to the kingdom of Kośala.[152]

## THE BULIS OF ALLAKAPPA

They no doubt had a republican form of government. But the importance of their republican state was not very great. Materials regarding them in Pāli literature are very meagre. It is very difficult to determine their exact location. Their capital Allakappa has been mentioned in a Pāli commentary as a kingdom. It was 10 leagues in extent and its king (chief) was in intimate relationship with king of Vethadipa,[153] which is said to have been situated on the way from Masār in the Shāhābād district to Vaiśālī. And it

150. *DN*, p. 167.
151. Giles, *op. cit.*, p. 41, Legge, *op. cit.*, pp. 70-71.
152. *AN*, I, p. 188; *Sutta Nipāta*, III, p. 65.
153. *Dhammapada-aṭṭhakathā*, I, p. 161.

has, therefore, been assumed that Allakappa lay not very far from Vethadipa.[154] In that case it must have been situated to the east of the kingdom of Vethadipa or Beta in Bihar. S. Chattopadhyaya on the authority of L. Petech has located the Bulis of Allakappa in the "Muzaffarpur and Sahabad districts"[155] of Bihar.

Cunningham has placed the capital city, Allakappa, in the neighbourhood of Gaṇḍak. According to him, it was inhabited by the Bulis or Bulukas. It has, therefore, been assumed that the city "lay somehwere near to Vaiśālī to the east of the Gandak".[156] He has drawn a conclusion which is rendered still more probable. According to Motichandra, the territories of the Bulis and Kālāmas (*gaṇa*s) were situated on the way from Kapilavastu to Vaiśālī.[157] One of the *Jātaka*s mentions the Bulis of Allakappa as neighbours of the Mallas of Kuśinārā,[158] which is also indirectly support by Fleet.[159] In face of these contradictory evidences it is not possible to draw any plausible conclusion about the location of their territory or capital.

Before we proceed to discuss one more republic of the Buddha's time, it is worthwhile to mention here that the independent status of the Koliyas of Rāmagāma, the Moriyas of Pipphalivana and the Kālāmas of Kesaputta like that of the Śākyas of Kapilavastu was reduced to that of Vassals (*anujātā*) after they acknowledged the supremacy of king Pasenadi of Kośala. And consequently their republican system of government could not last long. We do not have any information about the causes that led to the decline or disappearance of the Bulis of Allakappa.

## THE BHAGGAS OF SUṀSUMĀRA HILL

They were a small ruling clan. They have frequently been referred to in Pāli literature. They were absolutely identical with the Bhargas of Pāṇini (IV, 1, 178) and the *Mahābhārata* (Sabhā Parva, 27, 10-11). They were the eastern neighbours of the Vatsas of Kauśāmbī. Their close proximity can be proved by the testimony of the *Mahābhārata* given above. Their republican state was somewhere in the modern district of Mirzapur in eastern U.P. Their capital Suṁsumāra, which bore the resemblance of a hill fortress,

154. Law, *GEB*, p. 25.
155. *RANIT*, p. 80.
156. *CAGI*, p. 379.
157. *Op. cit.*, p. 49.
158. *Jāt.*, III, p. 157.
159. *JRAS*, (1906), p. 900, note.

has been identified with Chunar.[160] The *Apadāna* (II, p. 359) associates the Bhaggas with Karūṣa, which corresponds to an neighbourhood of the Vindhya range. In the latter half of the sixth century BC the Bhagga state was a dependency of the Vatsa kingdom. It seems that in the lifetime of the Buddha the Bhaggas passed under the sway of king Udena or Udayana of Kauśāmbī. We learn from the Buddhist records that his son, prince Bodhi, ruled over them as his father's viceroy.[161]

We find that a number of tribal republics or Oligarchies existed in the age of Buddha. The republics of this period fall mainly into two classes. In one class of republics the whole or a section of single clan, e.g., the Śākyas, the Koliyas, the Mallas, etc., were vested with powers to rule the state, and in other several clans like the Vajjis shared the power. The absence of single hereditary monarch constitues a common feature of these republics. All the free clans or tribes maintained their assemblies to transact the day-to-day business. The details of administrative procedures followed in big republican states like those of the Licchavis and the Śākyas are available in Buddhist literature. But the details of internal organisation or administrative system of the small ruling clans or republican clans like the Koliyas, the Moriyas, the Kālāmas, the Bulis and the Bhaggas are conspicuous by their absence in the available sources. We gather an impression that the constitutional machinery of small republican states was very simple.

The republics of the Buddhist tribes were undoubtedly well-organised, fully developed and prosperous. Of all the republics that existed in the time of the Buddha, the Licchavi and the Śākya republics became the most famous because of their magnificent constitution and excellent methods of administration. They were at the height of power and prosperity.

## Some Republics During and After the Time of Pāṇini

Here we shall deal with some of those republics which flourished in the Vāhika region (Punjab) and other parts of north-western India in the time of Pāṇini and further continued to exist. The republics mentioned by him as *āyudhajīvī saṁgha*s in his *Aṣṭādhyāyī* (*sūtra*s V, 3, 115-17) are described below:

### TRIGARTA-ṢAṢṬHA

The Trigartas inhabited a region comprising three valleys, viz., those of the rivers Rāvī,

160. R. Sānkṛtyāyana, *Buddhacaryā*, p. 412; R.B. Pandey, *op. cit.*, p. 42.

161. *MN*, I, p. 332; II, pp. 91, 97; *Jāt.*, III, p. 157; *AN*, II, p. 61; *Vinaya*, II, p. 127; IV, pp. 198-99.

Vyāsa and Sutlej. Their republican state seems to have comprised three sub-states. Pāṇini refers to a confederacy of six Trigartas known as Trigarta-Ṣaṣṭha (V, 3, 116). The six members of this confederacy mentioned by the *Kāśikā* are as follows : (1) Kauṇḍoparatha, (2) Dāṇḍakī, (3) Krauṣṭaki, (4) Jālamāni, (5) Brāhmagupta and (6) Jānakī.[162] This was one of the flourishing republics of Pāṇini's time. Patañjali also mentions the Trigartas (*Mahābhāṣya* VIII, 1, 15). Their descritption in the *Mahābhārata*,[163] the Purāṇas[164] and the *Bṛhat Saṁhitā*[165] of Varāhamihira leave behind an impression that they were inhabitants of the northern Himālayan region. The name Tigarta mentioned in the *Abhidhānacintāmaṇi* (IV, 24) of Hemachandra corresponds to Jalandhar. According to A. Cunningham, it is identical with the Kangra valley, situated near Jalandhar between the mountains of Cambā and the upper course of the Vyāsa,[166] which is also supported by an epigrahic evidence.[167] A copper coin issued by them, preserved in the British Museum, bears the inscription *Trakatajanapadasa* in Brāhmī characters on its reverse.[168] The legend on its obverse in Kharoṣṭhi is indicative of the fact that they came under the foreign influence, which may be that of Śaka Satraps. Its findspot is not yet known. The coin of the Trigarta republic on a palaeographic basis may be assigned to the second century BC. Their republican system of government might have eclispsed about the same time. They possibly migrated from the Punjab to Rājpūtānā in the second century BC itself.

VṚKA (V, 3, 115)

"An individual member of this *saṁgha* was called Vārkeṇya, and the whole *saṁgha* Vṛka."[169] It is very difficult to determine the exact location of the Vṛkas.

DĀMANĪ (V, 3, 116)

The members of his *saṁgha* known as Dāmanīs were a powerful warlike tribe "settled

---

162. *IP*, pp. 446-47, also 54-55.
163. Sabhā Parva, 29, 6; 48, 13; Droṇa Parva, 6, 2-7; 10, 16; Virāṭa Parva, 31, 1-124; 32, 3-7.
164. *Vy.*, 45, 136, *Mts.*, 114, 56; *Mkd.*, 54, 57; *Bmd.*, I, 16, 68.
165. *Br. Sam.*, IV, 24; IX, 19; X, 11; XIV, 25; XVI, 22; XVII, 16.
166. *Co. An. Ind.*, p. 66; *CASR*, vol. V (Calcutta, 1875), pp. 145-48; vol. XIV (Calcutta, 1882), p. 116.
167. *Ep. Ind.*, vol. I, pp. 102, 116.
168. Allan, *op. cit.*,, pp. cxxxix-cxl, 212, pl. xxix, 10.
169. *IP*, p. 445.

in the north-western portion of Baluchistan known as Chagai laying to the south of the Chagai Hills.[170]

PARŚU (V, 3, 117)

The Parśus of Pārśvas had their settlements somewhere on the borders of India and Persia. Nothing definite can be said about them.

The *āyudhajīvī saṁghas* are also mentioned in the *Gaṇa-Pāṭha*. Only some them are worth mentioning here:

BĀHLIKA

This is included in the list of the *saṁghas* of *parśvādi* group (V, 3, 117). The people of the Bāhlika region (mod. Balkh) in the extreme north of Afghanistan must have organised themselves as an *āyudhajīvī saṁgha* in Pāṇini's time.[171]

BHARATAS

They are mentioned as an *āyudhajīvī saṁgha*. They belong to *yaudheyādi* group which is repeated twice in the *Aṣṭādhyāyī* (IV, 1, 178; V, 3, 117). It is said that "these Bharatas lived round about Kurukṣetra as a *Saṁgha* in Pāṇini's time".[172]

Besides the *āyudhajīvī saṁghas* mentioned above, there were some other republican communities in Pāṇini's time which also deserve our notice here :

RĀJANYAS

They are mentioned not only by Pāṇini (IV, 2, 53; V, 3, 114)[173] but also by Kātyāyana, Patañjali (*Mahābhāṣya*, IV, 2, 52) and others. They also figure in the *Kāśikā* (IV, 2, 53). In the *Mahābhārata* (Sabhā Parva, 48, 13; 50, 14) they are mentioned along with other republican tribes like the Trigartas, the Yaudheyas, the Śibis, etc. Varāhamihira (*Br. Sam.* : XIV, 28) mentions them together with the Yaudheyas and other tribes of northen India. According to Pāṇini, the region occupied by them was called *rājanyaka*. They may undoubtedly be connected with the kṣatriyas.[174] They being the leaders of families were

170. *IP.*, p. 446.

171. *Ibid.*, p. 449.

172. *Ibid.*, p. 453.

173. *Ibid.*, p. 454.

174. Fleet, cf. *Ind. Ant.*, XXII, p. 182.

consecrated to rulership. A large number of their coins bearing the legend *rājña janapadasa* in both Brāhmī and Kharoṣṭhi characters have been found on the Manaswal plateau in Hośiārpur district of the Punjab, which on palaeographical grounds my be assigned to the second-first centuries BC.[175] This discovery proves beyond doubt that they were the inhabitants of eastern Punjab or the Vyāsa-Sutlej Doāb. It appears that in the post-Alexandrian period which witnessed large-scale tribal movements, a branch of the *rājanyas* had moved from Punjab to Mathurā region where also their coins have been found which are in fabric like the coins of Satraps of Mathurā.[176] It is also believed that one section of them had settled in eastern Rājpūtānā. However, this is still unproven. It seems that they must have come under the rule of Śaka Satraps sometime between the second and first century BC, which is evidenced by the similarity of their coins to that of the northern Satraps. Their absorption in the Punjab and the Mathurā Satrapa cannot be doubted. It transpires from the available evidence that they maintained their republican system of government in eastern Punjab (which was their homeland) from the time of Pāṇini until the beginning of the second century BC.

## MAHĀRĀJA

Pāṇini refers to *mahārāja* (IV, 3, 97) as an independent political community. Theirs was a democratic type of government. "Traces of the ancient name are probably still preserved in the collection of four large villages in the Moga Tahsil of Ferozpur district which is the headquarters of a Pargana and still called Mahārāja, held by the Maharajki clan of Jats".[177]

The existence of a *mahārāja janapada* is proved by their coins found in the Punjab. Such coins were first deciphered by Cunningham,[178] though there is no agreement among numismatologists about their provenance. We are given to understand that their coins originally bore legends in Brāhmī which was subsequently changed into Kharoṣṭhi. They came under the influence of Śaka Satraps by *c.* 100 BC.

---

175. For details see Allan, *op. cit*, p. civ; V.A. Smith, *CCIM*, vol. I, pp. 164-65, 179; E.J. Rapson. *Ind. Co.*, p. 12, Pl. III, 18 : Cunningham, *Co. An. Ind.*, pp. 69, 89; *CASR*, XIV, p. 151; J. Prinsep, *Essays on Indian Antiquities*, ed. E. Thomas, p. 223, pl. XLIV, 18 and 19.

176. Rapson, *op. cit.*, Smith, *op. cit.*, pp. 164-65; Cunningham, *Co. An. Ind.*, p. 85, Pl. VIII.

177. *IP*, p. 454.

178. *Op. cit.*, p. 69.

## Republics After the Buddha and Before Kauṭilya

The Kurus (of the Gaṅgā-Yamunā Doāb or Kurukṣetra), the Pañcālas (of Ahicchatra and Kāmpilya) and the Kāmbojas (on the Kābul river, modern Kamboha, in eastern Afghanistan) adopted the republican forms of government after the Buddha and before Kauṭilya or soemtime between fifth and fourth century BC. It is Kauṭilya who first mentions their *saṁgha*.[179] The former two had chiefs entitled to be called the *rājā* and the latter were the followers of military art and had no king or chief. They were no more under the regal form of government.

## Republics of North-West India in Pāṇinian, Alexandrian and the post-Alexandrian Period

### PRELIMINARY REMARKS

In order to get an accurate picture of the republics of north-west India (Afghanistan, the Punjab, Sindh and Baluchhistan) we can place our reliance on the combined testimony of Pāṇini and classical (Greek and Roman) writers. A perusal of their writings gives us an impression that they have taken enough pains to distinguish the different forms of government. The Greek historians had, of course, far greater knowledge of their constitutions and administration. As a matter of fact, some republics had already come into existence in Pāṇini's time which further received the notices of Alexander and his companions in course of their campaigns. In their times, the republics were highly organised and prosperous. They passed through different stages of political evolution. They reached the zenith of progress between the fifth and fourth century BC. The latter period may be reckoned as the peak period of north-western repblics. Alexander in course of his invasion of north-west India (*c*. 327-325 BC) came into contact with a number of independent tribes who were not under the authority of any king rather governed by their own headmen and saw with his own eyes the internal organisation and functioning of both republican and monarchical states. He and some of his companions left behind an eye-witness account of the subject which became the chief source of information for some Greek and Roman writers about the same. The republics which survived the attack of Alexander continued to thrive after him. The Punjab and the Indus valley were the two renowned seats of republics from *c*. 500 BC to AD 400.

At the time of Alexander's invasion, a large number of republics existes side by side

179. *Arth*., XI, I.

with kingdoms or monarchies in north-west India which can best be qualified in the statement of Megasthenes: "Most of the cities adopted the democratic form of government, though some retained the kingly until the invastion of the country by Alexander".[180] These republics were not much larger than the city-states of ancient Greece. The republican states on the whole fall under five categories, viz., free independent or autonomous states where the sovereignty was vested in the whole tribal community and popularly known as sovereign democratic republic; states governed by a body or council of members elected or unelected; confederate states where the representatives of two different states jointly shared the political power; states where there was aristocratic democracy being governed by members of a aristocratic type of community and the states where the executive power was held by members of a few families on hereditary principle but with circumscribed authority. There were different forms of republican government. Each state was free to choose its own form of government. The free city-states had "both oligarchical and republican constitution". The constitutions were framed according to needs and circumstances.

One of the noteworthy features of ancient Indian polity was the change in the form of government, i.e., from monarchy to republic. The north-west India was not an exception to this. Megasthenes has stated that "At last, after many generations had come and gone, the sovereignty (institution of kingship) was dissolved, and democratic gvernments were set up in the cities",[181] which has also been corroborated by Diodorus[182] and Arrian,[183] the two noted Greek historians. There are few available instances to justify the above statement. The Śivis and the Ambaṣṭhas of the Punjab before adopting the democratic form of government in the fourth century BC or in the time of Alexander were governed by monarchical constitution. The process of transformation in the political system of ancient India and Greece was almost the same. The free tribes in city-states of north-west India adopted the democratic constitutions in the same ways as in ancient cities of Greece (Athens and Sparta) the monarchies of the Heroic Age were succeeded by aristocratic republics sometime between the sixth and the fifth century BC.

Megasthenes as a keen observer of contemporary political system prevailing in India

---

180. *AIMA*, 1st edn., p. 40.
181. *Ibid.*, Fragm. I-B, p. 38; see also *Ind. Ant.*, vol. V, p. 89.
182. *Bib. Hist.*, III, 63 cf. *AIMA*, p. 38.
183. *Indika*, pt. I, Ch. XII cf. *AIMA*, p. 212.

refers to both monarchical and republican forms of government. He notes that "They . . . report everything to the king where the people have a king, and to the magistrates where the people are self-governed".[184] Arrian, has also expressed more or less the same view. He says : "The Councillors of State. . . who advise the king . . . or the magistrates of self-governed cities in the management of public affairs. . . ."[185]

Arrian on the authority of Megasthenes has made a statement of general nature which shows that in India up to the time of Sandrocottus (Candragupta) several kingdoms and republics were set-up out of which one state was thrice organised as a republic and two other republics continued to exist for 120 years and 300 years respectively.[186] Diodorus adds many extravagances about the republican institutions of India.[187]

V.A. Smith, while highlighting the value of the Greek accounts of the republics of north-west India, has aptly remarked that "For many centuries past India has not evolved any form of government other than the ordinary type of oriental despotism; but ancient India exhibited a greater variety of political constitutions and large areas were occupied by nations, tribes, or clans who managed to dispense with common place despot and governed themselves under some form of aristocratic or democratic constitution. The Greek writers give us glimpses of such communities . . . in the Punjab during the fourth century BC and later times. Occasional notices in inscriptions prove that the kingless peoples still held their grounds in various regions. To such peoples apparently must be assigned the curious coins. . . ."[188]

R. Fick's view that "the autonomous states of the Greek writers were individual cities or small states that maintained their independence in the neighbourhood of great monarchies like that of Magadha"[189] cannot be accepted *in toto*, as we find some inconsistency between facts. In fact, individual cities referred to by the Greek writers belonged to independent sovereigns and they formed parts of kingdoms and not autonomous states. The autonomous states mentioned by classical authors were, of

---

184. *AIMA*, p. 212.
185. *Indika*, Ch. XII, *AIMA*, p. 212.
186. *Ibid.*, ch. IX, *AIMA*, p. 203.
187. *Bib. Hist.* (ed. 1604), II, p. 124.
188. *Op. cit.*, vol. I, pp. 160-61, see also J.E. Schwartzberg (ed.), *HASA*, p. 169 f.
189. *The Social Organisation in North-East India in Buddha's time*, p. 137.

course, small but not individual cities. They were actually free cities. There were, of course, a number of small independent states in the neighbourhood of monarchical ones.

In Alexander's time some republican states had extensive territories within the limits of which a number of towns or cities and villages were included. One of the characteristic features of north-western republics was that both towns and villages were under the administrative control of such states. Some independent villages had more or less a republican type of government. We can further proceed to examine the relevance of McCrindle's statement that each of the rural or village units the Greeks took to be an independent republic.[190] A.S. Altekar[191] and K.P. Jayaswal[192] have dismissed his observation on the plea that the Greek authors hardly referred to the village government and never meant by the independent or autonomous states the village republics. But, on the other hand, we find that the above statement is not totally wrong. It rather contains some substratum of truth. Some big villages having a republican system of government were misconstrued by the Greek writers as city-states. There are few illustrations in classical literature to substantiate it. This fact has generally been lost sight of. Further, the Greek writers have not taken pains to make a clear-cut distinction between the cities and villages or between the two systems of government. That is why, they have not touched upon the village administration separately. But the fact remains that the free tribes living in cities and villages were under the republican form of government. In the light of above facts it is very difficult to accept the views of above two noted scholars. I am not in perfect agreement with them so far as this aspect of the subject is concerned. R.C. Jain's statement, that there was no central authority at the lower levels of administration, and the village community functioned like self-governing corporations and as a republic of cities and towns,[193] further lends support to McCrindle's view. McCrindle himself distinguishing the system of the village community from that of the urban ones remarks: "Whatever change may take place in the supreme authority, the peculiar constitution of each township remains unaltered. No revolutions affect it, no

190. *IIA*, p. 115, note 2.

191. *Op. cit.*, p. 111.

192. *Op. cit.*, p. 54.

193. Ed., *MAIMA*, p. xvii f.

conquest changes it. In such communities the Greeks recognised characteristics which forcibly reminded them of their petty independent republics which existed in their own country".[194] In this connction I cannot but quote the view of M. Elphinstone: "The number of independent governments seems to have been as great as at other times. Alexander, in his partial invasion, met with many . . . those which the Greeks called republics and aristocracies can easily be explained without supposing anything different from what now exists. There have always been extensive tracts without any common head, some under petty chiefs, and some formed of independent villages; in troubled times, also, towns have often for a long period carried on their own government. All these would be called republics by the Greeks, who would naturally fancy their constitutions similar to what they had seen at home. But what their authors had particularyly in view were the independent villages, which were in reality republics, and which would seem aristocratic or democratic as the village community was great or small in proportion to the other inhabitants."[195]

From the Greek accounts of the subject it appears that there were only few republics in Afghansitan. It was the Punjab in which there were a number of autonomous tribal republics to the east of the Hydraotes or Rāvī. The republics beyond the river Hyphasis or Vyāsa also could not escape the notice of Alexander, as we find some incidental references to them in the Greek sources. The Lower Indus Valley was another important centre of republics. There were also some minor republican communities in Baluchistan.

The classical accounts of the republican, oligarchical or democratic states with some details of their constitutions and administrative system are trustworthy to a great extent. Beni Prasad's doubt about the authenticity of Greek writers' accounts of the subject (*The State in Ancient India*, pp. 168-69) can not be entertained. The details of the republics of Afghanistan, the Punjab and the Indus Valley which follow here are entirely based on the accounts of Arrian, Curtius, Diodorus, Justin and Plutarch (the five well-known historians of Alexander), Megasthenes, Ptolemy, Strabo and Pliny, and on the data of Pāṇini available in his *Aṣṭādhyāyī*.

194. *AICL* (Westminster, 1901, rept. Delhi, 1984), p. 72, note 3.

195. 'The Greek Accounts of India' rept. from his *The History of India* (9th edn. 1911) in *Ancient India* (Delhi, 1983), p. 25; see also *AIMA*, p. 212, fn.

## AFGHANISTAN

### *The Nysaeans*

Their free city-state called Nysa was situated to the west of the Indus in the Swāt Valley or in the valley of the Kabul river near the Mount Meros. This city-state flourishing at the time of Alexander's invasion had an oligarchical form of government. According to Arrian, it was governed by a body consisting of 300 members of the aristocratic class and a president (chief) named Akouphis. It had 30 councillors or deputies.[196] The dwellers of the city tendered their submission to Alexander, and as a sequel to it the city also fell into his hands. The citizens of Nysa sent out to him their president accompanied by 30 of their most distinguished men (deputies) to solicit his clemency. The president imploringly said: "The Nysaeans beseech thee, O King . . . to allow them to remain free and independent . . . we inhabit Nysa, a free city, and we ourselves are independent conducting our Government with constitutional order".

Alexander gladly accepted the Nysaeans appeal and granted them clemency but he asked for three hundred horsemen from Nysa and one hundred aristocrates, who presided over the government, to accompany him. He ordered Akouphis to make the selection and appointed him governor of Nysa. Akouphis smilingly said: "How, O King can a single city if deprived of 100 of its best men continue to be well governed. But if you have the welfare of the Nysaeans at heart, take with you the 300 horsemen, or, if you wish, even more; but instead of the hundred of our best men you have asked me to select, take with you twice that number of our worst men, so that on your returning here you may find the city as well governed as it is now. . . ."[197] The Macedonian hero being highly impressed by the wisdom and prudence of Akouphis ordered him to send the horsmen only and waived the other demand, which enabled him and other citizens of Nysa to further carry on their oligarchical system of government. Arrian's narratives of the subject can also be supplemented and supported by that of Plutarch.[198] Their narratives show as to how much the Nysaeans loved independence. The city-state of Nysa presents a glaring example of aristocratic oligarchy in Afghanistan.

---

196. *Anab.*, V, 1 & 2, *IIA*, pp. 79 & 81.

197. *Ibid.*, V, 2, *IIA*, p. 81; see also *ibid*, Eng. trans. by E.J. Chinnock, p. 399; CAI, p. 21.

198. *Lif. Alex.*, ch. LVIII, *IIA*, p. 305; see also Curtius, *Hist. Alex.*, VIII, 10, *IIA*, pp. 191-93, Justin, *Hist. Phil.*, XII, 7, *IIA*, p. 321; B.C. Sinha, *Studies in Alexander's Campaigns*, p. 27.

### *The Dārteyas*

They were probably the inhabitants of a small city called by Arrian Dyrta[199] and identified by H.H. Wilson with Dhyr,[200] which was in the realm of the Assakénians or the Āśvakāyanas of the Swāt Valley. They are identical with the Dhārteyas of Pāṇini (IV, 1, 178; V, 3, 117). They are included in the list of the *āyudhajīvī saṁghas*. It is very likely that they had organised a republican type of state in the time of Pāṇini. They lost their independence at the time of the invasion of Alexander. Dyrta was one of the cities occupied by him. Our knowledge about them do not go beyond this.

## PUNJAB

### *The Kathaians (Skt. Kaṭhas)*

They were the most powerful Independent kṣatriya tribe of northern Punjab. According to the narrative of Arrian, they inhabited the regions lying to the east of the Hydraotes or Rāvī,[201] which is nearly if not altogether coextensive with the areas now covered by the districts of Lahore and Amritsar. According to the testimony of Alexandrian historians, their capital Sangala was situated between the Hydraotes (Rāvī) and the Hyphasis (Vyāsa).[202] Hence it was placed by Burnes at Lahore[203] and by Anspach at Jaṇḍīalā to the east of Amritsar.[204] It was probably situated in the Gurudāspur district (Lahore division) not far from Fathgarh.[205] The position of Sangala cannot be determined with precision and accuracy. Sangala of the Greek writers in accordance with the rules of transcription may be identified with Sāṅkala of Pāṇini (IV, 2, 75).[206] It is also described as the city-state of the Kathaians who are no doubt identical with the 'Kathaioi' of Ptolemy.[207] They

199. Arrian, *Anab.*, IV, 30, *IIA*, p. 76.
200. *Ar. Ant.*, p. 192.
201. Arrian, *Anab.*, V, 22, IIA, pp. 115-17.
202. *Ibid.*, V, 22-24, *IIA*, pp. 115-18; Curtius, *Hist. Alex.*, IX, I, *IIA*, pp. 217-18; Diodorus, *Bib. Hist.*, XVII, 91, *IIA* pp. 279-80; *IIA*, Append. pp. 347-48, notes L & M.; E.H. Bunbury, HAG, vol. I, pp. 444-45; *CAI*, pp. 47-50, 170, 259.
203. Cf. *IIA*, pp. 347-48, notes.
204. *CHI*, vol. I, p. 332, note 7.
205. *JRAS*, 1903, p. 687; V.A. Smith, *EHT*, 4th rev. edn., p. 81; *IMP*, *Gaz. Ind.*, vol. XII, p. 393 cf. *AIT*, pp. 365-66, note.
206. *IP*, p. 73; see also Sylvain Levi, *JA*, series VIII, vol. XV (1890), pp. 237-39.
207. *AIT*, pp. 122-24, 157-58.

"enjoyed the highest reputation for courage and skill in the art of war".[208] They along with some other republican tribes had defeated the combined forces of both king Poros and the *rājā* of Abhisāra shortly before their battle with Alexander.

> "The Kathaians were not ruled by kings like the tribes which lay nearer the Indus, but were autonomous, each of the communities into which they were divided being self- governed. In point of martial skill and prowess they were superior to all their neighbours. Their very name indeed indicates their warlike propensities and predominance, for it is doubtless a modified form of kṣatriya, the designation of the military caste."[209]

It is said that each of their ruling units-villages were independent republics.[210] Thus, it appears that both cities and villages were under the republican government. Their's was one of the largest republics in the Punjab.

The Kathaians left no stones unturned to preserve their republican institutions. They fought with such stubbornness against Alexander that even Poros had to come to the aid of the latter with "a force of 5,000 Indians". Sangala was stormed and finally razed to the ground. About 17,000 of the defenders sacrificed their lives and more than 70,000 were made captives.[211] Their territoy was made over to Poros or Paurava. They disdained to purchase peace by surrender and fought against the Greek invader to the last drop of their blood. However, their defeat at the hands of the Macedonian here struck a severe blow to their republican practice. Their love of freedom became a source of inspiration for the neighbouring republican tribes.

### *Saubhūti*

According to Onesikritos (who had accompanied Alexander on his Indian expedition), among the Kathaians beauty was highly valued and "the handsomest man was chosen as king" as quoted by Strabo.[212] But this remark is applicable to the subjects of Sophytes (Saubhūti), an independent sovereign, rather than to their neighbours, the Kathaians, whose institutions were republican. The classical accounts of the subject are full of confusions. However, its not very unlikely that in the kingdom of Sophytes and in the

208. Arrian, *Anab.*, V, 22, 2, *IIA*, p. 115.
209. *AICL*, p. 37, note 1.
210. *IIA*, p. 115, note 2.
211. Arrian, *Anab.*, V, 24, *IIA*, p. 119f.
212. *Geog.*, XV, I, 30, *AICL*, p. 38.

neighbouring republican state of the Kathaians lying between the Rāvī and the Vyāsa the political system was almost identical and the constitution almost similar. A. Cunningham remarks: "It seems highly probable thay they were one and the same people. They were certainly neighbours; and as both of them would appear to have had the same peculiar customs, and to have been equally remarkable for personal beauty . . . they must have been only different tribes of the same race of people".[213]

Strabo records that "some writers say that Kathaia and the country of Sopeithes, one of the petty kings, are situated in the tract between the two rivers (the Hydaspes and the Akesines, i.e., the Jhelum and the Chenab respectively). Others again place them beyond both the Akesines and the Hydraotes (the Chenab and the Rāvi), on the borders of the territory of the other Poros, the nephew of Poros. . . ."[214]

But these views are manifestly wrong. We find that their dominions lay between the Hydraotes and the Hyphasis.[215] It is not very clear whether Sophytes was an elected king or a regular monarch. However, it seems more probable that the administration of his state adjoining the territory of the Kathaians was based on the both monarchical and republican principles. There may have been some impact of the republican tradition of the Kathaians on their neighbours, the subjects of Saubhūti. As in the accounts of Curtius and Diodorus we find Sangala mentioned in connection with a king called Sophytes, so in appendix to Pāṇini's Grammar called the *Gaṇa-Pāṭha* Saubhūta is mentioned in the company of the people of Sāṅkala (Pāṇini, IV, 2, 75). Curtius avers that the people of Sophytes "excelled in wisdom, and lived under good laws and customs".[216] Diodorus observes that the cities subject to the rule of the Sopeithes "were governed by laws in the highest degree salutary" and "their political system was one to admire". "Beauty was held among them in the highest estimation". Further, "it follows that the inhabitants of these cities are generally held in higher estimation than the rest of their countrymen".[217]

From the narrative of Arrian it appears that Alexander before entering the territory of the Kathaians had already encountered several independent or republican tribes on

---

213. *CAGI*, p. 134.
214. *Geog.*, XV, I, 30, *AICL*, pp. 36-37; also Strabo's *Geog.*, Eng. trans. H.C. Hamilton and W. Falconer, vol. III, p. 92.
215. *IIA*, p. 133, note 2, pp. 348-49, 411, notes.
216. *Hist. Alex.*, IX, I, *IIA*, p. 219.
217. *Bib. Hist.*, XVII, 91-2, *IIA*, pp. 279-80.

the banks of the Rāvī.[218] But the details thereof are wanting. Besides the states of the Kathaians and Saubhūti, Arrian mentions two other city-states as republics,[219] but their names are not specified.

### *The Adraistai*

The Adraistai, Adrestae, Adraistoi or Arestae of the Greek writers may philologically be equated with the *Ariṣṭas* of Pāṇini (*sūtra*, VI, 2, 100; *Gaṇa-Pāṭha*, IV, 2, 80). They find mention in Ptolemy's Geography as "Adeisathra"[220] (Skt. Adhṛṣṭas?). They belonged to the Central Punjab. They were one of the free tribes. It is said that they were 'kingless' people.[221] They have been located by the historians of Alexander on the eastern side of the Rāvī. They had a very small state with a republican form of government. Their capital has been called Pimprama.[222] It has also been referred to by the Greek writers as their city-state. The Paurava (the Elder Poros) tried in vain to subdue them before Alexander. However, they ultimately submitted to Alexander after their capital was captured by him. They were later displaced by the foreign invaders (the Śakas and Kuṣāṇas), which led to their migration to a place which is still unknown to us.

### *The Oxydrakai-malloi (Skt. Kṣudraka-mālavas)*

Among five independent tribes ruling in the southern Punjab on the route of Alexander back to the Indus river who had republican form of government, the Kṣudrakas and the Mālavas were the most powerful and famous. Alexander without crossing the river Vyāsa retreated and on his way back down the Indus and up to the Indian frontier in Baluchistan came across a number of republican states.

The accounts of the Greek historians leave behind the impression that the Oxydrakai or Kṣudrakas occupied part of the territory on the Jhelum above its confluence with the Cenāb. They were evidently in the Upper Valley of these two rivers or in the higher region. They were the southern neighbours and allies of the Malloi or Mālavas who occupied the region situated between the lower Rāvī and the Cenāb extending up to the

218. *Anab.*, V, 21, *IIA*, pp. 114-15.
219. *Ibid.*, V, 24, *IIA*, p. 120.
220. *AIT*, p. 377, note.
221. *CAGI*, p. 181.
222. Arrian, *Anab.*, V, 22, *IIA*, pp. 115-16; Diodorus, *Bib. Hist.*, XVII, 91, *ibid.*, pp. 279-80; Justin, *Hist. Phil.*, XII, 8, *ibid.*, p. 323.

confluence of the latter river and the Indus.[223] To state the matter precisely, both these neighbouring republican communities in Alexander's time were settled in the region where the Rāvī joined the Cenāb. It is also said that the confederacy of free tribes lived between the Rāvī and the Vyāsa. The Kṣudrakas in particular are placed between these two rivers.[224] It is, however, doubtful whether this was their real position. Their respective location in the time of Alexander cannot be fiixed with perfect accuracy mainly because of the subsequent changes in river-courses concerned. The Kṣudrakas territory may have comprehended parts of the modern Jhang and Lyāllpur districts or some parts of the Montgomery district. The western extremity of the Mālavas territory lay to the south and south-east of the confluence of the Jhelum and the Cenāb. The latter were by and large in the valley of the Rāvī where they occupied the fertile lowlands. Their territory of great extent seems to have included the greater part of the Jhang district, the north-western portion of the Montgomery district,[225] and perhaps north Multān. According to H.H. Wilson, both these tribes inhabited the neighbouring districts of Multān and Bahāwalpur.[226]

The territories of the Oxydrakai and the Malloi were large and populous. Their states were fully independent or sovereign comprising several towns and cities, which were well organised and prosperous. They were the most famous for their military skill. Arrian says that they were the "most numerous and warlike of all the Indian tribes in those parts" (Punjab).[227] In the art of war they "were far superior to the other nations (peoples) by which Asia was at that time inhabited". They were confederate tribes. The Malloi in particular are called a race of independent Indians[228] against whom Porus and Abissares (an independent prince of Abhisāra) had once led their combined forces, and had been defeated.

---

223. Arrian, *Anab.*, VI, 4-6, *IIA*, pp. 138-41; Arrian's *Indica*, 1st pt. ch. IV; *AIMA*, 1st edn. p. 190; Curtius, *Hist. Alex.*, IX, 4, *IIA*, pp. 232-34; Diodorus, *Bib. Hist.*, XVII, 98, 99, *IIA*, pp. 287-88; Plutarch, *Lif. Alxe.*, ch. 63, *IIA*, pp. 311-12, Justin, *Hist. Phil.*, XII, 9, *IIA*, pp. 324-25; *IIA*, Append. pp. 350-51, note P ; *AICI*, p. 40, note 1; *CAI*, pp. 62, 64; Smith, *EHI*, 4th rev. edn., pp. 77-78, 98-99, *JRAS*, 1903, pp. 685-86.

224. *Imp. Gaz. Ind.* (The Indian empire), vol. II, p. 276; Arrian, *Anab.*, VI, 4; A.E. Anspach, *De Alexandri Magni Expeditione Indica*, note 316, cf. *CHI*, vol. I, p. 336 and note 2.

225. See the view of Smith, *JRAS*, 1903, pp. 698-99, also p. 631; G.H. Raverty, *NAB*, p. 364.

226. *Ar. Ant.*, p. 201.

227. Arrian, *Anab.*, VI, 4, *IIA*, p. 137.

228. *Ibid.*, VI, 6; VI XI, *IIA*, pp. 140-41 & 149; also *Ar. Ant.*, p. 200.

Arrian has incidentally referred to 137 independent cities of the Oxydrokai[229] but wthout specifying their names. Their capital city has been called by him Ucch[230] and by Diodorus Och or Och[231] (southern Punjab), which, according to Cunningham, "is situated on the eastern bank of the confluence of five rivers (pañcanada), 70 miles to the south-south-west of Multan, and 45 miles to the north-east of the present confluence with the Indus at Mithankot".[232] H.H. Wilson places it on the left bank of the Akesines (Cenāb).[233] St. Martin identifies it with Chuchpur on the eastern bank of the Indus right opposite Miṭhankoṭ.[234] The cities of Malloi were along the Cenāb and their capital was near the Rāvī. The clues provided by Arrian[235] about their capital enable us to identify it with ancient Mūlasthānapur or modern Multān — a city which owes its name to them. We cannot say anything definite about their etymological connection. But the fact remains that this fortified city, which was one of their strongholds, was situated in Alexander's time on opposite banks of an old bed of the Rāvī, and now it is on the Cenāb. Bunbury has clearly stated that Multān (the capital of the southern Punjab) was once the capital of the Malloi.[236] Cunningham[237] and McCrindle[238] have also accepted this identification. They hold almost identical views about its position. From thier statements it appears that this city in Alexander's time was situated at a distance of 15 miles above the confluence of the Rāvī and Cenāb. And now it is about 30 miles below the junctions of these two rivers.[239] St. Martin is inclined to identify their capital with Harappā,[240] situated to the east of the Rāvī in the Montgomery district of the west Punjab. But this may have been one of their towns and not the capital.

---

229. Arrian, *Anab.*, VI, 4.
230. *Ibid.*, VI, 15, *IIA*, p. 156, note 3.
231. *Bib. Hist.*, XVII, 98, IIA, pp. 287-88.
232. *CAGI*, p. 204.
233. *Ar. Ant.*, p. 200.
234. *E 'tude*, pp. 124-25 cf *IIA*, p. 156, note 3.
235. Arrian, *Anab.*, VI, 6, *IIA*, pp. 140-41.
236. *HAG*, vol. I, pp. 450-51.
237. *CAGI*, pp. 186, 194.
238. *IIA*, pp. 351-52, note Q.
239. *CAGI*, pp. 186, 194; *IIA*, pp. 351-52, note Q; see also *Ind. Ant.*, vol. V, pp. 87, 96, 333.
240. Cf. *IIA*, pp. 351-52, note Q.

The Kṣudrakas and the Mālavas were predominantly the kṣatriyas and the brāhmaṇas respectively. In their *gaṇa* states or *saṁghas* the non-kṣatriyas and non-brāhmaṇas were called Kṣudrakyas and Mālavyas, as it appears from one of the commentaries on Pāṇini (*Kāśikā*, V, 3, 114). In the *gaṇa* states the non-kṣatriyas were sharply distinguished from the members of the privileged kṣatriya order or the ruling aristocracy. Patañjali commenting on Pāṇini says that the Kṣudrakas and the Mālavas included only members of the kṣatriya caste and not other sections of the population such as labourers or slaves living there (IV, 1, 68).[241] Thirlwall opines that the Kṣudrakas (Sudracae of Curtius or Sydracae of Pliny) and the Mālavas were composed of widely different elements. The former were of śūdra caste — a tribe of aborigins of non-Āryan origin — and the latter were brāhmaṇas.[242] His statement only in respect of the Mālavas appears to be correct. In one of the early Pāli texts (*Apadāna*, II, p. 359) the Kṣudrakas called Khuddakas have been clearly distinguished from the Suddakas (śūdrakas or śūdras). In fact, R.G. Bhandarkar was the first to correct the mistaken identification of the kṣudrakas with the śūdras.[243] The Kṣudrakas and the Mālavas like the Kathaians belonged to the *āyudhajīvī saṁghas* (the corporations of warriors). Pāṇini (V, 3, 114-17) had made it abundantly clear that only brāhmaṇas and the kṣtriyas of the Vāhika region (comprising both the Punjab and the Indus valley) were members of said *saṁghas*. The *Kāśikā* (on V, 3, 114) not only bears the reflection of this truth but also associates these two tribes with the above-mentioned *saṁghas*.

The names of the two republican tribes, the Kṣudrakas and the Mālavas, are very often conjoined in the narratives of the historians of Alexander. They have been frequently mentioned together also in the *Mahābhārata*. Sometimes the name Kṣudraka-Mālavas occurs in a single appellation.[244] They are mentioned in combination by Pāṇini also (*Gaṇa-Pāṭha*, IV, 2, 45).

The geographical proximity of the territories of the Kṣudrakas and the Mālavas drew them close to each other which culminated in the formation of their confederation in the time of Pāṇini (the fifth century BC) which can be fairly attested to by his own

241. *Mahābhāṣya*, ed. Kielhorn, vol. II, pp. 268-69.

242. *History of Greece*, vol. VII, c. 54, p. 40 cf. *IIA*, pp. 350-51, note P; see also *IIA*, p. 287, note 2.

243. *Ind. Ant.*, vol. I, p. 23.

244. *Mbh.*, Sabhā Parva, 48, 14; see also E.W. Hopkins, *GEI*, pp. 392-94; B.P. Roy, *Political Ideas and Institutions in the Mahābhārata*, pp. 169-70.

reference to their united army as *kṣaudraka-mālavi senā* (*gaṇa-sūtra* of *sūtra* IV, 2, 45).[245] This confederacy obviously evolved out of their choice and not compulsion of any situation. It continued to exist till the time of the invasion of north-western India by Alexander the Great. It seems to have lasted for about a century. A. Weber's statement that Pāṇini's predecessor, Āpiśali, also speaks of their Union[246] seems to be untenable. V.S. Agrawala has correctly observed: ". . . the confederate military arrangement between the Kṣudrakas and the Mālavas was not a temporary make-shift, but permanent arrangement so as to find its way into current language in the phrase *Kṣaudraka-Mālavi Senā* as a special grammatical formation. There is, therefore, every likelihood that Pāṇini himself had composed the *Gaṇa-Sūtra Kshudraka-Mālavāt Senā-Saṁjñāyām* on the basis of his personal knowledge of such an army. In fact, the details given by the Greek writers rather Indicate that the joint army had existed before Alexander and was not the outcome of any emergency. . . ."[247] It is thus certain both on the testimony of Pāṇini and the Greek writers that the league of the Kṣudraka-Mālava army had been in existence long before Alexander.[248]

That the two states had formed a league in pre-Alexandrian period can also be proved by the commentaries on Pāṇini (Kātyāyana, *Vārttika*, IV, 2, 45; *Kāśikā*, IV, 2, 45). In the light of the above facts the general belief (which still holds ground) that there was no such league before the time of Alexander can be disposed of. The views of Lassen[249] and Weber[250] that the Kṣudrakas and the Mālavas were united into one nation for the first time by the invasion of Alexander cannot be upheld. It will not be correct to say that they formed a league just to avert an imminent danger, i.e., Alexander's attack on them. However, it can be admitted that the league of the Kṣudraka-Mālavas existed in the time of Pāṇini only in theory and not in practice. It is true that in Pāṇini's time the two states were separate. The confederate state virtually emerged in the time of Alexander. But it cannot be denied that they maintained soveregnity of the constituent parts even at that time.

---

245. *IP*, p. 471.
246. *HIL*, p. 222, note; also *JASB*, vol. LXI, pt. 1 (1892), p. 60.
247. *IP*, p. 472.
248. *Ibid.*, p. 473.
249. *Ind. Alt.*, vol. II, pp. 169-71.
250. *Ind. Stud.*, XIII, p. 375; also *HIL*, p. 222, note.

On the basis of the evidence recorded by Arrian[251] it is assumed that the Kathaians, who dwelt upon the eastern side of the Rāvī, had joined a confederation of the autonomous tribes — the Oxydrakai and the Malloi. It is said that they were neighbouring nations who were generally at war with each other, but were always ready to join against a common enemy.[252] As a matter of fact, the Kathaians were never allied with them. Since there is no evidence of such a confederation, we cannot accept it as a well-ascertained fact.

It is true that the Kṣudrakas and the Mālavas had been usually at war with each other. But they keeping in view their traditional league revied the old bond of friendship. They buried their hatchet, sank their differences, resolved to forget old enmities, joined the hands with each other and finally became allies to fight against the foreign invader. They decided to fight a common foe through a united army. The confederacy which they had formed earlier was already there to meet the invasion of Alexander. It is striking to note that like various other petty confederacies of free tribes or their chiefs, their confederacy also lasted for short period.

At the time of Alexander's invasion the two warlike tribes, the Kṣudraka-Mālavas, entered into a sort of military alliance. Curtius informs us that their combined army consisted of 90,000 foot-soldiers, 10,000 cavalry and 900 war-chariots.[253] They cemented the alliance by ten thousand intermarriages. Curtius clearly states that the confederating states in accordance with their custom had elected a Kṣudraka generalissimo to lead the united army against Alexander the Great. He was a brave warrior, an experienced general and noted for his courage and skill in the art of war. They rallied round one banner under the leadership of a common general to offer the stoutest resistance to Alexander.[254] It is also clear from the account of Aristoboulus (one of the companions of Alexander) that they mutually agreed to strike a blow to the Macedonian hero.[255] But Diodorus says that the two tribes "could not agree as to the choice of a leader and ceased

251. *Anab.*, V, 22, 2.

252. Smith, "The position of the autonomous tribes of the Punjab conquered by Alexander the Great", *JRAS*, 1903, p. 685 f; *CHI*, vol. I, p. 332, note 6; *CAGI*, p. 182; J. Talboys Wheeler, "Greek and Roman India". rept. from his *The History of India form the Earliest Ages*, 1st edn. London, 1881 in *Ancient India* (Delhi, 1983), p. 105, note 15.

253. *Hist. Alex.*, IX, 4, *IIA*, p. 234.

254. *Ibid.*, *IIA*, p. 236.

255. Cf Aelian, *A Collection of Miscellaneous History*, VI, II.

in consequence to take the field together against the enemy".[256] The personal jealousies in all ages have reduced to futility political combinations in India. Curtius almost confirms the version of Diodorus by saying that "overnight a dissension arose amongst them and they retired to their mountain recesses". The statements of Classical writers in this regard appear to be contradictory and inconsistent. However, there is no doubt about the fact that "They stood as an embodiment of Indian power and patriotism at that national crisis".[257] Alexander after having received the information about the confederacy of the Oxydrakai-Malloi and other independent tribes occupying the river valleys changed his strategy. He decided to break their union and to prevent the alliance from taking effect. Before they could combine their forces and their plan of fighting unitedly a common enemy could get materialised, Alexander ordered the fleet and the army to assemble at the next confluence that of the Rāvī and the Cenāb to operate against the Malloi who occupied the fertile valley of the lower Rāvī on both banks of the river. Thus, the two tribes eventually failed to become one in the most needed hour.

It is said that at the confluence of the Jhelum and the Cenāb Alexander was opposed by a confederacy of republican tribes led by the Oxydrakai and the Malloi.[258] But the details thereof are conspicuous by their absence in the classical accounts of the subject.

Alexander swooped down upon the Malloi who had well organised armed-forces. They had nearly 1,00,000 soldiers to resist the invasion. He extinguished their military power before the Oxydrakai could come to their aid. One of their towns with a citadel situated on a commanding height was stormed and 2,000 persons lost their lives. The other inhabitants escaping across the river Rāvī took shelter in a strongly fortified city of Brachmans or brāhmaṇas where Alexander hotly pursued them. The city was besieged. While defending this and other fortified towns in its neighbourhood, 5,000 in all were killed and very few of them were taken prisoners. Most of them were put to sword. The spell of disaster soon befell Alexander. He was in danger of losing his life from a deadly wound he received in the capture of a small town or the main stronghold of the Malloi. It was one of the most memorable incidents in his adventurous career. The Greek army had never experienced such heroic resistance and the fiercest attack of the Malloi. Consequently, the infuriated and enraged trops perpetrated terrible atrocities on the

256. *Bib. Hist.*, XVII, 98, *IIA*, p. 287; see also *IIA*, p. 236, note 1.

257. B.N. Puri, *India as Described by early Greek writers*, p. 53.

258. Arrian, *Anab.*, VI, IV.

innocent inhabitants sparing "neither man, woman nor child".[259] The small town where the tragic incident took place was situated north of the confluence of the Rāvī and Cenāb and hence it could not have been Multān, which lies south of the confluence. According to V.A. Smith, it was situated somewhere near the boundary of the modern Jhang and Montgomery district 80 or 90 miles to north-east of Multān.[260] A large number of them (the Malloi) were mercilessly stain. A city after city fell in the hands of Alexander and his general. According to the Greek historians, their crime was after all the "love of freedom". The Malloi completely broken bowed down to the Macedonian invader. The Oxydrakai after their separation from them had to bear the brunt of attack alone. Thus, they saw no better alternative than to submit to the invader. Eventually, both the tribes were compelled to send their envoys (including some of their headmen) with the authority to negotiate peace with Alexander. But Patañjali says that the Kṣudrakas fought alone against the foreign invader and won the laurels of victory (on Pāṇini, V, 3, 52).[261] This belief in Indian tradition does not go well in accord with Classical tradition.

According to the Greek writers, the two republican states deputed "hundred ambassadors to negotiate peace with Alexander. The former tendered their submission to the latter". It is said about the ambassadors that they "all rode in chariots and were men of uncommon stature and of a very dignified bearing. Their robes were of linen embroidered with in-wroguht gold and purple". "The gods, they said, were the authors of their submission and not fear." They were proud of their "liberty which for so many ages they had preserved inviolate". They, however, keeping in view their helplessness solicited the conqueror's clemency by offers of tribute and the delivery of valuable gifts. Alexander accepted the proposals and presents. He accorded the war reception, extended uncommon hospitality and meted out very decent and courteous behaviour to the ambassadors. He entertained them lavishly. And the "ambassadors were dismissed to their several homes".[262] Alexander was very ruthless to those who stood against him but very courteous to those who were submissive.

Arrian distinctly mentions that the Oxydrakai sent the leading men of their cities

259. For details see *ibid.*, VI, 6-11, *IIA*, pp. 140-49; Curtius, *Hist. Alex.*, IX, 4-7, *IIA*, pp. 232-48; Diodorus, *Bib. Hist.*, XVII, 98, 99, *IIA*, pp. 287-89; Plutarch, *Lif. Alex.*, Ch. 63, IIA, pp. 311-12; Justin, *Hist. Phil.*, XII, 9, *IIA*, pp. 324-25; Strabo, *Geog.*, XV, I, 33, *AICL*, p. 40; also Smith, *EHI*, 4th rev. edn. pp. 98-100 and note.; B.C. Sinha, *op.cit.*, pp. 50-52.

260. Smith, *EHI*, p. 100 and note.

261. *Mahābhāṣya*, ed. Kielhorn, I. pp. 83, 231; II, p. 412.

262. Curtius, *Hist. Alex.*, IX, 7-8, *IIA*, pp. 248-51; also Smith, *EHI*, pp. 101-2.

and their provincial governors, besides 150 of their most eminent men (representatives). They were entrusted with full powers to conclude a treaty.[263] The representatives declared that "they were attached more than others to freedom and autonomy, and their freedom they had preserved intact from the time Dionysius came to India until Alexander's arrival".[264]

After the Kṣudrakas and the Mālavas fell apart the confederacy automatically dissolved. It did not prove to be effective. Alexander appointed Philippos (or Philip) as satrap of the conquered "nations". The two "nations" which had submitted were attached to his satrapy.

The Greek accounts of the subject afford us a glimpse into the internal political organisation and constitution of the Kṣudrakas and the Mālavas. They had no king-consul which is proved by the fact they deputed 100 or 150 representatives to negotiate the treaty of peace with Alexander. They were obviously the leading members of their Central Assembly. The number of the members of their Assemblies may have been probably larger. They were governed by almost the same constitution, according to which the power was not vested in one man or a small body of men, but in a bigger body. It is noteworthy that the armies of two states elected a common general. Their *gaṇa*s did reserve in their own hands the executive powers instead of delegating it to their council or cabinet which betrays a defect of their constitutions. The form of government in their city-states was truely democratic. In the bigger republican state of the Kṣudrakas cities enjoyed full internal autonomy. They constituted separate administrative units, completely autonomous, and administered by their leading men. Their state was divided into provinces, each under a separate governor probably recruited from the privileged class. Both the cities and villages were self-governed. The Kṣudrakas later completely merged in the Mālavas.

A major section of the Mālavas (with whom the Kṣudrakas were fully amalgamated) after having come under the political pressure of the Indo-Greeks and Indo-Scythians (Śakas) or being dispossesed of their territories by them by the middle of the second century BC or sometime between *c*. 150 and 100 BC migrated from their original homeland in Punjab to eastern Rājpūtānā in search of a new home. They settled in the ancient town of Nāgar or Karkoṭa Nāgar situated in the modern Jaipur state at a distance of about 25 miles a little east of south from Ṭoṅk, which is proved by the discovery of a

263. Arrian., *Anab*., VI. 14, *IIA*, p. 154.

264. *Ibid*.

large number of copper coins there by A.C. Carlleyle sometime between 1871 and 1873.[265] The coins bear legends in Brāhmī: *mālavānāṁ jaya* ("Victory of the Mālavas"), *mālavaṇa jaya* ("Victory of the Mālavas" in Prākṛta), and *mālavagaṇasya* (of the Mālava *gaṇa*) dated between the second century BC and the fourth century AD.[266] It appears that coins were issued in the name of the *gaṇa* or the whole republic and not the king. Severals coins "with names of their chiefs" have also been found.[267] The place Nāgar after being occupied by them became popularly known as Mālavanagar which was probably their capital or main seat of power. They revived there their old republican tradition. The coins obtained by Cunningham at Pokhar in November 1864 were mainly from the Nāgar region.[268] More than six thousand coins issued by the Mālavas were discovered at Nāgar and adjoining region out of which about 35 coins were of foreign origin. Some coins were found bearing the inscriptions in Kharoṣṭhi. The coins on the whole have been assigned to a period which ranges from about the middle of the second century BC to the middle of the fourth century AD or from *c.* 150 BC to AD 330. However, there is a difference of opinion among the numismatists about the dating of the earliest coins.[269]

The Mālavas' occupation of eastern as well as central Rājpūtānā in the second century AD is a well proven fact. They occupied a tract near Ajmer where they came into conflict with the Uttamabhadras in the early part of the second century AD. While rescuing him, Uṣavadata, the son-in-law of Nahapāna, the Śaka Kṣatrapa of the Kṣaharāta family, inflicting a crushing defeat upon the Mālavas, which can be testified to by the Nāsik cave inscription of Uṣavadata.[270] It was Śrī-Soma or Nandīsoma who liberated the Mālavas from the Śaka domination by defeating the Śakas in AD 225. In fact, he was the Mālava general who is credited with having regained the independence for his state (Mālava-gaṇa-Viṣaya). He belonged to a family which was entrusted with the militray leadership at least for three generations. The political organisation of the Mālavas seems to have undergone radical change in the first half of the third century AD. The leadership of the Mālavas began to pass in the hands of hereditary family. The Mālavas' executive head

265. *CASR*, vol. VI (Calcutta, 1873), pp. 162 f, 173, 1776, 179; Smith, *CCIM*, vol. I, pp. 161-62.

266. Smith, *op. cit.*, pp. 162-63, 170-74; also Cunningham, *Co. An. Ind.*, pp. 77, 89, pl. VI, VII, *JBORS*, vol. XXIII, pt. III, pl. 317.

267. See Smith, *op. cit.*, pp. 170-78.

268. *CASR*, vol. XIV (Calcutta, 1882), p. 150.

269. Smith *op. cit.*, pp. 162-3, 170f; Allan, *CCBM*, p. cvi., *CASR*, VI, pp. 165, 174, 178, 182; Rapson, *Ind. Co.*, pp. 12-13; S.K. Chakrabortty, *AIN*, p. 192.

270. *Ep. Ind.*, vol. II, p. 78 f; vol. VIII, p. 44.

and military general (*mahāsenāpati*) belonged to the same family on the hereditary line. They were not elected by their assembly. However, their leaders or chiefs like Śrī-Soma were not permitted to have any regal title like *rājā* or *mahārājā* which indicates that the *gaṇa* tradition of the Mālavas even under the military regime was not affected. The Nandsā inscription[271] bears ample testimony to the facts stated above.

In the third century AD the region round about Nandsā, situated at a distance of 75 miles south-east of Ajmer or 110 miles east of Nāgar, was one of the seats of power of the Mālavas. The *viṣaya* of the Mālava *gaṇa* included a considerable portion of south-eastern Rājpūtānā comprising parts of the states of Udaipur, Jaipur and Ṭoṅk and the district of Ajmer. In the fourth century AD the Mālavas moved further southward and probably settled in Mewār and Koṭāh. They seem to have occupied the whole of the vast area to the south of Nāgar which was called Mālwā after them. They maintained their existence at Nāgar and the neighbouring areas sustaining independent life up to the fourth century AD. The *Mahābhārata* also mentions the Mālavas' settlements in the north and the west.

> "The migration from the fertile lands of the Punjab to dreary Rajputana is the testimony to the love of liberty which these unconquerable republicans bore "more than others", as one of them (the Mālavas) put it in the time of Alexander. They believed that the Yaudheya country or the Mālava country was wherever the Yaudheya or Mālava Gaṇa lived and lived as of Yore in freedom. They would sacrifice paternal homes and lands to preserve their political self and soul. They would go to deserts but live in democratic glory and rule in parliament. It is a settled principle of Hindu politics that freedom is more important than home and is to be preserved at the cost of the latter. The republics seem to have fully acted upon this principle".[272]

It is bit difficult to decide the antiquity of the settlements of the Mālava *gaṇa* in central India. It is generally believed that they defeated the Śakas near Ujjayinī (Ujjain), the capital of western Mālwā, in *c*. 58-57 BC and in order to commemorate this victoy introduced a new era known as Kṛta, Mālava or Vikrama, counted from that very date. On the basis of two Mandasor inscriptions, J.F. Fleet has also postulated that the "Vikrama Era" derived its origin from them,[273] which indicates that they had occupied Mālawā sometime

271. *Ep. Ind.*, vol. XXVII, pp. 252, line 4, and 266 f.
272. Jayaswal, *Hindu Polity*, p. 148.
273. *CII*, vol. III, pp. 70f, 87, 154, 158; also *Ind. Ant.* vol. XXII, p. 184; *Ep. Ind.*, vol. IX, p. 320.

before *c*. 58 or 57 BC. But this is debated on the ground that there is no definite evidence of the Śakas' settlements in western Mālwā before the second century AD. D.R. Bhandarkar does not take the Mālavas as the founders of the said era.[274] However, there is no doubt about the fact that some section of them while moving further southwards from south-eastern Rajasthan in the fourth century AD settled in Mālwā region[275] or in Vidiśā or Bhilsā, the capital of eastern Mālwā. After the fall of the Kuṣāṇa empire they further consolidated their position and maintained it up to the early Gupta period. In one of the later epigraphic records, the Mālavas having settlements in seven different regions of India, including those of Cis-Sutlej district of the Punjab, eastern Rājapūtānā and eastern Mālwā or Bhilsā region, have been mentioned as "Sapta-Mālavas".[276]

The republican system of government of the Mālavas no doubt continued to flourish till about the middle of the fourth century AD.

### *The Siboi Or Sibai (Śibis Or Śivis)*

They were originally governed by a monarchical constitution but sometime between the fifth the and fourth century BC adopted a republican constitution. They were known to Pāṇini (IV, 2, 109; Patañjali, IV, 2, 52). In the time of former Uśinara (IV, 2, 118; Patañjali, II, 4, 19), which formed part of the Vāhikadeśa, was their original home. It was situated between the Cenāb and the Rāvī in the south. The Śibis are often associated with the Uśinaras. Uśinara figures in the two lists of *āyudhajīvī saṁgha*s in the *Gaṇa-Pāṭha* (IV, 1, 178 and V, 3, 117). In his time it was probably under the *saṁgha*s government. The Śibis were definitely one of the *āyudhajīvīn*s or martial tribes of Punjab at that time.

At the time of Alexander's invasion, the Siboi or Śibis were settled in the region to the south of the confluence of the Jhelum and the Cenāb rivers on both the banks. They were in the neighbourhood of their republican friends, the Malloi or the Mālavas, as it appears from the account of Curtius.[277] They were undoubtedly the inhabitants of the Shorkoṭ region in the Jhang district at some distance above the junction of the above two rivers. It is also placed between the Rāvī and the Cenāb. Their big republican state appears to have included parts of southern, central and northern Punjab.[278] One of the

274. *Commemorative Essays*, presented to Sri R.G. Bhandarkar (BORI, Poona, 1917), pp. 187-94.
275. See *IHQ*, vol. I, p. 257.
276. *Ep. Ind.*, vol. V, p. 229p also *ABORI*, vol. XIII, pts. 3-4 (1931-32) p. 229.
277. *Hist. Alex.*, IX, 4, *IIA*, p. 232; also *AIMA*, 1st edn. p. 111, footnote.
278. *CAGI*, p. 171; B.C. Law, *HGAI*, pp. 66, 127-28.

historians of Alexander has located them between the Indus and the Akesines (Cenāb).[279] It is said that "The Sivis inhabited a district between the Hydespes and the Indus"[280] and their capital stood at a distance of about thiry miles from the former river above its confluence with the Akesines.[281] The ancient Śivapura of Patañjali (IV, 2, 2) or Śibipura of Shorkoṭ inscription (dated 83, Palaeograhically assignable to the fifth century AD : G.E. = AD 402-3) identified with modern Shorkoṭ was their capital. According to J. Ph. Vogel, who edited the said inscription, the mound of Shorkṭ marks the site of their capital city.[282] They were not only in the Punjab but also in Sind.

According to Diodorus, the Siboi had "a free city-state". They had full-fledged republican form of government. "There was no king amongst them, only the citizens filled the highest offices".[283] While forty thousand soldiers from this state were making preparation to oppose Alexander, the latter along with his troops reached at the confluence of the Jhelum and the Cenāb, situated not very far from the modern town of the Jhang (on the Cenāb), in order to subjugate the adjoining tribes called Siboi and Agalassoi and to prevent them from joining the powerful independent tribe, the Malloi, who were ready to offer the strenuous resistance to the inavader.[284] It is said that the citizens from the Śibi state after having offered their submission were allowed by Alexander to retain their freedom.[285]

In the *Mahābhārata* the "Śivigaṇa" have been mentioned along with other republican tribes like the Trigarttas, the Mālavas, the Ambaṣṭhas, the Yaudheyas and the Madras.[286]

The Śibis were one of those republican tribes who being hard pressed by the foreign aggressions left their original home in the Pubjab. They probably being displaced by the Śakas sometime in the second century BC migrated with the Mālavas from the Punjab to Rājapūtānā and settled in the town of Madhyamikā near Nāgarī or Cittor where a large number of their coins belonging to the second century BC have been found. The coins

---

279. Arrian, *Indika*, V. 12; see also *AIMA*, 1st edn. p. 196; *AIT*, p. 290.
280. Strabo, *Geog.*, XV, I, 33, *AICL*, p. 40; also *AICL*, pp. 199-200, note 11; *IIA*, p. 366.
281. *IIA*, p. 366, note Ee.
282. *Ep. Ind.*, vol. XVI (1921), p. 16; also Smith, *EHI*, 4th rev. edn. p. 97.
283. *Bib. Hist.*, XVII, 96, *IIA*, p. 285.
284. Curtius, *Hist. Alex.*, IX. 4, *IIA*, pp. 232-33; Justin, *Hist. Phil.*, XII, 9, *IIA*, p, 324; also Smith, *op. cit.*, p. 97; *CAI*, pp. 136, 174.
285. Diodorus, *Bib. Hist.*, XVII, 96, *IIA*, p. 285.
286. Sabhā Parva, 29, 5-6; 48, 13; Droṇa Parva, 6, 2-7; see also *Mbh. Ko.*, p. 673; *Bh. Sāv.*, vol. I, p. 158.

are struck in the name of their republic or the "country of the Śibis of Madhyamikā" (*majhamikāya śibi janapadasa*),[287] and not that of any king. We have no evidence of their political existence in the subsequent period.

*The Agalassians, Agalassoi, Agesinae Or Argasinae (Agra-Śreṇīs)*

They belonged to the southern Punjab. Their territory was situated at the confluence of the Jhelum and the Cenāb. They were very close to the Siboi on the eastern side.[288] Both the adjoining tribes were in the neighbourhood of the Kṣudrakas and the Mālavas.

The Agalassians of the Greek writers are identifiable with the Śreṇīs of Kauṭilya included by him in the list of *śastropajīvin saṁghas*. They had no king-consul. They lived by the profession of fighting. They were subdivided into more than one unit. Those who came into conflict with Alexander were the Agra-Śreṇīs or the First-Śreṇīs.

The Agalassians with the help of 40,000 foot-soldiers fought against Alexander with great vigour and valour. They barricaded their narrow streets. The latter "in pressing the attack lost a few Macedonians".[289] The former gallantly defended their capital or one of their principal towns, but it was ultimaltely captured by the invader. The citizens numbering about 20,000 offered heroic resistance to him, but realising their desperate position "set fire to their houses, and cast themselves along with their wives and childeren into the flames". They preferred death to surrender.[290] Thus, they sacrificed their lives for the sake of freedom. They have been identified with Ārjunāyanas which is absolutely wrong.[291] There is no valid reason to justify this identification. Because their state does not appear to have existed at that very time.

*Republics In The Neighbourhood Of The Kingdom Of The Elder Porus*

Plutarch, quoting Onesikritos, informs us that in the neighbourhood of the dominions of Porus (situated between the Jhelum and the Cenāb in N. Punjab) there were fifteen tribes with republican form of government in their cities.[292] But he has not specified their names. However, it is true that "Porus" immediate neighbours on every side were

287. *CASR*, VI, pp. 290-92; XIV, pp. 146; Allan, *CCBM*, pp. cxxiii-cxxv; Rapson *Ind. Co.*, p. 14.

288. St. Martin, *E'tude*, p. 115 cf. *IIA*, p. 367, note Ff.

289. Diodorus, *Bib. Hist.*, XVII, 96, *IIA*, pp. 285-86.

290. *Ibid.*; Curtius, *Hist. Alex.*, IX, 4, *IIA*, pp. 232-33; see also *CAI*, p. 175.

291. *IIA*, p. 367, note Ff.

292. *Lif. Alex.*, ch. 60, *IIA*, pp. 307-9 see also CAI, p. 197.

independent of him and most of them at war with him.[293] We are further fold that Alexander not only reinstated his faithful subordinate ally, Porus, in his kingdom with "the title of Satrap, but added a large province to it, subduing the inhabitants whose form of government was the republican".[294] Porus extended his sway over the cities of the said republican tribes.

### *The Glaukanikoi Or Glausai*

The free clan called the Glaukanikoi by the historians of Alexander or Galusai by Ptolemy are identical with the *Glauchukāyanakas* of the *Kāśikā* on Pāṇini (IV, 3, 99).[295] Arrian on the authority of Aristoboulos states that they occupied a tract to the west of the Cenāb which was coterminous with the dominion of Porus.[296] It is said that their "country lay in the fertile and populous regions lying in the south of Kāśmīr (the Bhimber and Rajauri districts) between the upper courses of the Jhelum and the Cenāb and the Rāvī".[297] The prevailing form of government in their state was by and large republican. They were independent of Porus. According to Arrian, they had 37 large cities the smallest of which contained not fewer than 5,000 inhabitants while many contained upwards of 10,000. There were also a great many villages which were not less populous than the towns. Alexander took them and put under the rule of great Porus, thereby adding much "country" to what he had before possessed.[298] They eventually became one of the dependencies of Porus. All other independent tribes bordering on the banks of the Hydraotes or Rāvī were reduced by Alexander's troops and placed under the rule of other Porus, nephew of the great Porus.[299]

### *The Abastanoi (Skt. Ambaṣṭhas)*

They were originally a monarchical people, and their state was under a monarchical government. The change in their constitution, from monarchy to republic, took place sometime between the fifth and the fourth century BC like the change in that of the Śibis.

---

293. Elphinstone *op. cit.*, p. 27, note.
294. Plutarch, *Lif. Alex.*, ch. 60, *IIA*, pp. 308-9.
295. *IP*, pp. 75-76.
296. *Anab.*, V. 20, *IIA*, p. 111-12.
297. *IP*, p. 76.
298. *Anab.*, V. 20, *IIA*, p. 112; Chinnock, *op. cit.*, p. 276.
299. *Ibid.*, V, 21, *ibid.*, pp. 114-15.

The Abastanoi or Arrian, Sambastai or Diodorus, Sabarcae of Curtius or Sabagrae of Orosius may undoubtedly be identified with the Ambaṣṭhas of Sanskrit literature. The Umbrittae of Megasthenes[300] or Ambastai or Ambautai of Ptolemy[301] may be taken as the same. The latter has placed them "in the east of the country of the Paropanisadai" (along the southern and eastern side of Hindukush or in the Kabul valley),[302] which must have been their habitat in the very early period.

The Ambaṣṭha of Pāṇini (*sūtra* VIII, 3, 97)[303] may definitely be taken as the Abastanoi or Sambastai of the Greek writers. The "Śaubhreyas" of former (identical with the Sabarcae of Curtius) belonged to an *āyudhajīvī saṁgha* (*Gaṇa-Pāṭha*, IV, 1, 178 and V, 3, 117).[304] They were brāhmaṇas by birth and kṣatriyas by profession. The Greek name may be descriptive of their warlike character. They had earned a high degree of reputation as warriors. They appear to have been divided into three clans. They were united as warriors in such a way as if they were formed of three allied tribes.

From the account of Arrian it distinctly appears that at the time of Alexander's invasion the Abastanoi, "one of the independent tribes", were settled on the lower Akesines or Cenāb above its confluence with the Indus.[305] They were apparently in the Cenāb valley in the neighbourhood of the Kṣudraka-Mālavas. H.H. Wilson has located them "in the Doāb between the Jhelum and the Cenāb".[306] They no doubt belonged to the southern Punjab. Curtius[307] and Diodorus[308] have placed them at the confluence of the Punjab rivers. Their territory seems to have extended along the bank of the Sindhu. They also lived in the northern part of Sind.[309] It has also been observed that "They were intimately connected with the Śivis and the Yaudheyas and were settled on the eastern border of the Punjab".[310]

---

300. *AIMA*, rev. 2nd edn. ed. R.C. Majumdar, pp. 152-53; Jain (ed.), *MAIMA*, Append. 4.
301. *AIT*, pp. 160-61, 376-77, note; see also R. Shafer, *EAI*, p. 117.
302. *Ibid.*, pp. 160-61, 311-12.
303. *IP*, p. 54, also Bohtlingk, *Pāṇini's Grammatik* (Leipzing, 1887) p. 464.
304. *IP*, p. 451.
305. *Anab.*, VI. 15, *IIA*, p. 155 and note 2; see also CAI, p. 75.
306. *Ar. Ant.*, p. 201.
307. *Hist. Alex.*, IX, 8, *IIA*, pp. 251-52.
308. *Bib. Hist.*, XVII, 102, *ibid.*, p. 292; see also *CAI*, pp. 75, 151, 180.
309. N.L. Dey, *GDAMI*, p. 6.
310. Law, *HGAI*, p. 60; *AIT* (London, 1934), vol. 1, pp. 34-36.

In the time of Alexander, the Ambaṣṭhas were a powerful tribe, and the form of their government was democratic and not regal. Diodorus expressly states that "They were a people inferior to none in India either for numbers or for bravery. They dwelt in cities in which the democratic form of government prevailed".[311] They were an independent tribe "without kings". They have been described as "one of the free nations of India".[312] Both banks of the river Cenāb were thickly studded with their cities and villages.

According to Curtius, the Sabarcae had a bigh republican state. Their army consisted of 60,000 foot-soldiers, 6,000 cavalry and 500 chariots. "They had elected three generals renowned for their valour and military skill"[313] to lead their armies to oppose Alexander the Great. But following the advice of their elders or leaders not to fight they ultimately decided to submit to him and to make peace proposal. They deputed fifty of the foremost citizens as ambassadors to negotiate peace with him "under the belief that they would be treated with all proper courtesy".[314] The elders on whose advice they decided to make peace with Alexander were not the members of an Upper House of Elders but senior persons of their own order. They elected not only the members of the executive but also the military leaders. It seems that like the Roman Senate their Central Assembly elected their own generals for launching campaigns in the fourth century BC. They had a Lower House composed of elected elders. According to their democratic constitution, every man in the community was free to exercise his franchise.

Alexander after having achieved victory over the Kṣudrakas and the Mālavas near the old junction of the Rāvī with the Cenāb moved down the rivers until he reached the confluence of the Akesines and the Indus where he waited for Perdikkas, one of his generals, who during the course of his march had subdued the Abastanoi or Sambasta.

The *Mahābhārata* mentions the Ambaṣṭhas along with the Śivis, the Kṣudrakas, the Mālavas and the other republican tribes of Punjab[315] Patañjali (on Pāṇini, IV, 1, 170, 171) refers to them only as a political community. The seems to have migrated from Punjab in later times to some place near the Mekala hill which is the source of the Narmadā.[316] They further moved to eastern India (Bihar and Bengal).

311. *Bib. Hist.*, XVII, 102, *IIA*, p. 292.
312. *CAGI*, pp. 202. 206; Smith, *EHI*, 4th rev. edn. p. 104.
313. *Hist. Alex.*, IX, 8, *IIA*, p. 252.
314. Diodorus, *Bib. Hist.*, XVII, 102, 292-93.
315. Sabhā Parva, 29, 5-6; 48, 14; Droṇa Parva, 6, 2-7.
316. Law, *HGAI*, p. 60; *TAI*, pp. 97, 374; see also *Ind. Ant.*, XIII, p. 361.

*The Yaudheyas*

They occupied very important position among republican peoples of north-western India. They adopted a republican form of government as early as the fifth century BC. The earliest reference to them as a republican community occurs in Pāṇini's *Aṣṭādhyāyī*. They mentioned therein as members of an *āyudhajīvī saṁgha* (*śutra*, V, 3, 117; *Gaṇa-Pāṭha*, IV, 1, 178; V, 3, 117) — a tribal republican organisation with sound military base. As already stated, the members of such *saṁgha* lived by the profession of war. Their very name indicates that they belonged to warrior class. They were undoubtedly the kṣatriya tribe. They further flourished as a republican people in the time of Alexander. In their times the Yaudheya republic was very prosperous and famous for its valour and love of independence.

The Yaudheyas had an extensive territory which covered large part of the Punjab. The areas occupied by them roughly correspond to south-eastern Punjab. They are often placed in the eastern Punjab.[317] They were basically divided into three distinct clans.

At the time of Alexander's invasion one of the prominent sections of the Yaudheyas had settlements on the opposite bank of the Hyphasis or Vyāsa. The latter did not come into conflict with the formed but definitely received his notice about which all positive indications are there. Arrian, one of Alexander's historians, mentions that the republican or oligarchic states to the east of the Hyphasis conducted their own political affairs in a regular and constitutional manner. He further observes that when Alexander reached the Hyphasis, he heard that beyond that river the country was "exceedingly fertile and the inhabitants were good agriculturists, brave in war and living under an excellent system of internal government; for the multitude was governed by the aristocracy, who exercised their authority with justice and moderation".[318] Thus, they were not only warriors but also agriculturists. They appear to have achieved prosperity by paying equal attention to warfare, agriculture, trade and industry. The account of the Greek historian more or less tallies with Kauṭilya's description of *vārttā-śastropajīvin saṁgha*s mentioned earlier. The missing links in the statement of Arrian can be restored by what the Roman geographer, Strabo, says: "All the country beyond the Hypanis (Hyphasis) is allowed to be very fertile, but little is accurately known regarding it. . . . They mention

317. Motichandra, *GEM*, p. 94.

318. *Anab.*, V. 25, *IIA*, pp. 121-22; see also CAI, p. 51.

also an aristocratical form of government, consisting of five thousand Councillors, each of whom furnishes the state with an elephant. . . ."[319]

The classical writers have not spelt out the name of a great republic on the other side of the Vyāsa or to the east of it. But this unnamed republic in all probability was of the Yaudheyas. The numismatic evidence also confirms our belief. Their dominions extended eastward up to Sahāranpur (Behaṭ) in U.P. where for the first time Captain Cautley in 1834 discovered some of their coins.[320]

After having analysed and interpreted the data supplied by Arrian and Strabo referred to above we obtain the result that the trans-Vyāsa republican state, which was not only powerful but also very big, belonged to the Yaudheyas. In their state the power was vested not in the whole body of the citizens but in a small aristocratic class. However, the sovereignty was vested in a very large Central Assembly or Parliament which consisted of as many as five thousand members. We do not know whether they were elected. Its membership was restricted to those who could supply at least one elephant to the state army. Arrian says that "These Indians had elephants in greater number and of superior size and courage".[321] The discovery of the earliest elephant type copper coin of the pre-Christian era belonging to the Yaudheyas[322] shows that the classical description of the trans-Vyāsa republic pertains to that of the Yaudheyas.

It is worthy of note that the Yaudheyas on the other side of the Vyāsa were the valiant warriors. They were invincible. Their very name, according to Alexander, struck terror in the minds of his soldiers. According to his own statement, the Macedonians "now for the first time" had to face really large armies. His own army "now began to lose heart" and "they began to hold conferences" and ultimately decided not to advance further. As a result of which the Macedonians hero had to crush his desire of crossing the Vyāsa. He had to retreat without conquering the Yaudheyas.[323] V.A. Smith observes that "the Beas was the boundary between the Yaudheyas east of that river and the Madrakas to the west".[324]

---

319. *Geog*; XVI. 37, AICL, pp. 44-5.
320. J. Prinsep, *ETA*, ed. E. Thomas, pp. 84-85, pls. IV, 11, 12: *JASB*, III (1834), pl. XVIII; IV (1835), pl. xxxiv; see also *JBORS*, vol. XXII (1936), p. 59.
321. *Op. cit.*
322. Smith, CCIM, pp. 165, 180-81.
323. Arrian, *op. cit.*, see also *IIA*, pp. 121-22.
324. *JRAS*, 1897, p. 889.

A large section of the Yaudheyas in Alexander's time were settled on both banks of the Hesydrus or Sutlej along the Bahāwalpur border which is known as Johiyawar or Yaudheyawara (the district round Multān). The modern Johiya Rājpūts who have been in occupation of both banks of the river since time immemorial are believed to be the descendants of the ancient Yaudheyas. They have been located in the southern Punjab. Cunningham connecting them with the Ossadioi of Arrian has inferred that Alexander may have carried his arms to Ajudhan, a town on the banks of the Sutlej. And the Yaudheyas tendered their allegiance to him at the confluence of the Punjab rivers.[325] In Alexander's time those regions were no doubt occupied by some autonomous tribes, including the yaudheyas. But keeping in view in fact that he did not traverse either the valley of the Vyāsa or that of the Sutlej it is very difficult to accept his hypothetical view that they were subdued by him.

In the *Mahābhārata* the Yaudheyas have been grouped with other republican peoples such as the Śibis, Trigarttas, etc.[326] Patañjali also mentions them in his *Mahābhāṣya* (IV, 1, 117). Varāhamihira has placed them in the northern division of India. He has also mentioned them along with other independent tribes like the Śibis, the Vasātis, the Ārjunāyanas, etc.[327]

The coins, seals and inscriptions of the Yaudheyas on the whole falling in between the period ranging from the middle of the second century BC to the middle of the fourth century AD throw some light not only on the extent of their territory but also on their administrative machinery and republican constitution. A large number of their coins (both copper and silver) and some clay seals or votive tablets have been found in the eastern Punjab and in the valley of rivers Sutlej and the Yamunā[328] the presentation of the details of which here is neither necessary nor desirable. They were a widely diffused republican tribe. In course of their diffusion they settled at different places at different periods of history.

---

325. *CAGI*, pp. 206-69; *Co. An. Ind.*, p. 76; *CASR*, vol. XIV, p. 140.

326. Sabhā Parva, 48. 13.

327. *Br. Sam.*, XVII, 19; see also V, 40, 67, 75; XIV, 28; XVI, 22.

328. For details see Cunningham *Co. An. Ind.*, pp. 75-79, also pl. VI; *CASR*, vol. XIV, pp. 139-44, pl. XXXI, 7-12; *CAGI*, pp. 206-8; Smith, *CCIM*, pp. 165, 180-83, Rapson, *Ind. Co.*, pp. 14-15, pls. III, 13-15; Allan, *CCBM*, pp. cxlvii-clix; *JNSI*, II, pp. 109-12; XIII, pp. 101-2; XVIII, p. 46f; XXIV, p. 138; XXVII, Pt. I, pp. 85-87; XXVIII, Pt. 2. p. 201, *JBORS*, XXII (1936), pp. 59-60; *JUPHS*, XXIII, pp. 171-74.

> "The Yaudheya republic was a fairly extensive state. The findspots of its coins show that it extended from Saharanpur in the east to Bahavalpur in the west, from Ludhiyana in the north-west to Delhi in the south-east. It was a confederation of three republics. Rohtak in the Punjab was the capital of one of them, and northern Panchala . . . was the centre of power of the second. Northern Rajputana seems to have been in the jurisdiction of the third".[329]

Their republican state seems to have comprised three sub-states. It was probably the largest republic in north-western India. We find that it was a great confederation of five republics which was known as the *Yaudheya Mahāsaṁgha*. The Yaudheyas, the Kuṇindas of north, the Agraśreṇīs of west, the Ārjunāyanas of south-east and the Bhadras of the Gaṅgā-Yamunā Doāb in the east and the Mālavas of the Rājpūtānā formed a confederacy sometime between the second and the first century BC to consolidate their position. But A.S. Altekar is of the view that it was a confederation of only three republican tribes, the Yaudheyas, the Kuṇindas and the Ārjunāyanas. The presidents of the three constituent republics elected by respective federating units had formed a Council to deal with military affairs and foreign policy.[330] V.A. Smith has opined that the Yaudheyas had organised a confederation in the "southern portion of the Punjab and the northern of Rajputana".[331]

The Yaudheyas' coins of three well-marked classes confirm their division into three sections.[332] Some coins were struck in the name of the *gaṇa* as well as the members of their Cabinet or the Executive Council. The coins bearing the legend in Brāhmī characters: *yaudheyagaṇasya jaya* (Victory of the Yaudheya *gaṇa*) assignable to the third-fourth century AD were found west of the Sutlej.[333] Coins of republics, where there was no king-consul, were generally struck in the name of the *gaṇa*. A group of coin-moulds with a legend *yaudheyānāṁ jaya-mantradharānāṁ* discovered at Sunet, 3 miles west of Ludhiana town, were brought to light by A.F.R. Hoernle.[334] These moulds are assigned

329. Altekar, *op. cit.*, p. 119; also *JNSI*, XI, p. 50.
330. Altekar and Majumdar (eds.), *The Age of the Vākāṭakas and the Guptas*, vol. VI, pp. 30, 246; see also *JNSI*, XI, p. 52
331. *JRAS*, 1897, p. 887.
332. Cunningham, *Co. An. Ind.*, p. 78; *CAGI*, pp. 206-8; Smith, *CCIM*, p. 165.
333. Cunningham, *Co. An. Ind.*, p. 77, pl. VI, 7; *CAGI*, pp. 206-8; *CASR*, XIV, pp. 141-42, 144.
334. *PASB*, LIII (1884), pp. 138-40.

to the third century AD. The legend stands for the members of the Executive Committee vested with power to formulate the policy (*mantra*) of the state.[335]

The stone inscription of the third century AD found at Bijayagaḍh near Bayānā in the Bharatpur state shows that an elected president (leader) of the Yaudheya *gaṇa*, who was the head of republic, was also called *mahārāja* or *mahāsenāpati* (. . . *yaudheya-gaṇa-puraṣkṛtasya mahārāja-mahāsenāpati*. . .).[336] A seal discovered at Agrohā with the legend in the Brāhmī characters conveys more or less the same information.[337]

The period extending from the fall of the Mauryas to the coming of the Kuṣāṇas to power may be taken as the period of the complete independence of the Yaudheyas. Towards the end of the first century AD they were temporarily overpowered by Kaniṣka I. A sizeable section of them being pressed by the foreign invaders migrated form their original seat in eastern Punjab to north-western Rājpūtānā in early Kuṣāṇa times or sometime before the second century AD. And they occupied the Bijayagaḍh region of the Bharatpur state, where they came in collision with the Śaka "Mahā-kṣatrapa", Rudradāman I (AD 130-50), who had possibly defeated them. In his Jūnāgaḍh Rock Inscription (AD 150), the Yaudheyas are described as "rendered proud, as they were, by having manifested their title of heroes among all Kṣatriyas"[338] which indicates the power and the prestige enjoyed by them during the period. The coins of the third century AD with the legend *yaudheyagaṇasya jaya* are indicative of the victory of the Yaudheyas (who had occupied the territory between the upper courses of the Sutlej and the Vyāsa) over the Kuṣāṇas. It is said that they "rebelled against the Kuṣāṇa hegemony. They not only reasserted their indepenence in *c*. AD 225, but dealt a powerful blow to the Kuṣāṇa empire from which it could not recover".[339] The large copper coins of the Yaudheyas datable to the third-fourth century AD show both in their fabric and in their types the influence of the Kuṣāṇas.[340]

The Yaudheyas surviving the northern Satraps and the Kuṣāṇas continued to flourish as a republican community till about *c*. AD 350.

---

335. See B.P. Mazumdar, "Political theory and practice in the Mālava and Yougheya republics", *JIH*, vol. 47, pt. 2, p. 306.

336. Fleet, *CII*, III, No. 58, p. 252.

337. *JNSI*, XXXII, pt. 2, p. 154 f.

338. *Ep. Ind.*, VIII, p. 44; Sircar, *SI*, vol. I, p. 178.

339. Altekar, *op. cit.*, p. 120.

340. Rapson, *op. cit.*, p. 15. pl. III, 14; Allan, *CCBM*, p. cl, P1. XL; p. Gardner, *CCBMG*, pl. XXVII, no. 10, cf. B.N. Mukherjee, "Some Interesting Yaudheya Coins", *JAS*, vol. XX, Nos. 1-4 (1978), pp. 36-37.

*The Ossadioi*

Among the Greek historians of Alexander it is only Arrian who describes them as an independent nation (a free people).[341] Cunningham is the only scholar to identify them with the Yaudheyas on the banks of Sutlej,[342] as far as my knowledge goes. But the validity of this identification may be doubted on certain resonable grounds. Firstly, Alexander did not come into direct contact with any republican tribe on the banks of that river nor do his historians refer to them. Secondly, Alexander in course of his voyage down the Indus met on his way some independent tribes, including the Ossadioi, before reaching the junction of that river with the Indus. "The Ossadioi were settled somewhere in the region of the confluence of the Chenab and Sutlej with the Indus".[343] McCrindle on the authority of Hemacandra's *Abhidhānacintāmaṇi* has placed them between the Indus and the Jhelum,[344] which comprised the modern district of Rāwalpiṇḍī.

The Ossadioi (or Ossadi) as such may be unhesitatingly identified with the Vasātis. St. Martin was perhaps the first scholar to propose this identification, which is strongly supported by McCrindle[345] and other scholars.[346] They were known to Pāṇini. They belonged to the group of republican *rājanyādi gaṇa* (the *Gaṇa-Pāṭha*, IV, 2, 53).[347] Kātyāyana and Patañjali mention them along with the Śibis (on Pāṇini, IV, 2, 52)[348] which shows their geographical contiguity. They have been mentioned in the *Mahābhārata* as neighbours of the Kṣudrakas, the Mālavas and the Ambaṣṭhas[349] which perfectly agrees with the accounts of Alexander's historians. In the Bhīṣma Parva they have been associated with the Śibis and Sindhu-Sauvīras of the Lower Indus valley. Cunningham says that it is highly probable that they tendered their allegiance to Alexander at the confluence of the Punjab rivers.[350] H.H. Wilson also holds more or less the same view. He says that "The Ossadii also sent ambassadors, tendering allegiance".[351]

341. *Anab.*, VI, 15, *IIA*, p. 156; see also Smith, *EHI*, p. 104; CAI, pp. 75-76.
342. *CAGI*, pp. 206-9; *CASR*, XIV, p. 140.
343. For their location see Curtius, *Hist. Alex.*, IX, 8, *IIA*, p. 253.
344. *IIA*, p. 156, note 2.
345. *Ibid.*
346. See *CAI*, p. 75.
347. *IP*, p. 455.
348. See also *Mahābhāṣya*, Kielhorn, vol. II, p. 282.
349. Sabhā Parva, 48, 14; see also Karṇa Parva, 30, 47-55.
350. *CAGI*, pp. 206-9.
351. *Ar. Ant.*, p. 201.

### *The Xathroi (Or Xathri)*

Arrian mentions them as an independent Indian tribe whose territories lay between the Indus and the lower course of the Akesines or Cenāb.[352] It is not possible to determine their geographical position with absolute certainty. However, the fact remains that their territories comprised parts of both the Punjab and Sindh. According to the laws of transcription, they may be identified with the kṣatriyas of the Sanskrit literature. They are absolutely identical with Kauṭilya's kṣatriyas of *śastropajīvin saṁgha*. They were no doubt a republican people. Ptolemy in his *Geography* (VII, 1, 64) mentions the same people as the Khatriaoi,[353] who, according to him, had in their possession six cities lying some east and west of the Indus. One of their cities called Soudasanna (Sadūsān) has been located in Sindh (to the west of the Indus). They were less hostile than others. They like the Abastanoi and the Ossadioi did not choose to fight. They in all likelihood either submitted to or were subjugated by Alexander. After the submission of the two independent tribes Ossadians and Xathrians to him, the junction of the Akesines and the Indus was fixed as the southern boundary of the Satrapy of Philip. The republican tribes came under his domination. The modern Khatrīs of the Punjab and Sindh are regarded as the descendants of ancient Xathroi or Xathri. But H.A. Rose does not support this generally accepted view. According to him, the "Kshatris, a low caste and distinct from the Kshatriyas, are unknown in the modern Punjab".[354]

## SINDH

Sindh comprised the whole valley of the Indus and the western part of the Punjab. It was another important centre of republics, which existed side by side with the monarchies. There were altogether four republics which are described below:

### *Sogdai Or Sogdi*

They were one of the republican tribes of Upper Sindh. At the time of Alexander's invasion, they were settled on the banks of the Indus to the northward of Alor, the capital city of Upper Sindh. They held an extensive territory extending to the Punjab. They along with other republican tribe are believed to have occupied northern Sindh with contiguous portions of the Punjab (Miṭhankoṭ area) and the Bahāwalpur state below the confluence of the Punjab rivers.

352. *Anab.*, VI, 15, *IIA*, pp. 156 and note 1, 347, note L; see also *CAI*, p. 75; Smith, *EHI*, p. 104.

353. Lassen, *Ind. Alt.*, vol. III, p. 141.

354. *GTCP*, vol. II, p. 505, note.

According to Arrian, on leaving the confluence of the Punjab rivers Alexander sailing down the Indus came to the capital of the Sogdi, who offered him no opposition.[355] One fact preserved in the account of Arrian is strongly in favour of the identification of the old site near Fāẓilpur with the town of the Sogdi. They have been identified with the Sohda or Sodha Rājpūts, who now occupy the south-eastern district of Sindh around Umarkoṭ.[356]

It is worthy of remark that the political organisation of the republican tribes along the Indus below the confluence of the Punjab rivers was completely different from that of the free tribes of the Punjab region.

### *The Sodrai Or Sodrae*

The Sodrai or Sodrae of the Greek historians is a closer transliteration of the śūdras of Sanskrit literature and the Suddakas (Śūdrakas) of Pāli literature. They may have been the remnants of the śūdra tribe of the Vedic age.[357] The *gaṇa*s of the śūdras were known to Pāṇini as the *Śaudrāyanas* (*Gaṇa-Pāṭha* IV, 2, 54). Diodorus mentions them as an idependent tribe. He locates them on the opposite banks of the Indus.[358] They were to the south of the Ambaṣṭhas. The Greek writers place them in the western part of the Punjab.[359] They were actually in the vicinity of the Sogdoi of Upper Sindh. H.H. Wilson, who is a most trustworthy guide on the subject, categorically states that the Sodgi of Arrian and the Sodrae of Diodorus have been described "as living under a republican form of government".[360] The latter opposed Alexander but ultimately submitted to him. The territories of both the free tribes were placed under the Greek Satrapy of Sindh. It was Peithon who was appointed by Alexander as the Satrap of the Indus valley. In the post-Alexandrian period the śūdras migrated from Sindh to western Rājpūtānā and occupied a tract near Vinaśana, identified with the area round Sirsā. They along with their neighbours, the Abhīras, were thus living in the region adjacent to the river

---

355. *Anab*; VI. 15, IIA, p. 157.
356. *CAGI*, pp. 213-14; *Ar. Ant.*, p. 210; *IIA*, p. 354 note R; Lassen, *Ind. Alt.*, vol. II, p. 174; St. Martin *Étude*, pp. 150-61.
357. For their identification see *IIA*, p. 354, note R; Lassen, *Ind. Alt.*, vol. II, pp. 144, 174, 177; St. Martin, *Étude*, pp. 150-61.
358. *Bib. Hist.*, XVII, 102, *IIA*, pp. 292-93; see also Smith, *EHI*, p. 104; *The Voyage of Nearchus*, tr. by W. Vincent, p. 141.
359. *CAI*, p. 181.
360. *Ar. Ant.*, p. 202.

Sarasvatī, which later on vanished. Cunningham has identified the Sodrae with the people of Seorai, whose exact geographical position cannot be ascertained but it was probably close to Fāẓilpur. According to him, "a village named Sirwahi . . . may possibly represent the Seorai of Sindhian history. It is 96 miles in a direct line below Uchh, and 85 miles above Alor, or very nearly midway between them".[361] He has admitted that "these identifications are not altogether satisfactory", but we find some elements of truth in his statement. This very region appears to be the place of the śūdras as evidenced by other reliable sources too.

*The "Brachmans"*

The bāhmaṇas of the Indus valley have been called by Alexander's historians "Brachmans" and the territory they inhabited "Brachmanoi" or "Brahmanoi" (the "country of the Brachmans"),[362] which is identical with *brāhmaṇaka* of Pāṇini (*sūtra* V, 2, 71)[363] and *brāhmaṇako* of Patañjali (*Mahābhāṣya*, IV, 2, 104).[364] In the commentatorial tradition (the *Kāśikā*), however, it is called the land of brāhmaṇas who were associated with *āyudhajīvī saṁgha* or followers of military profession. "Their military traditions continued up to the time of Alexander whose invasions they resisted with patriotic heroism".[365] Their territorial state comprised both middle and lower valley of the Indus. They were a republican community without any chief or king. The political sovereignty seems to have been vested in the whole community. They enjoyed privileged position in their own republican states, but whether they enjoyed the same position in the kṣatriya republics is difficult to say. This republic also received the notices of K.P. Jayaswal[366] and Motichandra,[367] but they have not provided the full details thereof.

Diodorus refers to "city of the brāhmaṇas"[368] which was probably the capital of their state. The city itself called brāhmaṇa at the time of Alexander's invasion is identical

361. *CAGI*, pp. 214-15.

362. Arrian, *Anab.*, VI. 16, 5, *IIA*, p. 159 & also note T, p. 355; Diodorus, *Bib. Hist.*, XVII, 102, *IIA*, p. 293.

363. *IP*, p. 51.

364. Puri, *India in the time of Patañjali*, p. 74; see also A. Mitra Śāstrī, *India as seen in the Bṛhatsaṁhitā of Varāhamihira*, pp. 51-52.

365. *IP*, p. 51.

366. *Op. cit.*, pp. 65-66.

367. *Sārthavāha*, p. 74.

368. *Bib. Hist.*, XVII, 102, 103, *IIA*, pp. 293-95; also Vincent, *op. cit*, p. 136.

with *Brāhmaṇavaha* ("abode of brāhmaṇas") of Rājaśekhara (ninth century AD)[369] Cunningham has identified it with the ruins situated near an old bed of the Indus at the distance of about 47 miles to the north-east of Hyderabad. It corresponds both in name and pisition with the great city of Brāhmaṇābād.[370]

The brāhmaṇas of Sindh were great lovers of freedom. They were the leaders of the patriotic movement for freedom from the Greek rule in north-west India. They appealed to the populace and potentates of their neighbouring kingdoms as well as the free tribes not to submit to Alexander but to maintain their independence. They themselves offered the stoutest resistance to him. According to the Greek historians, their capital city was stormed and captured by him and a large number of brāhmaṇas were put to death.[371] This can best be qualified in the statement of Plutarch, biographer of Alexander: "These philosophers were specially marked down for revenge by Alexander as they gave him no less trouble than the mercenaries, they reviled the princes who declared for him and encouraged the free states to revolt against his authority. On this account he hanged many of them".[372] He further adds that one of the revolutionary brāhmaṇas was asked just before his execution as to why he had incited the kings and the people of different states to raise the banner of revolt against the Macedonians. He boldly replied, "Because I wish them to live with honour or to die with honour".[373]

The brāhamaṇas of the Indus valley no doubt laid down their lives in defence of freedom, religion and culture, and by their heroic deeds and supreme sacrifices presented one of the earliest examples of patriotism. Their perfect sense of independence, warlike character, patriotic feelings and loyalty to the nation during the period concerned will always be remembered. "The suppression of Brahmanical opposition could not have been an easy task for Alexander, since the Brāhmaṇs were . . . respected throughout the land. . . . The taking up of arms by the meek Brāhmaṇs must not be regarded as a

---

369. *Kāvyamīmāṁsā*, ed. by G.S. Rai, p. 236.

370. *CAGI*, pp. 226-29; *CISSK*, p. 37; *IIA*, pp. 355-56, note T.

371. Arrian, *Anab.*, VI. 16, 5, IIA, pp. 158-59; Chinnock, *op. cit.*, p. 319; Diodorus, *Bib. Hist.*, XVII, 102, 1, *IIA*, p. 293.

372. *Lif. Alex.*, ch. 59, *IIA*, p. 306 & also note 2; see also *CHI*, vol. I, p. 339.

373. *Lif. Alex.*, ch. 64, *IIA*, pp. 313-14; see also G.P. Singh, "The Role of the Brāhmaṇas in Anti-Alexander Movement in North-West India *c.* 326-325 BC," SHC, III, 1, 1995, pp. 1-7.

strange phenomenon or a mere figment of Greek imagination. . . . The country was menaced with a calamity during the Macedonian avalanche, and so the Brāhmaṇs valiantly rose to defend their hounour and their hearth and home."[374]

*Pattala*

The city-state of Pattala in the lower Indus valley stood in close proximity to the city of brāhmaṇas or near the site of Brāhmaṇābād or Bahmanābād, only four miles south-west of Thatha. According to Holdich, it was situated about "30 miles south-east of Haidarabad".[375] The authorities on the subject are not at one about its exact geographical position. The city is also described as the capital of the province — Lower Sindh.[376] The constitution by which it was governed and the form of government that existed at the time of Alexander's invasion find the best description in the account of Diodorus: "A city of great note, with a political constitution drawn on the same lines as the Spartan; for in this community command in war was vested in two hereditary kings of two different houses, while a Council of Elders ruled the whole state with paramount authority".[377] The administration of the state bears striking resemblance to that of Sparta of Greece. This seems to have been a *dvairājya* state where two kings belonging to two different families were ruling simultaneously with the help of a powerful council. This is a typical example of aristocratic oligarchy or democracy. K.P. Jayaswal has observed that "The Patala kings were responsible to the Council which in turn was probably elected by the whole community, it being a democracy. Here we have in the Patala constitution a mixture of aristocracy and democracy. The ultimate political authority in all these cases rested with the *Gaṇa* or *Saṁgha*. . . . The states wherein the Greeks found Executive power held by a few families on hereditary principle, although the rulers were subject to a *Gaṇa*, they have described as aristocractic. In fact, they were a mixed constitution which may be called for want of a better term, aristocratic democracy. . . . The hereditary

---

374. R.S. Tripathi, *HAI*, p. 140.

375. Cf. *CHI*, vol. I, p. 339, note 4; also *AIMA*, 1st edn. p. 183, fn.

376. *IIA*, p. 356, note u; St. Martin, *Étude*, p. 168 f; Smith, *EHI*, p. 105 f; H.H. Wilson, *Ar. Ant.*, p. 207; *CAGI*, pp. 237-39; Ptolemy's *Geog.*, 7, 1, 59, *AIT*, pp. 146-47; 369-70, note; J. Ph. Vogel, notes on Ptolemy in *BSOAS*, vol. XIV, pt. I, p. 84, J. Wilson, *JBBRAS*, vol. III, (1850), p. 74; 'The Voyage of Nearkhos from the Indus to the Head of the Persian Gulf' described in Arrian's *Indica*, pt. II, chs. XVII ff, cf. McCrindle *CNES*, p. 156.

377. *Bib. Hist.*, XVII, 104, *IIA*, p. 296; see also *CAI*, p. 183.

kings were under the complete control of the House of Elders. It was an aristocracy in form but democracy in spirit".[378]

According to Curtius, one of its kings was called Moeres,[379] whom H.H. Wilson has identified with "Maha-raja" or "Maha-rai".[380] The name to be the derivative of Mura of the *Gaṇa-Pāṭha* (IV, 1, 151). From a comparison of the narratives of Arrian (based on the statements of Aristoboulos) and Curtius it appears that the same king offered his submission to Alexander at Brāhmaṇa of the city of brāhmaṇas, but before Alexander reached Pattala, he along with large part of the population abandoned the place and fled to the desert.[381] When Alexander reached Pattala he found the city wearing deserted look. He persuaded the fugitives to return. Most of them are stated to have returned. Long after Alexander's invasion it passed under the rule of the Bactrian Greeks.[382] But later on sometime between the first and second century AD it came in the hands of Indo-Scythian of Śaka rulers from the cultches of Indo-Greek rulers. About the middle of the second century AD it was one of the principal Indo-Scythian possessions.

The republics on the banks of the Indus described by the Greek historians find some reflection in the *Mahābhārata*. From the Sabhā Parva (29, 8) it appears that they were very powerful and prosperous. We find that those republics belonged to the kṣatriya, brāhmaṇa and śūdra community. Their towns and villages both were self-governed.

K.P. Jayaswal has expressed the view that "The major portion of the Punjab and Sindh, which came under the survey of the Greek writers, show only two or three monarchies . . . otherwise the whole country was republican".[383] But my own researches into classical accounts of the subject do not lead me to accept this view on the ground that in the Punjab and Sindh, besides a number of republics, about a dozen monarchies also existed. Since this aspect of the subject does not fall within the scope of this work, I would like to refrain myself from entering into its details.

---

378. *Op. cit.*, pp. 70-72.

379. *Hist. Alex.*, IX, 8. 28, *IIA*, p. 256.

380. *Ar. Ant.*, p. 206.

381. Arrian, *Anab.*, VI. 17, *IIA*, p. 161; Curtius, *op. cit.*, *IIA*, p. 256; also *Ar. Ant.*, p. 206, *CAGI*, p. 239.

382. Strabo, *Geog.*, tr. Hamilton and Falconer, vol. II, pp. 252-53.

383. *Op. cit.*, p. 67.

## BALUCHISTAN

There were some republican tribes of Indian descent in Baluchistan. The classical writers have unanimously placed them to the west of the Lower Indus. From their accounts its transpires that their territories were included within the geographical limits of India. In the time of Alexander such tribes were only two number:

### *Arabitae*

The Arabii of Arrian,[384] the Arabitae of Curtius,[385] the Ambritae of Diodorus[386] or Arbies of Strabo[387] correspond to Sanskrit Arabhaṭa. They were populary known as Aravya. They were one of the independent tribes. Their territory was situated to the east of the river Arabis (now Purali, which falls into the Sonmiani Bay, west of Karachi). This river formed the boundary between the Arabitae and Oritae. Both Arrian[388] and Strabo[389] have clearly stated that their country also formed a part of India.

### *Oritae*

The Oritae or Oreitai of classical authors may be undoubtedly identified with *Vārteya* of Pāṇini. They were one of those nine republican tribes who belonged to the *āayudhajīvī saṁghas* mentioned in the *Gaṇa-Pāṭha* (*Aṣṭādhyāyī*, IV, 1, 178; V, 3, 117).[390] They were the next neighbours of the Arabitae. They occupied an extensive territory to the west of the river Arabis or Purali. The district which they occupied is now known as Las. According to Alexander's historians, they were of Indian origin.[391] It is Strabo (a Roman geographer) who on the authority of Nearchos (who had accompanied Alexander as an admiral of

384. *Indica*, pt. II, chs. 21 and 22.

385. *Hist. Alex.*, IX, 10, 33.

386. *Bib. Hist.*, XVII, 104, 7-8.

387. *Geog.*, XV, 2, 1, *AICL*, p. 81; see also Pliny. *Hist. Nat*, VII, 2; A.H.L. Heeren, *Historial Researches* vol. I, *Asiatic Nations*, p. 297; Elphinstone, *op. cit.*, p. 11.

388. *Indica*, pt. II, ch. 22.

389. *Geog.*, XV, 2. I, *AICL*, p. 82; see also A. Stein, "An Archaeological Tour in Gedrosia", *MASI*, No. 43 (Calcutta, 1931).

390. *IP*, p. 452.

391. Curtius, *Hst. Alex*, IX, 10, 33; Diodorus, *Bib. Hist.*, XVII, 104 & 105, *IIA,* pp. 296-99; Arrian, *Indica*, pt. II, chs. 22, 23; see also stein, "On Alexander's Route to Gedrosia — an archaeological tour into Las Bela", *Geog. Jour.* (JRGS), vol. 102 Nos. 5-6 (1943) pp. 193-227.

fleet) categorically states that "Then succeeds the nation of the Oritai, which is autonomous".[392] From the accounts of the Greek writers we learn they they had long maintained their independence in those parts of India. They had no king. The power was vested in the hands of their leaders which reflects their republican (or *Saṁgha*) character. One of their large villages or small town, Rhambakia, which served them as a capital city, was occupied by Alexander. They made their submission to him and negotiated peace through ther leaders. The conqueror appointed Apollophanes their Satrap or governor to exrcise control over them. The Satrapy of Gedrosia or Baluchistan included the country of the Oritae. Shortly after Alexander's departure from their country towards the end of October in 325 BC, they raised the banner of revolt against the Greeks to regain independence. Apollophanes was slain, but they were defeated by Leonnatus (one of the chief captains) in one fierce battle and 6,000 of them including their all leaders killed.[393] According to V.A. Smith "The Oreitai are supposed to be now represented by the Lumri tribes of Las Bela, who claimed Rājūpt descent".[394]

K.P. Jayaswal did not describe the above two republics being guided by the beliefs that they were not Indian which is not true. He says that "There were some minor communities on the frontier of Baluchistan which it would not be accurate to describe as Indian".[395]

## SOME OTHER REPUBLICS OF THE PUNJAB AND SINDH

### *The Madras*

They existed as republican community as early as the Vedic age. A passage in the *Aitareya Brāhmaṇa* (VIII, 3, 14) states that the Uttara (northern) Madras were living beyond the Himālaya "without a king (vairājyam), and called Virāj, i.e., without king".[396] This shows that they had a republican type of state which had no king. They were governed by a

---

392. *Geog.*, XV, 2, 1, *AICL*, p. 82.
393. Arrian, *Anab.*, VI, 21 & 22, *IIA*, pp. 167-69; *Indica*, Pt. II, ch. 23; Curtius, *Hist. Alex.*, IX, 10, 34; Diodorus, *Bib. Hist.*, XVII, 104, 8.
394. *EHI*, pp. 111-12.
395. *Op. cit.*, p. 67.
396. *Aitareya Brāhmaṇa*, ed. and trans. by M. Haug, vol. I, p. 203; vol. II, p. 518 and note 3.

democratic constitution. They were originally a people of Bāhlika (mod. Balkh in Afghanistan) from where they shifted to Vāhikadeśa (Punjab). They seem to have occupied the central portion of the Punjab. Their territory was situated between the Rāvī and the Cenāb which corresponds roughly to modern district of Siālkoṭ and the adjoining regions. Their capital city, Śākala, finds mention in the *Mahābhārata*[397] and the Purāṇas.[398] It was situated on the banks of the river Āpagā (or Ayak)[399] at a distance of about 60 miles to the west of the Rāvī. It has been identified with Siālkoṭ,[400] which stood on the river Ajakula (mod. Aji).[401] The people of Madradeśa were an ancient kṣatriya tribe of Vedic time. They were a branch of Pauravas. Their prevailing form of government in the time of Pāṇini also seems to have been republican. He not only refers to them (*Aṣṭādhyaāyī*, IV, 2, 131) but also mentiones their two divisions, Pūrva (eastern) and Apara (western) (VII, 3, 13; IV, 2, 108). "Purva-Madra extended from the Ravi to the Chenab and Apara-Madra from the Cenab to the Jhelum."[402]

The Madras, republican form of government seems to have undergone significant change in the post-Pāṇinian period. According to Kauṭilya, they belonged to *rāja-śabdopajīvin saṁgha*.[403] It appears that their chiefs or rulers enjoyed the status of *rājās*.

Some scholars mistakenly identifying the Madras' captial, Śākala, with the Kathainans' Sangala mentioned by Alexander's historians have suggested that the former offered brave resistance to Alexander.[404] It is equally wrong to say that the Madras' dominions with the capital Śākala passed under the sway of Alexander,[405] who placed them under the Satrap of the adjacent territory between the Jhelum and the Cenāb. We do not have even the slightest evidence in the classical accounts of the subject of either their defeat at the hands of the Macedonian conqueror or of the occupation of their

397. Sabhā Parva, 29. 13; Karṇa Parva, 30, 26-30, 33.

398. *Brh.*, 19, 18; *Vṣṇ.*, *Dh.*, 1, 156, 24-28; I, 207, 55-60.

399. Karṇa Parva, 30, 14; see also Lassen, *Ind. Alt.*, vol. I, p. 801; *Pent. Ind.*, pp. 73-74 cf. *CAGI*, pp. 155-56.

400. *CASR*, XIV, pp. 44-46; *AIT*, p. 395, note; Fleet, *PIOC*, 14th session; Law, *HPL*, vol. II, pp. 555-56; *GEB*, pp. 53-54; *Geographical Essays*, p. 67.

401. J. Przyluski, *JA*, 1926, pp. 3-7.

402. *IP*, p. 53.

403. *Arth.*, XI, 1.

404. Altekar, *State and Government in Ancient India*, p. 120, *CAGI*, p. 151 f; *AIT*, pp. 365-66, note; T.W. Rhys Davids, *BI*, pp. 38-39.

405. See *CHI*, vol. I, p. 496; Law, *HGAI*, pp. 105, 122.

territory by him. However, it is absolutely correct that their territory with its capital Śākala came under the sway of the most powerful Indo-Greek ruler, Menander or Milinda (165-145 BC). Consequently, the name of the capital was changed from Sanskrit Śākala to Pāli Sāgala,[406] which is exactly identical with Ptolemy's Sagala (VII, 1, 46),[407] which belonged to the Mardyenoi (Madras).[408]

The Madras continued to maintain their existence as a republican community at least up to the fourth century AD. At a later date in the early part of the sixth centuy AD (or in AD 532) Śākala became the capital of the Hūṇa conqueror, Mihirakula. It was he who probably destroyed it.

### *The Audumbaras Or Udumbaras*

Pāṇini includes them in the *rājanya* group of republics (*Gaṇa-Pāṭha*, IV, 2, 53). The find-spots of their coins indicate that they had occupied an extensive territory which comprised the Kāṅgarā valley between the Rāvī and the Vyāsa, Paṭhānkoṭ in Gurdāspur district and Hośiyārpur district of the Punjab. Paṭhānkoṭ at one time was their capital. The coins bear legends both in Brāhmī and Kharoṣṭhi and belong to the period extending from the second century BC to the first century AD. Their coins were struck both in the name of the leader (or the king) and the community.[409] They also find mention in the *Mahābhātata*.[410] They are identical with Odomboerae of Megasthenes[411] and Ptolemy[412] and Odombeores of Pliny.[413] Pliny has placed them on the mouth of the Indus.[414] They have been described as independant people. They appear to have been divided into two or three sections.[415] They belonged to the north-eastern and north-western parts of the

406. *Milindapañha*, ed. V. Trenckner, vol. I, pp. 2-3; trans. T.W. Rhys Davids, SBE, XXXV, p. 6; Law, *HPL*, vol. II, pp. 354, 356, 368; Rahula Sāṅkṛtyāyana, *Pāli Sāhitya kā Itihāsa*, pp. 182-83.

407. *AIT*, pp. 12-24, 157-58 & 395, note.

408. Bunbury, *HAG*, vol. II, pp. 641-42.

409. Allan, *CCBM*, pp. lxxxii-lxxxvii; Smith, *CCIM*, vol. 1, pp. 160-61, 166; Cunningham, *Co. An. Ind.*, pp. 66-67; *CASR*, XIV, pp. 115-17; *CISSK*, p. 37; Rapson, *Ind. Co.*, p. 11, pl. III. 8.

410. Sabhā Parva, 48, 12.

411. *AIMA*, 1st edn., p. 146, fn.

412. *AIT*, p. 149.

413. *Nat. Hist.*, VI, 1, 23; VI, 75.

414. *Ibid.*, VI, 75.

415. See J. Przyluski, App., p. 12f.

Punjab. Their independent state in northern Punjab continued to flourish till the end of the second century BC. The Kharoṣṭhi script is indicative of the fact that about 100 BC they like their neighbours of the Punjab came under the influence of the Satraps and were finally absorbed. The domination of both the Indo-Greeks and the Kuṣāṇas over them stood as barriers in the way of smooth functioning of their republican state. A branch of theirs migrated to Cutch region sometime before the first century AD, as it appears from analysis of the data supplied by Pliny.[416]

### *The Kulūtas*

They are one of the republican communities of the Punjab.[417] They dwelt in the upper valley of the river Vyāsa which is now known as the Kullu Valley. Its ancient capital was at Nāgara on the Vyāsa which was known to Pāṇini. The name is included in the Katryādi *gaṇa* (IV, 2, 95).[418] Their territory formed the central portion of Trigartta region. The confederation of six states mentioned by Pāṇini as Trigartta-Ṣaṣṭha (V, 3, 116) included not only their state but also that of the Auḍumbaras of the Kāṅgarā Valley. The Kulūtas have been mentioned in the *Mahābhārata* as an indepedent tribe.[419] They are identical with the Colubae of Megasthenes[420] and Pliny.[421] They very likely maintained their republican tradition up to the second or first century BC, though they existed in the subsequent period too.

### *The Kuṇindas Or Kulindas*

They were known to Pāṇini as Kuluna (*Gaṇa-Pāṭha*, IV, 2, 133 and IV. 3. 93).[422] They were originally settled in the districts of Kullu on the Vyāsa and Kunāwar on the Sutlej. They were neighbours of the Kulūtas. "They seem to have occupied the hill districts on both sides of the Satlej from time immemorial." Their name is still preserved in the Kunets of Kullu, Kunāwar and all the hill districts around Shimla. Their capital has

416. See Cunningham, *CISSK*, p. 37.
417. Law, *Geographical Essays*, p. 129.
418. *IP*, p. 55; see alo P. Gupta, *GNAII*, p. 72; N.L. Dey, *GDHMI*, p. 106; St. Martin, *Étude*, p. 217; Rapson, 'The Kulutas, a people of Northern India', *JRAS*, 1900, p. 529.
419. Sabhā Parva, 24, 5-9.
420. *AIMA*, 1st edn., p. 137.
421. *Hist. Nat.*, VI, 22.
422. *IP*, p. 55.

been located at Srughna on the west bank of the old Yamunā.[423] Ptolemy calls them *Kylindrine* and locates them in the region of the lofty mountains wherein the Vyāsa, the Sutlej, the Yamunā and the Gaṅgā had their sources.[424] A large number of their coins, both copper and silver, bearing legends in both Brāhmī and Kharoṣṭhi characters datable to 150 BC to AD 100 have been discovered from the Kāṅgarā valley, Ambālā, Rupar and other parts of the Punjab, and Sahāranpur and Garhwal districts in U.P.[425] Their coins on the whole have been found in eastern and north-eastern Punjab and north-western parts of U.P. On the basis of the find-spots of their coins Allan concludes that they "occupied a narrow strip of land at the foot of the Siwalik hills between the Jumna and the Sutlej and the territory between the upper courses of the Beas and the Sutlej".[426] On the basis of the provenance of their coins it can be affirmed that they were a widely diffused tribe. The legends on some of their coins afford very valuable and concrete evidence of the political system that prevailed in their republican state. The coins were struck both in the name of the king and the community. According to their constitution, their ruler was called *rājā*. One of their rulers named Amoghabhūti was also called *mahārājā*. They followed the same type of constitution between 150 BC and AD 100.

The Kuṇindas have been mentioned in the *Mahābhārata* along with some republican tribes of the Punjab.[427] According to Varāhamihira, the leaders or chiefs of the *gaṇa* of the Kuṇindas were also called the *rājās*.[428]

The Kuṇindas maintained their independence till they were compelled to acknowledge the suzerainty of the Kuṣāṇas in the first century AD. They, however, regained their indepedence in the third century AD. The second group of their coins may be assigned to the same period.[429] A confederacy of the Yaudheyas, the Kuṇindas and the Ārjunāyanas was formed against the Kuṣāṇas. They struck and effective blow to the Kuṣāṇa power. The Kuṣāṇas were gradually ousted from the eastern Punjab. The

---

423. Cunningham, *Co. An. Ind.*, p. 66, 70-71; *CASR*, XIV, p. 126, see also pp. 125-35; G. Oppert, *OIB*, pp. 143-44, note 43.

424. *Geog.*, VII. I. 42, cf. *AIT*, pp. 109-10, 360-61, note.

425. Cunningham, *Co. An. Ind.*, p. 70, pl. V, 1-5; *CASR*, XIV, pp. 134-35, 137, pl. XXXI, 5, 6; Allan, *CCBM*, pp. ci-civ; Smith, *CCIM*, pp. 161, 167; Rapson, *Ind. Co.*, p. 12, pl. III, 9; *JASB*, 1875, p. 89 f; 1886, p. 161; *PASB*, 1875, p. 164; *PASB*, 1893, p. 174; Prinsep, *EIA*, pp. 203, 208, pl. XIX, 16.

426. *CCBM*, p. ciii.

427. Sabhā Parva, 23, 13-15; 48, 3.

428. *Br. Sam.*, IV, 24; XIV, 33, see also XIV, 30.

429. Rapson, *Ind. Co.*, p. 12, pl. III, 10.

Kuṇindas like the Yaudheyas rose in power as the Greek an Kuṣāna supremacies successively declined. The Kuṇinda republic continued to flourish till about the end of the third century AD.

*The Ābhiras*

They were also a republican people. They had their settlement in the Indus valley. They are generally associated with the śūdras, who are most likely identical with the Sodrai of the Greek historians of Alexander. McCrindle, while identifying Ptolemy's *Abiria* with the Ābhīras, says that "their country . . . lay to the east of the Indus where it bifurcates to form the delta".[430] One of their branches migrated from the Indus valley to western Rājpūtānā and settled in the neighbourhood of the śūdras in the Sarasvatī valley. The tract occupied by them was known as Vinaśana which can be identified with the modern Sirsā region. The *gaṇas* of the śūdras and Ābhīras were living in the Matsyadeśa near the river Sarasvatī (*Mbh.*, Sabhā Parva, 29, 9). They retained their independent political status up to the fourth century AD.

## Republics Under the Mauryas

Those non-monarchical, republican or self-governing communities who came under the Maurya rule were the Kāmbojas, the Nābhas and the Pāladas or Pāradas (the Paradene of Ptolemy or Paraitakenai of Arrian) of Afghanistan (northern India), and the Rāṣṭrikas, the Bhojas and the Pitinikas of Gujarat (including Cutch) in western India. They find mention in Aśoka's inscriptions (Rock Edicts V and XIII).[431] It appears that their territories were within the geographical limits of the Maurya empire. Some of them have passed out of history.

## Some Republics in the Śuṅga Period

Those old republics which survived the Maurya imperialism and further flourished in the Śuṅga period have already been described. Here we shall present the details of those new republican states which were founded particularly during the period concerned.

430. *AIT*, p. 140; see also Law, *TAI*, pp. 79-81.

431. *Aśoka ke Dharmalekha*, ed. by Janardan Bhatt, pp. 30 and 45; for details see Jayaswal, *Hindu Polity*, pp. 115-42 and his paper 'Places and Peoples in Asoka's Inscriptions' bearing on the identification and location of the republics mentioned in his proclamations, *Ind. Ant.*, vol. LXII (1933), pp. 121-33.

## THE GAṆAS OF UTSAVA-SANKETAS

The earliest reference to them occurs in the *Mahābhārata*.[432] They were said to have been divided into seven classes. It has been observed that "the Utsava-saṅketa republic was situated in the Himalayan region in the vicinity of Kashmir".[433] They have been placed by some scholar in "Rāmapura Baśahara region of the valley of Satluj".[434] Kālidāsa also mentions this tribal republic.[435] M.R. Kale has categorically stated that "The Utsava-saṅketas were a hill-tribe living in Ladak north of Kāśmere or in the north-east region of Ladak".[436] They were probably in the neighbourhood of the Kinnaras of Kanaur in the upper valley of the Sutlej.[437] It is well-nigh impossible to determine their exact location. However, it is significant to note that they had organised a republican type of state roughly about *c*. 100 BC.

## THE ŚĀLAṄKĀYANAS

The details furnished by Patañjali (on Pāṇini, V, 1, 58)[438] show that they were composed of three sections (*trika*). It appears that their league of *saṁgha* consisted of three small state-units. We are told by the *Kāśikā* that they were in the Vāhikadeśa (Punjab) and belonged to *rājanya* class. Their constitution was similar to those of the members of the *āyudhajīvī saṁgha*s.

## THE VĀMARATHAS

The republic of the Vāmarathas has also been mentioned by Patañjali (on Pāṇini, IV, 1, 151). The *Kāśikā* (on Pāṇini, IV, 1, 151) refers to their *saṁgha*. Nothing definite can be said about their seat. They were in all likelihood the *rājanya*s of the Vāhikadeśa.

## THE ĀRJUNĀYANAS

They flourished as a republican community roughly about *c*. 150 BC. On the basis of the findspots of their coins (all copper) it has been suggested that they were settled in the

---

432. Sabhā Parva, 29.8.
433. B.P. Roy, *op. cit.*, p. 176.
434. S.N. Pande, *Geographical Horizon of the Maābhārata*, p. 127.
435. *Raghuvaṁśa*, (ed. with Eng. trans. and notes by M.R. Kale, Delhi, 1972), IV, 78, p. 96.
436. *Ibid.*, p. 116, note.
437. See B.S. Upādhyāya, *India in Kālidāsa*, p. 62; *POC*, sixth session, pp. 111-12.
438. *Mahābhāṣya*, ed. Kielhorn, II, p. 352.

region lying west of Agra and Mathurā which corresponds roughly to Bharatpur and Alwar states in Rājpūtānā. They have also been placed in the Agra-Jaipur tract. Some of their coins which palaeographically have been assigned to *c.* 100 BC bear the legend in Brāhmī script *ārjunāyanānā(ṁ) jaya* ("victory to Ārjunāyanas").[439] These coins bear witness to the fact that in their republican or autonomous state there was no place for any king or general. The political sovereignty seems to have been vested in the whole community. They were by and large governed by the democratic constitution. The ruling class were probably the *rājanyas*. In the first century BC they like their northern neighbours, the Yaudheyas, reached the height of glory. But later on their power gradually began to decline because of the frequent attacks of the Śakas. They, however, revived their glory after the downfall of the Kuṣāṇas and continued to maintain their republican character till about the middle of the fourth century AD.

## Republics During the Time of Samudragupta

Only a few republics lingered on in the Gupta period. During the time of Samudragupta (*c.* AD 335-380), the Punjab, Rājpūtānā and Central India for the most part were in possession of tribes who were governed by republican constitution. The republican tribes mentioned in the Allahabad Pillar Inscription[440] are described below :

### THE MĀLAVAS

They were settled in south-east Rājpūtānā or Mālwā region.

### THE YAUDHEYAS

They probably occupied northern Rājpūtānā and south-eastern Punjab. Their territory stretched from Bharatpur right up to the lower course of the Sutlej on the border of the Bahāwalpur state where Johiyāwar still bears the stamp of their name.

### THE ĀRJUNĀYANAS

They lived in Bharatpur and the eastern part of Jaipur and Alwar states.

---

439. For details see Smith, *CCIM*, pp. 160, 166, pl. XX, 10; *JRAS*, 1897, p. 886; Cunningham, *Co. An. Ind.*, pp. 89-90; pl. VIII, 20; Rapson, *Ind. Co.*, p. 11, pl. III, 20, *JRAS*, 1900, p. 106, pl. 6; Allan, *CCBM*, pp. lxxxiii-lxxxiii, pl. XIV, 11 and 12.

440. Fleet, *CII*, vol. III, p. 8, line-22; *SI*, vol. I, pp. 265-66, line 22, note 4.

### THE MADRAKAS

They were immediately to the north of the Yaudheyas. They held the central parts of the Punjab. Their territory was situated between the two rivers, the Rāvī and the Cenāb, which corresponds to modern Siāḷkoṭ district and the surrounding regions. Their capital Śākala (Siāḷkoṭ) lay to the west of the Rāvī.

### THE ĀBHĪRAS

They were probably settled in the territory of Ahirwāḍā between Jhānsī and Bhilsā.

### THE PRĀRJUNAS

They belonged to the Narasiṁhapur district of Central Provinces.

### THE SANAKĀNIKAS

They were in the Īśāgarh district near Bhilsā (eastern Mālwā).

### THE KĀKAS

They were the neighbours of the Sanakānikas. The modern Kākpur town, which is within 20 miles from Bhilsā, was their seat of power.

### THE KHARAPARIKAS

They occupied the Damoh district of Central Provinces.

The above republican communities submitted to Samudragupta of their own accord, acknowledged his supremacy and agreed to offer him tribute, but retained their autonomy to a considerable extent. V.A. Smith's statement that "The free tribes of Rajputana and Malwa were attached to the empire of Samudragupta by bonds of subordinate alliance"[441] appears to be a mere supposition. We do not have any evidence to prove the authencity of his statement. The republic of the Mālavas exceptionally continued to thrive in the modern Mandasor region under the patronage of the Gupta rulers up to the fifth century AD.

K.P. Jayaswal has listed total eighty-two republics.[442] But some republics are missing

441. *EHI*, 4th rev. edn., pp. 302.3.

442. *Hindu Polity*, pp. 361-63.

in his list and some non-republican tribes are mistakenly included in it. We actually find it difficult to ascertain the exact number of republics that flourished in ancient India.

## A Critical Assessment of the Functioning of Republics

We do not have sufficient data at our disposal to enlighten us on the constitution and the administrative machinery of ancient Indian republics. However, after having deeper insight into the details furnished above we can recapitulate some general idea about them.

In ancient Indian republican states, the sovereignty was vested note in one individual but in a small class or in a fairly bigger body. The real power was vested in the Central Assembly. Its members frequently met together to discuss all the important issues relating to administration of the state. All matters whether political, social, economic, religious or military were thoroughly deliberated and unanimously decided. Every issue was decided by the votes of majority. The Central Assemblies also controlled the foreign affairs, decided the momentous issues of peace and war and elected the members of the Executive Council. Different rules and procedures were followed for transacting business of the state. The administration of the state was normally carried on in accordance with its constitution. The members generally worked in harmony and concord to promote the growth of the state. All cantankerous and contentious issues were avoided, and only the motion before the House was thoroughly debated. In the time of the Buddha, in the small states of north-eastern India the members of the Central Assembly used to meet frequently in the Assembly Halls (*santhāgāras*) in the capitals to transact business of the state. The head of the state functioned as the chief executive officer. The number of the members of the Central Assembly varied from state to state. The Central Assemblies of big states like those of the Licchavis of Vaiśālī and the Yaudheyas on the other side of the Vyāsa consisted of as many as 7,707 and 5,000 members respectively. The Central Assembly of the Kṣudrakas had more than 150 members. The city-state of Nysa had a governing body of 300 members of the aristocratic class besides 30 councillors. The governing class in the *gaṇa* state was as large as it was in ancient republics of Greece and Rome. In Greece the contemporary Athenian Assembly consisted of 42,000 members but in actual practice only 2,000 to 3,000 of them attended its session and took part in the administration of the state.

It is striking to note that the membership of the Central Assemblies was confined to only a few privileged class of the aristocratic order. In a purely aristocratic republics or oligarchies, the supreme power was vested not in the whole populace or whole body of the citizens but in a small aristocratic class. Generally speaking, in the republican states only the two copper classes, the brāhmaṇas and the kṣatriyas, were given the citizenship, and the other sections of the population like the artisans, farmers, slaves and the hired labourers were excluded from it. The commoners had no voice in the momentous decision of the central government on important issues like peace and war which effected the whole population. They had to merely carry out the decision of privileged class. Thus, it is apparent that the political power in such states was not shared equally by all which point to the serious defect or weakness of the republican constitution. The basic spirit of democracy was not maintained. The political sovereignty was centralised in the hands of the dominant kṣatriyas. They actually belonged to the ruling class. There is sufficient evidence to show that in the *gaṇa*-states the non-kṣatriyas were sharply distinguished from the ruling aristocracies. In the kṣatriya republics every chief was entitled to call himself the *rājā*. The chiefs or *rājās* were elected only in some cases. They were generally chosen by the people. The fact that the brāhmaṇas in their own states like that of the lower Indus Valley were vested with sovereign power should also not be lost sight of. The śūdras of Sindh exceptionally had their own republican state.

In the oligarchical state the kings or nobles controlled only diplomatic or military affairs. The paramount authority in fact rested in the Council of Elders. It is a fact to be reckoned with that in all types of republics or oligarchies the kings or chiefs never governed the state in utter disregard of the will of the common people.

In the state having the *gaṇa* form of government (*gaṇa-rājya*) the supreme power was vested in the *gaṇa* or whole community. The coins of states of the Mālavas, the Yaudheyas and the Ārjunāyanas were issued not in the name of any king but in the name of the respective *gaṇa*. However, in some states like that of the Kuṇindas coins were struck both in the name of the king and the whole political community.

The *saṁgha* states functioned in a different way. The jurisdiction of the Federal Assembly of such states in all responsability was confined only to foreign policy and declaration and prosecution of war. The confederating states also used to elect the general to lead the joint army against a common enemy. But each constituent unit retained its sovereignty.

The Assemblies or Parliament of some states reserved the right to deal with executive policy and did not delegate it to their council or cabinet which was a weak point in the *gaṇa* constitution. Some states like those of the Kṣudraka-Mālavas and the Ambaṣṭhas were governed by such constitution. However, some states had their own Executive

Council. The Licchavis and the Mallas had or example and Executive Council each consisting of nine members. The Yaudheyas too had an Executive body which can fairly be attested by their coins. The Executive was entrusted with the task of formulating the policy of the state with particular reference to foreign affairs. The evidence recorded in one of the Pāli texts (*Mahāvagga*, IX, 4) and in Patañjali's *Mahābhāṣya* (V, 1. 58-59) shows that the number of its members generally varied from four to twenty. They were probably elected from amongst the members of their respective Assembly. The Executive was thus under the complete constitutional control of the Central Assembly in the republican states. Some states after having formed a confederation set-up a Federal Council to strengthen their own position or for their own self-defence. The Licchavis and the Mallas had such council which consisted of eighteen members, nine being elected by each confederating unit. The matter relating to their mutual defence was usually discussed in it. However, we get only a dim and blurred picutre of its constitution and working.

The small states like those of the Koliyas and the Moriyas included besides their capitals a few villages in their jurisdiction. But bigger states like those of the Śākyas, the Yaudheyas, the Kṣudrakas and the Mālavas included within their extensive territories a number of cities and villages which enjoyed complete autonomy. It appears that some states were divided into a number of small administrative units, and possessed complete machinery for carrying on the local administration. The Punjab and Sindh republics were studded with numerous free cities. Most of the city-states adopted a democratic form of government. They were famous for their love of freedom. In some states the sovereignty was vested in the whole tribal community. The confederate states and aristocratic oligarchies also existed in north-west India. Like cities villages had their own councils which were represented by the people of all classes, castes and professions.

The business of the state as a whole was entrusted to a popular Assembly consisting of heads of different administrative units under the guidance of a chief, the president or king elected for a definite period. In case the assembly was very large, and Executive Council was constituted to assist in carrying out the administration of the state. This form of government bears striking resemblance with the Athenian and Spartan constitutions.

The ancient Indian *gaṇa*-states functioned almost like ancient states of Greece and Rome. In these republics a small minority governed a vast majority. None of them actually possessed full democratic character. The concept of a republic or democracy in ancient times was totally different from what we understand today.

There were *āydhajīvin* or *śastropajīvin saṁghas* in ancient India which denote those martial republics which considered military art as a vital principle of their constitution. One of the distinguishing features of their constitution was the compulsory military training for both men and women. It was the primary duty of citizens to acquire military skill. They cultivated military art as a way of their life. In these republics a type of military democracy prevailed. The citizens attached the highest importance to military matters. However, there was constitutional provision for them to devote their attention also to trade, industry and agriculture. Thus, the members of these republics lived not only by the profession of arms but also by trade and agriculture. The most powerful and influential leader was elected as the head of a martial republic. The republics of this class had no king which is the antithesis of *rājaśabdopajīvin saṁghas*. As already stated, only the brāhmaṇas and kṣatriyas were the members of *āyudhajīvin saṁghas*. They mainly belonged to the Punjab and Sindh. The most prominent among them were the Trigarttas, the Kaṭhas, the Śibis, the Agraśreṇīs, the Kṣudraka-Mālavas, the Yaudheyas and Ambaṣṭhas of the Punjab and the "Xathroi" or the kṣatriyas and the brāhmaṇas of the Indus valley. Their states were rich, strong prosperous. The other sections of population like the śūdras and the dāsas or slaves were not allowed to become the members of these republics. Such *saṁghas* existed in India up to *c*. 300 BC.

The Assemblies of some republics like the modern Parliament were torn by party factions, group rivalry and mutual jealousies. The disunity and discord among members constitute main weakness of the *gaṇa* states. On the testimony of the *Mahābhārata*, the Buddhist literature and Kauṭilya's *Arthaśāstra* it can be pointed out that internal dissensions among members of an Assembly often afforded opportunity for the enemy to foment troubles to weaken their strength. The republics of the Andhaka-Vr̥ṣṇīs and the Licchavis of became victims of such situation.

In fact, it was the bond of unity, spirit of equality or sense of fraternity that kept the the republican institutions alive on the whole for about thousand years.

Each republican state retained its sovereignty and independence till absorbed into neighbouring kingdoms or destroyed by internal and external forces.

## General Causes of the Decline and Disappearance of Republics

The factors that led to the decline and disappearance of republics were variant in nature.

The internal dissension was the root cause of the downfall of some republics of which the Andhaka-Vṛṣṇī *saṁgha* is the most glaring example. Such dissension acutally led to breaking-up of *gaṇas*, which need not be dilated upon here again.

The republics faced both internal and external dangers. One of the vital factors which led to the gradual decline of republics was the emergence and growth of kingdoms. The rise and expansion of kingdoms stood as barriers in the way of survival of republics. There was general tendency on part of the rulers of monarchical states to make the neighbouring republican or oligarchical communities subjet to their authority by conquering their territories and absorbing them in their respective kingdoms. For instances, the Vajjian or Licchavis power was destroyed by the Magadhan king, Ajātaśatru. The Śākyas or Kapilavastu acknowledged to the suzerainty of king Prasenajit of Kośala and became his vessals. The kingdom of Kośala also included the territory of the Kālāmas of Kesaputta. The Bhaggas of Suṁsumāra Hill were under the sway of prince Bodhi, son and successor of king Udena (or Udayana) of Kauśāmbī.

The conflict between kingdoms and republics ensued in the age of the Buddha and continued down to the time of Samudragupta of course, with some gaps in between.

In the time of Alexander, the Elder Porus (the ruler of vast kingdom on the other side of the Jhelum in the plains of Punjab) in alliance with the *rājā* of Abhisāra (a hill country between the upper Jhelum and the Cenāb extending to the Indus) made several attempts to subjugate the neighbouring free tribes in order to extend his sway over them. Quite a few of them came under his political hegemony, and consequently their status was reduced to that of Vassals. In such a situation it was not possible for the republics to function smoothly. We are informed by Arrian that "Poros and Abisares were not only enemies of the king Taxila but also of neighbouring autonomous tribes. On one occasion they marched against the Kṣudraka-Malavas. . . ."[443]

The republican tribes of the Punjab were facing threats both from within and without simultaneously in the fourth century BC.

Alexander's invasion of north-western India proved to be destructive mainly for the republics of the Punjab and the Indus valley. The military operations carried on by him and his troops against the people of the Punjab and Sindh between *c*. 327 and 325 BC resulted in the destruction of a number of flourishing independent tribes and their towns and cities and republican institutions. The survivors moved form one place to another for seeking shelter or to save their life. The Punjab and Sindh, the two noted

443. Chinnock, *op. cit.*, p. 279.

centre of republics, were destabilised. Every attempt of the republican tribes to protect their freedom went in vain. Some of them were only subjugated but eventually lost their internal autonomy. We are told by Plutarch that Alexander after subduing the inhabitants whose form of government was republican ceded their territories to his faithful ally Porus which formed part of his kingdom and his dependencies.[444] The conquered republican states were attached to the Greek Satrapies. Alexander appointed Greek Satraps in the Punjab, Sindh and Baluchistan to rule the conquered territories, including those of the republican tribes. However, it is admitted that Alexander did not destroy all the republics. Actually those republican communities who tendered their submission to him were allowed to carry on their republican system of government. He allowed some of them like the Nysaeans of Afghanistan and the Śibis of Punjab to retain their freedom. On the valuable testimony of some contemporary Greek writers here it may be added that at the time of his invasion north-west India did not know political unity. It was rather parcelled out into a number of petty states, monarchical and republican, convulsed by internecine feuds. The independent tribes were disorganised and disunited. They could not form a powerful confederacy like the one formed by the east Indian states against Ajātaśatru which resulted in their defeat and destruction at the hands of the Macedonian invader. Their *saṁghas* became unpopular. Some of the small states, which were dissolved, became wiser after their discomfiture and formed a confederation which lasted only for a few decades.

Further, the establishment of the powerful Maurya empire proved ruinous to a number of non-monarchical communities. They succumbed to Maurya imperialism. Some isolated states were obliterated during the Maurya rule. The Kāmbojas of eastern Afghanistan, the Bhojas, the republics of Saurāṣṭra region in Gujarat, etc. soon lost their independence and their territories were absorbed into the Maurya empire. The oligarchies or republics in the neighbourhood of Magadha vanished for ever. Kauṭilya's theory with regard to the destruction of *saṁghas* had some impact on the policy of the Maurya rulers towards republics.

Kauṭilya being strong champion of centralised monarchy advocates the destruction of *saṁghas* by all possible means knowing it fully well that they being united are relatively more powerful than the *gaṇa* which are separated and divided. He says that the monarch should conquer the *saṁghas* either by disuniting them or by creating dissension among them or through intrigues or by employing other means of decay and destruction.

444. *Lif. Alex.*, ch. 60, *IIA*, pp. 308-9.

According to his theory, a monarchical state provide better protection to citizens against invasions than a republican state.[445] On the other hand, in the Śānti Parva of the *Mahābhārata* arguments have been advanced in favour of preservation and prosperity of republics. The *gaṇas* are advised to form confederacies or *saṁghas* for safety and longer life. It is said that disunion leads to destruction of republics.[446] Ancient Indian political thinkers had diametrically opposite views about the life of republics which need not be elaborated here.

The republican tradition went on becoming feeble and feeble in the post-Maurya period. The period form 150 BC to AD 350 saw the decline and decay of a number of republics in the Punjab, Sindh, Rājpūtānā and central and western India.

The later foreign invaders, the Indo-Greeks, the Indo-Scythians (or the Śakas) and the Kuṣāṇas were largely responsible for the destruction of republics in the Punjab, Sindh and other parts of western India. The independence of many republican tribes had been completely eclipsed during their rule (second century BC to third Century AD). In the presence of northern and western Satraps it was not possible for the republics to flourish. The situation prevaling in north-west India which was then under foreign rule was not conducive to the growth of republics. In order to liberate them form the foreign domination, to maintain their freedom and to preserve their age-old republican tradition they started migrating from Punjab to Rājpūtānā. The Mālavas, the Śibis and the Yaudheyas were compelled to quit their original homeland and to move to Rājpūtānā sometime in the latter half of the second century BC. It was their love of liberty which inspired them to move to a place where they could further carry on their republican system of government. However, in Rājpūtānā they existed not as *saṁghas* but merely as *gaṇas*. They had self-government without well-organised states and states whatsoever were without power.

The foreign invasions of north-west India on the whole proved to be disastrous for the republics. It is significant to note that whenever the republican tribes found that their freedom was threatened they formed confederations to make a combined front against a common enemy. But they failed to form a big north-western federation embracing the Punjab, Sindh and Rājpūtānā which could stand as a bulwark against the foreign invader.

---

445. *Arth.*, XI, 1.

446. Ch. 108, vv. 6-32; see also ch. 82.

The decline of republics may also be attributed to some extent to the imperialistic policy of Samudragupta. It is true that the republican communities like the Mālavas, the Yaudheyas, the Madras, the Ārjunāyanas and the Ābhīras merely accepted his suzerainty and their autonomy remained intact. But it can scarcely be doubted that during his reign their freedom was always in peril and their republican spirit was dampened. K.P. Jayaswal has rightly pointed out that "Samudragupta, like Alexander, killed the free spirit of the country. He destroyed the Mālavas and the Yaudheyas, who were the nursery of freedom, and many others of their class". But A.S. Altekar maintains that "Their territories were never directly administered by the Guptas, and so their republican institutions could not have been much affected. . . . The Gupta imperialism had not interfered with their autonomy and it is, therefore, difficult to understand how it could have been fatal to their democratic institutions".[447] There may be some contradictions in the statements of scholars but it is a fact that some of the republican tribes found it difficult to maintain their autonomy during the time of samudragupta because of his favour to monarchy and opposition to republic.

Most of the republics declined and finally disappeared from the pages of ancient Indian history by the end of the fourth century AD.

---

447. *State and Government in Ancient India*, p. 137.

# 2

# The Sixteen Mahājanapadas of Northern India in the Age of the Buddha

IT was the age of the Buddha (*c.* 563-483 BC)[1] which really witnessed the formation of large territorial states in northern India. The sixteen great *janapadas* were no doubt in existence in the seventh or early sixth century BC anterior to the rise of Buddhism. But the actual process of territorial expansion began in the time of the Buddha. Some states as exceptions like Kuru and Pañcāla had already become territorial before the advent of Buddhism. The geographical limits of states underwent changes from time to time. The sixth century BC saw major changes in the political boundaries of some states. In all ancient *janapadas* (territorial units or regions) the *janas* or the tribes held the important position, but gradually the territory started assuming greater importance than the former. Thus, the transition from the tribal identity to territorial identity facilitated the formation of large states which comprised both monarchies and repulics. The great *janapada* was no longer merely the territory; it included villages, towns and cities. When Buddha appeared on the scene there was no paramount sovereign in India, rather there were congeries of states whose rulers and chiefs were fighting among themselves for establishing supremacy. These states were, indisputably, of considerable extent and power. The political divisions of northern India at or shortly before the time when Buddhism arose are well exemlified by the following list of sixteen large states (*Solasa Mahājanapadas*): Aṅga, Magadha, Kāsi (Kāśī), Kosala (Kośala), Vajji (Vṛji), Malla, Ceti (Cedi), Vaṁsa (Vatsa), Kuru, Pañcāla, Maccha (Matsya), Śūrasena, Assaka (Aśmaka), Avantī, Gāndhāra and Kāmboja, as mentioned in one of the Canonical Pāli texts.[2] Each

1. The date is based on the Buddhist Chronology, as determined by W. Geiger in the introduction to his translation of a Pāli Chronicle, *Mhv.*, pp. xl-xlvi.

2. *AN*, ed. R. Morris and E. Hardy, vol. I, p. 213; IV, pp. 252, 256, 260; See also *Vinaya Texts*, II, p. 146. The *Janavasabha Suttanta* of the *Dīgha Nikāya* (*DN*, II, cf. B.C. Law, *HPL*, vol. II, p. 654; *GEB*, p.3, note) gives a list of the following ten *janapadas*: Kāśī-Kośala, Vajji-Malla, Ceti-Vaṁsa, Kuru-Pañcāla and Maccha-Śūrasena, omitting another six of them. Besides the Pāli canonical →

one of them is named after the people who settled there or colonised it. According to Buddhist conception of the geographical divisions of India, the first fourteen are included in the Majjhimadesa (Madhyadeśa) and the last two in Uttarāpatha (Northern Region).[3]

## Aṅga

The Kingdom of Aṅga, situated to the east of Magadha, comprised the modern Bhāgalpur and Monghyr districts of Bihar, and also extended northwards up to the river Kosī. Its capital Campā stood at the confluence of the river of the same name (*Jātaka*, No. 506), i.e., modern Chandan, and the Ganges. According to the *Campeyya Jātaka*,[4] the river Campā formed a boundary between Aṅga in the east and Magadha in the west. The actual site of the capital Campā is probably marked by two villages, Campānagara and Campāpura, that still exist near Bhāgalpur. According to A. Cunnigham, the capital must have stood either on the site called Patharghāṭa, 24 miles to the east of Bhāgalpur, or in its immediate vicinity.[5] The *Mahājanaka Jātaka* (No. 539) refers to Campā which, according to the *Mahāparinibbāna Sutta*, was one of the six great cities of India. Another *Jātaka*[6] records that the wealth of Campā gradually increased and traders sailed from her banks to Suvaṇṇabhūmi (Lower Burma) for trading purposes. In the *Mahāgovinda*

---

→ texts, the Sanskrit Buddhist texts also abound in references to the sixteen major states. One of the oldest Sanskrit Buddhist texts, the *Mahāvastu* (ed. E. Senart, vol. II, p. 2, line 15), refers to the '*Soḍaśahi Mahājanapadehi*' without enumerating them. This text, however, in a different connection provides a list of sixteen *mahājanapadas* (*ibid.*, vol. I, p. 34), but includes Śibi and Daśārṇa (in the Punjab and Central India respectively) in place of Gāndhāra and Kāmboja. Another Buddhist Sanskrit work, *Lalitavistara* (ed. S. Lefmann, p. 22), simply makes an allusion to '*Soḍasa Jānapadesu*'. No traditional list is furnished therein.

The Jain canonical text (the *Viyāhapaṇṇatti* or *Vyākhyāprajñapti* popularly known as *Bhagavatī Sūtra*, sec. XV cf. J.C. Jain, *LAIJC*, p.338) gives a slightly variant list of the sixteen *mahājanapadas* which follows: Aṅga, Baṅga (Vaṅga), Magaha (Magadha), Malaya, Mālava (Avantī), Accha, Vaccha (Vatsa), Koccha, Pāḍha (Pāṇḍya or Pauṇḍra), Lāḍha (Lāṭa or Rādha), Bajji (Vajji), Moli (Malla), Kāsi (Kāśī), Kośala, Avāha and Sambhuttara (Suhmottara ?).

The Buddhist and Jain tradition seem to be almost identical in respect of the sixteen political divisions of India but are at variance with each other with regard to their distribution and order of enumeration. However, the Buddhist list of the sixteen great states is comparatively more reliable.

3. See *DPPN*, vol. II, p.494.
4. *Jāt.*, IV, p. 454.
5. *CAGI*, p. 402.
6. *Ibid.*, VI, p. 539.

*Suttanta*[7] we find that Mahāgovinda built the city of Campā. The Pāli texts[8] frequently refer to the visit of Buddha with a large number of *bhikkhus* to Aṅga and Campā. We are also told that the Buddha was once dwelling among the Aṅgas in a city named Assapura in the kingdom of Aṅga.[9] At the time of the Buddha Campā was a big town and not a village.[10] The town of Āpana is also said to have been included within the dominions of Aṅga (Aṅguttarāpa).[11] In one of the Pāli commentaries it is explicitly stated that Aṅga was a prosperous kingdom containing money merchants, and the people from here used to go to trade with many caravans full of merchandise to Sindhu-Sovīradeśa.[12] The celebrated Buddhist scholar and commentator, Buddhaghoṣa, in his Pāli commentary[13] on the *Dīgha Nikāya* incidentally refers to the kingdom concerned.

In the pre-Buddhist period Aṅga was a very powerful kingdom. It was fully independent.[14] But in the Buddha's time Aṅga lost her political power for ever, and it became subject to Magadha. The *Jātakas* contain several references to Aṅga both as an independent kingdom and as a Vassal of Magadha. We are told in one of the *Jātakas*[15] that Magadha was once under the sway of Aṅgarāja. During the days of the Buddha Aṅga and Magadha, the two neighbouring kingdoms, were constantly at war. Once the Magadhan king was defeated and pushed by the army of Aṅga, but he defeated king of Aṅga, recovered his lost kingdom and conquered Aṅga as well.[16] There is no doubt that the Magadha kingdom once came under the suzerainty of Aṅga. But towards the end of the sixth century BC Bimbisāra, the famous ruler of Magadha, after having defeated and killed Brahmadatta, the last independent ruler of Aṅga, occupied its capital Campā and

---

7. *DN*, ed. T.W. Rhys Davids and J.E. Carpenter, vol. II, p. 235.
8. *Ibid.*, vol. I (*Sonadaṇḍa Suttanta*) cf. *GEB*, pp. 7-8; *Vinaya Piṭaka*, ed. H. Oldenberg, vol. I pp. 312-15.
9. *MN*, ed. V. Trenckner and R. Chalmers, vol. I, pp. 271 ff; *Dhammapada-aṭṭhakathā*, a commy. on the *Dhammapada*, ed. H.C. Norman and L.S. Tailang, vol. I, p. 384.
10. *DN*, vol. II, p. 146.
11. *SN*, ed. L. Feer and Mrs. Rhys Davids, vol. V, p. 225.
12. *Vimānavatthu* commentary, pp. 332, 337 cf. *GEB*, p. 8.
13. *Sumaṅgalavilāsinī*, ed. T.W. Rhys Davids and J.E. Carpenter, vol. I, p. 279.
14. *Jāt.*, V, p. 316; VI, 271.
15. *Ibid.*, VI, p. 272.
16. *Jāt.*, IV, pp. 454-55.

resided there as his father's viceroy.[17] That Aṅga passed under the sway of king Bimbisāra is clearly proved by the fact that a certain brāhmaṇa named Sonadaṇḍa with whom the Buddha had a discussion on the subject of caste lived at Campā on the grant made by the king and also used to enjoy the revenues of the town which he received from him.[18] Thereafter Aṅga lost her independent political status and became an integral part of the Magadhan empire. The Pāli text[19] as well as the Sanskrit-Buddhist text[20] confirm it that the Aṅga kingdom with its capital Campā was brought within the territorial limits of the Magadhan kingdom. Aṅga continued to be a dependency of Magadha till the second century BC.

## Magadha

The kingdom of Magadha in the Buddha's time corresponded to the modern Patna and Gayā districts of south Bihar. The evidences furnished in the Buddhist literature gives us an impression that it was broadly divided in to two *khettas*, viz., Gayā and Magadha.[21] It was bounded on the north by the Ganges, on the south by the Vindhya mountain, on the east by the river Campā and on the west by the river Sona. Its capital during the period concerned was Rājagaha (also known as Giribbaja, Girivraja or Rājagṛha) the site of which is marked by ruins which are still extant at modern Rājagīr. The kingdom reached the height of glory during the reigns of its two powerful monarchs, Bimbisāra (*c.* 558-491 BC) and Ajātaśatru called Ajātasattu (*c.* 491-459 BC), the contemporaries of the Buddha.

Bimbisāra adopted the policies of matrimonial alliances, conquest, annexation and aggrandisement not only for strengthening his own position and extending his influence far and wide but also for establishing political hegemony of Magadha over neighbouring states. He married Kośala Devī, daughter of Mahākośala, father of king Pasenadi (Prasenajit) of Kośala. The pin-money or wedding gift was the village of Kāśī yielding a revenue of a hundred thousand for bath and perfume.[22] One of his principal queens was

17. S. Hardy, *A Manual of Buddhism*, p. 163, note. (The account is based on the Tibetan text *Dulva*.)
18. *DN*, vol. I, p. 111.
19. *Ibid.*, vol. I (*Sonadaṇḍa Suttanta*) cf. *HPL*, vol. II, p. 652.
20. *Mahāvastu*, vol. I, pp. 288 ff.
21. *Paramatthajotikā* (a commentary on the *Suttanipāta*) ed. H. Smith, vol. II pp. 301, 583; *Therīgāthāṭṭhakathā*, (a commy. on the *Therīgathā*), ed. E. Muller, p. 225; *Lalitavistara*, ed. R. Mitra, XVII, 309.
22. *Jāt.*, II pp. 237, 403; IV, pp. 342 ff; See also *ibid.*, Nos. 239, 283 and 492.

Cellanā (called Vedehi or Vaidehī), daughter of Cetaka, the then king of Videha. In the time of the Buddha he was a chieftain of the Licchavis (Licchavi-nāyaka) of Vaiśālī.[23] His third wife was Khemā, daughter of the king of Madda (or Madra) in Central Punjab.[24] These marriages paved the way for the expansion of Magadha both northward and westward and enabled Bimbisāra to add a part of Kāśī to his dominions. In pursuance of his expansionist policy, he defeated king Brahmadatta of Aṅga in or about *c*. 500 BC, conquered his kingdom and annexed it to that of his own. The *Vinaya Mahāvagga*[25] offers a reasonable evidence to prove that the kingdom of Aṅga came under Bimbisāra's sway. The *Sonadaṇḍa Suttanta* of the *Dīgha Nikāya*[26] by mentioning the bestowal of Campā, the capital of Aṅga, as a royal fief on the brāhmaṇa Sonadaṇḍa also proves the same thing. This was effected through a land-grant made by the Magadhan king. During Bimbisāra's lifetime his son Ajātasattu (a crown-prince) governed Aṅga as a separate province with Campā as its capital in the capacity of a *uparājā* or viceroy. The annexation of Aṅga was a turning point in the political history of Magadha. It marked the first significant step towards its advance to greatness and the position of eminence which it attained in the fifth century BC. Bimbisāra can be regarded as the real founder of the Magadhan imperial power. His territory inclusive that of Aṅga with its capital Campā embraced villages and towns whose numbers combined together have been estimated as many as 80,000 (eighty thousand) over which he held his sovereignty.[27] The two kingdoms taken together covered an area of three hundred leagues (*yojana*),[28] i.e., about twenty-three hundred miles. The whole of the United Kingdom of Magadha in the time of Ajātasattu covered an area of five hundred leagues. After having ruled for exactly 52 years[29] (*c*. 543-491 BC) Bimbisāra was put to death by his own son, Ajātasattu.[30]

Ajātasattu, the eldest son and successor of Bimbisāra, ascended the throne of Magadha in 491 BC. He has been called Vedehiputto or Vaidehīputra (being the son of Cellanā, also

23. Jacobi, *Jaina Sūtras*, I, XII-XV.
24. *Therīgāthā-aṭṭhakathā*, pp. 131, 139-43.
25. Trans. by T.W. Rhys Davids and H. Oldenberg, SBE (ed. F. Max Müller, Oxford, 1882), vol. XVII, pt. II, p.1.
26. *DN*, I, p.111f.
27. *Vinaya Piṭaka*, I, p. 179, *Vinaya Texts*, SBE, II, pp. 1, 4.
28. *Sumaṅgalavilāsinī*, I, p. 148.
29. *Mhv.*, ed. W. Geiger, p. 15; tr. W. Geiger, II, 29, 30. *Dip.*, ed. and tr. H. Oldenberg, III, 50-60.
30. Different stories have been narrated in the Pāli literature (*Vinaya*, II, p.190; *Sāmaññaphala Sutta*, Dīgha, I, p. 86; *Sumaṅgalavilāsinī*, I, pp. 133-36) about the death of Bimbisāra. He was either imprisoned by his son Ajātasattu and starved to death or murdered by him with a sword.

known as Licchavi princess).[31] He followed his father's policy of annexation through military conquest. On the death of Bimbisāra, his wife, Kośala Devī, died of tremendous shock and grief.[32] Ajātasattu then began to enjoy the revenues of the Kāśī village, which had been settled upon her by her father as pin-money or dowry on her marriage. But Pasenadi of Kośala was not inclined at all to allow the parricide monarch to do so. He accordingly confiscated the township of Kāśī the revenues of which had been granted to his sister. He finally stopped the payment of revenues to him which ultimately resulted in a war between the two royal families. In the first three rounds of battles Pasenadi suffered humiliating defeats at the hands of Ajātasattu, but in the fourth and last one he avenged his defeat and took possession of Kāśī. Ajātasattu after being defeated in the fourth campaign was made prisoner by Pasenadi and not released until he had relinquished his claim. However, the latter treated the former generously giving him his daughter Vajirā in marriage and even bestowing the disputed village of Kāśī on her as a wedding gift. In the end Ajātasattu succeeded in extending his sway over Kāśī and Kośala. The two kingdoms of Magadha and Kośala were once more closely united by matrimonial alliance. The Pāli texts[33] and a commentary[34] present an account of a war between Pasenadi of Kośala and Ajātasattu of Magadha. As a matter of fact, there took place many a fierce fight between the sons of Mahākośala and Bimbisāra, Pasenadi and Ajātasattu respectively. But the two kings entered into a short of agreement. Magadha during the reign of Ajātasattu came into conflict also with the Vajjis of Vesāli or Vaiśālī.

The next important political achievement of Ajātasattu was his voctory over the Licchavis of Vaiśālī. Various causes are attributed to the war that brocks out between the two. One of the primary causes was that there was a port near the Ganges extending over a *yojana* half of which belonged to Ajātasattu and half to the Licchavis. And at the foot of the mountain which was not far from it there was a mine of precious gems. Both the parties entered into a mutual agreement over the equal distibution of the produce of mine. But the Licchavis did not honour the terms of agreement and took the lion share of gems unilaterally. The flagrant violation of the agreement enraged the feelings of

---

31. *SN*, II, p. 268; *Sumaṅgalavilāsinī*, I, p. 47; *Papañcasūdanī* (*aṭṭhakathā* or commy. on the *Majjhima Nikāya*) ed. J.H. Woods, D. Kosambi and I.B. Horner, I, p. 125; *Sāraṭṭhappakāsinī-aṭṭhakathā* (commy. on *Saṁyutta*), II, p. 215.
32. *Jāt.*, II, p. 403.
33. *Kosala Saṁyutta*, *SN*, I, pp. 82-86; *Jāt.*, IV, pp. 342 ff.
34. *Dhammapada-aṭṭhakathā*, III, p. 259.

Ajātasattu. The quarrels intermittently flared up between the two over the possession of a mineral mine on the boundary of the two territories. The Ganges formed the boundary between the kingdom of Magadha and repulican territory of the Licchavis, and that both the Magadhans and the Licchavis had equal rights over the river. This may have furnished merely the pretext of the hostility between the two. In fact, the real motive of Ajātasattu was to destroy the power of the Vajjians. He was not only jealous but also scared of the Licchavis on account of their numerical strength and national solidarity. Accordingly he became bent upon uprooting them. Being fully conscious of the strength of the Licchavis as *gaṇarājās*, he deputed his chief minister, Vassakāra (or Varṣakāra who was a brāhmaṇa) to sow the seed of dissensions among the Licchavis princes and to break their unity which, according to the Buddha, was the real source of their strength. After reaching Vaiśālī he took three or four years to accomplish his task. Taking advantage of internal dissensions and disunity of the Licchavis effected through the machination and stratagem of his minister, Ajātasattu waged war against them. When he decided to attack the Vajjibhūmi the then most poweful leader Cetaka summoned the eighteen *gaṇarājās* of Kāśī, Kośala, the Licchavis and the Mallas together at Vaiśālī to chalk out a strategy of fighting unitedly against the Magadhan king. Ajātasattu after making counter preparation swooped down upon the Licchavis with an overwhelming force, defeated them and their allies and conquered Vaiśālī, the capital of the Vajjians. The Licchavis were forced to acknowledge the suzerainty of Ajātasattu and to pay him tribute as a token of their submission. But they were in all probability independent in their internal politics. The facts stated above can undoubtedly be confirmed by the evidence of the Pāli text[35] as well as by the Pāli commentatorial tradition preserved in the *Sumaṅgalavilāsinī*.[36] We have also positive evidence to show that Vaiśālī soon became a "Magadhan town" and later became independent.[37] We are also told that he employed two of his ministers, Sunidha and Vassakāra, to build a fort at Pāṭaligāma (a village near Pāṭaliputra or in its

35. *DN*, II, pp. 72ff; *Mahāparinibbāna Suttanta*, Pāli text with Hindi tr., ed. S.G. Prajñānanda, pp. 1-4. See also T.W. Rhys Davids and C. A.F. Rhys Davids (tr.), *Dialogues of the Buddha*, vol.II, p. 78; Rahula Sānkṛtyāyana, *Pāli Sāhitya Kā Itihāsa*, pp. 38-39.

36. *Sumaṅgalavilāsinī*, ed. S. Hewavitarne, Burmese edn. Bequest series No. 1, rev. by Nānissara, p. 99. The Sanskrit Buddhist texts (*Mahāvastu*, vol. I, pp. 34, 289; II, p. 419; III, pp. 47, 90; *Avadāna Śataka*, ed. J.S. Speyer, *Divyāvadāna*, ed. E.B. Cowell and R.A. Neil, p. 425) also make mention of the kingdom of Magadha in different context.

37. *Suttanipāta*, ed. D. Andersen and H. Smith, PTS (London, 1913) and tr. V. Fausboll, SBE, vol. X, 2nd edn. (Oxford, 1898), Verse 1013.

vicinity) on the Ganges with a view to repelling the attacks of the Vajjians and crushing them.[38] Vaiśālī situated in the north opposite Pāṭaliputra on the Ganges was a standing menace to Pāṭaliputra and stood in the way of the expansion of the Magadhan kingdom. It is said that the Licchavis were in the habit of entering the Magadhan territory, Pāṭaliputra, by crossing the Ganges to make an attempt to subdue Ajātasattu.[39] This was one of the reasons why the former were reduced to submission by the latter. Ajātasattu is credited with having established his supremacy over Kāśī, Kośala and Vaiśālī. The Magadhan kingdom attained the greatest political importance in northern India during his reign.

Ajātasattu is said to have fortified his capital Rājagaha in anticipation of an attack by king Pajjota of Avantī, but this attack was never materialised.[40] Ujjain had become subject to Magadha afterwards, probably in the fourth century BC. Ajātasattu's minister Vassakāra is stated to have begun the work of repairing the fort of Rājagaha.[41]

The *Mahāvaṁśa* assigns a reign of thirty-two years to Ajātasattu,[42] while the *Vinaya* commentary fixes it only twenty-four years.[43] However, he met the same tragic end as his father being put to death by his son, Udayi-Bhadda.[44] The Buddha passed away in the eighth year of Ajātasattu's reign (i.e., 483 BC).

During the times of Bimbisāra and Ajātasattu Magadha rose to great eminence end virtually became a paramout power. The absorption of Aṅga, Kāśī, Kośala, Vaiśālī and surrounding territories into Magadha made it the mightiest kingdom in northern India. It gradually turned into an empire in the first half of the fifth century BC.

## Kāśī

The Kāśīs were one of the most ancient peoples of northern India. They can undoubtedly be placed in the Brāhmaṇical mid-land. They founded a kingdom named Kāśī after them

---

38. *DN*, II, pp. 86-87; *Sumaṅgalavilāsinī*, PTS, II, pp. 516-17, 540; *Vinaya* Texts, SBE, II, p. 101; *DPPN*, II, p. 178.
39. W.W. Rockhill, *The Life of the Buddha* (based on the Tibetan text, *Dulva*), p. 97; Rāhula Sāṅkṛtyāyana, *Buddhacaryā*, pp. 520, 527.
40. *MN*, III, p. 7.
41. *Vinaya Piṭaka*, III, p. 41f.
42. *Mhv.*, II vv. 29, 31-32.
43. *Sāmantapāsādikā*, ed. J. Takakusu and M. Nagai, p. 72.
44. *Mhv.*, ch. iv. v. I.

which was bounded by Vatsa on the west, Kośala on the north and Magadha on the east. The extent of the kingdom as a whole is mentioned in the *Jātakas* as 300 leagues or *yojana* (i.e., about twenty-three hundred miles),[45] and that of its capital city, Vārāṇasī (mod. Banāras), as 12 *yojana* (i.e., over ninety miles).[46] This city (whose earliest name was Kāśī itself) stood, as it now does, on the left bank of the Gangas between the river Varaṇā on the north-east and the Assi Nālā on the south-west. The city was known by different names in the past ages, as told in the *Jātakas*.[47] The city of Vārāṇasī is distinctly mentioned in the *Vinaya* commentary as one of the important cities of the Buddha's time,[48] whereas the *Jātaka* refers to it as the chief city in India.[49] The Kāśīs of Varāṇasī also finds mention in the *Majjhima Nikāya*.[50] The kingdom of Kāśī with its capital Vārāṇasī is referred to not only in Pāli literature but also in Sanskrit-Buddhist texts.[51]

It appears from the Pāli texts that before the time of the Buddha Kāśī was a great political power, absolutely independent and the most powerful kingdom in the whole of northern India.[52] Brahmadatta was the dynastic name of the kings of Kāśī which is evident from the *Jātakas*[53] as well as other work.[54] Many *Jātakas* testify to the unsurpassed glory of the city of Vārāṇasī and to the ambition of its potentates for paramount sovereignty over the whole of India.[55] The most important event in the history of the Kāśīs during the period preceding the rise of Buddhism was the frequent wars and repeated struggle for supremacy between the kings of Kāśī and Kośala. Sometimes Kāśī extended its suzerain power over Kośala and sometimes Kośala conquered Kāśī. The vicissitudes of their fortunes always took different turns.[56] In the time of the Buddha, Kāśī lost its independent political status. The series of struggles of

---

45. *Jāt.*, IV, p. 442; V, p. 41; *Jāt.*, No. 391.
46. *Ibid.*, VI, p. 160; IV, p. 74; also *Jāt.*, Nos. 483, 515, 543.
47. *Ibid.*, IV, pp. 15, 119-20.
48. *Sāmantapāsādikā*, vol. I, p. 201.
49. *Guttila Jāt.*, No. 243.
50. *MN*, vol. I, p. 473.
51. *Lalitavistara*, pp. 405-6; *Mahāvastu*, vol. III, p. 402; *Divyāvadāna*, p. 73; *Bodhisattvāvadāna Kalpalatā*, 6th Pallava, pp. 31-32.
52. *Jat.*, I, pp. 262 ff; III, pp. 115ff; *Vinaya* Texts, SBE pt. II, pp, 30ff.
53. *Dummedha Jāt.*, vol. I, pp. 259, 285; *Gaṅgamāla*, *Jāt.*, No. 421; *Kosiya Jāt.*, vol. I, p. 463.
54. *DPPN*, II, p. 332.
55. *Bhaddasāla Jāt.*, No. 465; *Dhonasākha Jāt.*, No. 353; *Sonananda Jāt.*, No. 532.
56. *Jāt.*, III, pp. 115ff; *Vinaya* Texts, II, pp. 30ff, 301ff; *DPPN*, I, p. 592; *Mahāvastu*, III, p. 349.

the pre-Buddhistic phase culminated in its fall in the age of the Buddha. First it was annexed to the Kośalan kingdom and formed part of it during the reign of Pasenadi,[57] and then it was finally conquered and incorporated into the Magadhan kingdom when Ajātasattu defeated the Kośalans and became the most powerful king of northern India.[58]

## Kośala

In the time of the Buddha the kingdom of Kośala (northern Kośala) with its capital, Sāvatthi (Śrāvastī), was under the rule of its king Pasenadi, the son of Mahākośala. It was one of the most powerful kingdoms in northern India.[59] It was "bounded on the west by the Gomatī, on the south by the Sarpikā or Syandikā (Sai) river, on the east by the Sadānīrā which separated it from Videha, and on the north by the Nepal hills".[60] The total extent of Kośala is said to have been "little less than that of France today".[61]

The ancient Kośala kingdom was divided by the river Sarayū into two great parts, that to the north being called Uttara (northern) Kośala and that to the south Dakṣiṇa (southern) Kośala. An evidence to the effect is also furnished in the Sanskrit Buddhist texr, *Avadānaśataka*. It may be taken for granted that Ayojjha (Ayodhyā) on the river Sarayū was the earliest capital of undivided kingdom of Kośala. And then during the Buddhist period it was the capital of Dakṣiṇa Kośala. It distinctly appears from some of the early Buddhist texts that during the lifetime of the Buddha both Sāketa and Sāvatthi were the capital cities of the northern Kośala. However, Ayojjha did not escape the notice of the Buddha. He is said to have visited this particular city twice. He preached there *Phena Sutta* and *Dārukkhandha Sutta*.[62] But according to G.P. Malalasekera, this refers to another settlement made by colonist from the original Ayojjha.[63] Sāketa is mentioned sometimes as an important city and sometimes as a capital of Kośala.[64] It is

57. *DN*, 1, pp. 288; *MN*, II, p. 111; *Vinaya* Texts, SBE, vol. XIII, pp. 294-99; *Kunāla Jāt.*, No. 536, *Kosambi Jāt.*, No. 428.

58. *SN*, I. pp. 82-85.

59. The *Kosala Saṁyutta*, *SN*, I, pp. 70-97; The *Ambaṭṭha Suttanta*, *DN*, I cf. *HPL*, vol. II, p. 652, *Jāt.*, III, pp. 211-13, 237, *Dhammapada-aṭṭhakathā*, I, pp. 211, 337-38; *Bodhisattvāvadāna Kalpalatā*, 100th Pallava, p. 2.

60. *PHAI*, p. 99.

61. *CHI*, vol. I, p. 159.

62. *SN*, III, pp. 140ff; IV, p. 179f; V, p. 73.

63. *DPPN*, I, p. 165.

64. *Jāt.*, III, p. 270; *Mahāvastu*, I, p. 348.

said to have stood on a high road between Sāvatthi and Kośāmbī.[65] The identity of this city as a second capital of Kośala may also be inferred from the *Nandiyamiga Jātaka* (No. 385). The most important and permanent capital of the Kośala kingdom in the Buddha's time was Sāvatthi. This capital city has been frequently mentioned in the early Pāli texts.[66] It is said to have been situated on the banks of the Acirāvatī (mod. Rāptī).[67] It was six league (about forty-five miles) north of Sāketa.[68] It is further said that the distance between the two could be covered in one day.[69] Sāvatthi is identical with the great ruined city on the south bank of the Rāptī called Sahet-Mahet, which is situated on the borders of the Bahraich and Goṇḍā districts (about 70 miles north-west of modern Gorakhpur) in U.P.[70] Sāvatthi during the period concerned was the seat of the government. This city, according to one of the Sanskrit-Buddhist text, was full of kings, princes, their councillors, ministers and followers, kṣatriyas, brāhmaṇas, householders, etc.[71] In the Buddha's time there were fifty-seven thousand families in this city, if the account given thereof in the *Vinaya* commentary[72] is to be relied upon. The *Jātaka* stories also speak of the wealth and glory of this city.[73] This was the third and the last capital of Kośala. It is curious to note that Lord Buddha out of forty-five years of his homeless life or wanderings (after having attained Buddhahood at the age of thirty-five) spent altogether twenty-five years in Sāketa and Sāvatthi and remaining twenty years in other parts of northern India. It is said that he lived at Sāketa either six or sixteen years and at Sāvatthi either nine or nineteen years.[74] There are innumerable references to the Buddha's visit to Kośala in Buddhist literature. The general impression, that Ayodhyā and Sāketa, two of the earlier capitals of this kingdom, lost their importance during the early Buddhist period, can be dispelled in the light of the facts stated above. Both the cities existed in the Buddha's time and retained their importance. And "They were possibly adjoining, like London and Westminster", as observed by T.W. Rhys Davids.[75]

65. *Sutta-nipāta*, verses 1011-13.
66. *AN*, II, p. 100; III, p. 356; V, pp. 193-96.
67. *Vinaya,* I, pp. 191, 293.
68. *Vinaya Texts*, II, p. 147; see also *DPPN*, II, p. 1084.
69. *MN*, I, p. 149.
70. *CASR*, vol. I, p. 331.
71. *Lalitavistara*, Ch. I and pp. 20-21.
72. *Sāmantapāsādikā*, III, p. 614.
73. *Jāt.*, IV, pp. 144ff, 236ff; VI, p. 68.
74. Turnour, *JASB*, vol. VII, p. 790, cf. *CAGI*, pp. 339-40.
75. *BI*, p. 39.

However, in a comparative manner it will not be unfair on our part to uphold the view that "In Buddha's time, Ayodhyā had sunk to the level of an unimportant town, but Sāketa nad Sāvatthi were two of the six great cities of India".[76]

Besides the two cities of Sāketa and Sāvatthi, some other minor town like Setavya,[77] Ukkaṭṭha,[78] Ulumba or Ulumpa (in the territory of the Śākyas of Kapilavatthu or Kapilavastu in the Nepalese Tarai), Nagaraka (bordering on the Śākya territory)[79] Daṇḍakappaka,[80] Nalakapāna,[81] Paṅkadhā,[82] and a village named Toraṇavatthu (between Sāvatthi and Sāketa)[83] were also included within the territorial limits of the kingdom of Kośala.

In the pre-Buddhsit period the Kośala was only "a poor and tiny estate with slender resorces".[84] But during the days of the Buddha it apparently became an extensive kingdom.

During the time of Pasenadi the Kośala kingdom turned into an empire, which can be authenticated by the details available in the early Pāli texts. The kingdom or an empire of his time comprised five territories including Kośala proper, the remaining four being Kāśī with Vārāṇasī as its capital, Uttara Pañcāla with Kāmpillapura (better Ahicchatra) as its capital. Ālavī and a principality with Polāsapura as its capital. Pasenadi has been called as the chief of a group of five *rājās*.[85] Kāśī after becoming subordiante to Kośala was placed by him under the viceroyalty of his brother. The territory of the Śākyas of Kapilavatthu was also included within the kingdom of Kośala. They claimed to be Kośalans. They had acknowledged the supremacy of king Pasenadi in the latter half of the sixth century BC, which is quite evident from some of the Pāli texts.[86] The territory

76. B.C. Law, *GEB*, p. 5; *Mahāparinibbāna Sutta*, SBE, XI, p. 99, quoted in *ibid*., also Law, *ABORI*, XVII, pt. III (1936), p. 225.

77. *Pāyāsi Suttanta*, cf. *GEB*, p. 5.

78. *Ambaṭṭha Sutta*, *DN*, I, p. 87.

79. *Dhammacetiya Sutta*, *MN*, II, p. 118f.

80. *AN*, III, pp. 402ff.

81. *Ibid*., V. pp. 122ff.

82. *Ibid*., I, p. 236; See also Law, "The Kosalas in Ancient India", *IHQ*, vol. 1, Nos.1-2 (Delhi, 1979), p. 165.

83. *SN*, IV, pp. 374ff.

84. *Vinaya Mahāvagga*, SBE, XVII, pt. II, p. 294.

85. *SN*, I, p. 80; for details See Law, "Śrāvastī in Ancient Literature", *MASI*, No. 50 (Delhi 1935), p. 12.

86. *Aggñña Suttanta*, *DN*, III, p. 83; *Dialogues of the Buddha*, III, p. 80; *Jāt*., IV, p. 145; *Bhaddasāla Jāt*., No. 465; *DPPN*, I, p. 696; *Suttanipāta*, verse 422.

of another republican community known as Kālāmas of Kesaputta is also said to have formed part of the Kośalan kingdom.[87] The Licchavis of Vaiśālī were, however, on friendly terms with king Pasenadi of Kośala.[88]

We are told that Pasenadi once in his old age went to see the Buddha, who was then at Ulumba in the territory of the Śākyas. Taking advantage of his absence from the capital, his son Viḍūḍabha (Virūdhaka) being instigated by his minister or commander-in-chief, Dīgha-Cārāyana, raised the banner of revolt, deposed his father and usurped the throne. Pasenadi having found himself deserted by all his people rushed to Rājagaha to seek help from Ajātasattu, but being worn out by worry and fatigue he fell ill and died outside the gates of the city.[89] The latter gave the former a state funeral. The last interview of Pasenadi with the Buddha is said to have taken place in their eightieth year. They were not only the contemporary of each other but were also born on the same data and died in the same year.[90] We are also informed that it was king Viḍūḍabha who exterminated the Śākyas who he hated much. But spell of disaster soon befell him and his army, as they got drowned in the river Acirāvatī (Rāptī) while returning from Kapilavatthu.[91] We know nothing more of him or of his successors. In the Buddha's time Kośala was no doubt a predominant kingdom. But its battles with kings of Kāśī and Magadha, as already noted, caused a great setback to it and consequently its political power gradually started dwindling. It was eventually eclipsed by the growing power of Magadha.

## Vajji

This *mahājanapada* actually stands for a confederacy of eight allied clans (*aṭṭhakula* or *aṭṭhakulakā*)[92] represented by the Videhas, the Licchavis, the Vajjis proper, the Jñātrikas, the Ugras, the Bhogas, the Aikṣvākas and the Kauravas.[93] The Vajjis (Skt. Vṛjis) themselves formed one of the constituent clans of that confederacy after whom the *mahājanapada* was named as Vajji. All the clans were collectively called the Vajjis, and

87. *AN*, I, p. 188.
88. *Aṅgulimāla Sutta*, *MN*, II, pp. 100-1.
89. *Jāt.*, II, p. 403; IV, pp. 144ff, 152, 343; *SN*, I, p. 83; *Avadānaśataka*, p. 51.
90. *Dhammacetiya Sutta*, *MN*, II, p. 118f.
91. *Jāt.*, IV, pp. 144ff; *Dhammapada-aṭṭhakathā*, I, p. 359; *Mhv.*, VIII, 18.
92. *Sumaṅgalavilāsinī*, II, p. 519.
93. *PHAI*, pp. 118-20; B.C. Law, *GEB*, p. 12 and note 1; *Some Kshatriya Tribes of Ancient India*, Ch. II, See also Ch.V; *CAGI*, pp. 375-77.

the confederacy became popularly known as the Vajjian confederacy. Turnour while giving an interesting account of the Vajjis from his commentary on the *Mahāvaṁśa*, one of the Pāli chronicles of Ceylon, also says that they were "Samvajji", i.e., "the united Vajjis",[94] which is said to be "a descriptive title of the whole nation of eight clans".[95] Of the aforesaid eight confederate clans, the Videhans, the Vajjis and the Licchavis were the most important. In the Sanskrit-Buddhist text,[96] the Vaiśālakas (Vajjis) and the Licchavis are clearly described as two different confederate clans.

This *mahājanapada* appears to have comprised the principalities of all eight clans which lay by and large in Vaiśālī and Videha regions of north Bihar. It may have extended northwards as far as Nepal.

The Videha clan had its seat at Mithilā, the capital city,[97] which is usually identified with the small town of Janakapura (now within the Nepal border). It was about thirty-five miles north-west from Vaiśālī (Pāli Vesāli). The extent of the city is mentioned as seven leagues (about fifty miles).[98] During the time of the Buddha a section of them may have settled in Vaiśālī and joined the Vajjain confederation. The Videhas and the Vajjis became politically knit together. Videha roughly corresponds to ancient Tirabhukti or modern Tirhut. The Videhan territory in a wider sense embraced the modern districts of Muzaffarpur, Darbhaṅgā and Madhubanī and the adjoining Nepalese Tarai. At the time of the Buddha the Videha country with the capital at Mithilā was one of the eight constituent principalities of the Vajjian confederacy. However, the Videhas of Mithilā like the Licchavis of Vesāli found an important place in the annals of Buddhism for obvious reasons.

The Pāli works expressly speak of Vajjigāma,[99] i.e., a locality of the Vijjis proper near about Vesāli which is clearly mentioned as Vajji town.[100] The Licchavis' capital was undoubtedly at Vesāli. The Vajjis and the Licchavis are often associated with the city of Vesāli which was not only their capital but also the metropolis of the entire confederacy.[101]

94. *JASB*, VII, pp. 992-3, cf. *CAGI*, p. 377.
95. *CAGI*, p. 377.
96. *Divyāvadāna*, pp. 55-56, 136.
97. *Mahāvastu*, III, p. 172.
98. *Gāndhāra Jātaka* (No. 406), *Jāt.*, III, p. 365; Cowell's *Jāt.*, III, p. 222; *Suruchi Jāt.*, No. 489; *Jāt.*, IV, pp. 315-16; VI, p. 246.
99. *SN*, V, p. 348.
100. *DN*, III, pp. 12ff.
101. *MN*, II, p. 101.

Vesāli (to the north of the Ganges or to the east of the Sadānīrā or Gaṇḍak) is identical with the ruins at and near the modern village or Besārh in the Muzaffarpur district of Bihar. Vesāli at the time of the Buddha was not only one of the most flourishing and populous cities but also the seat of famous republic in northern India. The Jñātrika clan had thcir seats at Kuṇḍapura or Kuṇḍagrāma and Kollāga, suburbs of Vesāli. But the dwellers of the suburban areas were also called "Vesālie", i.e., inhabitants of Vesāli. According to Buddhist tradition, the city of Vesāli consisted of three districts which "were probably at one time the seats of three different clans".[102] In the *Aṅguttara Nikāya* the Ugras are associated with Vesāli[103] and with Hatthigāma.[104] The Bhogas probably resided in a town of Bhoganagara. This town because of its peculiar geographical position had fallen under the joint occupation of the Vajjis and Mallas. This being a border town touched the realm of both. The *Mahāparinibbāna Suttanta* locates some villages or towns like Hatthigāma, Bhoganagara, Bhaṇḍagāma, Ambagāma and Jambūgāma on the way from Vesāli to Pāvā.[105] The Bhogas had also settled between Vesāli and Sāvatthi. The Aikṣvākas of Vesāli were in all probability the descendants of Ikṣvāku. The Kauravas represent those Kuru brāhmaṇas who had settled in the capital of Videha long before the rise of Buddhism. The Vajji territory seems to have included not only Vaiśālī but also the larger adjoining realm of Videha and villagers and towns of neighbouring areas belonging to different clans. The importance of the "Vajjibhūmi" has been highlighted in the *Vinaya* commentary.[106]

According to Hiuen-Tsang, the extensive region of Fu-Li-Chih (Vṛji) was above 4000 *li* (or 667 miles) in circuit, long from east to west and narrow from north to south. He further adds that the people of the north called it the San-fa-chih (or Samvajji) country.[107] Cunningham, while placing his reliance on the Chinese account of the subject, observes that "This description corresponds exactly with the tract of country lying between the Gaṇḍak and Mahānadī rivers which is 300 miles in length and 100 miles in breadth. Within these limits there are several ancient cities some of which may possibley have been the capitals of the eight different clans of the Vrijis".[108] He includes among them

102. Rockhill, *op.cit.*, p. 62.
103. *AN*, 1, p. 26; III, p. 49; IV, p. 208.
104. *Ibid.*, IV, p. 212.
105. *DN*, II, pp. 122-26, for details see pp. 72-168; also *Sutta-nipāta*, p. 194.
106. *Sāmantapāsādikā*, 1, p. 207.
107. *YCTI*, II, p. 81.
108. *CAGI*, p. 378.

the ancient cities of Vaiśālī, Kesariya, Janakapur, Navandgarh, Simrun and modern towns of Darbhaṅgā, Motihārī, etc. Kesariya, an old ruined town, according to him, was just 30 miles to the north-west of Vaiśālī. Navandgarh is identical with a ruined fort situated in close proximity to the large village of Lauriya, "15 miles to the north-west of Bettiah and 10 miles from the nearest point of the Gandak river".[109] He also mentions that "In the Buddha's time the Balays or Bulukas, one of the eight clans of the Vr̥jis, were situated in the neighbourhood of the Gandak or in the east of Bettiah".[110] Simrun (Simraon) was included in the Videhan territory bordering Nepal. V.A. Smith observes that "The Vr̥ji (Fu-li-Chih) country evidently is roughly equivalent to the northern part of the Darbhanga District and the adjoining Nepaless Tarai. A possible site for the capital is offered by the ruins at Baligarh or Kshemagarh, some 16 miles north of Madhubani. . . ."[111] The site suggested by him for the capital may have possibly formed part of the Vajji territory. The actual site of the capital was at Vaiśālī, as noted before.

The political organisation of the Vajjis was fundamentally based on the principle of republicanism. This republican state called *gaṇasaṁgha* in the contemporary sources was jointly ruled by the chiefs or princes of all the clans called *rājā*s. The ruling class belonged to the kṣatriya clan. It has been rightly pointed out that "the union of the Vajjian states consisted of a confederation of chiefs".[112] Their unity was destroyed and they, particularly the Licchavis, were conquered by the Magadhan king Ajātasattu not long after the demise of the Buddha in 483 BC. However, they continued to exist as an independent or autonomous clans.

## Malla

The republican state of the Mallas had two territorial divisions. Kuśinārā (identical with Kuśāvatī or Kuśinagar) was the capital of one division and Pāvā of the other.[113] The first abutted on the Śākya territory and the second on the Vajji. The Mallas of Kuśinārā were called Kosināraka and those of Pāvā Pāveyyaka Malla.[114] The Malla territory (called in the *Jātaka*s Mallaraṭṭha, i.e., Mallarāṣṭra) was situated to the north of the Vajjians of

109. *CAGI*, pp. 376, 378.

110. *Ibid*., p. 379.

111. Cf. *YCTI*, II, p. 340; S. Beal, *The Life of Hiuen Tsiang*, (Delhi, 1973), Appendix 1, p. 230.

112. *CAGI*, p. 377.

113. *Kusa Jāt*., No. 531; *Mahāparinibbāna Suttanta, Dialogues of the Buddha*, pt. II, pp. 136ff, 161-62; *DPPN*, 1, p. 653; II, pp. 453-54.

114. *DPPN*, II, p. 453.

Vesāli or to the south-east of the Śākyas of Kapilavatthu. It not only touched the northern border of the Vajji states but also the realm of the Uttarakośala. Their chief capital city, Kuśinārā, is identical with modern Kasiā (on the smaller Gaṇḍak), situated at a distance of exactly 35 miles to the east of Gorakhpur in U.P.[115] The another capital, Pāvā, has been identified with Padarāonā (now in Deoriā district), 12 miles to the north-east of Kasiā.[116] The ancient city of Kuśāvatı or Kuśinārā was the most flourishing and magnificent city in bygone ages. It was 12 *yojana* in length from east to west, and 7 *yojana* in breadth from breadth from north to south.[117] According to Pāli commentary on the *Dīgha Nikāya,* this city was 25 *yojana* from Rājagaha.[118] This is the city where Lord Buddha attained *nirvāṇa* or passed away.[119] According to Cunningham, the old capital "occupied a circuit of about 2 miles".[120] Pāvā was also famous as one of the eight cities during the period concerned.

At the time of the rise of Buddhism the Mallas were divided into many sections. The Pāli canonical texts bring into prominence the territories of just two of them with their two chief cities Kuśinārā and Pāvā. But we find that besides these two cities, the Malla territory included other important towns namely, Bhoganagara, Anupiyā and Uruvelakappa in the neighbourhood of which there existed a wide forest called Mahāvana.[121] In fact, there was a great belt of a Himālayan forest called Mahāvana which covered some portions of the Vajji and Malla territories. Bhoganagara was between Jambūgāma and Pāvā on the high road connecting Vasāli with Kapilavatthu.[122] Anupiyā was evidently on the same high road between Kuśinārā and the river Anomā,[123] the latter serving as a dividing line between the Śākya and Malla territories. It appears from the Sanskrit-Buddhist text that Anomiya was another important Malla town, situated to the south of Kapilavastu at a distance of 12 *yojana*.[124]

---

115. *CAGI*, p. 363; *CASR*, I, p. 76.
116. *Ibid*., p. 366; *ibid*., 1, p. 74.
117. *DN*, II, pp. 146-47.
118. *Sumaṅgalavilāsinī*, II, p. 609.
119. *Sāmantapāsādikā*, I. p. 4f; *Divyāvadāna*, pp. 208-9.
120. *CAGI*, p. 364.
121. *AN*, IV, p. 438; *SN*, V, p. 228; Law, *Some Kṣatriya Tribes of Ancient India*, p. 149.
122. *DN*, p. 123; *Sutta-nipāta*, verses 1012-13.
123. *Jāt*., I, pp. 65, 140; *DN*, III, p. 1; *Vinaya*, II pp. 180, 184.
124. *Mahāvastu*, II, p. 164.

The Mallas were governed by their own chiefs, who had formed a confederation or *saṁgha*. They also belonged to the kṣatriya clan. Their state has been called *saṁgharājya*.[125] The political relation between the Mallas and the Licchavis was on the whole very cordial. "But there were occasional rivalries between the two".[126]

## Ceti (Cedi)

The kingdom of the Cetis or Cedis called Cetiraṭṭha (Cetirāṣṭra) lay near the Yamunā contiguous to that of the Kurus. It corresponds roughly to the eastern part of modern Bundelkhaṇḍ (M.P.) and the adjoining region. We learn from the *Cetiya Jātaka*[127] that the capital city of this kingdom was Soṭṭhivatinagara which is most probably identical with the Sūktimatī (on the bank of the river of the same name) in the neighbourhood of Bāṅdā (U.P.). Other important towns of the Cedi kingdom include Sahajāti[128] or Sahañcanika,[129] which probably stood on the right bank of the Yamunā,[130] and Tripurī close to the Narmadā not far from modern Jabalpur. The reference to Cedi as one of the sixteen *janapadas* is also made in the Buddhist Sanskrit work.[131] We are also told that the Cedis had two distinct settlements. One probably the older was in the mountains in what is now Nepal.[132] The other probably a later colony was near Kośāmbī to the east.[133] Their territory appears to have been situated midway between the kingdoms of the Kurus and Vaṁsas.[134]

## Vaṁsa (Vatsa)

The kingdom of the Vaṁsas or Vatsas was situated along the right bank of the Yamunā (Allahabad district), immediately to the north of Avantī. It was bounded on the east by Magadha, on the south by Avantī and on the west by Śūrasena. The kingdom with its capital at Kośāmbī (or Kauśāmbī) on the Yamunā ruled over by king Udena (Udayana),

125. *MN*, I, p. 231.
126. *Dhammapada*, Fausboll, old edn., pp. 218-20, cf. *GEB*, p. 15.
127. *Jāt.*, III (No. 422) , pp. 454, 460-61.
128. *AN*, III, p. 355.
129. *SN*, V, p. 436f.
130. *DPPN*, II, p. 1080.
131. *Lalitavistara*, p. 22.
132. *Jāt.*, V, pp. 514, 518.
133. *Vinaya*, I, p. 108; *Jāt.*, 1, p. 360; *Divyāvadāna*, pp. 184-91.
134. For further details see Law, *Ancient Mid-Indian Kshatriya Tribes*, vol. 1, ch. V.

the contemporary of the Buddha, has been frequently referred to in Buddhist literature.[135] The said capital is identical with modern Kosam (the name born by two adjacent villages, Kosam Inam and Kosam Khiraj) on the right bank of the Yamunā, 30 miles south-west of Allahabad.[136] In the Buddha's time it was regarded as one of the six chief cities of India.[137] It is described as a land which was very rich and prosperous.[138] There were four distinct settlements by the order of the Buddha in the suburbs of Kośāmbī — the Badarika, Kukkuṭa, Ghoṣitārāma and Pāvāriya.[139] Vatsa was one of the powerful kingdoms of the sixth century BC. Its ruler, Udayana (son of Parantapa), in order to strengthen his position entered into matrimonial alliances with the royal families of Avantī, Magadha and Aṅga. The Buddhist tradition preserved in the Pāli work[140] as well as in the Sanskrit text[141] also confirms that he had three wives. However, we are in a better position to affirm that king Pajjota (Pradyota) of Avantī invaded Vatsabhūmi but after being defeated by king Udayana gave his daughter Vāsuladatla (Vāsavadattā) in marriage to him. This fact can be positively attested to by Buddhist sources.[142] The two contemporary rulers of adjoining kingdoms always remained enagaged in war but ultimately became united by bond of marriage. The royal marriages were absolutely necessary for the maintenance of the political independence of Kośāmbī which, however, served as a buffer state between Avantī and Magadha. The marriage alliances of king Udayana saved Kośāmbī from falling an easy prey to the overgrowing power of Avantī and Magadha. During his reign the Bhagga (i.e., Bharga) state of Suṁsumāragiri was a dependency of the Vatsa kingdom.[143] The location of Suṁsumāragiri has been firxed "between the Yamunā and the lower valley of the Son".[144] Some parts of the Cedi territory were also included

135. *Udāna*, tr. D.M. Strong, VII, 10, *SN*, IV, pp. 110-13, *MN*, 1, p. 513; *Jāt.*, IV, p. 28; VI, p. 236, *Mahāvastu*, II, p. 2; *Lalitavistara*, p. 27; *Bodhisattvāvadāna-Kalpalatā*, Pallava 35th, p. 3; *DPPN*, 1, p. 692f; Turnour's *Mahawanso*, p. 16; Csoma de Koros, *As. Res.* XX, p. 299, cf. *CAGI*, p. 331; see also Law, *op.cit*, 1, Ch. VI; 'Kausambi in Ancient Literature', *MASI*, No. 60 (Delhi, 1939).

136. *CAGI*, p. 332.

137. *DN*, II, pp. 146, 169.

138. *AN*, IV, pp. 252, 256, 260; *Manoratha Purāni* (*aṭṭhakathā* or Commy. on the *Aṅguttara Nikāya*) ed. M. Walleser and H. Knopp, 1, p. 306f; Hardy, *op. cit.*, p. 501.

139. *Vinaya*, IV, p.16; *Sumaṅgalavilāsinī*, p. 319.

140. *Udena-Vatthu* in *Dhammapada commentary*, I, pp. 161-230.

141. *Divyāvadāna*, pp. 515-44.

142. The Commentary on verses 21-23 of the *Dhammapada*;*Vinaya Mahāvagga*, VIII, 1-23.

143. *Jāt.*, No. 353.

144. *PHAI*, p. 133.

within the limits of the kingdom. The territory of Śūrasena round modern Mathurā to the west of the Vatsa kingdom was also brought under the rule of Udayana's son Māthur called Avantiputto. One of the sons of king Udena named Bodhi Kumāra also figures in some of the Pāli texts.[145] We are on firmer ground to establish that in the lifetime of the Buddha this prince ruled over the Bhaggas as his father's viceroy.[146] Udena continued to rule even after the death of the Buddha.[147] He built a large number of forts on the borders of his kingdom and till he remained alive he paid utmost attention to the defence of his kingdom. This kingdom was as extensive as Kośala was. In the mutul struggle of Magadha, Vatsa and Avantī for supremacy Vatsa suffered several reverses. After the death of Udayana his successors did not prove to be worthy enough to defend the integrity of the kingdom. It resulted in its downfall. As Kośala was merged into the kingdom of Magadha, likewise the Vatsa kingdom was annexed to Avantī after his death.

## Kuru

In the time ofthe Buddha, the Kurus settlement was confined to the land between the Gaṅgā and the Yamunā (Gaṅgā-Yamunā Doāb). This was, of course, a new phase of settlement in the sixth century BC. The Kuru kingdom has been mentioned in Pāli literature as "Kururaṭṭha",[148] i.e., Kururāṣṭra. And it is said that its kings were called as Kurus.[149] This kingdom was three hundred leagues in extent, and its capital, Indapatta (Indraprastha on the Yamunā and a part of modern Delhi), extended over seven leagues in circuit).[150] It is stated in the *Jātakas* that the ruling dynasty of this city belonged to the Yudhiṭṭhilagotta (i.e., the family of Yudhiṣṭhira).[151] This capital city probably continued to be the seat of kings claiming to belong to this family. We find that Kuru kingdom was split up broadly into two parts, one part had its capital at Indapatta and another at Hatthipura or Hatthinipura (Hastināpura). The latter one also finds mention in the Pāli text.[152] It was seven hundred leagues in circumference. It was the capital of that part of the Kuru realm which was situated on the bank of the Gaṅgā. It is traditionally identified

145. *Vinaya*, II, p. 127; IV, p. 198; MN, II, p. 97; *Jāt.*, III, p.157.
146. *MN*, II, p. 91; *Jāt.*, III, p. 157.
147. *Peta-Vatthu Commentary*, ed. E. Hardy, p. 140.
148. M.L. Feer, *A Study of the Jātakas*, p. 22; *Dhammapada-aṭṭhakathā*, II, p. 99.
149. *Papañcasūdanī*, 1, p. 225.
150. *Mahā-Sutasoma Jāt.*, No. 537; *Vidhurapaṇḍita*, *Jāt.*, No. 545; *Jāt.*, V, pp. 57, 484; VI, p. 255.
151. *Dhūmkāri Jāt.*, No. 413; *Dasabrāhmaṇa Jāt.*, No. 495; *Jāt.*, III, p. 400; IV, p. 361.
152. *Apadāna*, II, p. 359; *DPPN*, II, p. 1319.

with the ruins of an old town on the old bed of the Gaṅgā, about 22 miles north-east of Meerut in U.P. The importance of the city called Hastināpura has been highlighted particularly in the Sanskrit Buddhist texts[153] as one of the capitals of this *mahājanapada*. We are also informed that at the time of the Buddha it was being ruled by the Kuru kings descended from the Pāṇḍava race.[154] This capital is said to have been visited by the Buddha himself who was received and praised by an excellent brāhmaṇa there.[155] This visit probably might have taken place sometime in the latter half of the sixth century BC.

It appears from the Pāli texts that the Kuru kingdom comprised several smaller towns (*nigamas*), villages and districts besides the above-mentioned two capital cities. Of smaller towns mention may first be made of Kammāssadhamma, where the Buddha once dwelt for sometime. The *Mahānidāna* and the *Mahāsatipaṭṭhāna Suttantas* of the *Dīgha Nikāya*[156] bear witness to the fact. One of the Kuru nobles named Raṭṭhapāla was born in the town of Thullakoṭṭhika.[157] Of kings and princes of the Kurus mention is made of the following four: Dhanañjaya Koravya,[158] Raṭṭhapāla,[159] Koravya[160] and Sutasoma.[161] They were probably the titular chieftains by whom the Kuru territory was being ruled during the period concerned. According to the *Jātaka* tradition, there was a time when Kuru was one of the three most powerful kingdoms.[162] But in the Buddha's time it had very little political importance. The potentates did not have the importance which they had attained in the later Vedic age. However, the populace continued to enjoy their ancient reputation for political wisdom and sagacity.[163]

---

153. *Bodhisattvāvadāna-Kalpalatā*, 3rd Pallava, p. 116; *Divyāvadāna*, p. 435.
154. *Lalitavistara*, Ch.III.
155. *Divyāvadāna*, p. 72.
156. *DN*, II, cf. *HPL*, II, p. 654.
157. *Psalmas of the Brethren* (trans. of the *Theragāthā*), by Mrs. Rhys Davids, pp. 302-7.
158. *Kurudhamma Jāt.*, No. 276; *Dhūmakari Jāt.*, No. 413; *Sambhava Jāt.*, No. 515; *Vidhurapaṇḍita Jāt.*, II, p. 65f.
160. *Ibid.*, *Dasabrāhmaṇa Jāt.*, No.495; *Mahāsutasoma Jāt.*, No.537.
161. *Jāt.*, No. 537.
162. *Jāt.*, II, p. 214.
163. *Papañcasūdani*, I. p. 184f.

## Pañcāla

This kingdom as a whole roughly corresponds to Rohilkhaṇḍ, Bareilly, Badaon, Furrukhābād and the Central Gangetic Doāb in the modern Uttar Pradesh. It was divided by the Ganges into two parts, the northern and the southern, each forming a kingdom by itself. The *Divyāvadāna* (p. 435) also attests to these two divisions of the realm of the Pañcālas. This text speaks of two Pañcāla *viṣayas* : Uttra Pañcāla and Dakṣiṇa Pañcāla. The former comprised the districts lying east of the Ganges and north-west of Avadha, and the latter included the territory to the east and south-east of the Kurus and the Śūrasenas or the region extending from Mākandī on the Ganges to the river Cambal.

The northern Pañcāla had its capital at Ahicchatra, which is identical with a large ruined fortress, seven miles to the north of Aonlā near the modern Rāmnagar in the Bareilly district or twenty miles to the west of Bareilly. It must have comprised the eastern half of Rohilkhaṇḍ.[164] And the southern Pañcāla had its capital at Kāmpilya, which is now represented by ruins at modern Kāmpil on the south bank of the old Ganges nearly opposite Badaon in the Furrukhābād district.[165] It is situated exactly at distance of 28 miles north-east of Fatehgarh. In the Buddha's time the Uttara Pañcāla attained proportionately greater importance than the southern one. It was outside the town of Ahicchatra that the Buddha had preached the law for seven days.

It appears that when Uttara Pañcāla was included in Kururaṭṭha, i.e., the realm of the Kurus,[166] it had its capital at Hastināpura.[167] The apparent discrepancy in the two evidences furnished here can be reconciled after taking into account the struggle between the Kurus and the Pañcālas for the possession of Uttara Pañcāla. It is said that at other times it formed a part of Kampillaraṭṭha.[168] According to one of the *Jātaka*s, its capital was Kāmpillanagara[169] (and not Ahicchatra). This may be possibly an error in the Buddhist account of the subject. But then the fact, that sometimes king of the Kampillaraṭṭha held court at Uttara Pañcālanagara and at other times kings of Uttara Pañcālaraṭṭha held court at Kāmpilla, cannot be overlooked. From the analysis of the data available in

164. *CAGI*, pp. 305-6.
165. A. Cunningham, *Co. An. Ind.*, p. 79.
166. *Somanassa Jāt.* (No. 505), *Jāt.*, IV, p. 444.
167. *Divyāvadāna*, p. 435.
168. *Brahmadatta Jāt.*, No. 323; *Jayaddisa Jāt.*, No. 513; *Gaṇdatindu Jāt.*, No. 520.
169. *Kumbhakāra Jāt.*, No. 408, III, p. 379; *Cowell's Jāt.*, III, p. 230; *DPPN*, I, p. 525.

Buddhist literature it appears that the traditional division of the kingdom was not strictly maintained in Buddhist period.

The two noted kings of the Buddha's time were Viśākha[170] and Cūlani Brahmadatta.[171] The latter was a very poweful king of Kāmpilla, which formed very important part of the Pañcāla kingdom during the period concerned.[172] In the Buddha's time Pañcāla was being ruled by a king of its own, although like the Kuru realm it lost its political importance.

**Maccha (Matsya)**

This kingdom was situated to the south of the Kurus and to the west of the Śūrasena. It comprised within its limits the whole of the present territory of Alwar with a portion of Bharatpur and some parts of modern Jaipur in Rajasthan. Its capital Bairāta or Virāṭanagar lies at the distance of 41 miles to the north of Jaipur. This kingdom also finds a place in the list of sixteen *mahājanapadas* enumerated in the *Lalitavistara* (p.22). The *Janavasabha Suttanta* makes a mention of the Macchas or Matsyas in connection with the account of the Buddha's stay at Nādika.[173] They had, however, no political importance in the Buddha's time.

**Śūrasena**

It was located immediately to the south of the Kurus and to the east of the Matsyas. Its capital Madhurā on the right bank of the Yamunā is generally identified with Maholi, five miles to the south-west of the present town of Mathurā. In the Buddha's time it was called "Uttara Madhurā".[174] In one of the *Jātakas* we are told that Mahāsāgara was the king of Upper Madhurā and he had two sons whose accounts are well recorded therein[175] as well as in one of the Pāli commantary.[176] The Pāli text bears testimony to the Buddha's visit to Mathurā.[177] The king of the Śūrasenas during his time bore the title of Avantiputto,

170. *Psalms of the Brethren*, pp. 152-53.
171. *Mahā-Ummagga Jāt.*, No. 546; *Uttarādhyayana Sūtra*, SBE, XLV, pp. 57-61.
172. *Mahāvastu*, 1, p. 283; *Bodhisattvāvadāna Kalpalatā*, 68th Pallava, p. 9.
173. *DN*, II, p. 200.
174. *Vimānavatthu Commentary*, pp. 118-19.
175. *Ghata Jāt.*, Cowell's *Jāt.*, IV, pp. 50-52.
176. *Petavatthu Commentary*, pp. 111ff.
177. *AN*, II, p. 57.

which is indicative of the fact that he was a prince born of a princess from the royal family of Avantī. It is said that he was the king in the time of Mahākaccāna,[178] one of the chief disciples of Śākyamuni through whose agency Buddhism gained ground in the Mathurā region.[179] Mathurā at that time was predominantly a centre of Buddhsit religion and culture. The political subjection of this kingdom to both Vatsa and Avantī for a considerable period of time presented stumbling-block in the way of its further expansion.

### Assaka (Aśmaka)

At the time of the Buddha the Assaka territory was situated on the banks of the Godāvarī immdiately to the north of Patiṭṭhāna or in close proximity to Alaka or Mūlaka in the Dakkhināpatha,[180] which lay contiguous to the kingdom of Avantī.[181] Thus, this kingdom comprised the district round modern Paiṭhan in the Auraṅgābād district of Mahārāṣṭra. The capital city of the Assakas or Aśmakas is named in the ***Mahāgovinda Suttanta*** of the *Dīgha Nikāya*[182] Potana, in the *Assaka Jātaka*[183] Potali and in the *Vimānavatthu* commentary[184] Potanagara, which can be identified without any hitch and hesitation with Patiṭṭhāna, (i.e., ancient Pratiṣṭhāna or modern Paiṭhan). Their identity has always been accepted without doubt. Its identification with "Bodhan in the Nizam's dominions"[185] is not acceptable to us.

> "In early Pāli literature Assaka has been distinguished from Mulaka which lay to its north, but has always been associated with Avanti which lay immediately to the north-east".[186] It has been suggested that "Assaka included at that time Mulaka and some neighbouring districts and its territory approached the southern frontier of Avantī".[187]

---

178. *MN*, II, p. 83f.
179. *PHAI*, pp. 142-43.
180. *Sutta-nipāta*, p. 190, verse 977; See also Law, *HGAI*, pp. 141-42; *DPPN*, I, p. 222.
181. *Jāt.*, V. p. 317.
182. *DN*, II, p. 235.
183. *Jāt.*, II, p. 155.
184. *Vimānavatthu-aṭṭhakathā*, p. 259.
185. *PHAI*, p. 143.
186. *GEB*, p.22.
187. *PHAI*, p. 143.

> The Assaka kingdom "is mentioned with Avantī in the same way as Aṅga is with Magadha",[188] "and its position . . . between Sūrasena and Avantī makes it probable that when the list was drawn up, its position was immediately north-west of Avantī. In that case the settlement on the Godhāvari was a later colony".[189]

In one of the Pāli commentaries we are told that the ruler of Assaka at the time of the Buddha was a king whose son was prince Sujata. It is further stated therein that an Assaka king was ordained by Mahākaccāyana.[190] From the *Culla-Kāliṅga Jātaka* we learn that the relationship between king Assaka of Potana and king Kāliṅga of Dantapura was at first hostile, but afterwards the two kings lived amicably.[191] The *Jātaka* mentions a king of Assaka named Aruṇa and his minister Nandīsena, and refers to a victory which they won over the king of Kaliṅga.[192] As stated in the *Assaka Jātaka*, there was a king named Assaka who reigned in the city of Potali, which at one time was included in the kingdom of Kāśī.[193] This evidence gives us an impression that prince Assaka was once a Vassal of the Kāśī monarch.

## Avantī

This kingdom roughly corresponds to modern Mālwā (western), Nīmar and adjoining parts of the Central Provinces. It was divided into two parts : the northern part had its capital "Ujjeni"[194] (Skt. Ujjayinī = mod. Ujjain) on the bank of the Śiprā and the southern part had its capital at "Māhissati"[195] (Skt. Māhiṣmatī) on the right bank of the Narmadā, which has been identified with Maheśvara or Māndhātā (Nīmar district), about 40 miles to the south of Indore.[196] It must be noted here that Māhissati was the capital of this kingdom in pre-Buddhist India. In the time of the Buddha the kingdom with its capital at Ujjeni was reigned over by king Canda Pajjota ("Pajjota the Fierce" or Pradyota), who was one of the powerful rulers of northern India. He was at daggers drawn with the

188. *Jāt.*, V. p. 319, cf. *BI*, p. 27.
189. *BI*, pp. 27-28.
190. *Vimānavatthu-aṭṭhakathā*, p. 259f.
191. *Jāt.*, III, pp. 3-5.
192. *Ibid.*, p. 3.
193. *Jāt.*, II, p. 155.
194. *Dīpavaṁsa*, p. 57.
195. *Mahāgovinda Suttanta*, *DN*, II, p. 235: See also *Suttanipāta* commy., II. p. 583.
196. Fleet, *JRAS*, 1910, pp. 444-47.

neighbouring rulers of Vatsa and Magadha.[197] He tried to extend his supremacy over Udena of Kośāmbī, but he could not achieve his objective. In the end he gave his daughter in marriage to him. This matrimonial alliance save Kośāmbī from being conquered by Pajjota, as has already been stated. He, however, succeeded in extending his sway over Śūrasena round Mathurā. He also established matrimonial relation with this kingdom. He is said to have given his sister in marriage to a king of Mathurā.[198] His power and influence grew to such on extent that the Magadhan king Ajātasattu had to fortify his capital Rājagaha shortly after the death of the Buddha in anticipation of an attack by him.[199] The king Pālaka, one of the successors of Pajjota, appears to have annexed Kośāmbī to his realm during the lifetime of the Buddha.

Besides the capital city of Ujjeni, some other minor towns of Avantī have also been referred to in Buddhist works of which mention may be made of Kuraraghara and Sudarśanapura.[200] It is said that Kaccāyana the great or Mahākaccāyana was born at Ujjeni in the family of the Chaplain of king Pajjota. He is said to have converted the king to the Buddhist faith.[201] When "Mahākaccāna was living at the city of Kuraraghara in Avanti he ordained an Upasaka named Sonakutikaṇṇa".[202] Avantī was no doubt one of the noted centres of Buddhism.

## Gāndhāra

The kingdom of Gāndhāra included within its boundaries some parts of modern eastern Afghanistan, the whole of the districts of Peśāwar and Rāwalpiṇḍi in the north-western Punjab and the vale of Kashmir. In fact, it extended from the Kabul valley in the west of the Indus to Takṣaśilā region in the east of the Indus. According to V.S. Agrawala, "Gāndhāra extended from Takshaśilā, its eastern capital, to the river Kunar, its western boundary, and from the river Kābul in the south to Swāti in the north".[203] It was undoubtedly one of the most extensive kingdoms in northern India. In the *Gandhāra Jātaka* it is wrongly mentioned as a part of Kashmir.[204] The fact remains that Kashmir

197. For details see *DPPN*, I, p. 379.
198. *Ibid.*, p. 195.
199. *MN*, III, p. 7.
200. See Law, *Ancient Mid-Indian Kṣatriya Tribes*, p. 148.
201. *Psalms of the Brethren*, pp. 238-39.
202. *Dhammapada-aṭṭhakathā*, V, p. 101.
203. *IP*, p. 49.
204. *Jāt.*, III, pp. 222-23.

was partly included within the limits of this kingdom. That is why, the same *Jātaka* sometimes refers to the "Kāshmir-Gandhāra kingdom" as one kingdom.[205] Only the eastern part of the latter may have once formed a part of the former.

The western capital of this kingdom, Puṣkalāvatī or Puṣkarāvatī called Utpalāvatī in the *Divyāvadāna* (p. 470), is represented by the ruins that still exist at Chārasadda (near Parang) little above the junction of the Swāt with the Kābul river at the distance of about 17 miles north-east of Peśāwar. And its eastern capital called "Takkasilā" in Pāli literature (or modern Taxila) is identical with the ruins located near modern Shahdheri or immediately north-east of Sarai-Kela, about 20 miles north-west of Rāwalpiṇḍi. The eastern capital finds mention also in the *Bhimasena Jātaka*.[206] According to some other *Jātakas*, it lay 2,000 leagues from Banāras.[207] This city flourished as a seat of learning and as a centre of trade and commerce.

It is significant to note that in the time of the Buddha "Takkasilā" was the capital city of the Gāndhāra kingdom,[208] and Utpalāvatī or Puṣkalāvatī was one of its chief towns. The latter (western capital) lost its political importance in the latter half of the sixth century BC after it was conquered by Darius (*c.* 522-486 BC) and incorporated into an Achaemenian empire. His Behistun inscription (*c.* 520- 518 BC) testifies to the subjection of the Gāndhārians to his empire.

The rulers of Gāndhāra are mentioned simply as Gāndhārarāja.[209] We are told by Buddhaghoṣa (the greatest Pāli commentator of the fifth contury AD) that the king ruling in Gāndhāra contemporaneously with king Bimbisāra of Magadha was Pukkusāti (Puṣakarasārin), who sent an embassy and a letter to his Magadhan contemporary as a mark of friendship. He is also said to have waged a war on king Pajjota (or Pradyota) of Avantī who was defeated.[210] Here there are some gaps which still exist in our knowledge. In an attempt to fill in this gap with the help of some other relevant sources, we have come across the truth that Pukkusāti sent an embassy to Bimbisāra with the object of invoking his assistance against the threatened advance of the Achaemenian ruler.[211] We

205. *Jāt.*, pp. 363-69; See also R. Fick, *The Social Organisation of North-East India in Buddha's Time*, p. 273.

206. *Jāt.*, I, pp, 356fff.

207. *Telapatta Jāt.*, No. 96; *Susima Jāt.*, No. 163.

208. Cowell's *Jāt.*, vol. II (Delhi, 1973), *BK.*, II, No. 163, pp. 36, 47, 50f; BK-II, No.229, p. 152.

209. *Jāt.*, I, p. 191; II, p. 219; III, p. 364, IV, p. 98.

210. *Papañcasūdanī*, II, p. 982; BI, p. 28; *GEB*, p. 50; *DPPN*, II, p. 215.

211. *Modern Review* (Calcutta, Octob., 1930), p. 438.

learn from the Jain sources that a young general who led Bimbisāra's army was merchant prince, Jambū Kumar, who returned from the campaign triumphantly.[212] The conflicts of the Gāndhārian kings with their contemporaries are conspicuous by their absence in Pāli literature, but Sanskrit Buddhist literature[213] contains some legendary accounts of the subject. In all probability, the Gāndhāra kingdom had regained its independence before the downfall of the Persian empire. It passed under several hands but by and large retained its independence.

### Kāmboja

The exact location of the Kāmboja kingdom, as it existed in the Buddha's time, has not yet been saisfactorily determined. Nowhere in early or later Pāli literature there is any mention of the location of this kingdom or of its capital city. This kingdom is referred to in one of the *Jātakas* devoid of any details.[214] Placing our reliance on all the available sources at our disposal we can state with absolute certainty that it was situated in north-west India as a neighbouring kingdom of "Kashmir-Gāndhāra". The frequent association of the Kāmbojas with the Gāndhāras in ancient Indian literature and inscriptions enables us to establish their closeness. This large kingdom must have comprised within its western boundaries Balkh-Badakhshan and Pāmīr regions or Kafiristan in eastern Afghanistan, and within its eastern boundaries the province round about ancient Rājapura or modern Rajauri to the south or south-east of Punch. The Kāmbojas seem to have occupied also the Hazārā district of the North-Western Frontier Province.

In the *Petavatthu*[215] as well as in the commentary (*Paramatthadipani*)[216] on it, Dvārakā (or Dvāravatī) occurs along with Kāmboja. But it is nor expressly stated whether Dvārakā was the capital of Kāmboja. Some scholars are divided in their opinion about the identity or the former as a city of the latter though both were connected by a road.[217] But Rhys Davids is of the firm opinion that Kāmboja adjoining Gāndhāra in the extreme north-west had Dvārakā as its capital.[218] N.L. Dey is also more or less of the same view. While

212. See K.P. Jain, *Some Historical Jaina Kings and Heroes*, p. 11.
213. See *Vinayavastu*, Gilgit Manuscript, vol. III, pt. 2 (Srinagar, 1942), pp. 31-32.
214. *Jāt.*, IV, p. 208.
215. Ed. Minayef, II, p. 9.
216. *Peta vatthu* Commentary, ed. E. Hardy, p.113.
217. See *DPPN*, I, pp.526, 1126; *GEB*, p. 50; *PHAI*, p.150.
218. *BI*, p. 28.

associating Kāmboja with Afghanistan, he has correctly suggested that its capital Dvārakā should not be confounded with the place of the same name in Gujarat.[219] It is Motichandra who has identified this capital with Darwaz placing the Kāmbojas in the Pāmīr-Badakhsan region.[220] Lassen and others have also identified Kāmboja with the Pāmīr region.[221] H.C. Raychaudhuri on the authority of Elphinstone has suggested that "The western boundaries of Kāmboja must have reached Kafiristan, and therre are still in that district tribes like the "Caumojee", "Camoze", and "Camoje" whose names remind us of the Kāmbojas'.[222] According to D.C. Sircar "The Kamboja capital was connected by road with the headquarters of Gandhāra and Rawalpindi, Peshawar region . . . the Kamboja country was near Gandhāra and more easily accessible from it than the distant and inaccessible Pamirs were. . . ."[223] Wilson has located Kāmboja in the Ghazni region to the south of Kabul,[224] and Stein has identified it with the eastern part of Afghanistan.[225] In one of the *Jātakas* it is clearly stated that the Kāmbojas were a north-western tribe who were outside the pale of Aryanism.[226] From the *Assalāyana Sutta* of the *Majjhima Nikāya* we learn that during the time of the Buddha the Kāmbojas inhabiting the north-western frontier of India belonged to two classes, viz., masters and slaves.[227] From H. Lüders' inscriptions (Nos.176 and 472)[228] it appears that Nandīpura was very important city of the Kāmbojas. But its location is not yet determined.

The capital of the Kāmbojas in the epic period was Rājapura which can be substantiated by the evidence of the *Mahābhārata*.[229] Their settlement might have

---

219. *GDAMI*, p. 87.
220. *Geographical and Economic Studies in the Mahābhārata, Upāyana Parva*, p. 38, See also pp. 32ff.
221. *Ind. Ant.* (1923), p. 54; *IP*, p. 49; *Purāṇa*, vol. V, No. 1. p. 172.
222. M. Elphinstone, *An Account of the kingdom of Kabul*, vol. II, pp 375-77; *PHAI*, p 149.
223. *Purāṇa*, vol. VI, No. 1, p. 220, See also p. 210.
224. *JASB*, 1838, pp. 252, 267.
225. Kalhaṇa's *Rājataraṅgiṇī*, vol. 1, p. 136, notes.
226. Cowell's *Jāt.*, VI, p. 110, note.
227. *MN*, II, p. 149.
228. See his "List of Brāhmī Inscriptions from Earliest times to the Second Century AD", *Ep. Ind.*, vol. X, Appendix.
229. Droṇa Parva, 4, 4.

continued at this place in the later period too. Cunningham has identified Rājapura with Rajauri to the south of Kashmir.[230] Taking one particular evidence furnished in the *Mahābhārata*[231] as worthy of our credence we can suggest that the Kāmbojas had their settlements in two different parts of northern India : one to the east of the Indus called Kāmboja which comprised the region near about modern Kashmir, and the other to the west of the Indus called Paścimī (western) Kāmboja, which probably comprised the eastern part of Afghanistan or Gāndhāra region and Pāmīr-Badakhshan region. Taking all the facts stated above into account we can plausibly conclude here that in the early Buddhist period the kingdom of Kāmboja included within its boundaries Kafiristan in eastern Afghanistan and the adjoining regions of Gāndhāra in the west with its capital at Dvārakā or Darwaz and Rājapura or Rajauri to the south of Kashmir in the east. The Kāmbojas had their main settlements in the territories of eastern Afghanistan on the river Kābul or modern Kamboha.

From the foregoing description of the subject it is quite evident that in the time of the Buddha (sixth and fifth centuries BC), India was politically divided into sixteen independent states. With the exception of two republican states of the Vajjis and the Mallas all others were the kingdoms. The four most powerful kingdoms of considerable extent were Magadha, Kośala, Vatsa and Avantī. The early Buddhist records reveal that there was rivalry among these powers, each trying to extend its supremacy at the cost of another. In the mutual contest among the contemporary rulers of these four monarchical states for political hegemony, the Magadhan monarchs achieved greater success than their counterparts. And consequently Magadha emerged as the mightiest among all the kingdoms. There was a general tendency among the rulers towards the gradual absorption of each other's domain and also of the neighbouring republican territories. Besides these four, there were other ten kingdoms both big and small. Those kingdoms which were smaller in extent and power had hardly any political importance in the Buddhist period. The normal relations between them were hostile. It is worthy of note that politically these states were, of course, divided but culturally and commercially they were united.

---

230. *CAGI*, pp. 108-9.

231. Sabhā Parva, 24, 22-25.

# 3

# Trends and Patterns of Urbanisation and the Growth and Decline of Towns and Cities in Ancient India

## From the Post-Harappan Period to the Gupta Age with Special Reference to the Gaṅgā Valley

THE term urbanisation in its broader sense is indicative of the process of transition from ruralism to urbanism. It also implies various trends of growth and development of purely rural or semi-urban areas into full-fledged urban centres, patterns of the urban settlement, town-planning, evolution of towns, etc. The city and urbanism can be used somewhat interchangeably. But some sort of distinction can definitely be maintained between the two to a certain extent. "Urbanism implies the characteristics that distinguish cities from simpler community form. It also refers to the organisation of an entire urban society which includes not only cities but also towns and villages".[1] A city, on the other hand, is resultant symbol of urban growth. However, the underlying bond between the two or their correlation cannot be denied. The urbanisation and the towns or cities were the two wheels of the chariot of progressive civilization in ancient India. As a matter of fact, the evolution of urban tradition and the emergence of towns and cities went on not in isolation from but in collaboration with each other.

This Chapter is an humble attempt at reconstruction of history of urban civilization in ancient India from the post-Harappan period to the age of the Guptas. The period under review witnessed the growth and decline of a number of towns and cities in different parts of northern, eastern, central, western and southern India. An attempt has been made to make an empirical approach to the study of the subject as far as possible.

---

1. Charles L. Redman, *The Rise of Civilization*, p. 215, cf. G.L. Possehl, "Archaeological Terminology and the Harappan Civilization", in B.B. Lal and S.P. Gupta (ed.), *Frontiers of the Indus Civilization*, p. 29.

The picture which emerges from the researches carried out so far on the subject is, of course, very comprehensive but not complete in historical perspective. There are still some gaps in our existing knowledge of the subject which can be bridged up with the help of literary sources, classical (Greek and Latin) literature, the accounts of two famous Chinese travellers, Fa-hian and Hiuen-Tsang, archaeological evidence and some other standard historical records.

The towns and cities emerged in diverse contemporary geo-political situation without any uniformity of pattern or designs. The ten criteria essential for urbanisation, as suggested by V. Gordon Childe,[2] are the following:

(1) population in terms of both size and density,

(2) surplus food produced by the peasants in villages to support and sustain the non-food producing urban communities,

(3) rural economy, taxation, etc.,

(4) monumental public buildings,

(5) ruling class,

(6) temples,

(7) invention of writing,

(8) artists-sculptors, painters, architects, seal-engravers, etc.,

(9) trade and industry, and

(10) specialised craftsmen, merchants, different occupational groups, guilds, etc.

These factors proved to be helpful in the evolution of towns and cities and efflorescence of urban culture in ancient India. Arnold Toynbee[3] has postulated that corporate social life, public buildings, defensive city wall with towers, gates and ramparts, transaction of commercial and political business, presence of administrators, temples of tutelary gods, etc., constitute the hallmarks of urban civilization. G. Sjoberg[4] and Lewis

---

2. "The Uraban Revolution", reprinted from *Town Planning Review*, vol. XXI, No.1 (Liverpool, 1950), pp. 3-17 in G.L. Possehl (ed.), *Ancient Cities of the Indus*, pp. 12-17; See also his *What Happened in History*, pp. 30-31, 90f, 99; *Man Makes Himself*, p. 109; "Civilisation, Cities and Towns", *Antiquity*, vol. XXXI (1957), pp. 36-37.

3. Ed., *Cities In Destiny*, p. 13.

4. *The Preindustrial City of Past and Present*, pp. 69-75.

Mumford[5] have opined that political factor is the primary factor in effecting the change from a decentralised village economy to a highly organised urban economy. "The towns and cities even commercial ones cannot flourish without direct or indirect support of a well established state system. Urban growth in societies is highly correlated with the consolidation and expansion of a political apparatus whether it be the result of a kingdom or an empire." The industrialisation and commercialisation associated with urban growth were for centuries subordinate factors. Commercial organisation is necessary if a political system is to be maintained but it is not a crucial factor for urbanisation. The king is "polar Magnet" so far as the urban explosion is concerned. Gordon Childe,[6] on the other hand, suggests that economic factor (related to trade and commerce, surplus food production and improved agricultural technology) plays more vital role than political factor in the growth of urban centres. The political and economic factors no doubt played an equally important role in urban transformation. However, the importance of other factors like religious, educational, military and artistic, which also contributed to the growth of towns, cannot be dismissed. In ancient India, a number of political, administrative, commercial, religious, educational and artistic centres developed into big cities. Different scholars[7] have suggested different criteria as prerequisites for urbanism and expressed different views about determinants of urban culture. In the ancient Indian context, it will not be reasonable to lay emphasis on one particular approach. In ancient India, in fact, different factors influenced the growth of towns and cities at different periods of history.[8]

In ancient times, the common term used for a city or town was *nagara* or *pura*. However, some variations in this regard are discernible in ancient Indian literary texts. In the *Ṛgveda* there are copious references to *pura*s (forts and not *nagara*s or towns) which were built by the Āryans and non-Āryans of so-called Sapta-Sindhu region to fortify their respective villages for their defence against the attacks of each other.[9] The

5. *The City in History : Its Origin, its trasformation and its prospects*, pp. 31f, 35, 51-60, 64-65.
6. *Man Makes Himself*, pp. 109, 154; *What Happened in History*, p. 99.
7. Philip M. Hauser and L.F. Schnore (ed.), *The Study of Urbanization*, pp. 216, 269-70; Robert Adams, *The Evolution of Urban Society*, pp. 45-47.
8. B.B. Dutt, *Town Planning in Ancient India*, p. 25f; See also S. Piggott, *Some Cities of Ancient India*, p. 90f; B.N. Puri, *Cities of Ancient India*, p. 5f.
9. *ṚV*, 1, 130, 10; 1, 174, 2 & 8; 1, 189, 2; 2, 19, 6; 4, 16, 13; 4, 30, 20; 5, 19, 2; 5, 41, 12; 6, 18, 5; 7, 18, 13; 7, 99, 5; 8, 98, 6.

officials employed to look after these *puras* were called either *paur*[10] or *puparti* (*purpati*). The text contains allusions to well-guarded and protected forts of enormous size,[11] iron-built (*āyasi*) *puras* of the Dasyus (Danhu of *Avesta*, Dahae of Achamenian inscription, Daoi of Herodotus (I,126) or Dasai of other Greek writers),[12] the forts with hundred walls[13] and mansions or large buildings supported by thousand pillars.[14] The famous Dasyu king named Shambara had ninety-nine[15] or one hundred stone-built forts[16] with force to protect his people against the attack of his arch enemy, king Indra, who is said to have destroyed a large number of strongholds (whose number varies from seven to ninety-nine) of the Dasyus called *pura*.[17] Because of having destroyed *puras* of the Dasyus he has been called *purandra*. Yāska (the first to etymologically interpret the Vedic hymns) in his *Nirukta*[18] also refers to king Indra as destroyer of *pura* (*purandra iti*). In the Āryan-non-Āryan conflicts of about forty years a large number of *pura* of the latter were destroyed by the former. F. Max Müllar, who holds the prominent position in the galaxy of the Vedic scholars, also refers to the destruction of "town after town" by mighty Indra.[19] H.H. Wilson in his rendering of the R̥gvedic hymns also observes that Indra while fighting against his political adversaries in battles destroyed mighty "city after city".[20] Louis Renou, a French Vedic scholar, further mentions that the Dasyus, the aborigines, lived in fortress and *pura* — perhaps small primitive forts surrounded by a fence. The terms *alaka* and *puraya* have been identified by him with towns.[21] The evidences furnished in the *R̥gveda* about the subject concerned have also been brought to light by

10. *R̥V.*, 5, 74, 4.
11. *Ibid.*, 1, 189, 2.
12. *Ibid.*, 2, 20, 8; 4, 27, 1; 7, 95, 1.
13. *Ibid.*, 1, 166, 8; 7, 15, 14.
14. *Ibid.*, 2, 41, 5; also 7, 88, 5.
15. *Ibid.*, 2, 19, 6; 7, 99, 5.
16. *Ibid.*, 2, 14, 6; 4, 30, 20.
17. *Ibid.*, 1, 130, 7 & 10; 1, 63, 7; 2, 20, 7 & 8; 4, 16, 13; 6, 20, 10; 7, 99, 5; 8, 98, 6.
18. Ed. and tr. By Uma Shankar Sharma, VII, III, 12-13.
19. *The Vedas*, p. 31.
20. *Ibid.*, p. 30.
21. *Vedic India*, tr. from the French by Philip Spratt, pp. 126-27.

A.A. Macdonell and A.B. Keith,[22] P.V. Kane,[23] Abināś Chandra Das,[24] Rāhul Sāṅkṛtyāyana,[25] Pt. Biśveśvaranāth Reu,[26] A.K. Majumdar,[27] Motichandra,[28] and Ācārya Priyovarta Vedavācaspati,[29] but they have not drawn any plausible conclusion. It is very difficult to affirm that the stone forts, iron forts, walled cities, stone houses and brick edifices were known to the early Vedic people. Many *pura*s were earthern walls or mere earth work fortifications.[30] Like the Dasyus the Āryans also had a hundred cities (*ṚV*, VI, 48, 8; VII, 3, 7; VII, 15, 14). The early Vedic society was basically a rural society. There is no positive evidence of the urban life of early Vedic Āryans. Nor is there any reference to a particular town or city. There is no archaeological evidence either to confirm the existence of any town in the Ṛgvedic age. The Ṛgvedic references to the Dasyus (degraded Āryans or non-Āryans) or Āryans as city dwellers can be passed over as an inferential evidence. However, exclusively on the testimony of the *Ṛgveda* it can conclusively be proved that military factor relating to defence and warfare was a factor of vital importance for the erection of forts. Some of the Ṛgvedic hymns fairly illustrate the truth that several strong forts of stone and iron were erected for the defence of *rāṣṭra* as well. One of the later Vedic texts[31] also portrays a vivid picture of well fortified and impregnable stone-built and iron-built *pura*s.

The *pura* (a town or city) mentioned in the *Śatapatha Brāhmaṇa* (6, 3, 3, 25) can be easily distinguished from *mahāpura* (a large city) which occurs in the *Taittirīya Saṁhitā* (6, 2, 3, 1). The *Taittirīya Āraṇyaka* mentions *nagara* (1, 11, 8) as town. In the *Vālmīki-Rāmāyaṇa*, the city or town has been frequently mentioned as *pura* and *nagara*,[32] and its dwellers as *paura*.[33] The association of city merchants figures therein as *naigama* which

22. VI, vol.1, pp. 356-57.
23. *Dharmaśāstra Kā Itihāsa*, vol. II, p. 664.
24. *Ṛgvedic India*, p. 87.
25. *Ṛgvedic Āryans*, pp. 14-17, 95-106.
26. *Ṛgveda Para ek Aitihāsik Dṛṣṭi*, p. 218.
27. *Early Hindu India : A Dynastic Study*, vol. 1, pp. 163, 337.
28. *Sārthavāha*, p. 37.
29. *Vedon ke Rājnitika Siddhānta* (A Study in Vedic Polity), pp. 649-50.
30. See E.W. Hopkins, *JAOS*, vol. XIII, pp. 174-76.
31. *AV*, 5, 10, 1-7; 19, 58. 4; See also S.C. Sircar, *Some Aspects of the Earlier Social life of India*, p. 14, note 6.
32. Ayodhyā Kāṇḍa, 6, 26; 33, 22; 40, 18-20; 48, 37; 49, 13.
33. *Ibid.*, 2, 19; 6, 19; 14, 55.

goes in perfect harmony with what we find in the *Jātaka* records. The *Mahābhārata* refers to *pura* as *nagara* or capital city.[34] A branch city or small town has been mentioned therein as *Śākhānagara*.[35] It is said that cities were centres of both political and commercial activities. All adequate measures were taken by the king for their protection. They were protected with storng forts, ramparts and gateways. All necessary steps were taken by the state for their administration. The officer-in-charge of city administration has been referred to as *nagarādhikṛta* or *nagarapāla*.[36] The information relating to laying out of cities, market management, administration of cities, etc., are also available in the text.[37] Both the epics make pin-pointed references to the role of sovereigns and potentates in the growth of cities in the early phase of urbanism. Some of the Purāṇic texts[38] also speak of *puras*, *nagaras*, etc., in the sense of towns.

Pāṇini (fifth century BC) makes clear-cut distinction between the two terms — *grāma* (village) and *nagara* (town) which were two different units of settlements (IV, 2, 142). He mentions separately the villages and towns of eastern India (VII, 3, 14; *Kāśikā* on that VI, 2, 100). The term *pura* (IV, 2, 122; also *Kāśikā* IV, 2, 122) has been employed for fortified capital town. He uses the term *mahānagara* (VI, 2, 89) which comprises some big towns of middle Gaṅgā Valley. By the time of Pāṇini many towns had come into existence which also attest to the progress in the art of town-planning (*nagara-māpana*) and architecture (*vāstuvidyā*). His *sūtras* (V, 1, 17-18) point to regular town-planning. The most important parts of a city were its moat (*parikhā*), rampart (*prākāra*) and gates (*dvāra*), which served the purpose of defence. Kātyāyana (fourth century BC) also mentions the same (*Vārttikas*, V, 1, 16; VI, 3, 122). According to the *Jātakas* (I, p. 262; III, p. 415), "the plan of the ancient walled cities was rectangular, usually square, pierced with four gates, one in the middle of each wall, facing the four quarters". Pāṇini also describes the principle which governed the naming of city-gates (*sūtras*, IV, 3, 85-86). A well laid-out city was equipped with a multitude of buildings for its defence as well as for residence and business. The fortification consisted of the moat, parapet wall and gateways. The towns, according to him, were generally intersected by streets (III, 3, 119) and had

34. Śānti Parva, 69, 6-7, 20, 25-26, 42-58; 87, 1-3.
35. *Ibid.*, 69, 33; 88.8.
36. Ādi Parva, 134, 1-10.
37. Śānti Parva, 58, 9; 67, 51; 69, 8-58; for details see B.P. Roy, *Political Ideas and Institutions in the Mahābhārata*, pp. 375-82.
38. *Mts.*, 217, 1-9; *Agn.*, 222, 1-4; *Vy.*, 8, 108; 94, 40; *Pdm.*, Svargakhaṇḍa, (ed. Ashoka Chatterjee Śāstri), 38, 59-60.

residential buildings, business quarters (*āpaṇa*, III, 3, 119), royal store-house (IV, 4, 70), king's council-hall (*rājasabhā*) and a number of other buildings and places of dramatic performance (IV, 2-80), dancing, music, concerts and sports. The lists attached to the two *sūtras* (IV, 2, 75 and IV, 2, 80) and the other *gaṇas* contain the names of more than 500 towns (including some old and forgotten ones) which more less goes in accord with the testimony of classical authors. The accuracy of number of towns, as mentioned by Pāṇini and the Greek writers, is not beyond doubt. Their lists include some big and prosperous villages too. However, it is true that ancient India possessed a large number of flourishing cities and towns which were centres of trade industry. Many of these were forts or centres of defence. Patañjali (*c.* 184-148 BC) has also differentiated between villages (*grāma*) and big cities (*nagara*) by citing several examples thereof (*Mahābhāṣya*, IV, 2, 104; II, 4, 7; 1, 3, 25; II, 1, 1; II, 1, 16).

According to Kauṭilya (fourth century BC) the *nagara* or town was laid-out in a planned manner conforming to the rules of *Vāstuśāstra*. It generally consisted of walls of bricks and stones, forts and fortifications (*durgas*), gates, roads and streets, king's palace in the centre, residential buildings, market complex, military cantonments, etc. He refers to *sthānīya-nagara* as a main town or capital which consisted of 800 villages, *droṇamukha* as a town consisting of 400 villages and *saṁyānīya* for an emporium or a centre of trade and commerce. He clearly distinguishes and ordinary town from a *nagara* or *pura*.[39]

Manu (*c.* 200-100 BC) uses both the terms, *nagara* and *pura* in the sense of fortified capital city.[40] According to him, the people used to live in towns and cities which were built out of mud brick, stone and timber with several stories, several rows, lanes and roads between them. The towns contained several temples, tanks, ponds, fountains, gardens, etc. The cities were the centres of various activities. They had their assembly hall (*sabhā*), various shops, artisans' dwellings (*kārukāveśana*), brothels (*veṣa*), meeting places and theatres (*samājāḥ prekṣaṇāni ca*) "where conclave of people assembled and prowled with varied engagements". The capital cities possessed royal store-houses (*koṣṭhāgāra*) and magazines (*āyudhāgāra*). "They were surrounded by Palisade walls (*prākāra*) intersected with gates (*dvāra*) and by a ditch (*parikhā*)" which reflect the defence mechanism.[41] During the time of Manu, traders, merchants and craftsmen played very

39. *Arth.*, ed. with Hindi tr. by Vācaspati Gairola, 1, 15, 19, pp. 65-68; 2, 19, 3, pp. 85-89; 2, 20, 4, pp.91-94.

40. *Manu.*, 7, 70, 76; 9, 294.

41. *Ibid.*, 9, 264-65, 280, 289; See also V.S. Agrawala, *India as Described by Manu*, pp. 15-16.

conspicuous role in furthering the growtn of urbanism. Varāhamihira (*c*. AD 505-87) mentions eight different kinds of fortified cities which include *nagara*, *pura*, *nagarī* and *paṭṭana*.[42]

Amarasiṁha (sixth century AD) categorically refers to *pura*, *purī* and *nagarī* (fortified town), *paṭṭana* (port town), *puṭṭavedana* (an emporia or a large commercial centre in a big city for breaking the seals of packed articles or parcels of merchandise and for their sellings to small traders), *sthānīya* (local town surrounded by ditch and defensive walls and a place of abode of the officials of king), *nigama* (commercial town predominantly inhabited by traders, merchants an artisans), *mūla-nagara* (main city, probably the capital) and *śākhānagara* (branch city or small towns near the capital city).[43] According to him, the capital city was characterised by its fortifications king's palace, residential buildings, markets (*āpaṇa*) temple complex, assembly hall, entrance gates (*toraṇa*), magnificent gateways (*puradvāram* or *gopuram*), strong wall studded with bones, irons, wood, tin, etc. (*edukam*), stone or iron pillars, *prācīra*, nearby place fenced with barbed wire, political and economic activities, etc.[44] The above description testifies to the existence of different types of town or city in ancient India.

One of the Jain canonical texts also mentions different types of urban settlement such as a town with an earthen wall, a town with small wall, an isolated town, a large town, a sea-town and a capital town.[45] In the Purāṇas, the *pura* or *nagara* has been described as a place which wore cosmopolitan look; which was inhabited by the people of different castes, different religious groups and different professions and occupations; which was centre of trade and commerce and which was adorned by multi-storeyed buildings, gates, forts, gardens, etc. Three different types of town, viz., *droṇamukha* (situated on the bank of a river near the sea-coast and where the trade was carried on both by land and water routes, e.g., Tāmralipti and Bharukaccha), *jalapaṭṭan* (on the

---

42. *Br. Sam.*, ed. and tr. by Pt. Baladeva Prasad Mishra, Chs. 53 & 56.
43. *Amarakoṣa* with "*Maṇiprabhā*" Hindi commentary of Pt. H.G. Śāstrī, 2, 2, 1; 2, 2, 2, p. 113, notes 1-2; See also V.S. Apte, *The Students Sanskrit English Dictonary*, pp. 312, 339, 341, 623.
44. *Amarakoṣa*, 2, 2, 2-6, p. 113, notes 4-7, p. 114, note 2; 2, 2, 16, p.119, notes 1-3.
45. *Kalpasūtra* of Bhadrabāhu, tr. H. Jacobi, SBE, vol. XXII (Oxford, 1884), p. 89.

sea) and *puṭṭavedana* are also mentioned therein.[46] The texts also bear witness to peoples' acquaintance with the art of planning of a city.[47] The Pāli canon proves the existence of *mahānagara* in ancient times.[48] One of the Buddhist Sanskrit texts also refers to different types of town applying different appellations for them.[49]

The period extending from the latter half of the second millennium BC to the early fourth century AD can undoubtedly be considered important in the early history of urbanisation (post-Harappan) in India. In the post-Harappan period, on the whole, there were three distinct phases of urbanisation in early India, viz.,

(a) latter half of the second millennium BC (*c.* 1500-1000 BC),

(b) first half of the first millennium BC (*c.* 1000-600 BC), and

(c) from the sixth century BC to the end of the third century AD from the point of view of the growth of towns.

The ancient Indian history is replete with two glaring instances of urban revolution, one in the Indus valley in the west representing the Bronze age culture and other in the Gangetic valley in the east representing the Iron age culture. The urban civilization which flourished in the Gangetic valley in the first millennium BC is often referred to as the second urbanisation.[50] The statements of A. Ghosh,[51] R.S. Sharma[52] and Walter Ruben[53] that after the decay and disappearance of the Indus cities the urbanisation in the Gangetic region took place around *c.* 600 BC or in the sixth century BC can fairly be disputed. On the basis of the archaeological reports of some excavated sites in the Gangetic

46. *Mahāpurāṇa* (*Ādipurāṇa* of Jinasena & *Uttarapurāṇa* of Guṇabhadra), 16, 163, 169-70, 172, 175; 62, 267; 71, 25; *Padma Purāṇa* of Raviṣeṇa, 2, 39-45, 49; 3, 169-70; 41, 57; *Harivaṁśa Purāṇa* of Jinasena, 2, 3; 8, 147-48.; See also *Mānasāra* (non-Jain Sanskrit text), ed. P.K. Ācārya (Oxford, 1933), ch. 10.

47. *Mahāpurāṇa*, 19, 68-70; *Harivaṁśa*, 5, 264-66; see also U.N. Rai, *Prācīna Bhārata mein Nagara tathā Nāgarika Jīvana*, p. 231.

48. *DN*, ed. Rhys Davids & J. Carpenter, vol. II, p. 146.

49. *Divyāvadāna*, ed. P.L. Vaidya, p. 181.

50. See D.K. Chakrabarti, "Concept of Urban Revolution in the Indian Context", *Purātattva*, No. 6 (1972-73), pp. 27-32; S.P. Gupta, "Two Urbanisation in India", *Purātattva*, No. 7 (1974), pp. 53-60.

51. *The City in Early Historical India*, Introduction.

52. "Iron and Urbanization in the Ganga Basin", *IHR*, vol.1, no. 1 (1974), pp. 98-103.

53. "The Development of the Town in Ancient India", in D.P. Chattopadhyaya (ed.), *History and Society*, pp. 229-30.

basin as well as literary evidence the date can be pushed back much earlier to what has been proposed. In the post-Harappan period it was actually *c.*1000 BC which marked the beginning of the process of urbanisation in the Gangetic valley and not the sixth century BC (the earliest historical period) as erroneously supposed by some scholars. The period falling in between *c.*1000 BC and 600 BC cannot be considered as barren from the standpoint of study of urban tradition and evolution of towns and cities in the Gaṅgā valley. Moretimer Wheeler's view that urbanisation and the organised city-life began in the Gaṅgā-Yamunā valley during the earlier half of the first millennium BC (*c.*1000-600 BC)[54] is absolutely correct. While dealing with the Gangetic civilization he has unequivocally stated that some towns came into being in the "Yamunā-Ganges basin" during this period. Most of the towns which came into existence in the Gangetic Doāb during the first millennium BC were successively associated with PGW (Painted Grey Ware) and NBPW (Northern Black Polished Ware) cultures. The stage of urbanisation in the Gaṅgā valley synchronising with the advent of NBPW culture and the growth of material culture towards the middle of the first millennium BC represents the beginning of the second phase of urbanisation and not the first phase. By AD 300 urbanism in the Gaṅgā valley reached its climax but thereafter the process of decline began.[55] Some cities had declined, of course, much earlier.

The later Vedic phase was a turning point in the history of Gangetic urbanisation. With the expansion of the Āryans in the Gangetic Doāb the whole socio-economic and political scenario underwent significant changes. The thick forests of the upper, middle and lower Gangetic basin were cleared with iron axes which paved the way not only for cultivation but also for setting up of the state capitals, kingdoms and delightful urban localities. The knowledge of iron technology helped a lot to the Āryans in bringing about innovations in the urbanisation process in the Gangetic valley. The use of iron-tipped plough cultivation led to the increase in the production which fulfilled the requirement of surplus food for the city population of high density. The iron no doubt played a vital role in accelerating the pace of urbanisation in the Gangetic valley sometime between *c.* 800 BC and 600 BC. Some scholars are of the opinion that the introduction of iron technology did not bring about any revolutionary change in the pattern of urban settlement nor had any impact on the growth of urban centres prior to 500 BC which marks the beginning of

54. *EIP*, pp. 127, 132, 149.
55. For details see M. Lal, *Settlement, History and Rise of Civilization in Ganga-Yamuna Doab from* 1500 *BC*-300 *AD* (Delhi 1984); T.N. Roy, *The Ganges Civilization* (Delhi 1983).

NBPW phase of culture.[56] The iron finds mention in the early Vedic text as *ayas*[57] and in the later Vedic text as *śyāma-ayas*[58] as well as *kṛṣṇa-ayas*. The archaeological evidence proves that the upper Gangetic basin was inhabited by the people associating themselves with PGW phase of culture in the first half of the first millennium BC and iron phase of culture in the second half of the first millennium BC. The variety of iron objects have been discovered from Hastināpura, Ahicchatra, Kauśāmbī, Atrañjikhera, Ālamgīrpur, Noh, Jakhera and other urban sites.

The later Vedic age saw the transformation of tribal pastoralism into well-settled peasant society and city life of urban character. In the wake of the Āryan expansion and colonisation many non-Āryan ethnic groups were absorbed by them as a result of which their wealth and territory steadily increased. Many extensive kingdoms and stately cities came into existence. With the growth of the extensive kingdoms and large cities the political and cultural sway of the Āryans further extended towards the east. The Āryans and non-Āryans played an equally important role in the process of urban transition in early Indian society. As a matter of fact, the Āryans expanded from the Punjab over the vast tract of land between the Yamunā and the Gaṅgā popularly known as the Gaṅgā-Yamunā Doāb or Madhyadeśa. These areas were occupied by the Kurus, the Pañcālas and other adjoining tribes. The Kurus occupied Delhi and the upper portion of the Doāb called Kurukṣetra and set-up their capital at Hastināpura on the bank of the Gaṅgā in the district of Meerut. The Pañcālas occupied the middle portion of the Doāb

---

56. For details see R.S. Sharma, "Class Formation and its Material Basis in the Upper Gangetic Basin (*c.*1000-500 BC)", *IHR*, vol. II, no. 1, (1975), p. 2; "Iron and Urbanization in the Ganga Basin", *IHR*, vol. 1, no. 1 (1974) pp. 98-103; Romila Thapar, *The Past and Prejudice*, pp. 27, 51-52; *From Lineage to State* (Social Formations in the Mid First Millennium BC in the Ganga Valley), p. 94; D.K. Chakrabarti, "Beginning of Iron and Social Change in India", *Indian Studies : Past and Present*, vol. XIV, no. 4 (Calcutta, 1973), pp. 329-38; "The Beginning of Iron in India", *Antiquity*, vol. 50 (1976), pp. 114-24. N.R. Ray, "Technology and Social Change in Early Indian History — A Note posing a Theoretical Question", *Purātattva*, no. 8 (1975-76), pp. 132-38; V.K. Thakur, "Role of Iron in the Origin of Second Urbanisation in India : A Resurvey of Evidence", PIHC, Bodh Gaya Session, 1981, pp. 61-69; N.R. Banerji, *The Iron Age in India*, pp. 15ff, 216; D.D. Kosambi, "The Beginning of the Iron Age in India", *Journal of the Economic and Social History of the Orient*, vol. VI, pt. 3 (1963), pp. 309-18; *The Culture & Civilization of Ancient India in Historical Outline*, pp. 88-91; Vibha Tripathi, *The Painted Grey Ware : An Iron Age Culture of Northern India* (Delhi, 1976).

57. *ṚV*, 1, 52, 8; 1, 57, 3; 1, 80, 12; 2, 20, 8; 4, 27, 1; 7, 15, 14; 7, 95, 1; 10, 9, 101; 10, 96, 3-4; 10, 101, 8; 10, 113, 5.

58. *AV*, 9, 5, 4; 11, 3, 1, 7; see also D.K. Chakrabarti, "Iron in Early Indian Literature", *JRAS*, no. 1 (1979), pp. 22-28.

and established their kingdom comprising the modern districts of Bareilly, Badāun and Farrukhābād with northern capital at Ahicchatra and southern at Kāmpilya (Kāmpil). By the end of the Vedic period the Āryans had thoroughly conquered and subdued the fertile plains of northern India watered by the Yamunā, the upper Ganges and Sadānīrā (the Rāptī or Gaṇḍak). They gradually spread over the areas covered by Kośala, Kāśī and Videha where they established their respective kingdoms with capitals and began a new phase of urban life.

During the later Vedic period both political and economic factors gave fillip to the process of urbanisation in the Gaṅgā valley. The formation of ruling class, the territorial state formation, the emergence of administrative machinery, the introduction of taxation system, agrarian economy, technological advancement, material prosperity, foundation of few cities, etc., were the initial stages of progress towards urbanism.[59] However, it may be admitted that it was faint beginnings of town life. The urbanisation in the later Vedic age based on the literary evidence can also be confirmed by the archaeological evidence. The archaeological excavations and explorations in the Gangetic valley have brought to light a number of PGW sites, including Hastināpura and Ahicchatra, which were inhabited by the people who used earthen bowls and dishes made of painted grey pottery. They simultaneously used iron weapons in the so-called early iron age. On the basis of the combined evidence of the later Vedic texts and PGW iron-phase of culture we can form an idea of the urban life of the people in the first half of the first millennium BC. R.S. Sharma is of the view that the total picture of PGW settlements does not reflect an urban way of life in the later Vedic age. He, however, admits that towards the end of the PGW period there was proto-urban of semi-urban way of life.[60]

## Northern India

The towns and cities of northern India include those of the upper and middle Gaṅgā valley also. Ayodhyā, situated on the banks of the river Sarayū near Faizābād in Uttar Pradesh, is one of the oldest cities of India. The earliest allusion to this city with eight *cakra* (palaces) and nine gateways occurs in one of the later Vedic texts.[61] It was the earliest capital of the undivided kingdom of Kośala. This celebrated city (in the mid-

59. See also R.S. Sharma, *Aspects of Political Ideas and Institutions in Ancient India*, pp. 273-75.

60. "The Later Vedic Phase and the Painted Grey Ware", *Purātattva*, no. 8 (1975-76), pp. 63-68; D.P. Chattopadhyaya (ed.), *op. cit.*, pp. 135-36.

61. *AV*, 10, 1, 2-31.

Gaṅgā valley) was the capital of the rulers of Ikṣvāku dynasty of the Solar race. From the *Rāmāyaṇa* of Vālmīki it appears that the primaeval king Manu (father of Ikṣvāku) was the builder of this city, which reached the pinnacle of glory in the time of king Daśaratha, the father of Rāma. It covered an area of twelve *yojana* (about ninety-six miles) in length and three *yojana* (about twenty-four miles) in breadth. It was a well-planned city. It was intersected by broad streets. It had magnificent buildings, high mansions adorned with waving flags, ornamental gates, pillars, towers, beautiful gardens, markets, etc. It was also well fortified with strong walls, deep trenches, garrison of arches and well-equipped with sophisticated weapons. It was full of artisans, traders, merchants and craftsmen. It was large and densely populated city.[62] From demographic, economic, political, religious and cultural points of view Ayodhyā may undoubtedly be reckoned as a classic example of an early urbanism in India. It was both administrative and religious centre which led to its urban growth.

Ayodhyā is described in some of the Purāṇas also as a great city with an extent of ten *yojana* and a circumference of three *yojana*.[63] It is one of the seven sacred cities of India (the other six being, Kāśī, Mathurā, Ujjain, Dvāravatī (Dvārakā), Kāñcī and Māyāpura or Kāntipurī).[64] According to the Jain Purāṇas, this ancient city was twelve *yojana* in length, nine *yojana* in breadth and 38 *yojana* in circumference.[65] There are numerous references to this city (called Ayojjha) in Pāli literature.

H.D. Sankalia holds that Ayodhyā of the *Rāmāyaṇa* in a true historical perspective was a well-fortified city ascribed to *c.* 1000 BC-800 BC. In 1967 he discovered sherds of PGW.[66] There has been no systematic and extensive archaeological excavations in and around Ayodhyā. However, some minor excavations were carried out at this site in the late sixties and seventies which proved that the city had all the characteristic features of urbanism in the late NBPW phase. The excavation at the site in 1969-70 showed that it was later occupied in NBPW times (fifth-second centuries BC). The upper level of this phase brought to light six terracotta human figurines, two Ayodhyā coins, some iron

---

62. *Vāl. Rām.*, Bāla Kāṇḍa, V, 5-23; VI, 5-28; *Vāl. Rām. Ko.*, p. 25; see also S.C. De, *Historicity of Rāmāyaṇa and the Indo-Aryan Society*, pp. 157-58.
63. *Vṣṇ. Dh.*, 1, 13, 1-12; *Vy.*, 1, 8. 100-07; see also *Pdm.*, Uttarakhaṇḍa, 242, 41-42.
64. *Bmd.*, 4, 40, 91: see also *PK*, p. 29.
65. *Mahāpurāṇa*, 7, 41; 71, 416; *Pdm.*, 3, 169-72; 81, 120; *Hv.*, 10, 163.
66. *ABORI*, vols. LVIII-LIX (1977-78), pp. 893-919.

objects, etc.[67] There is an unmistakable evidence of town planning in the late NBPW phase which is confirmed by the discovery of structures of baked bricks, ring wells, etc., in 1979-80.[68] M. Wheeler has also included Ayodhyā in the list of cities of the Gaṅgā-Yamunā Doāb and other areas representing NBPW phase of culture.[69] K.D. Bajpai has opined that Kośala with its capitals at Ayodhyā and Śrāvastī might have represented an advanced phase of material culture about *c.* 600 BC.[70] B.B. Lal, who undertook an excavation work in March-April 1975, arrived at the conclusion that it was built posterior to Hastināpura. The lay out of the city, according to him, might have begun in early historical period (*c.* 250 BC-AD 350).[71] The baked brick wall of the Śuṅga period and house complex of Gupta times have also been discovered in the scrappy excavations at the site. The archaeological evidences available to use show that there were different phases of settlement at this city which broadly covers the Śuṅga, Kuṣāṇa and Gupta periods. The city had reached a high watermark of its grandeur during the reign of imperial Guptas (sometime between AD 402 and 467). It continued to flourish in post-Gupta times as a temple city.

Fa-hian visited the city of Ayodhyā in the fifth century AD. He found it entirely in excellent state of preservation. The brāhmaṇas and Buddhists were among the inhabitants of the city.[72] This city was visited by Hiuen-Tsang in the seventh century AD. According to him, the capital city of *A-yu-te* (Ayodhyā) was above 20 *li* (or upwards of 3 miles) in circuit. There were more than 100 Buddhist monasteries, 10 Hindu temples, etc. And the non-Buddhists were few in number.[73] Both of the them in the course of their visits to the city did not find any sign of its decay. It is believed that this city suffered a blow because of being besieged by the Bactrian Greeks sometime in the second century BC. But we do not have any positive evidence at our disposal to confirm it.

The old city of Ayodhyā seems to have decayed at much later period. V.A. Smith has clearly pointed out that the ancient city of Ayodhyā famous as the capital of Rāma was replaced by the modern city of Faizābād. The latter was built in no small degree from

---

67. *IAR*, 1969-70, p. 41.
68. *Ibid.*, 1979-80, p. 77.
69. *Op. cit.*, p. 30f.
70. *ABORI*, LVIII-LIX, pp. 434-37.
71. *Ibid.*, pp. 893-919.
72. H.A. Giles, *RBK*, pp. 29-30; see also J. Legge, *RBK*, pp. 54-55.
73. *YCTI*, 1, pp. 354-55.

the materials of Rāma's capital. The inscribed copper coins obtained at Faizābād datable to *c.* 150 BC-AD 100 belonged to the contemporary rulers of Ayodhyā.[74] A. Cunningham held these coins not older than the second century BC. Inscribed punch-marked coins and other cast pieces may be older.[75] He observes: "The present city of Ajudhya, which is confined to the north-east corner of the old site is just two miles in length by about three quarters of a mile in breadth; but not one half of this extent is occupied by buildings, and the whole place wears a look of decay. There are no high mounds of ruins, covered with broken statues and sculptured pillars, such as mark the sites of other ancient cities, but only a low irregular mass of rubbish heaps, from which all the bricks have been excavated for the house of the neighbouring city of Faizābād. This . . . city is built chiefly of materials extracted from the ruins of Ajudhya. The two cities together occupy an area of nearly six square miles, or just about one-half of the probable size of the ancient capital of Rama. . . ."[76]

The another important city was Sāketa, which appears in one of the Purāṇas[77] and the *Raghuvaṁśa*[78] of Kālidāsa to be the same as Ayodhyā. Ptolemy's (*c.* AD 150) Sageda (Sāketa)[79] or Fa-hian's *Sha-chi* or *Sha-ki* (Sāketa)[80] has also been identified with Ayodhyā. Both the cities were considered to be the same down to the fifth century AD. F.E. Pargiter,[81] Cunningham[82] and Csoma de Koros[83] have also described them as identical. In fact, they were the twin capital cities of the whole Kośala kingdom. "They were possibly adjoining cities like London and Westminster."[84] The site of Sāketa has been identified with the ruins (as yet unexplored) at Sujān Koṭ on the river Sai in the Unnāo district.[85] In the

---

74. *CCIM*, vol. 1, pp. 144, 148-51.
75. *Co. An. Ind.*, p. 90, Pl. IX, 1-3, 7-11; P1. XIX, 13; see also E.J. Rapson, *Ind. Co.*, p. 11 and P1. IV. 24; *JRAS*, 1903, p. 287; *JASB*, vol. XLIX, pt. 1 (1880), p. 27 and P1. XVI.1.
76. *CAGI*, p. 342.
77. *Bmd.*, 3, 54, 54.
78. V. 31; XIII, 79; XIV 13; XVIII, 36; S.C. Banerji, *Kālidāsa Kośa*, pp. 27, 30.
79. *AIT*, VII, I, 71, pp. 164-66; VII, 2, pp. 228-29.
80. *YCTI*, 1, p. 354-55.
81. *PDKA*, p. 53.
82. *CAGI*, p. 341; *CASR*, 1, p. 318.
83. *As. Res.*, vol. XX, p. 442.
84. T.W. Rhys Davids, B1, p. 39.
85. A. Führer, *MAINW*, p. 275.

Buddha's time, Ayodhyā had sunk to the level of an unimportant city. But Sāketa rose into prominence as one of the six great cities of India (the other five being Sāvatthi or Śrāvastī, Kośāmbī, Vārāṇasī, Rājagaha or Rājagṛha and Campā).[86] Sāketa has been categorically mentioned in some of the early Buddhist texts as another capital of the Kośala kingdom.[87] This city is said to have been adorned with domes.[88] According to some of the Jain canonical texts, this city called Sākeya was one of the ten ancient capital cities of India, the other nine being Sāvatthi, Hatthinaura (Hastināpura), Kośāmbī, Vārāṇasī, Kāmpilla, Mahurā (Mathurā), Rāyagiha (Rājagṛha), Campā and Mihila (Mithilā).[89] Some of the Jain Purāṇas also refer to Sāketa as one of the ancient capitals of India.[90] In the *Abhidhānapaddīpikā* of Moggalan Thera,[91] this city is included in the list of twenty ancient cities of India as follows: 1. Vārāṇasī, 2. Sāvatthi, 3. Vesāli, 4. Mithilā, 5. Ālavi, 6. Kosāmbī, 7. Ujjeni, 8. Takkasilā, 9. Campā, 10. Sāgala, 11. Sumsumāragiri, 12. Rājagaha, 13. Kapilavatthu, 14. Sāketa, 15. Indapatta, 16. Ukkatthā, 17. Pātaliputra, 18. Jetuttara, 19. Saṁkassa, and 20. Kusinārā.

The city, Śrāvastī, situated on the right bank of the Acirāvatī (modern Rāptī), according to Purāṇic evidence, was originally founded by a king named Śrāvasta, the son of Yuvanāśva I of Ikṣvāku family.[92] The city was built anterior to Rāma. According to epic,[93] Purāṇic[94] and Buddhist tradition (contained in the Sanskrit text, *Avadānaśataka*),[95] it was during the time of Rāma that the kingdom of Kośala was divided into two parts, viz., northern with its capital at Śrāvastī and the southern with its capital at Kuśāvatī.

---

86. *DN*, II, p. 146; see also B.C. Law, *GEB*, p. 5; *Geographical Essays*, p. 130; also *JGRI*, vol.1, pp. 423-43.

87. *Jāt.*, 3, p. 270; *Mahāvastu-Avadāna*, ed. E. Senart, vol. 1, p. 348.

88. *Bodhisattvāvadāna Kalpalatā*, 3rd Pallava, p. 2.

89. *Thānāṅga*, 10, 718; *Niśitha Sūtra*, 9, 19 cf. J.C. Jain, *LAIJC*, pp. 339-40.

90. *Mahāpurāṇa*, 48, 40; 60, 33; 61, 92; *Hv.*, 8, 150; *Pdm.*, 20, 16.

91. Ed. by Muni Jin Vijaya (Ahmedabad), p. 32.

92. *Vy.*, 88, 24-27; *Vṣn.*, IV, 2, 36-37; *Mts.*, 12, 29-30.

93. *Vāl. Rām.*, Uttara Kāṇḍa, 107, 5, 17; 108; 4; also *Vāl. Rām. Ko.*, pp. 73, 82.

94. *Vy.*, 88, 198-200; *Vṣn.*, IV, 4, 104; *Mts.*, 12, 40-44; *Bmd.*, 2, 16, 41, 64; 3, 53, 199; *Pdm.*, VI, 208, 46-47; VI, 271, 10-12; *Vmn.*, 16, 32. 38; *PK*, p. 133; see also Law, "The Kośalas in Ancient India", *IHQ*, vol. 1, Nos. 1-2 (Delhi, 1979), pp. 137-65; *IETBJ*, pp. 23, 43-44; "Śrāvastī in Ancient Indian Literature", *MASI*, no. 50 (Delhi, 1935), p. 9f.

95. Cf. *SBLN*, p. 20.

The former was occupied by one of his sons, Lava, after deserting the city of Ayodhyā, and the latter by his other son named Kuśa.

Śrāvastī, the capital of northern Kośala, became famous as one of the six great cities of India during the lifetime of the Buddha. It was six leagues (about forty-five miles) north of Sāketa. There are copious references to this city in Buddhist literature. It is described in Pāli canon[96] and commentaries[97] as one of the principal cities of Buddhist India. If Pāli commentatorial tradition is to be believed, there were fifty-seven thousand families in this city in Buddha's time.[98] In one of the Sanskrit Buddhist texts we are told that "it was full of kings, princes, ministers, councillors and their followers, Kṣatriyas, Brāhmaṇas, etc."[99] The towns and cities described in Buddhist literature as a whole number about sixty out of which twenty, including Śrāvastī, were great cites. It is said that "The material prosperity of the city was due to the fact that it was a meeting place of the three main trade-routes and a great centre of trade. . . . It was surrounded by a wall provided with gates on four or more sides. Within the wall the city must have three broad rings or divisions. There must have been proper allocation of sites for quarters of officials, religious and educational institutions, private houses, markets and even prostitutes" quarters. The road arrangements must have been so planned as to facilitate patrol duty. . . . It was not only a great emporium of Indian trade but also a great centre of religion and culture".[100] It was a famous commercial town.[101] At the same time it was a seat of Brāhmaṇical learning as well as a centre of Buddhism. This great city also attracted the notice of Pāṇini (IV, 2, 97)[102] and Kālidāsa.[103] In the Jain Purāṇas it is mentioned as a capital city.[104.]

---

96. See Law, *HPL*, II, p. 654.
97. *Dhammapada-Aṭṭhakathā*, ed. H.C. Norman, vol. II, p. 99f; *Suttanipāta-Aṭṭhakathā* (*Paramatthajotikā*) of Buddhaghoṣa, ed. H. Smith, vol. II, p. 448f.
98. *Sāmantapāsādikā* (Comm. on *Vinayapiṭaka*), ed. J. Takakusu and M. Nagai, vol. III, p. 614.
99. *Lalitavistara*, ed. R.L. Mitra, ch.I.
100. Law, *Geographical Aspect of Kālidāsa's Works*, p. 8.
101. Rāhula Sāṅkṛtyāyana, *Purātattva Nibandhāvalī*, pp. 33, 35; *Sārthavāha*, p. 18.
102. V.S. Agrawala, *IP*, p. 74.
103. *Raghuvaṁśa*, XV, 97.
104. *Mahāpurāṇa*, 49, 14; *Hv.*, 28, 5; *Pdm*, 20, 39; 91, 23.

Śrāvastī has been identified by Cunningham with the great ruined city on the south bank of the Rāptī called Sahet-Mahet, which is situated between Akaona and Balarāmapur at 5 miles from the former and 12 miles from the latter, and at nearly equal distances from Baharaich and Goṇḍā. Here he discovered a colossal statue of Buddha with an inscription containing the name of Śrāvastī itself.[105] This ruined city is at a distance of 58 miles from Ayodhyā. The limited vertical excavations carried out at Śrāvastī under the guidance of John Marshall and Daya Ram Sahani brought to light the remains of *stūpa*s and other structures.[106] The further excavation at the site by K.K. Sinha brought to light a mud rampart, brick wall, etc. It was a fortified city. The rich deposits of NBPW (whose Carbon-14 date ranges from 275 to 200 BC) show the growth of the city during this phase.[107] The city was in a flourishing state in the first century AD. Two inscriptions of Kaniṣka have also been found here.

Śrāvastī continued to flourish as a great city to the end of the third century AD. It declined in wealth, population and political importance probably during the fourth century AD. It lost its metropolitan character. In AD 400 the city contained only about two hundred families, as stated by Fa-hian, who visited it in the same year.[108] In AD 632, Hiuen-Tsang found it almost deserted. In his own words: "The capital (*Shih-lo-fa-si-ti* = Śrāvasti) was a wild ruin . . . . the old foundations of the palace city were above twenty *li* in circuit, and although it was mostly a ruinous waste yet there were inhabitants. . . . There were some hundreds of Buddhist monasteries of which the most were in ruins. . . . There were 100 Deva-Temples and the non-Buddhists were very numerous. This city was in the Buddha's time the seat of government of King Prasenjit and the foundations of this king's old palace remained in the old palace city. . . ."[109]

The ancient city of Kuśāvatī mentioned in the Purāṇas (*Vy*., 88, 198-200; *Mts*., 12, 40-44) and the *Raghuvaṁśa* (XV, 97; XVI, 25) of Kālidāsa was the capital of southern Kośala. It can be identified with Kuśapura, about 30 miles from the present city of Ayodhyā. There was another Kuśāvatī which became popularly known as Kuśinārā (Kuśinagara) in the time of the Buddha. In his time it was one of the capitals of Mallas'

105. *CAGI*, p. 345; *CASR*, 1, p. 331.
106. *ASIAR*, 1907-8, p. 84; see also *ASIAR*, 1910-11, pp. 1ff; *JRAS*, 1908, pp. 971-75; 1901, pp. 1061ff.
107. Excavation at Śrāvastī (1959), Vārāṇasī, 1967; *IAR*, 1958-59, pp. 47-48.
108. Giles, *op. cit*., pp. 30-31.
109. *YCTI*, 1, p. 377.

kingdom. This capital city was 12 *yojana* in length from east to west and seven *yojana* in width north to south. It had seven ramparts, four gates, etc.[110] It is identical with the ruins near the modern village of Kasiā (on the smaller Gaṇḍak), about 35 miles to the east of Gorakhpur. It was a famous centre of Buddhism. It being an administrative and religious centre did not take much time to grow up into an urban complex. The city appears to have declined much before the fifth century AD, as attested to by Fa-hian. At the time of his visit, it was in utter ruin and there were only few inhabitants scattered here and there.[111] The same desolation prevailed in the city at the time of Hiuen-Tsang's visit to it. The city has been called by him *Kou-Shih-na-ka-lo* (Kuśinagara). He found that "The city walls were in ruins and the towns and villages were deserted. The brick foundations of the old city (which had been the capital) were above ten *li* in circuit; there were very few inhabitants the interior of the city being a wild waste".[112]

One of the famous cities of the Buddha's time was Kapilavatthu (Kapilavastu), which stood close to the western bank of the Rohiṇī at a distance of about 90 km to the east of Śrāvastī. It was the renowned capital of the Śākyas. It is often identified with Tilaurakoṭ and the widely scattered ruins in its vicinity, about two miles from Tauliva in the Nepal Terai. In one of the Sanskrit Buddhist texts the story of its foundation and settlement of the Śākyas there is prolixly narrated.[113] It was surrounded by seven walls.[114] We are further told that it was a *mahānagara* or great city. It was populous and immensely rich. It was adorned with four gates, towers all over the palaces, arched gateways, pinnacles, gardens, market places, etc.[115] The burnt brick structure discovered by D. Mitra in the course of a minor excavation and exploration at the site belongs to the early phase of NBPW.[116] This city was destroyed by Prasenajit's son, Viḍuḍabha (Virūdhaka) towards the end of the Buddha's life. He not only destroyed the city but also killed a large number of its inhabitants who mostly belonged to the Śākya race. Consequently, the survivors started deserting the city which led to its gradual decline. Fa-hian found it "desolate and barren with few inhabitants".[117] Hiuen-Tsang after crossing the distance of

110. *DN*, II, pp. 146-47.
111. Giles, *op. cit.*, p. 41.
112. *YCTI*, II, pp. 25-26.
113. *Mahāvastu*, vol. 1, pp. 350 ff.
114. *Ibid.*, vol. 11, p. 75.
115. *Lalitavistara*, pp. 58, 77-78, 98, 101-2, 113, 123, 128.
116. Cf. Ghosh, *op. cit.*, pp. 60-72.
117. Giles, *op. cit.*, pp. 36-38.

about 500 *li* or so to the south-east of Śrāvastī reached Kapilavastu. He describes it as above 4000 *li* (about 800 miles) in circuit or circumference, and as containing more than ten deserted cities all in utter ruin. The royal city was also found in ruins. But the solid brick foundations of the "palace city" within the "Royal city" still remained and were above fifteen *li* in circuit. The capital city had been left desolate for a very long time and it was very sparsely inhabited.[118]

Hastināpura in the upper Gaṅgā valley was the earlier capital of the Kuru kingdom. There are some evidences to take back its antiquity to the time of the king Duṣyanta or his on Bharata of Paurava dynasty.[119] However, according to epic and Purāṇic tradition of a very reliable nature, it was Bharata's fifth successor, Hastin, the son of Suhotra in the same Paurava line, who founded this city on the bank of the Gaṅgā and made it his own capital.[120] It was evidently so named after him. It had an extent of ten *yojana*.[121]

The *Mahābhārata* provides very positive evidence of the evolution of Hastināpura as a city in ancient times which covers both the pre- and post-Bhārata war period. It is said to have been the most magnificent of all the cities existing during the former period.[122] It continued to be the chief capital city of the Kauravas until their annihilation in the Great Bhārata battle. In the post-war period it came into possession of the Pāṇḍavas. Yudhiṣṭhira along ruled over the kingdom with its capital at Hastināpura for nearly thiry-six years — the period during which it had attained all the paraphernalia of a prosperous city. The Great epic provides a pictureque description of this city of his time. It contains the description of the settlement patterns of the dwellers of the city, the magnificent buildings on both sides of the road, the royal palace protected by an enclosure with a main gate, other city gates, the houses of common citizens on the main roads, the broad streets in the city, assembly-hall, market places, reservoirs, drains, etc.[123] It definitely wore a look of an urban centre during his time. It was no doubt a grand city.

---

118. *YCTI*, II, p.1.

119. *Abhijñāna-Śākuntalam* of Kālidāsa, p. 128; see also B.S. Upādhyāya, *India in Kālidāsa*, p. 71; F.E. Pargiter, *AIHT*, p. 273.

120. *Mbh.*, Ādi Parva, 90, 36; *Mbh. Ko.*, p. 737; *Bh. Sv.*, vol.1, p.84; *Mts.*, 49, 42; *Vy.*, 99, 165; *Vṣṇ.*, IV, 19, 27-28; *Bhāg.*, IX, 21, 20; *Bhv.*, 1, vv. 45-47, pp. 303-4; *PK*, p. 550.

In the *Vāl. Rām.* (Ayodhyā Kāṇḍa, 68,13) also Hasināpura has been mentioned as a city.

121. *Bhv.*, 1, v. 46, pp. 303-4.

122. *Ādi Parva*, 94, 10; 102, 22; *Mbh. Ko.*, p. 737.

123. Śānti Parva, 38, 37-38, 43, 45-49; 39, 1-10; Udyoga Parva (173, 2) also refers to Hastināpura.

However, the information supplied in the text about the layout of the city is very meagre. It appears to have passed through certain stages of its transition from a rural to an urban area. J. Talboys Wheeler oberves: "The old domestic life at Hastinapur may be easily realized if the probable surroundings are first taken into consideration. A large village seems to have been constructed of mud and bamboos on the bank of the upper stream of the Ganges. This was known as the city of Hastinapur. It was probably inhabited by the cultivators of the neighbouring lands, and all the dependants and retainers of the colony. Whilst the Raja, with his family and immediate kinsmen, dwelt in a so-called palace or fort, which was most likely built in a rude square, with a council-hall and inner quadrangle after the fashion of Hindu forts. The Aryan colony at Hastinapur was not, however, without its neighbours . . . who dwelt in cities, and had perhaps attained a certain stage of civilization".[124]

Hastināpura continued to exist as a great city up to the time of an illustrious Paurava king, Adhisīmakr̥ṣṇa. It was his son and successor named Nicakṣu (also called Nirvaktra, Nemicakra, etc.) who abandoned the city because of being washed away by heavy floods in the Gaṅgā and shifted his capital therefrom to Kauśāmbī, as stated in the *Mahābhārata*[125] and the Purāṇas.[126] This event has been ascribed by F.E. Pargiter to *c.* 820 BC.[127] The transfer of the capital from Hastināpura to Kauśāmbī might have taken place sometime after *c.* 800 BC or between *c.* 800 BC and *c.* 600 BC which can archaeologically be also proved. However, the former was rebuilt sometime in the early sixth century BC but never attained the status of other cities in the middle Gaṅgā valley. However, it continued to flourish in the succeeding period.

Hastināpura (Pāli Hatthipura or Hatthinipura) has been frequently mentioned in Buddhist literature as the capital city of both the Kuru kings and Pāṇḍavas.[128] In one of the Sanskrit Buddhist texts it is described as a rich, prosperous and populous city.[129] In

---

124. *India from the Earliest Ages*, p. 29.

125. Ādi Parva, 95, 54; 100, 12.

126. *Vy.*, 99, 270-71; *Mts.*, 50, 78-70; *Vṣṇ.*, IV, 21, 6-8; *Bhāg.*, IX, 22, 39-40; Pargiter, *PDKA* (Oxford, 1913), p. 5.

127. *AIHT*, p. 285.

128. *Apadāna*, II, p. 359; *DPPN*, p. 1319; *Bodhisattvāvadāna-Kalpalatā*, 3rd Pallava, p. 116; 64th, p. 9; *Lalitavistara*, ch. III; *Mahāvastu-avadāna*, III, p. 361; *Kalpadruma-avadāna* cf. *SBLN*, p. 297.

129. *Divyāvadāna*, p. 435.

the Jain tradition it was one of the ten capital cities of India, as stated before. In the Jain Purāṇas it is mentioned as large city.[130] Pāṇini mentions the Kuru kingdom (IV, 1, 172) as well as the town of Hastināpura (VI, 2,101) which was its capital.[131] The Kuru kingdom of the Āryāvartta and its capital Hastināpura also find mention in Patañjali's *Mahābhāṣya* (I, 4, 51 and II, 1, 16 respectively). The said capital has been mentioned along with other towns of north India like Kauśāmbī, Vārāṇasī (II, 1, 16 ), Mathurā (II, 4, 7) Ahicchatra and Kānyakubja.[132]

Hastināpura has been identified with a ruined site (about eight km long and over one km wide, still called Hasti kā nagara) on the old bed of the Gaṅgā, about 22 miles north-east of Meerut in Uttar Pradesh. The excavations carried out by B.B. Lal at the site in 1950-52[133] have revealed that there were as many as five occupational periods with stratigraphical gap in betwen all of occupational periods with stratigraphical gap in between all of them which are given below with their respective Carbon-14 dates:

| | |
|---|---|
| Period I | to 1200 BC |
| Period II | *c.* 1100 BC to *c.* 800 BC |
| Period III | *c.* early sixth century BC to the third century BC |
| Period IV | early second century BC to the end of the third century AD |
| Period V | late eleventh century to early fifteenth century AD |

The earliest period I was represented by a thin layer with no structures but with a few much-worn fragments of the OCP associated with copper hoards. The period II contained the PGW together with remains of mud or mud-brick walls but with no clear evidence of the use of baked bricks. Copper was found in the form of an arrow-head, etc. There were no iron objects, though in the uppermost levels lumps of iron ore were encountered. The excavation has shown that the site was abandoned due to flood sometime after the second period, i.e., *c.* 800 BC. The habitation was renewed in period

130. *Mahāpurāṇa*, 43, 74, 76; *Pdm.*, 4, 6; 20, 52; *Hv.*, 9, 157; 34, 456.

131. *IP*, pp. 55, 73.

132. B.N. Puri, *India in the time of Patañjali*, p. 79; *Mahābhāṣya*, ed. by F. Kielhorn, vol. 1, pp. 139, 216, 225, 378, 380, 474; vol. II, pp. 206, 233, 280-1; P.V. Kane, "Ancient cities and towns mentioned in the *Mahābhāṣya*", *JBBRAS*, vol. XXVII, pt. 1, (1951), pp. 38-42.

133. "Excavations at Hastināpur and other explorations in the Upper Ganga and Sutlej Basins", *AI*, Nos. 10 & 11, 1954-55, pp. 5-151.

III. This period is marked by the discovery of over a hundred sherds of NBPW (ascribed to the fifth-second century BC) baked-brick structures alongside mud and mud brick, soak-pits; ring-wells and iron objects — all characteristic of Indian towns from the latter half of the first millennium BC onwards. In the period III money came into use in the shape of punch-marked rectangular pieces of silver with some symbols. A number of cast copper coins both rectangular and round bearing similar symbols were also used. The coins of some rulers attributed to the second century BC belonged to the period IV.[134]

It is generally inferred that the people representing the earliest phase of settlement at Hastināpura using OCP and copper-hoards were semi-nomadic and food-gathering communities.[135] But, on the other hand, on the basis of the distribution of OCP in the upper Gaṅgā valley and the excavation of some sites the above statement is contradicted and it is further held that the OCP people were not nomads but had a settled life and lived in "simple mud walled as well as sophisticated brick houses"![136] The archaeological examination of some samples from several sites in the upper Gangetic basin by B.B. Lal led him to postulate that OCP sites were abandoned because of long exposure to dry climate or a deluge in the Gaṅgā-Yamunā valley after the seventeenth century BC.[137] But this theory is no longer tenable.

In the second phase of settlement, other people using PGW were mainly dependent on agriculture and cattle-breeding, and their economy was essentially a rural one. Elements of urbanisation, as is generally accepted, such as large-size settlements with regular town-planning, commercial activities, system of writing, etc., were conspicuous by their absence. The people lived in houses of mud or wattle and daub plastered with mud. They used mainly iron objects such as spear-heads, daggers, sickles, etc., though arrow-heads of both copper and iron were used. It, of course, marked the faint beginnings of town life. But Mortimer Wheeler is of the opinion that "The civic life in recognisable

---

134. "Excavations at Hastināpur and other explorations in the Upper Ganga and Sutlej Basins"; M. Wheeler, *op. cit.*, pp. 26-30, 117, 120, 129, 130 and P1. 27, 131.

135. M. Wheeler, *op. cit.*, pp. 117, 124, 126, 129.

136. B.B. Lal "The Copper Hoard Culture of the Ganga Valley", *Antiquity*, vol. XLVI (1972), pp. 282-87; "Further Copper Hoards from the Gangetic Basin and a Review of the Problem", *AI*, No.7, 1951, pp. 20-39; H.D. Sankalia, *PPIP*, pp. 397-400.

137. "The Ochre-Coloured Pottery — A Geochronological Study", *Purātattva*, no. 5, 1971-72, pp. 49-58.

from began at Hastinapur in the painted Grey Ware level, that the culture represented by that ware was urban in character and that urban life began in the doab in about 1000 BC".[138] He admits that Hastināpura was established before the *Mahābhārata* war for which he accepts the date *c.* 950 BC, as suggested by others. But, on the other hand, he ascribes the PGW found at Hastināpura to the eighth century BC. The date *c.* 1100 BC assigned to it by B.B. Lal is also not disputed by him.[139] But he is of the firm opinion that the remains of Hastināpura of the PGW period constitute the evidence of "a developed township with an economy based on mixed farming, and with adequately constructed houses of which at present little is known".[140] In this regard the views expressed by H.D. Sankalia are also worth-quoting: "For the first time the small and big places — towns and villages mentioned in the *Mahābhārata* seemed to be truly living. Their antiquity was being established for the first time. But the archaeologists after probing the depth of Hastinapur and Ahicchatra little said about sociological background of the people, their houses, the layout of their settlement, habits, customs or manners. . . . The Carbon-14 dates from Hastinapur and other sites proved the culture not older than 7-8th century BC. The authors of the Painted Grey Ware culture whom the archaeologists associate with the *Mahābhārata* heroes — the Pandavas, Kauravas . . . should have lived only 2700 years ago and not 5000 years ago. . . ."[141] On the basis of the discovery of pottery from each successive layers of deposits at Hastināpura and other identical pottery from the places mentioned in the *Mahābhārata* he further associates the PGW phase of culture in the Gaṅgā-Yamunā Doāb with the early Āryans or the Kauravas and the Pāṇḍavas and their contemporaries in the region. He has brought to light subsequent Carbon-14 dates of the PGW (*c.* 800-400 BC and sixth to fifth century BC, etc.), but it seems that he does not totally accept its lower dating. He has also not discarded the historical value of the traditional accounts of the subject as provided in the epics and Purāṇas. Traditionally he seems to be inclined to place the epic details concerned anterior to the PGW period but archaeologically he does not consider the PGW phase of culture or the Gangetic

138. *Civilization of the Indus Valley and Beyond*, p. 98.

139. *EIP*, p. 26f.

140. *Ibid.*, p. 130.

141. *PPIP*, pp. 400-1.

culture older than the seventh or sixth century BC.[142] In any case, Hastināpura, of the *Mahābhārata* does not fall within the range of the later C-14 dates of the PGW. There is no perceptible link between the two.

The settlement of the PGW phase of Hastināpura actually came to an end after the second period for the reason already stated before. It remained in the state of decay for about two centuries after *c.* 800 BC. After a break in habitation the site was reoccupied in the third phase of NBPW — using people, who abandoned it after a conflagration. The NBPW phase ascribed to the latter half of the second millennium BC (*c.* 500-200 BC) was a blooming period for its growth like other towns of the Gaṅgā-Yamunā Doāb. It continued to flourish till the end of the third century AD. Thereafter it gradually began to decline. However, after a gap of about seven centuries or so it again came into limelight in early medieval period. It appears to have lost its existence sometime in early fifteenth century AD.

Both the literary and arachaelogical evidence attest to the phase-wise growth of Hastināpura as a city. On the combined testimony of both, which are supplementary to each other, we can have an overall picture of this city from the beginning to its end.

The another great city founded in the pre-Bhārata war period on the Yamunā was Indraprastha, which was the later capital of the Kuru kingdom. The history of its foundation as well as its layout is well recorded in the *Mahābhārata*. Dhṛtarāṣṭra, Kaurava king, in order to avoid the rivalry or conflict between the two branches of the Kuru family divided the kingdom and ceded half to Pāṇḍavas assigning to them the small principality of Khāṇḍavaprastha, a part of Khāṇḍavavana, on the bank of Yamunā, and retaining Hastināpura proper with him to continue his rule over it. The Pāṇḍavas led by Yudhiṣṭhira left Hastināpura for destination. After clearing the jungle called Khāṇḍavavana by setting it on fire they established a colony, built a palace and made it their new capital, which became popularly known as the city of Indraprastha. It was well fortified with deep moats, a high rampart, numerous gateways and towers. It was protected by weapons, iron-wheels, etc. Near the city entrances there were beautiful mansions. The city was provided with wide roads connecting one another and dividing the enclosed area into sections for palaces, buildings, houses of citizens, lakes, reservoirs, gardens and parks abounding in trees and plants enhancing its beauty. The traders, merchants,

---

142. *PPIP.*, p. 403; *AIHA*, pp. 277, 308; see also *PPIP*, Appendix II, Table 6, p. 566 and his "Traditional Chronology and C-14 dates of excavated sites", *JIH*, vol. 42 (1964), pp. 635-50 for different C-14 dates of Hastināpura in PGW phase and that of other urban centres in the Gaṅgā Valley.

artisans an craftsmen flocked to it from all directions in search of wealth. It had a splendid look.[143] It appears to have been a well-planned city. Thirty-six years after the war the Yādavas of Dvārakā in Gujarat entered into a fratricidal stirfe in which many of them lost their lives. Thereafter Arjuna came to Dvārakā and took the bulk of the surviving population back to Indraprastha.[144] The re-settlement of the Yādavas at Indraprastha was a significant event. Because the increase in population led to the growth of this city. The descendants of Pāṇḍavas at Indraprastha continued to rule there long after the destruction of their principal metropolis, Hastināpura, and the migration of the older line of kuru kings to Kauśāmbī.

About two cities, Hastināpura and Indraprastha of the epic fame, it has been rightly pointed out by B.C. Law that "the former was the earlier as well as the later capital of Kuru kingdom and it was one of the 19 great cities of ancient India while the latter was the capital of Pandavas or later capital of the Kuru kingdom founded by Pandavas on the bank of the Yamuna, 2 miles south of modern Delhi".[145]

We learn from some of the Purāṇas that from east to west the city, Indraprastha, was one *yojana* in extent and to the south its boundary had an extent of four *yojana*.[146] The Pāli literature also throws some light on this city of both pre-Buddhist period and of the Buddha's time. We are told in the *Jātaka*s that the Kuru kingdom, which was three hundred leagues in extent, comprised several towns and villages and its capital Indapatta (Indraprastha) was seven leagues (about 50 miles) in extent.[147] The said capital was one of the three chief cities of "Jambudipa" (India), the other two being "Uttarapañcala" (possibly the famous Ahicchatra) and "Kekaya" (which stands for its capital Girjak). Indapatta in particular is said to have been a lofty city.[148] In the time of the Buddha as well as in the post-Buddha times this was a prosperous city.[149]

Ptolemy while referring to the kingdoms and towns and cities of upper Gangetic

---

143. Ādi Parva, 55, 23-25, 35; 199, 24-50; *Bh.Sv.*, vol. 1, p. 129; vol. II, p. 143; see also *Bmd.* (4, 12, 44) for the origin of the name Indraprastha.

144. Maūsala Parva, 8, 10-11, 32-47, 68-74; also *Bhāg.*, 10, 58, 12; 11, 30, 48; *PK*, p. 51.

145. "Hastinapur and Indraprastha in Ancient India", *Journal of the Asiatic Society of Bombay* (New Series), vol. XXX, pt. 1. 1955, pp. 9-16; see also his *HGAI*, p. 86.

146. *Pdm.*, VI, 196, 5; VI, 200, 5, 75-77; *Vsn. Dh.*, 1, 80, 14.

147. *Jāt.*, V, pp. 57, 484; VI, pp. 160, 255; also II, pp. 365f; Law, *IETBJ*, p. 35.

148. *Jāt.*, II, pp. 213-14.

149. See *Mhv. Comm.*, pp. 128-29; *Buddhavaṁsa*, tr. Law, ch. XXVIII, V.11.

Doāb clearly mentions "Pandoouoi" (Pāṇḍavas) and their capital cities Hastināpura on the bank of the Gaṅgā and also "Indabara" or "Indabatta" (Indraprastha of which the Prākṛt form is Indrabattha) on the bank of the Yamunā in the neighbourhood of Delhi.[150]

Indraprastha now called Indrapat is archaeologically identified with ancient mound on which stand the Purana Qila (a fort of the sixteenth century) at Delhi. M. Wheeler has correctly stated that the first half of the first millennium BC (*c*. 1000-600 BC) "witnessed the emergence of a comfortable and organised city-life in the Yamuna-Ganga basin, and to this period belongs the earliest settled occupation . . . in the Delhi region at the Purana Qila (Indrapat) which may fairly be described as the first Delhi. . . . We may recognise in it the general urban background of the *Mahābhārata* period. . . ."[151] This can also be corroborated by archaeological evidence. The excavations at Purana Qila were first carried out in 1954-55 which revealed that the site (on the eastern side) had been under occupation round about 1000 BC, when the people used distinctive bowls and dishes of the PGW. Some copper tools were also found.[152] The later excavations were carried out in its vicinity and at other places adjacent to the tomb of Humāyun in 1969-73. In 1971-72, a few fine and thin greyware pot-sherds closely affiliated to PGW were found. The occurrence of the NBPW datable to *c*. fourth-third century BC shows the second phase of settlement at the city. The archaeological evidence as a whole goes to show its gradual expansion.[153]

Indraprastha was no doubt an important city during the rule of the Mauryas, Śuṅgas, Kuṣāṇas and Guptas. However, there is no evidence of continuous habitation of the site during the period concerned. The city was in a dilapidated condition during the time of Candragupta II (*c*. AD 375-414). There is also an evidence to show the poor nature of settlement at the city during the Gupta period (AD 400-600). The city might have been possibly attacked and destroyed first by the Śakas in the early fourth century AD and then by the Hūṇas towards the end of the fifth century AD or in early sixth century AD. It was Anaṅgapāla I of the Tomara dynasty who rebuilt it in about AD 791. It had, of course, a chequered history like some other cities in ancient India. However, its history of the subsequent period does not fall within the scope of this work. Suffice it to say that

---

150. *AIT*, pp. 121-22, 128-29, 212; see also Lassen. *Ind. Alt.*, vol. III, p. 151.

151. *EIP*, p. 132.

152. *IAR*, 1954-55, pp. 13-14, 17; see also *AI*, Nos. 10 &11, 1954-55, p. 140.

153. *IAR*, 1969-70, pp. 4-6; 1970-71, pp. 8-11; 1971-72, pp. 7-8; 1972-73, pp. 8-9.

modern Delhi was known altogether by seven different names at different periods of History. Its most ancient name was Indraprastha which is also supported by a fourteenth-century inscription found in a village called Sarban, New Delhi.[154]

In the beginning, the Āryans formed rural settlements at Hastināpura and Indraprastha on the upper streams of the Gaṅgā and Yamunā respectively. But in the course of time the increasing population, construction of forts, growing influence of iron-technology, etc., led to the transformation of the places concerned from rural to urban centres. Actually, there were several stages of their growth as two different cities in the succeeding period.

The archaeological data do confirm the existence of Hastināpura and Indraprastha, the two famous capital cities of the Kuru kingdom, as described in the *Mahābhārata* and the Purāṇas. But the literary and archaeological description of the cities do not go in harmony with each other. However, the archaeological evidence help us determine their approximate antiquity. It also fairly attests to the various phases of settlement of the people at these two great cities in the remote past. Over and above it throws light on the evolution of urban culture in the entire Gangetic valley during the period concerned. But we cannot solely depend on the C-14 dates of the PGW phase of culture ranging sometimes form *c*. 1100 to 800 BC and sometimes from *c*. 800 to 400 BC for the purpose of determining the exact antiquity of the cities concerned. The people using PGW were undoubtedly the Āryans. Their expansion in the Gaṅgā-Yamunā Doāb in the later Vedic age is a well-proven fact. Their cities at PGW level have higher antiquity. Some of the C-14 dates can be readjusted by applying MASCA[155] correction factor.

Kauśāmbī in central Gaṅgā valley was the capital city of the Vatsa kingdom called Vatsabhūmi in the *Mahābhārata* and the Purāṇas. According to epic and Purāṇic tradition, the city was founded by Kuśāmba (one of the kings of Puru dynasty),[156] but its fame begins only with the reign of Nicakṣu who made Kauśāmbī his capital after Hastināpura had been swept away by the Gaṅgā.[157] Cunningham while supporting it observes that

154. *EP. Ind*., vol. 1 (1892), pp. 93-95.

155. This is a corrective factor evolved by the Museum Applied Science Centre for Archaeology, University of Pennsylvania, USA.

156. *Mbh*., Ādi Parva, 57, 28-29; *Bh. Sv*., vol. 1, p. 59; *Vāl. Rām*., Bāla Kāṇḍa, 32, 6; *Vāl. Rām. Ko*., p. 73; *Mts*., 50, 26-28; *Vy*., 99, 220-22; *Vṣṇ*., IV, 19, 80-81; *Bhāg*., IX, 22, 6-7; *Hv*., 1, 32, 54; Pargiter, *AIHT*, p. 118; *PK*, p. 121; see also Law, *IETBJ*, p. 133; "Kauśāmbī in Ancient Literature", *MASI*, no. 60, Delhi, 1939.

157. Ādi Parva., 95, 54; 100, 12; *Vy*., 99, 270-71; *Mts*., 50, 78-79; *Vṣṇ*., IV, 21, 6-8; *Bhāg*., IX, 22, 39-40.

"The city of Kosambi was one the most celebrated places in ancient India, and its name was famous amongst Brahmans as well as Buddhists".[158] About twenty-three Paurava kings succeeding Nicakṣu ruled over their kingdom, Vatsabhūmi, with its capital at Kauśāmbī till the time of Udayana, a contemporary of Buddha. In the Buddhist literature Kauśāmbī figures as one of the great cities of the time of the Buddha.[159] In his time it was an entrepot or emporium of trade.[160] Before and after the time of the Buddha it was the capital of the said kingdom. In the Jain Purāṇas it has been distinctly mentioned as the capital of the Vatsas.[161] Both Pāṇini (IV, 2, 97) and Patañjali (II, 1, 1) mention it as a great city of their times. Ptolemy also refers to this city as a capital of the Pauravas ("Porouaroi").[162]

Cunningham was the first archaeologist to locate Kauśāmbī's extensive ruins lying near the village Kosam on the right bank of the Yamunā, about 30 miles south-west of Allahabad.[163] Daya Rama Sahani also found the ruins of the city in the vicinity of same village.[164] This identification can also be confirmed by an epigraphic evidence, i.e., Kauśāmbī pillar Edict of Aśoka.[165] According to Cunningham, "The present ruins of Kosambi consist of an immense fortress formed of earthern ramparts and bastions, with a circuit of 23,100 feet, or exactly 4 miles and 3 furlongs. The ramparts have a general height of from 30 to 35 feet above the fields; but the bastions are considerably higher, those on the north face rising to upwards of 50 feet, while those at the south-west and south-east angles are more than 60 feet. . . ."[166] In the course of an archaeological exploration in 1887 he obtained six coins from Kosam which have been assigned to second or third century BC.[167] The archaeological excavations systematically carried out

158. *CAGI*, p. 330
159. *DN*, vol. II, pp. 146, 169; *Sutta-Nipāta Commentary*, vol. II, p. 584; *Mahāvastu*, vol. II, p. 2; *Bodhisattvāvadāna-Kalpalatā*, 35th Pallva, p. 3; *Mhv. Comm.*, p. 128; see also *Jāt.*, 4, 28; 6, 236.
160. *BI*, p. 36.
161. *Mahāpurāṇa*, 52, 18; *Pdm.*, 20, 16; 91, 30; *Hv.*, 14, 2.
162. *AIT*, p. 72.
163. *CASR*, vol. 1 (1871), pp. 302-3; *CAGI*, p. 332.
164. *JRAS*, pt. IV (1927), pp. 689-98.
165. D.C. Sircar (ed.), *SI*, vol. I, p. 70, note 2; *Ind. Ant.*, vol. XVIII, p. 30f; vol. XIX, pp. 122ff.
166. *CAGI*, p. 334.
167. *Co. An. Ind.*, P1. V, 7-10; also Smith, *op. cit.*, pp. 146, 155; Rapson, *op. cit.*, p. 12.

by G.R. Sharma at the site in between 1949 and 1959 reveal that the ramparts armed at regular intervals by bastions of mud revetted externally with a battered facing of baked bricks bearing the influence of Harappan citadel were built before the introduction or NBPW (C-14 date 450-95 BC) witnessed the radical transformatrion of Kauśāmbī city. This phase is characterised by the use of burnt brick structures, coins, erection of fortifications or defensive walls around the city, increase in the size of settlement, enlarged population, etc. In the course of excavations, potteries, jars, ring-wells, iron objects, the remains of a palace complex and other monumental buildings, Buddhist monasteries and *stūpa*s, evidence of drainage system, etc., were found. Some relics of Kuṣāṇa time as well as of the Gupta age were also discovered.[168] The excavations have brought to light 25 structural periods the buildings of which are represented by the remnants of walls and floors lying over one another. The four structural periods are dated as follows.[169]

| | |
|---|---|
| I | *c*. 1165 BC to *c*. 885 BC |
| II | *c*. 885 BC to *c*. 605 BC |
| III | *c*. 605 BC to *c*. 45 BC |
| IV | *c*. 45 BC to *c*. AD 580 |

The date suggested by the excavator with regard to the founding of Kauśāmbī has not been accepted by some archaeologists on the ground that it shows its very high antiquity.[170] H.D. Sankalia is also of the view that the "beginnings of this city go back to 8th century BC, but with its moat and encircling protection wall over 3½ miles (5.7 km) in length and provided with bastions and watch towers . . give idea of a city in the Ganga Valley from the 6th century BC to 2nd century BC. . . . These indicate the kind of civic life people had at this period. In the earliest phase (*c*. 700 BC) as well as in the first five

168. G.R. Sharma, *The Excavations at Kauśāmbī*, 1957-59 (Allahabad, 1960), pp. 6-25, 37-45; *IAR*, 1953-54, p. 9; 1954-55, pp. 16-17; 1955-56, p. 20; 1956-57, pp. 24, 28; 1957-58, p. 47; 1960-61, pp. 16, 18, 20f, 46-47, 53-58; *MASI*, no. 74 (Delhi 1969), pp. 24-27; also M. Wheeler, *EIP*, pp. 128-29 and Pls, 26 & 28.

169. G.R. Sharma, *op. cit*., pp. 17, 22.

170. K.K. Sinha "Stratigraphy and Chronology of Early Kauśāmbī — A Reappraisal", in D.P. Agrawal and A. Ghosh (eds.), *Radiocarbon and Indian Archaeology*, pp. 231-39; A. Ghosh, *op. cit*., pp. 11, 62, 80-81.

phases of period II, which is associated with the NBPW, the houses had mud walls. Around 400 BC appear the first brick structures and the first road with bylanes. . . ."[171] The city was an administrative, commercial and religious centre.

From the reports of archaeological excavations it appears that Kauśāmbī must have been a large city in ancient times. All the positive signs of urbanism have been found here. Sankalia had excepted that when fully excavated it will rival Takṣaśilā. His expectation has come almost true. At the time of Fa-hian's visit to the city only some monasteries were found in ruins.[172] According to Hiuen-Tsang, *Kiao-shang-mi* (Kauśāmbī) was above 30 *li* in circuit. At the time of his visit all the ten Buddhist monasteries were in utter ruin but the temples which were more than fifty in number were flourishing. The non-Buddhists were very numerous.[173] The city appears to have only partly declined by his time.

Bhītā, not far distant from Kauśāmbī or about 18 miles south of Allahabad, was a fortified town. The scrappy excavations carried out at the site in the past proved the occurrence of NBPW which hints at its antiquity. Its thick brick-walls are seen resting on an earthern rampart. It covers an area of 400 yards square with mound. It was one of the famous commercial towns of the Maurya age. Here in 1887, Cunningham found a coin of the second or third century BC. It was excavated by J. Marshall (*ASIAR*, 1911-12, pp. 29ff). It was in a flourishing state in the Kuṣāṇa period (first and second centuries AD). It gradually began to decline from the fourth century AD onwards.

Pratiṣṭhānapura, situated on the confluence of the Gaṅgā and Yamunā or on the northern bank of the Yamunā near Prayāg, was the capital city of Pururava Aila and his lineage of the Lunar dynasty where they ruled for a long time, as it appears from the epics[174] and the Purāṇas.[175] The city also finds mention in the *Vikramoravaśīyam* (II, 9, 17; IV, 73, 1) of Kālidāsa. It is identical with the immense mound at modern Jhūṅsī near Allahabad. Here some sherds, including NBPW have been found. It must have been a

171. *AIHA*, p. 240.

172. Giles, *op. cit.*, pp. 61-63.

173. *YCTI*, I, pp. 365-66.

174. *Vāl. Rām.*, Uttara Kāṇḍa, 90, 22-23; *Vāl. Rām. Ko.*, p. 184; *Mbh.*, Ādi Parva, 90, 7-9.

175. *Vy.*, 91, 1-8, 18; *Vṣṇ.*, IV, 1, 12, 16; *Bhāg.*, IX, I, 35, 42; IX, 14, 1ff; IX, 15, 1; *Mts.*, 12, 18; *Bmd.*, 3, 60, 21; 3, 65, 45-46; 3, 66, 1-2, 19-22; *PK*, pp. 315 & 331.

very small town. The site has not yet been fully explored from the archaeological point of view. However, it may be considered as one of the urban sites of Madhyadeśa. It continued to flourish till the fourth century AD. Śṛṅgaverapur near Allahabad was a centre of Brāhmaṇical religion. It assumed an urban character in the Kuṣāṇa period.

Ahicchatra and Kāmpilya were two of the famous cities of upper Gaṅgā Valley. Both the cities came into being in pre-Bhārata war period. The former (also called Chatravatī), north of the Gaṅgā, was the capital of north Pañcāla kingdom and the latter, south of the Gaṅgā, was that of south Pañcāla kingdom which included the upper half of the Doāb.[176] The Gaṅgā formed the dividing line between these two cities.

In one of the Purāṇas, we find a graphic description of Ahicchatra as a city inhabited by brāhmaṇas and other people.[177] According to Cunningham, "Its history reaches back to BC 1430, at which time it was the capital of northern Panchala".[178] The local legend attributes its foundation to Rājā Ādi. The grand old fort believed to have been built by him is also called Ādikoṭ. Ptolemy not only refers to the Paurvas ("Porouaroi" or "Porvaroi"), who reigned over the realms between the upper Gaṅgā and Yamunā, but also to the "Passalae" (Pañcālas) of lower Gangetic Doāb and their northern capitals Ādisadra which has been equated with Ahicchatra.[179] It is Adhicchatra of the Pābhosā inscription.[180]

The ruins of Ahicchatra are stiuated about half a mile to the north-east of the village of Rāmnagar and about seven miles to the north of Aonla town in Bareilly district of U.P. Ahicchatra was first visited by Hodgson in 1833. He found the ruins of an ancient fortress several miles in circumference, which had 34 bastions, and was known in the neighbourhood by the name of the "Pāṇḍus Fort". Cunningham in his survey of the site in 1862-63 noticed 32 towers varying in height from 28 to 47 feet. In 1891, he obtained six coins at Rāmnagar which have been assigned to the second or third century BC.[181] A. Führer in the course of minor excavations at the site in 1891-92 and 1893-94 discovered

---

176. *Mbh*., Ādi Parva (5th edn. Gorakhpur, Samvat, 2044), 137, 73-76; *Bh.Sv*., vol. 1, p. 85; Pargiter, *AIHT*, pp. 111-13; *PK*, p. 41; see also Cunnigham, *Co. An. Ind*., p. 79; N.L. Dey, *GDAMI*, pp. 2, 145; Law, "The Pāñcālas and their capital Ahicchatra", *MASI*, no. 67, Delhi, 1942.

177. *Pdm*., Sṛṣṭikhaṇḍa, 34, 38; Pātālakhaṇḍa, 12, 40-41.

178. *CAGI*, p. 303.

179. *AIT*, pp. 131, 133, 161, 368-69 (notes).

180. *Ep. Ind*., vol. II, p. 242; *SI*, vol. 1, p. 97.

181. *Co. An. Ind*., P1. V, 11, 14; Smith. *op. cit*., pp. 146, 155.

the remains of the Hindu and Jain temples, *stūpas*, etc., of the Kuṣāṇa period. The city appears to have been inhabited by the followers of Hinduism, Jainism and Buddhism.

In 1940-44, the Archaeological Survey of India, Delhi, conducted extensive excavations at selected places within the precinct of the fortification at Ahicchatra. Two successive earthern ramparts below a stout-wall of baked brick came to the notice of excavators, and PGW is said to have been found below as well as in the earlier rampart. On the basis of the findings it is conjectured that rampart may be little earlier than 500 BC. It is also presumed that city's brick wall was built sometime betwen 300 BC and 200 BC when it became the capital. As at Hastināpura, coins (square and round) came into use during the NBPW period. The excavators recognised nine main strata in the total life-span of the city[182] which are given below with their respective dates:

| | |
|---|---|
| Stratum IX | Before BC 300 |
| Stratum VIII | BC 300 to 200 |
| Stratum VII | BC 200 to 100 |
| Stratum VI & V | BC 100 to AD 100 |
| Stratum IV | AD 100 to AD 350 |
| Stratum III | AD 350 to AD 750 |
| Stratum II | AD 750 to AD 850 |
| Stratum I | AD 850 to AD 1100 |

The later excavations carried out at Ahicchatra in 1963-65 also brought to light the mud ramparts of PGW period and burnt brick structures of NBPW phase (C-14 date 160 ± 95 or 475 ± 105 BC). The evidence of habitation at the site from the Kuṣāṇa to Gupta period (*c.* AD 100-350) has also been brought to light.[183] The excavations have so far not revealed anything which may enable us to connect the city with Ahicchatra of the *Mahābhārata*. However, the antiquity of the city may be pushed back much earlier to the dates suggested by archaeologists.

Ahicchatra was one of the flourishing cities of northern India in the Maurya, Kuṣāṇa, Gupta and post-Gupta times. It was visited by Hiuen-Tsang. According to him, the capital,

---

182. A. Ghosh and K.C. Panigrahi. "The Pottery of Ahichchhatra", *AI*, no. 1 (1946), pp. 37-40; *AI*, no.8 (1952), p. 34; M. Wheeler, *op. cit.*, pp. 131-32.

183. *IAR*, 1963-64, pp. 44-64; 1964-65, p. 39f; see also *PPIP*, App. II, Table 6, p. 566.

which was in a strong position, was 17 or 18 *li* (or just about three miles) in circuit. There were above 10 Buddhist monasteries, and more than 1000 monks. The Hindu temples were 9 in number, and there were above 300 professed adherents of the Pāśupatas who worshipped Īśvara (Śiva).[184] It retained something of its metropolitan status till about AD 1100. Today, the deserted city looms majestically over the plain with towering ramparts 3½ miles in circuit.

According to Purāṇic evidence, Kāmpilya, one of the five sons of Haryaśva (in Paurava line of Lunar dynasty) founded a city which was so named after him.[185] In the *Rāmāyaṇa* of Vālmīki this city has been referred to as Kāmpilapur.[186] The *Harivaṁśa* also makes a mention of this city.[187] It finds mention in the Buddhist literature[188] and the Jain Purāṇas[189] as the capital ctiy. Modern Kāmpila on the old bank of the Gaṅgā, about 5 miles from Kāimgañj or about 28 miles north-east of Fatehgarh in Farrukhābād district of U.P., still preserves its ancient name, Kāmpilya. The site is said to have been visited by Śrī Rāma Babu who collected the PGW from there.[190] Like Ahicchatra Kāmpliya also represents both PGW and NBPW site. Here the urban settlements continued up to AD 300.

The city of Vārāṇasī (modern Banāras), situated on the left bank of the Gaṅgā between the river Varaṇā or Varaṇāvatī on the north-east and the Asi on the south-west, was the capital of the Kāśī kingdom. It was encompassed by the walls. It was one of the principal cities of the central or mid-Gaṅgā Valley. The said capital city, according to epic and Purāṇic tradition, was founded Divodāsa, one of the celebrated kings of Kāśī, on the northern bank of the Gaṅgā (on the southern side of Gomatī).[191] According to the *Mahābhārata*, the city had the semblance of Amarāvatī of Indra. And it is said to have been populated by the brāhmaṇas, kṣatriyas, vaiśyas and śūdras.[192] The city is described

---

184. *YCTI*, I, p. 331.
185. *Vy.*, 99, 196-99; *Vṣṇ.*, IV, 19, 57-59; *Bhāg.*, IX, 21, 32-35; *Mts.*, 50, 2-4; *Hv.*, 1, 32, 26-29; *PK*, p. 102.
186. Bāla Kāṇḍa, 33, 19; *Vāl. Rām. Ko.*, p. 57.
187. 1, 23, 28.
188. *Jāt.*, III, p. 230; *Bodhisattvāvadāna Kalpalatā*, 66th Pallava, p. 4.
189. *Mahāpurāṇa*, 59, 14; 72, 197; *Pdm.*, 8, 281.
190. *AI*, nos. 10-11, p. 140.
191. *Mbh.*, Anuśāsana Parva, 31, 15-17; *Vy.*, 92, 3-9, 18-28; *Vṣṇ.*, IV, 8, 1-21; *Bmd.*, 3, 67, 1-79; *Bhāg.*, IX, 17, 2-10; *Hv.*, 1, 29, 25-72.
192. Anuśāsana Parva., 31, 16-18.

in several Purāṇas.[193] From both the Purāṇic and *Jātaka* records it appears that the city was known by different names in ancient times.[194] Before the rise of Buddhism it had an extent of twelve leagues or *yojana* (about eighty-five miles).[195] The township actually grew in Buddha's time. Vārāṇasī continued to be the capital of the kingdom of Kāśī during the days of the Buddha. From Buddhist literature (both Pāli and Sanskrit Buddhist texts) it distinctly appears that it was magnificent, extensive, prosperous and populous city at that time.[196] The city is frequently referred to in the *Jātaka* records where it is said to have been over two thousand miles in circuit.[197] Many *Jātaka*s testify to the unsurpassed glory of the city. In one of the Pāli chronicles, Vārāṇasī is included in eight principal capital cities of India.[198] The *Vinaya Mahāvagga* (X, 2, 3) also bears testimony to the former greatness and prosperity of the city which can be corroborated by the evidence furnished in the commentary on the *Vinaya*.[199] There are abundant references to the city in Buddhist sources as a great centre of both internal and external trade and commerce and indigenous industry. It had also a town-hall for the transaction of public business. It flourished as a political, commercial and religious centre. The city is also mentioned in the Jain Purāṇas.[200] Pāṇini also mentions the Kāśī kingdom (IV, 2, 116) and its capital Vārāṇasī in a *gaṇa* (IV, 2, 97). Ptolemy's Kassida has been equated with Kāśī which is also used as a name for Vārāṇasī.[201] His Erarasa, a metropolis, has been identified by Saint-Martin with capital Vārāṇasī,[202] But this identification seems to be of doubtful nature as it has not been supported by other scholars.

In the early fifth century AD, Vārāṇasī was a flourishing city, as stated by Fa-hian.[203] On the basis of an eye-witness account of Hiuen-Tsang it can be further added that in the seventh century AD the capital city on the western side of the Gaṅgā was about 18 *li*

193. *Mts.*, 183, 62; *Bhāg.*, X, 66, 41; *Pdm.*, Uttara. 35, 87.

194. *Vṣṇ.*, V, 34, 14, 21-40; *Bmd.*, 3, 67, 26-62; *Jāt.*, IV, pp. 15, 119-20.

195. *Jāt.*, VI, p. 160.

196. *DN*, II, pp. 220, 235; *AN*, I, p. 213; *Divyāvadāna*, p. 73; *Lalitavistara*, pp. 405-6; *Mahāvastu*, III, p. 402; *Bodhisattvāvadāna Kalpalatā*, 6th Pallava, pp. 31-32; Law, *IETBJ*, p. 42.

197. *Jāt.*, IV, p. 442; V. p. 41.

198. *Mhv. Comm.*, p. 67.

199. *Sāmantapāsādikā*, I, p. 201; also Law, *HPL*, II, p. 406.

200. *Mahāpurāṇa*, 16, 151; 43, 121; 60, 70; *Hv.*, 3, 3; *Pdm.*, 6, 317.

201. *AIT*, p. 228.

202. *Ibid.*, pp. 129, 228.

203. Giles, *op. cit.*, p. 60.

(or 3 miles) in length and from 5 to 6 *li* (or 1 mile) in breadth. The inhabitants were very numerous and had boundless wealth. There were above 30 Buddhist monasteries with more than 3000 monks, and above 100 temples wtih more than 10,000 professed adherents of the sects, the majority being devotees of Śiva. Within the capital there were 20 temples. They had towers of many stories, and magnificent chapels built of stones elaborately carved and of wood richly painted.[204]

The ancient city of Vārāṇasī was situated on the place which is identical with the ruins of the fort of Rājghāṭ. An extensive excavation was carried out at Rājghāṭ first by A.K. Narain (of the Banaras Hindu University) in 1957[205] and then jointly by him and T.N. Roy in 1960-61 which revealed the various phases of settlement at the site. The most notable discovery was that of an enoromous clay rampart dating back to the earliest occupation of the site.[206] The dates assigned to the different periods of occupation at Rājghāṭ are as follows:[207]

| | |
|---|---|
| I a | *c.* 800 BC to 600 BC |
| I b | *c.* 600 BC to 400 BC |
| I c | *c.* 400 BC to 200 BC |
| II | *c.* 200 BC to the beginning of the Christian Era |
| III | From the beginning of the Christian Era to *c.* AD 300 |
| IV | *c.* AD 300 to AD 700 |
| V | AD 700 to AD 1200 |
| VI | AD 1200 to AD 1700 |

The further excavations at Rājghāṭ were carried out in 1962-65.[208] The archaeological evidence shows the earliest occupation of the site early in the first millennium BC. D.L. Eck on the basis of excavations carried out at the site in the mid-1960s also supports the view that the old city wall is datable to the ninth century BC.[209] The C-14 date of NBPW

204. *YCTI*, II, pp. 46-47.
205. *IAR*, 1957-58, p. 86.
206. *Ibid.*, 1960-61, pp. 35-37.
207. *Ibid.*, p. 37.
208. *Ibid.*, 1963-64, p. 16; 1964-65, p. 17.
209. *Banaras: City of Light*, p. 46.

phase is 490 ± 110 BC.[210] Some of the remarkable features of urbanism had become noticeable here by the dawn of the sixth century BC. The city was in the flourishing state in the Kuṣāṇa period. By AD 300 it reached the zenith of progress. The uppermost phase of settlement at the site could be dated to the seventeenth century AD.

Kānyakubja, a famous city in the Gangetic Doāb of Purāṇic antiquity situated to the south-east of Sankāsya, also deserves our notice. According to Purāṇic evidence, it was a capital of the kingdom founded by Amāvasu, the son of Purūravas (the progenitor of the Lunar dynasty).[211] It is identical with modern Kanauj in Farrukhābād district of U.P. It has been identified with *Kalinipaxa* of the Greek writers.[212] Ptolemy has also mentioned it. Fa-hian visited it in AD 400[213] and Hiuen-Tsang in AD 636. The latter describes the *Ka-no-ku-she* (Kānyakubja) kingdom as being above 4000 *li* (or 667 miles) in circuit. The capital, which had the Gaṅgā on its west side, was above 20 *li* (or 3½ miles) in length and 4 or 5 *li* (or ¾ of a mile) in breadth. It was surrounded by strong walls and deep ditches. It was very strongly defended and had lofty structures everywhere. The inhabitants were well off and there were families with great wealth. There were above 100 Buddhist monasteries with more than 10,000 monks and more than 200 temples. The non-Buddhists were several thousands in number.[214] At the time of Hiuen-Tsang's visit, Kanauj was the capital of Harṣa, the most powerful sovereign in northern India. The existing remains of the great city of Kanauj, which for many centuries was the Hindu capital of northern India, are few and in important. "According to tradition, the ancient city contained 84 wards or Mohalas, of which 25 are still existing within the lilmits of the present town."[215]

Mathurā on the Yamunā was the capital of the Śūrasena kingdom. According to epic and Purāṇic tradition, it was originally founded by Madhu, king of the *daitya*s, and named Madhupura of Madhurā after him. Śatrughna, one of the four sons of Daśaratha, after having defeated and killed Lavaṇa, the son of Madhu, conquered it and made it his own capital. He took twelve years to make it a beautiful and prosperous city. That is why, he is generally described in the texts concerned to have been the builder of the

210. Ghosh, *op. cit.*, pp. 60-72.

211. *Vy.*, 91, 51-96, 103; *Br.*, 10, 13-60, 68, *Bmd.*, 3, 66, 22-68, 75; *Vṣṇ.*, IV, 7, 2-17, *Bhāg.*, IX, 15, 3-16, 36.

212. Lassen, *Ind. Alt*, 2nd edn, I, p. 760; Saint Martin, *Étude*, pp. 271-78.

213. Giles, *op. cit.*, p. 29.

214. *YCTI*, I, p. 340.

215. *CAGI*, p. 321.

city. It was well-organised and well-planned city. It was adorned with magnificent houses, markets, crossroads an broad streets. It was also famous as a centre of trade and commerce. It was inhabited by the people of all the four *varṇas*.[216] The ancient literary tradition is supported by Thomas Watters,[217] J.W. McCrindle[218] and B.C. Law.[219] The holy citiy of Mathurā is one of the most ancient places in India. In the age of the *Mahābhārata*, it was under the rule of the Yādavas of the Śūrasena. In the time of Śrī Kṛṣṇa it developed as a temple town. The old city is generally identified with Maholi, five miles to the south-west of the present town of Mathurā in U.P.[220]

Mathurā as the capital of the Śūrasenas was known to Pāṇini (*Aṣṭādhyāyī*, IV, 2, 82), Patañjali (*Mahābhāṣya*, 1, 1, 2; 1, 3, 1; 2, 4, 1) and Kālidāsa (*Raghuvaṁśa*, VI, 48; XV, 28, 36). From one of the canonical Pāli texts it appears that the city prospered during the days of the Buddha.[221] In the *Milindapañho*, an extra canonical Pāli work,[222] it is described as one of the three chief cities of India. In one of the Buddhist Sanskrit texts, it is described as rich, flourishing and populous city.[223] According to Jain texts, it was one of the ten capital cities of India. The city prominently figures in the Jain Purāṇas.[224]

The city of Mathurā developed not only as a religious centre of the Hindus, the Buddhists and the Jains but also as a centre of artistic excellence. The city also attracted the notice of classical writers. Megasthenes mentions Methora (Mathurā) and Carisobora also called Cleisobora ("Kṛṣṇapura", identified with Vṛndāvana, about 6 miles to the north of Mathurā) as two of the important cities of hoary antiquity.[225] Arrian, on the

216. *Vāl. Rām.*, Uttarakāṇḍa, 70, 5-14; *Vāl. Rām. Ko.*, p. 219; *Vy.*, 88, 184-87; *Vṣṇ.*, IV, 4, 100-1, 104; *Bmd.*, 3, 63, 186; 4, 10, 19; *Bhāg.*, IX, 11, 14; *PK*, p. 393.

217. *YCTI*, I, p. 301.

218. *AIT*, pp. 129, 367, note.

219. *GEB*, p. 20, note 1; see also his "Mathura in Ancient India", *JRASB* (L), vol. XIII, No.1 (1947), pp. 21-30.

220. Law, *Geographical Essays*, p. 26.

221. *AN*, II, p. 57.

222. Ed. V. Trenckner, p. 331.

223. *Lalitavistara*, p. 21.

224. *Mahāpurāṇa*, 57, 79; 70, 331; *Pdm.*, 1, 95; *Hv.*, 33, 25.

225. J.W. McCrindle, *AIMA*, 1st edn., p. 139 and note; also R.C. Majumdar, *CAI*, pp. 342-43; E. J. Rapson (ed.), *CHI*, I, *Ancient India*, p. 367; D.C. Sircar, *SGAMI*, p. 109.

authority of Megasthenes, explicitly states that these two large cities belonged to the Sourasenoi (Śūrasenas).[226] Pliny also makes a mention of these two towns.[227] Vṛndāvana on the left bank of the Yamunā is also included in the list of towns and cities furnished by Kālidāsa (*Raghuvaṁśa*, VI, 50). Ptolemy mentions Mathurā under the form of Modoura and calls it as "the city of gods" or one of the most sacred cities of India.[228]

In the course of excavation carried out at Mathurā by joint effort of Shri M. Venkataramayya and Shri Ballabhsaran in 1954-55, mud-rampart citadel was discovered. The PGW was also obtained. The Ware also lay strewn over the top of the mounds around the town. The urban settlement at the site in the latter half of the first millennium BC is proven by the occurrence of NBPW and the presence of structures of this very phase. Mathurā is one of those urban sites which represent both PGW and NBPW phase of culture.[229] In fact, it was the NBPW period which witnessed the growth of this urban centre.

The Śūrasena kingdom with its capital at Mathurā was possibly included in the Mayura empire. It was governed by native princes whose names are known from their coins of the second century BC. But later the capital came under that sway of the Bactrian Greeks, the Śaka Satraps and Kuṣāṇas. Coins, inscriptions and archaeological remains show that Madhurā became one of the important urban centre in the first century AD which is attested by archaeological discovery of brick structures, roofing tiles, fortifications, etc., in the course of further excavations carried out at the site in 1970s.[230] The old city is said to have "extended from the Nabi Masjid and Fort of Raja Kansa on the north to the mounds called Tila Kans . . . on the south. . . . The city is surrounded by numbers of high mounds; several of which are no doubt old brick kilns; but many of them are the remains of extensive buildings, which having been dug over for ages in search of bricks, are now mere heaps of brick dust and broken brick. . . . But this unpromising-looking mound has since yielded numbers of statutes and inscribed pillars, which prove that it is the remains of at least two large Buddhist monasteries of as early

---

226. *Indica*, Ch. VIII, *AIMA*, p. 201; also *AIT*, p. 98.

227. *Nat. Hist.*, VI, 19.

228. *AIT*, p. 129.

229. *IAR*, 1954-55, p. 15; *AI*, Nos. 10-11 (1954-55), p. 140; see also *ABORI*, LVIII-LIX (1977-78), pp. 882-83.

230. *IAR*, 1973-74, pp. 31-32; 1974-75, pp. 48-50; 1975-76, pp. 53-55; 1976-77, pp. 54-56.

a date as the beginning of the Christian era".[231] In the third and early fourth century AD Mathurā was the capital of the rulers of the Nāga dynasty.

Fa-hian in the course of his visit to Mathurā found 26 monasteries with about 3000 monks.[232] In the seventh century, the famous city of *Mo-t'u-lo* (Mathurā) was the capital of a large kingdom which is said to have been 5000 *li* (or 833 miles) in circuit. The capital city, according to Hiuen-Tsang, was above 20 *li* (or 3½ miles) in circuit (which agrees with its size at the present day). There were above twenty Buddhist monasteries and above 2000 monks. There were also five Brāhmaṇical temples and the professed adherents of the different non-Buddhist sects.[233]

Soṅkh, at a little distance from Mathurā, was excavated relatively at larger scale by a team of archaeologists form Berlin University led by Prof. Haertel. The excavations have so far revealed total 37 layers of habitation. The house walls excavated prove that there was probably uninterrupted habitation down to level 27 or 32. The two blocks of large houses seem to have been constructed separated by either a broad street or narrow bylanes. The Kuṣāṇa houses were constructed one on top of the other. There were as many as seven levels of the Kuṣāṇa phase and only one of the Gupta phase. Terracottas, seals, coins, and other objects of the Maurya, Śuṅga and Kuṣāṇa periods have been unearthed here. The monumental buildings and some temple complexes (which are two of the essential criterias for urbanisation) have also been brought to light. It was basically a religious place. At a short distance from the mound and apsidal temple has been unearthed which dates back to the first century BC. It has been conclusively proved that worship of Nāga Deva flourished here at the time of Kaniṣka in the first century AD. Nāga motifs appear on temple railings, pillars and *toraṇas*. It is interesting that a little modern Nāga shrine stands nearby. Soṅkh had no doubt come into existence in the age of the Mauryas but, in fact, flourished as a urban centre in the Kuṣāṇa period (first-second centuries AD). It continued to flourish till the early phase of the Gupta rule. Thereafter it began to decline and was completely deserted in post-Gupta times.

Atrañjikhera in the western Gaṇgā Valley was one of the important urban centres. It was situated on the right bank of Kālinadī, about 10 km north of Aligarh. It was a commercial town. It was excavated by R.C. Gaur of Aligarh University in 1960s. In the

---

231. *CAGI*, p. 315.
232. Giles, *op. cit.*, pp. 20-21; Legge, *op. cit.*, p. 42; *YCTI*, I, p. 301.
233. *YCTI*, 1. p. 301; see also *BRWW*, I, p. 179.

course of excavations, OCP, Black and Red Ware (BRW *c.* 1200 BC) and PGW (C-14 dates upper 1025 ± 110 BC or 890 BC and lower 535 ± 100 BC) were successively found at the site which show different phases of settlement and sequence of cultures.[234] The increase in the size of settlement, enlarged poulation and widespread use of iron during the NBPW period (C-14 date 260 ± 105 BC) led to its growth as a town. It continued to flourish till about AD 300. It was in a state of decadency in Gupta and post-Gupta times.

Ālamgīrpur in the Yamunā basin, 19 miles west of Meerut or 30 miles away from Delhi, was a small town. The cursory digging at the site in 1958 revealed the occurrence of both PGW and NBPW. Some material discovered here bear unmistakable influence of Harappan culture.[235] Mason in Ghazipur in eastern U.P. and Sohagaura in the district of Gorakhpur were prosperous towns of Kuṣāṇa times. They probably declined in the Gupta period.

Allāhapur in Badāun district of U.P. was excavated in 1969-70. It was one of the towns of Doāb region. The two important phases of settlement at this site, according to C-14 dates, were between 820 and 225 BC and between 225 and 110 BC.

The urban settlement at Khairaḍīh in Baliā district of U.P. started around *c.* 800 BC. It was a commercial centre. The horizontal excavation carried out at the site in 1981-82 showed that it was a flourishing town in the Kuṣāṇa period. The positive sign of urbanism here in the first three centuries of the Christian era has also been found.[236] It started decaying from the fourth century AD onwards.

Jakhera, situated on the left bank of the Kālinadī about 8 km to the north-west of modern town Kāsgañj in Eṭāh district of U.P., was one of the earliest urban centres of the Gaṅgā Valley. The excavation carried out at the site by M.D.N. Sahi in 1970s and late 1980s have revealed the following sequence:[237]

Period I — Characterised by the occurrence of OCP in a small number.

---

234. *IAR*, 1960-61, p. 35; 1968-69, p. 37; see also B.P. Sinha (ed.), *Potteries in Ancient India*, pp. 95-100, 185-6.

235. *IAR*, 1958-59, pp. 50-54.

236. *Ibid.*, 1981-82, p. 69.

237. For details see *IAR*, 1971-72, p. 42; Sahi, "New Light on the Life of the Painted Grey Ware People as revealed from the Excavations at Jakhera", *Man and Environment*, vol. II (1978), pp. 101-5; "Excavations at Jakhera — 1985-87 : An Interim Report", in N.C. Ghosh and S. Chakrabarti (eds.), *Adaptation and other Essays* (Visvabharati, Santiniketan, 1990), pp. 217-22.

| | |
|---|---|
| Period II | Characterised by the unpainted BRW. |
| Period IIIA | Proto-PGW phase marked by the introduction of iron. |
| Period IIIB | Mature PGW phase. Jakhera during PGW period no longer represented a rural settlement rather it had grown into a township |

The ancient towns and cities of Rajasthan are also worth mentioning here. Noha developed as an urban centre during the first half of the first millennium BC and continued to flourish till the end of the second century AD. It was a centre of trade and commerce. In course of a scrappy excavation at the site in 1963-64 BRW was found with PGW.[238] Virāṭ, Virāṭanagara or Virāṭapura, the ancient capital of the Matsya kingdom, was a very large city. It finds mention in the Virāṭa Parva (1, 14; 5, 6-7) of the *Mahābhārata.* It is identical with the present town of Bairāt (or Bairath), about 41 miles to the north of Jaipur. It has had a glorious past. Archaeologically, the site is associated with PGW and NBPW phase of cultures. It was a flourishing city during the Maurya and the Kuṣāṇa period. Among the important archaeological discoveries of this place are the remains of a circular brick temple ascribed to the third century BC and a large Buddhist monastery and some coins of Indo-Greek origin. It was an important centre of Brāhmaṇical as well as Buddhist religion and culture. The earliest historical notice of this place is that of the Chinese pilgrim Hiuen-Tsang in AD 634. According to him, the capital was 14 *li* (or just 2½ miles) in circuit, which corresponds almost exactly with the size of the ancient mound on which the present town is built. There were eight Buddhist monasteries but they were much ruined, and the monks were very few in number. The brāhmaṇas of different sects, about 1000 in number possessed about 12 temples. The city continued to flourish till its destruction by Mahmud of Ghazni sometime between 1009 and 1014.[239]

Mandor, the ancient capital of Marwar dating back to the fourth century AD, was another great city in Rajasthan. It was occupied successively by the Mauryas, Kuṣāṇas, Guptas, Hūṇas and Parihāras.

Architectural finds, temples and stone pillars, some with inscriptions, sculptures and terracottas discovered a several important sites have helped historians filling the gaps in history or urbanisation. Among these mention may be made of the remains of

---

238. *IAR*, 1963-64, p. 29f.

239. *YCTI*, 1, p. 300; *CAGI*, pp. 288-89.

brick structures dating from the beginning of the Christian era found at Rairh and Nagar (in Ṭoṅk district), Sambhar (in Jaipur district) and Bhīnmal (in Jālore district). Somewhat later, temples of the Gupta period have been located at Nāgrī (in Cittor district) and Mandor (in Jodhpur district). However, we do not know anything about the system of their town-planning.

A.C. Carlleyle, a distinguished archaeologist, discovered sometime between 1871 and 1873 the remains of an ancient town of Karkoṭanagara covering an area of four square miles at a distance of about twenty-five miles from Ṭoṅk. According to him, it was of high antiquity. He also discovered the remains of old temples, buildings of huge bricks and a large number coins ranging from 250 BC to AD 350.[240] These discoveries fairly attest to emergence of an urban complex in and around Karkoṭanagara about the middle of the third century BC which continued to flourish till about the middle of the fourth century AD.

Sanghol in Punjab was a spectacular town in ancient times with its well-planned fortresses and monasteries, its impressive gates and palaces, urban community, etc. Its history goes back to nearly 3700 years. It is situated in tehsil Samarālā of district Ludhiana. It is about 40 km west of Chandigarh or 32 km from Ropar which lies on the left bank of the Sutlej. The excavations at the site revealed six different phases of settlement extending from the late Harappan period (*c.* 1700 BC) to the Gupta age. The late Harappan dwellers of Sanghol lived in beautiful and artistically furnished and decorated houses. The painted pottery, copper chisels and bells bangles and ear-rings and necklaces discovered from the site belong to this period. Sanghol was a flourishing town in the age of the Buddha. It again rose to prominence during the Kuṣāṇa and early Gupta period when the settlement not only sprawled over the entire expanse of the present mound but also extended over the neighbouring areas. The coins, bangles, ivory combs, beads, a pentagonal fort with massive ramparts and corner towers, Buddhist statues and standing figure of a Jain *tīrthaṅkara* unearthed in the course of excavation belong to this age. The defence complex is unique in character. The archaeological findings leave no room for doubt about the urban life of the people of Sanghol during the period concerned. The town was perhaps destroyed in the course of the Hūṇa's invasions in the late fifth century AD or early sixth century AD. In the seventh century AD it was in utter ruins. It was probably the *She-to-lulu* of Hiuen-Tsang.

---

240. V.A. Smith, *Co. An. Ind.*, pp. 161-63; *CASR*, XIV, p. 150; Rapson, *JRAS*, 1897, p. 643.

Rājagṛha or Girivraja, the capital of the Kekays in western Punjab, has been described in the *Rāmāyaṇa* of Vālmīki as a populous and wealthy city.[241] It has been identified by Cunningham with ancient Girjak or modern Jalālpur on the river Jhelum in the province of the Punjab in west Pakistan.[242] This identification has been supported by H.C. Raychaudhuri[243] and B.C. Law.[244] The evidence of the *Rāmāyaṇa* that the capital city of the Kekayas lay beyond the river Sudāmā[245] may also be corroborated by the statement of the Greek writer, Arrian, that the river Saranges (Sudāmā) also flowed through the territory of the Kekians.[246] The ruins of the old city was traced by Cunningham. The ruins consist of two large mounds just half a mile apart, with two smaller mounds about midway between them. The city appears to have covered an area of about one mile in length by half a mile in breadth.

Rājapura, the metropolis of the Kāmboja kingdom, may also be mentioned here. It earliset mention may be found in the Droṇa Parva (4,4). It was situated to the north-west of the Indus. It was very much in existence in the epic age but developed as an urban complex in the sixth century BC. It was the centre of both Brāhmaṇism and Buddhism. It continued to flourish till the seventh century AD.

It is very difficult to say as to what extent the Harappan civilization, which was distinctively urban in character, had spread into the valley of the Gaṅgā. The revival of urban tradition of the Indus Valley in the Gaṅgā Valley has been much discussed by some scholars but without drawing any plausible conclusion. Their views need to be critically examined. Mortimer Wheeler's view about impact of the Indus tradition on Gangetic urbanisation on the basis of colonisation of the Gaṅgā basin by refugees and displaced persons from the Punjab and Sindh in the north-west during the time of the break-up of the Harappā empire[247] cannot be totally accepted for certain valid reasons.

---

241. Ayodhyā Kāṇḍa, 67, 7: 68, 21-22; 70, 26.
242. *CASR*, II, p. 14; See also *JASB*, 1895, pp. 250ff; A.K. Chatterjee, "The Kekayas in Ancient India", *JIH*, vol. LVI, pt. II (1978), pp. 197-202.
243. *PHAI*, 6th edn., p. 63.
244. *HGAI*, p. 98.
245. Āyodhyā Kāṇḍa, 71, 1.
246. *Indika*, IV; see also *Ind. Ant.*, V, p. 332.
247. *Op. cit.*, p.125.

Such view seems to be highly speculative. Bridget and Raymond Allchin,[248] S.C. Malik[249] and W.A. Fairservis[250] have also propounded the theory relating to the survival, resurgence and continuity of urban tradition of the Indus basin in the Gaṅgā-Yamunā Doāb. Their theory is based on the arguments that some urban sites in the Gangetic Valley like Hastināpura Ahicchatra and Atrañjikhera are associated with OCP phase of late Harappan age, and some objccts discovered from there are of Harappan origin. They have tried to establish that there was movement of urbanisation from the west to the east in north India.The rampart of Kauśāmbī having similarity with Harappan citadel and pattern of settlement at Ālamgīrpur of the late Harappan period, of course, show some unmistakable evidence of influence of Harappan urban tradition on them but it does not necessarily mean that all the sites in the Gangetic basin came under the impact of the urban culture of the Indus Valley. D.P. Mishra was also led to believe that the authors of the Harappan civilization moved into the Gaṅgā-Yamunā mid-region. He also held that we may continue to believe that the urbanisation of the Gangetic Plains "must have followed the founding of Harappa and Mohenjodaro".[251] It is very difficult to accord our assent to the theory concerned. The poeople of the Gaṅgā Valley were not ignorant of urban life. The Gangetic urbanisation can claim its indigenous origin because of certain considerable reasons. Firstly, there was long gap between the fall of Harappan urban culture and the evolution of urban culture in the Gangetic Valley. Secondly, the urnab pattern and structural designs of both the centres of urban culture were not exactly the same. In fact, both the Indus and the Gaṅgā Valley represent two different urban traditions. A. Ghosh has also admitted that there was no perceptible link between the two.[252] The impact of the urban culture of the Indus can be admitted only on the early phase of urbanisation in the Gangetic Doāb and the Punjab and Rajasthan because of their geographical proximity. The great bulk of Indian population far advanced in civilization for ages lived in large and splendid towns and cities of the Gaṅgā Valley in northern part of India, played significant role in urban movement and attained high degree of perfection and excellence in most of the arts of common life.

---

248. *The Birth of Indian Civilization — India and Pakistan before 500 BC*, pp. 179-206.
249. *Indian Civilization: The Formative Period*, pp. 12-13, 105-9, 144-54.
250. *The Roots of Ancient India*, p. 379.
251. *Studies in the Proto-History of India*, p. 92.
252. *Op. cit.*, pp. 80. 85.

The towns and cities of north-west India, including Takṣaśilā and Puṣkalāvatī, have been described in a separate chapter included in this volume.

## Eastern India

There were some small towns and large cities in eastern India. One of the most important cities of the mid-Gaṅgā Valley was Rājagṛha (Pāli Rājagaha = Prākṛt Rāyagiha = mod. Rājagīr in south Bihar). It was the earliest capital of the kingdom of Magadha. It had many names in the course of its long history. The oldest name was Girivraja. It was a well fortified city being protected by five hills.[253] Because of being a hill fortress it was popularly known as Girivraja or Giribbaja. The city was named Vasumatī after its founder, the king Vasu, as recorded in the *Rāmāyaṇa* of Vālmīki.[254] In the age of the *Mahābhārata* it was called Bārhadrathapura (after the most famous king Bṛhadratha)[255] as well as Māgadhapura.[256] The latter is described in one of the Sanskrit Buddhist texts as a *mahānagara* or great city.[257] It was also named Kuśāgrapura after the king Kuśāgra, one of the successors of Bṛhadratha.[258] It is *Kiu-she-kie-la-po-lo* of Hiuen-Tsang which, according to him, was an old capital of Magadha. In olden times many rulers and kings lived in it. The high hills surrounding it on every side formed its outer walls or external ramparts. "Within it was another little town the foundation walls being about 30 *li* round (or 5 miles in circuit)".[259] We are further told by him that king "Bimbisāra (*c*. 543-491 BC) had his capital at Kuśāgrapura which was constantly afflicted by disastrous fires. When a fire broke out in the palace he made his heir king and went to live in the cemetery. Hearing this the king of Vaiśālī proceeded to invade Magadha, whereupon the new capital city was built" at the foot of the hills, and all the inhabitants of Kuśāgrapura were shifted to it. The new city because of being the abode of the king or royal palace

---

253. Sabhā Parva, 19, 2-3.

254. Bāla Kāṇḍa, 32, 7-9; *Vāl. Rām. Ko.*, p. 103; see also *Étude*, pp. 108-11.

255. Sabhā Parva, 17, 4; 22, 44; *Mbh. Ko.*, p. 503.

256. *Ibid.*, 18, 30. The City has been mentioned as Magahapura in Jain canon (*Āvasyaka Cūrṇi*, p. 459) as well as in non-canonical text (*Vasudevahiṇḍi*, 2, 16; 16, 4; 20, 5; 54,10).

257. *Lalitavistara*, pp. 239, 243, 246.

258. Law, "Rājagṛha in Ancient Literature", *MASI*, no. 58 (Delhi, 1938) p. 1f; see also Jain *Padma Purāṇa*, 2, 32.

259. S. Beal (tr.), *The Life of Hiuen-Tsiang* by S. Hwui Li and *Yen Tsung*, p. 113; see also *YCTI* II, p. 148.

came to be called Rājagr̥ha.[260] Its another name was Bimbisārapurī by which the Buddhist writers designated the city.[261]

Both Fa-hian[262] and Hiuen-Tsang[263] have distinguished the old Rājagr̥ha city called Kuśāgrapura from the new city of Rājagr̥ha, which, according to the former, was built by Bimbisāra's son Ajātaśatru (*c.* 491-459 BC) who made it his capital. It continued to be the capital of his immediate successor, Udāyin, for another three or four years. It is said that "The old city called Rājagr̥iha is represented as a very ancient one, the third in the history of the world. That New Rājagr̥iha was the work of Bimbisara or his son and successor seems to agree with some of the Buddhist scripture".[264] Sir John Marshall in the course of his archaeological exploration in 1905-6 saw the ruins of the city at the village of Rājagīr.[226] He observes: "The mighty ruins of the older city of Kuśāgrapura, the capital and centre of the great Magadha kingdom, go back to an antiquity of which no other monuments are left to us in India".[266]

The city of Rājagr̥ha had a massive cyclopean wall, about 40 km in circuit, inner fortifications and a gate. The stone walls of Giribbaja are the specimens of the oldest extant stone buildings in India. It was Ajātaśatru who began fortification of the ctiy. It is said that the city had a fort which was once repaired by his chief minister, Vassakāra.[267] The fortifications of both Giribbaja and Rājagaha are still extant 4½ and 3 miles in circumference respectively. The remains of the walls can still be seen.

The Buddhist literature abounds in valuable information about the glory of the ancient city of Rājagaha. It was at the height of its prosperity during and immediately after the Buddha's time. According to commentatorial tradition of the Buddhist, it is

---

260. *YCTI*, II, p. 162.
261. Law, *The Life and Works of Buddhaghosa*, p. 87, note cf. *GEB*, p. 9.
262. Legge, *op. cit.*, pp. 81-82; Giles, *op. cit.*, p. 49.
263. *YCTI*, II, pp. 148, 162; Beal, *op. cit.*, p. 113; *BRWW*, II, pp. 149-50.
264. Cf. *YCTI*, II, p. 162.
265. *ASIAR*, 1905-6, pp. 86ff.
266. *Ibid.*, p. 58.
267. *Vinaya Piṭaka* III, p. 41f cf. *HPL*, II, pp. 648-49.

believed that the city was originally laid out by Mahāgovinda, the famous architect.[268] It is placed at a distance of "five leagues (about 35 miles) from the Ganges".[269] As a matter of fact, it was situated south of the Gaṅgā at a distance of "one league (or *yojana*, i.e., about 7 miles) from Nālandā". In one of the Sanskrit Buddhist texts it is mentioned that it was rich, prosperous ad populous capital city at the time of Bimbisāra and Ajātaśatru.[270] It was an important centre of inland trade where merchants flocked from different parts of the country to buy and sell their merchandise.[271] We learn from the Pāli canon that at the time of the Buddha it was one of the big cities of India.[272] It figures in the list of all imortant towns given in one of the Pāli chronicles.[273] Buddhaghoṣa, the celebrated commentator of the fifth century AD, also mentions Rājagaha as a city the inner and outer areas of which contained a large number of people. It had thirty-two gates and sixty-four posterns.[274] According to one of the biographical works, "The city was adorned with beautiful palaces, well-guarded, decorated with mountains, supported and hallowed by sacred places and distinguished by the five hills."[275]

The noted Jain scholar, Jinaprabhasūri, informs us that Rājagṛha city contained 36,000 splendid houses of merchants half of which belonged to the Buddhists while the other half belonged to the Jains. It was centre of trade. It was a the capital of kings and princes, including Jarāsandha, Śreṇika (Bimbisāra) Kuṇika (Ajātaśatru) and their successors.[276] Some of the Jain texts describe the city rich, happy and thriving. The three principal schools of religion, Hinduism, Jainism and Buddhism, thrived here.

Rājagṛha because of being religious, administrative and commercial centre speedily grew up into a city. It must have lost its glory with the removal of the capital to Pāṭaliputra by Udāyin in the fifth century BC.

---

268. *Sumaṅgalavilāsinī* (commentary on the *Dīghanikāya* by Buddhaghoṣa), ed. Rhys Davids, I, p. 132; *Vimānavatthu Comm.* (by Dhammapāla), p. 82; *Sutta-Nipāta Comm.*, p. 413.
269. *Dhammapada Comm.*, III, p. 439f.
270. *Divyāvadāna*, p. 545.
271. *Ibid.*, p. 307.
272. *DN*, II, pp. 146-47.
273. *Mhv.*, p. 125; *Mhv. Comm.*, pp. 128-29, 54-56.
274. Spence Hardy, *Manual of Buddhism*, p. 323 cf. Law, *The Magadhas in Ancient India*, p. 29.
275. *Buddhacarita Kāvya*, Bk. X, verse 2 cf. *Geographical Essays* p. 15.
276. *Vividhatīrthakalpa* (Bombay, 1934), p. 22.

The archaeological excavations at Rājagīr carried out by A.C. Banerjee in 1950s have unearthed the remains of earthen rampart, brick and stone structures, inner and outer fortifications, etc., (of both old and new city).[277] A. Ghosh in the course of excavations at the site discovered besides other things a rubble wall, the remains of burnt brick structures, few black sherds with rich iron ore deposites of NBPW phase (carbon date 265 ± 105 BC), Buddhist monasteries and *stūpas*, monumental buildings, etc.[278] The archaeological finds have also revealed that there were different phases of urban settlement at the site between the first century BC and first century AD.

The process of decline of Rājagṛha city began in the later phase of the Kuṣāṇa rule which continued in Gupta and post-Gupta times. At the time of Fa-hian's visit it was a deserted city. He says: "inside the city all was emptiness and desolation and no man dwelt in it. The old city, according to him, was 5 or 6 *li* from east to west and 7 or 8 *li* from north to south (i.e., 24 to 28 *li* = 4$^{1}/_{3}$ miles). And the new city was 4 *li* (or two-thirds of a mile) to the north of the old one"[279] which agrees exactly with the position of the ruined fortress now called Rājagīr. Hiuen-Tsang also visited the place. According to him, the foundation of the inner wall of the old city was 30 *li* (or 5 miles) in circuit. The outer wall of the new Rājagṛha city was "utterly destroyed". But "the foundation of the inner wall stood out prominently and were above 20 *li* (or 3½ miles) in circuit with one gate".[280]

Another important city in the middle Gaṅgā Valley was Pāṭaliputra (identical with modern Patna), the later or second capital of the Magadha kingdom. The Buddhist tradition ascribes the foundation of the city to Ajātaśatru. It is said that he employed two of his ministers, Sunidha and Vassakāra, to fortify the village of Pāṭali called Pāṭaligāma on the confluence of the Gaṅgā and Sone to repel the attacks of the Vajjis (Licchavis of Vaiśālī).[281] It had its own strategic importance. This marked the beginning of the process of urbanisation there. The said fort was constructed exactly eight years before the *nirvāṇa* of the Buddha or in 491 BC (the year in which Ajātaśatru was crowned

---

277. *IAR*, 1953-54, p. 9; 1954-55, p. 16; 1957-58, p. 11; also 1969-70, pp. 40-44.

278. *Op. cit.*, pp. 60-72; "Rajgir-1950", *AI*, no. 7, pp. 66ff; see also M. Wheeler, *op.cit.*, pp. 30f, 173, P1. 47; J. Marshall, "Rajagriha and its Remains", *ASIAR*, 1905-6, pp. 86ff.

279. Legge, *op. cit.*, pp. 81, 2; Giles, *op. cit.*, p. 49.

280. *YCTI*, II, pp. 148, 162; *BRWW*, II, pp. 149-50; S. Beal, *op. cit.*, p. 113.

281. *DN*, II, pp. 86-87; *Mahāparinibbāna Suttaṁ*, ed. with Hindi tr. by S.G. Prajñānanda (Lucknow, 1981), vv. 37-39, pp. 33-35; *Sumaṅgalavilāsinī*, II, pp. 516-17, 540; *HPL*, II, pp. 648, 650, 654; *DPPN*, II, p. 178; Rāhula Sāṅkṛtyāyana, *Pāli Sāhitya kā Itihāsa* (Lucknow, 1973), p. 39.

as a king). This is attested by the fact that the Buddha on his way from Rājagṛha to Vaiśalī *en route* Pāṭaliputra saw with is own eyes the fortification work in progress. Pāṭaligāma gradually developed into a township which later became popularly known as Pāṭaliputra. This is one of the glaring example of transition from ruralism to urbanism. It was Udaya, Udāyin or Udāyibhadra (*c.* 459-443 BC), the son and successor of Ajātaśatru, who transferred the capital from old Rājagṛha to Pāṭaliputra twenty-eight years after the Buddha's demise or in the fourth year of his reign and founded the city of Kusumapura (called because of abundance of Kusuma flowers that grew in the royal enclosures) on the south bank of the Gaṅgā (in the immediate neighbourhood of the fortress at the village of Pāṭali) and made it his new capital and continued to rule there till about 443 BC which can be established on the combined testimony of three traditions, Purāṇic,[282] Jain[283] and Buddhist.[284] This is the reason why he is also described as the founder of the city. If Buddhist chronology is to be relied upon, the said transfer of capital and the founding of a new city of Kusumapura took place in AD 455. There is positive evidence to show that the orignial name of the city was Kusumapura which was later changed to Pāṭaliputra.[285]

The two most famous names of Pāṭaliputra city in ancient times were Kusumapura and Puṣpapura (city of flowers). The former is mentioned by Viśākhadatta (sixth century AD) with rampart and city gates[286] and in Pāli chronicles[287] of the fifth century AD and Jain Purāṇas[288] and the latter by Kālidāsa[289] and Daṇḍin (*c.* AD 500-650), who speaks of it as the foremost of all the cities (in the middle Gangetic basin).[290] The *Mahāvastu* refers to it as Puṣpāvatī[291] which is probably identical with Puṣpapura. The *Garga Saṁhitā*

---

282. *Vy.*, 99, 319-20; *Mts.*, 272, 8-11; *Hv.*, 32, 61; *Bmd.*, 3, 74, 132; *PK*, pp. 59-60, 122; F.E. Pargiter, *PTDKA*, pp. 67-69.

283. *Pariśiṣṭaparvan* of Hemacandra, ed. by H. Jacobi, p. 42; J.C. Jain, *LAIJC*, p. 472; also *Ind. Alt.*, II, p. 63.

284. *Sāmantapāsādikā*, pp. 72-73; see also *AIIC*, p. 29.

285. *YCTI*, II, p. 87.

286. *Mudrārākṣasa*, ed. with *Śaśikalā* Sanskrit & Hindi commentaries by S.V. Singh, II, 13, pp. 89-90.

287. *Mhv.*, IV, 31; *DIP*, XI, 28; see also *CII*, III, p. 1.

288. *Mahāpurāṇa*, 6, 127; 76, 398; *Hv.*, 60, 240; see also *As. Res.*, IX (Delhi, 1979), p. 43.

289. *Raghuvaṁśa*, VI, 24; also Banerji, *Kālidāsa Kośa*, p. 30.

290. *Daśakumāracarita*, ed. with Eng. tr. by M.R. Kale, I, 2.

291. III, p. 231.

(composed sometime after *c.* 144 BC) but not later than the first century BC) mentions both Kusumapura and Puṣpapura for Pāṭaliputra.[292]

The tradition recorded in the Sanskrit Buddhist text shows that Pāṭaliputra was a great city at the time of the Buddha.[293] It was prosperous and populous. It is also described as an emporium of trade and commerce.[294] This city, though the least ancient of all the greater capitals in Gangetic India, was destined to become the most famous of them all.

It is striking to note that Pāṭaliputra "was a vast metropolis with two divisions which the *Kāśikā* (a commentary on Pāṇini's *Aṣṭādhyāyī*) records as Pūrva-Pāṭaliputra (eastern, on the Ganges) and Apara-Pāṭaliputra (western, on the Sone, VII, 3, 14)"[295] Patañjali also speaks of the grandeur of the city.[296]

Pāṭaliputra as a capital city has long history of its own. It flourished as an imperial capital of the Mauryas. During the reign of great Maurya emperor Candragupta (*c.* 321-297 BC), it turned into a historic city, and its name and fame spread far and wide. Megasthenes, who was sent by Seleukos as an envoy to the court of said Maurya emperor at Pāṭaliputra where he lived for five years (*c.* 303-298 BC), has presented and eye-witness account of the city called Palimbothra or Palibothra. According to him, it was situated on the confluence of the Ganges (Gaṅgā) and Erannoboas (Hiraṇyavāha = Sone). It "stretched in the inhabited quarters to an extreme length on each side of eighty stadia (9½ or about 10 miles), and that its breadth was fifteen stadia (1¾ or about 2 miles) and that a ditch (or moat) encompassed it all round, which was 600 feet in breadth and thirty cubits (about 60 feet) in depth, and that the wall (or wooden palisade) was crowned with 570 towers and had sixty-four gates".[297] He was highly impressed by the immense size

---

292. Cf. *Br. Sam.*, *op. cit.*, Introd. p. 10.

293. *Divyāvadāna*, p. 544; see also *Mhv.*, XVIII, 8; *Buddhavaṁsa*, p. 68.

294. *Mahāparinibbāna Suttaṁ* (supra), v. 39, pp. 34-35.

295. *IP*, p. 75; see also Kātyāyana's *Vārttika* (on Pāṇini), 4, 3, 66; 4, 3, 134.

296. *Mahābhāṣya*, ed. Kielhorn, I, p. 380; II, p. 321.

297. *Indika*, Bk. II, Fragm. XXVI, *AIMA*, p. 68; see also J. Talboys Wheeler, "Greek and Roman India", rept. from his book, *The History of India form the earliest Ages*, 1st edn. (London, 1881) in *Ancient India* (Delhi, 1983), pp. 117-18; E.R. Bevan, "India in Early Greek and Latin Literature", in *CHI*, I, p. 369.

In the course of research it was brought to light that the Sone was not only identical with the Erannoboas, but that up to the year 1379, when it formed a new channel for itself, it had joined the Gaṅgā in the neighbourhood of Patna.

and splendour of the city. It extended for about ten miles along the right bank of the Gaṅgā in a fashion similar to that of the modern Patna. It was adorned by splendid buildings. It contained a market complex, industrious artisans of every class, soldiers, etc. He has portrayed a vivid picture of the royal palace at Pāṭaliputra and that of the urban life of the people there. The wooden wall which he speaks of continued to exist till about the beginning of the fifth century AD.

The fragments of the *Indika* of Megasthenes relating to Pāṭaliputra city are preserved in the works of classical writers of later period. Arrian (*c.* AD 96-180) on the authority of Megasthenes calls it "the greatest city in India".[298] He also informs us that the cities situated on the banks of the rivers were built of wood instead of brick, and the cities which stood on commanding situations and lofty eminences were built of brick and mud. His description of the city is similar to that of Megasthenes. He further adds that the number of Indian cities is so great that it cannot be stated with accuracy and precision (*Indika*, 1, 10). This statement like that of Megasthenes (*Indika*, Fragm. XXVI) is about the cities of the Maurya age.

The Palibothra or Pāṭaliputra city was a vast and splendid metropolis of the great Maurya empire. It, according to Strabo (*c.* 64 BC-AD 21), was of the shape of parallelogram and was surrounded by a wooden wall pierced wtih loopholes for the discharge of arrows. It had a ditch in front for defence and for receiving the sewage of the city.[299] This passage has been extracted from the work of Megasthenes. He calls it "a very large city".[300] Pliny (*c.* AD. 23-79) also calls it "a very large and wealthy city".[301] Diodorus (second half of the firsrt century BC) in his epitome of Megasthenes tells us that it was the most renowned and the greatest of all the cities. It was adorned with many sumptuous palaces, and within its walls a numerous population were settled. It was a fortified city with trenches of notable dimensions which were filled with water introduced from the river.[302] It became

298. Cf. Megas. *Fragm.* XXVI, *AIMA*, pp. 67-68; also his *Indika*, Eng. tr. (Leipzig, 1867), 1, 2 and 10 , cf. *ibid.*, pp. 184, 204-5.

299. Cf. Megas. *Indika*, Bk. II, *Fragm.* XXV, *AIMA*, p. 66; also his *Geog.*, XV, 1, 36, cf. McCrindle, *AICL*, p. 42; see also H.F. Tozer, *A History of Ancient Geography*, p. 150.

300. *Geog.*, XV. 1. 13, *AICL*, p. 19; see also Eng. tr. of his *Geog.* by Hamilton and Falconer, vol. III, p. 106.

301. *Nat. Hist.*, VI. 21. 22; *CAI*, p. 342; also cf. Megas. Fragm. LVI, *AIMA*, p. 139; see also *As.Res.*, V (Delhi, 1979), pp. 273-74 for Strabo's and Pliny's description of the city.

302. *Bib. Hist.*, II, 39, *AICL*, p. 42 note 3, also p. 205; *CAI*, p. 236; cf. Megas. Fragm. 1, *AIMA*, p. 39; see also *As. Res.*, V, p. 270.

the capital of the celebrated Sandrakottos (Candragupta Maurya). Solinus (first half of the third century AD), who derived nearly all his materials from the works of Megasthenes and Pliny, makes only incidental reference to this city inhabited by extremely powerful people.[303] Ptolemy (middle of the second century AD) refers to the city as a Palimbothra[304] which has been identified with "Pāṭaliputra, the ancient capital of Magadha, and a name still frequently applied to the city of Patna which is its modern representative. In the times of Chandragupta (the Sandrokottos of The Greeks) and the kings of his dynasty Palibothra was the capital of a great empire".[305]

Aelian, who flourished about the middle of the second century AD, informs us that "In the Indian royal palace where the greatest of all the kings of the country resides, besides much else which is calculated to excite admiration, and with which neither. . . . Susa with all its costly splendour, nor Ekbatana with all its magnificence can view, there are other wonders besides. . . ."[306] The royal palace described in this passage has been conclusively identified with the famous Sugāṅga palace of Candragupta at Pāṭaliputra[307] which as stated above was more magnificent than the palaces of Susa and Ekbatana. "The whole description is significantly reminiscent of a Persian paradise."[308] The said imperial palace probably stood close to the modern village of Kumharar of Kumrahār on the outskirts of modern Patna. The capital city of Palibothra also attracted the attention of a Greek merchant and traveller of the first century AD.[309]

For about eight centuries after the time of Candragupta Maurya, Pāṭaliputra continued to be a great and flourishing city, adorned with a magnificent palace, many temples and monuments and other public buildings of great splendour. Aśoka (*c.* 272-232 BC), who

---

303. *Collectanea rerum memorabilium*, 52, 6-17, of. *CAI*, pp. 457-58; also cf. Megas. Fragm. LVI.B, *AIMA*, p. 155.
304. *Treatise on Geography*, VII, 76, *AIT*, p. 169.
305. *AIT*, p. 169.
306. *On the Peculiarities of Animals*, XIII, 18, *AICL*, p. 141; *CAI*, pp. 414-15, 421, note 3.
307. *JRAS*, 1923, p. 587.
308. M. Wheeler, *op. cit.*, p. 176f.
309. *Periplus*, 64, p. 270.

was third in succession from him, and who made Buddhism the state religion, in his inscription on the rock at Dhauli gives it the title of *Metropolis of the Religion*, i.e., the chief city of Buddhism. The replacement of wood by stone as building material and the use of stone pillars in the royal palace during his time added to the beauty and splendour of the city. He had installed two stone pillars there to propagate Buddhism the fragments of one of which have been discovered in the excavations. According to one of the Pāli chronicles, Pāṭaliputra in his time was the chief city of the whole continent of India.[310] We are told in one of the Pāli commentaries that the city had four gates and his income from them being 400,000 *kahāpaṇa*s daily.[311] We are further informed by one of the Sanskrit Buddhist texts that he had erected all over the country altogether eighty-four thousand *stūpa*s and *caitya*s out of which the first and the largest *stūpa* was installed at Kukkuṭārāma Vihāra in Pāṭaliputra which magnified its beauty.[312] Pāṭaliputra continued to be the capital of his successors up to *c.* 184 BC.

The archaeological discoveries of a column capital with central palmettes and two stone legs of a throne, and a large pillared hall representing some eighty or hundred monolithic columns and monumental staircase of a familiar Achaemenid pattern in the excavations of 1896 and 1912 led Mortimer Wheeler to warrant the belief that the ancient Pāṭaliputra city was modelled on the famous Persian city of Persepolis. He has distinctly acknowledged the contributions of Persian artists and craftsmen to the masonry architecture of the Maurya age. He was perhaps under the impression that there was Persianisation of the urban pattern in the Gangetic Valley.[313] Nihar Ranjan Ray in his famous article "Rural-urban dichotomy in Indian tradition and history" has also admitted that Pāṭaliputra city was a prototype of Achaemenian model. But at the same time he has reasonably doubted the transplantation of Achaemenid craftsmanship at this place.[314] The resemblance of the Maurya palace at Pāṭaliputra to the Persian palace at Persepolis cannot be definite established. We do not have much positive evidence to show the impact of Persian urban tradition on urbanisation process of the Maurya period. Nor do we have any clue to show its impact on the pattern of Gangetic urbanisation. The Gaṅgā

310. *Mhv.*, ch. XV.

311. *Sāmantapāsādikā*, I, p. 52.

312. *Bodhisattvāvadāna Kalpalatā*, 69th Pallva, pp. 6-7.

313. *Op. cit.*, p. 177, also pl. 49.

314. *ABORI*, LVIII-LIX (1977-78), pp. 873-74.

Valley, in fact, had its own urban tradition which does not bear stamp of any Persian influence.

In the post-Maurya age, Pāṭaliputra was the capital of both the Śuṅgas (*c*. 184-72 BC) and the Kaṇvas (*c*. 72-27 BC). It further flourished as an urban centre during the times of the Kuṣāṇas (first to third century AD).

It is generally believed that Pāṭaliputra continued to be the capital of the Gupta empire till the time of Candragupta II (*c*. AD 375-414). During his reign it was still a magnificent and populous city. He is called "Lord of Pāṭaliputra, the best of cities". V.A. Smith's view, that it ceased to be an important city after Samudragupta,[315] is no longer tenable. Vātsyāyana in his *Kāmasūtra*,[316] while making an incidental reference to sophisticated life of an aristocratic class in urban areas, specialised crafts and various other features of towns and cities of the Gupta period, speaks of the urban life in Pāṭaliputra city. Vararūci in his *Prākṛt Prakāśa* has also referred to the magnificence of the city.

Pāṭaliputra was not only a seat of government but also a great and opulent seat of commerce, which inreased its wealth and prosperity. It was also a centre of learning. Patañjali, Vararūci and Āryabhaṭṭa II acquired fame as scholars by passing their examination at this city of learning. It was also a centre of art and culture. It being an administrative, commercial, religious and educational centre rapidly grew into a big city. All the amenities were available here for leading an urban life. It was the largest of all the cities in the middle Gangetic plains. It has the same place in Asia which Rome has in Europe.

Fa-hian visited the imperial city of Pāṭaliputra called *Pa-lian-fu* about the beginning of the fifth century AD. He is believed to have stayed there for about three years (AD 406-8). He was so much impressed by the glory and splendour of the city. He calls it the greatest of all the cities in Madhyadeśa. According to him, the city was the capital of king A-you (Aśoka). The palaces of the king which were in the city had stone walls and gates. The elegant carvings and inlaid sculptures were of such a high order as they really bear testimony to superhuman workmanship. The inhabitants of the city were rich, prosperous and righteous.[317] At the time of his visit, the city was in a excellent

315. *EHI*, p. 309.

316. Eng. trans. by Ishwar Datt (Delhi, 1964), pp. 19, 24, 29-30, 32.

317. Legge, *op. cit.*, pp. 77-78; Giles, *op. cit.*, pp. 45-47.

state of preservation. It had not then experienced any diminution of its prosperity. The wooden wall by which it is said to have been surrounded was seen still standing by the said Chinese pilgrim.

There were several causes of the downfall and decay of Pāṭaliputra city. The Indo-Greek ruler, Menander (*c*. 165-144 BC), was the first to strike a blow to this city during the Śuṅga period. It was apparently not ruined until the time of the Hūṇa's invasion in the fifth century AD. During the time of Skandagupta (*c*. AD 455-67), the Hūṇas after crossing over the Punjab and U.P. reached Pāṭaliputra and plundered, pillaged and destroyed it which has been confirmed by the excavation at Kumharar. It received blow after blow. It had also caught the fire which reduced the entire wooden city to ashes which can also be confirmed by the archaeological evidence. In the excavation of 1912, the presence of a thick layer of ashes just below the Gupta walls was noticed. The city being situated at the confluence of the two big rivers, the Gaṅgā and the Sone, was always subject to floods. It is believed that in the latter half of the sixth century AD it was swept away by the floods in the said two rivers. The prophecy of Buddha regarding the ruin of this city that "Three dangers will hang over it, that of fire, that of water, and that of mutual dissension"[318] almost came true. It is also said that about AD 600. Śaśāṅka Narendragupta, king of Gauḍa with its capital at Karṇasuvarṇa, demolished many Buddhist temples and monasteries at Pāṭaliputra.[319] The fall of the Magadhan imperial capitial, Pāṭaliputra, was accomplished by the year AD 632. Its glory had virtually eclipsed in the post-Gupta period. The place where the splendid metropolis had once stood, Hiuen-Tsang found there nothing but heaps of ruins and a village containing about two or three hundred miserable houses. At the time of his visit, the city wore a deserted look. According to him, "South of the Ganges . . . was an old city about 70 *li* (about fourteen miles) in circuit, the foundations of which were still visible although the city had long been a wilderness".[320]

The ruins of Pāṭaliputra city witnessed by the Chinese traveller, Hiuen-Tsang, remaind lying buried deep below the foundations of modern Patna till its discovery in 1876. It was in this very year that the workmen employed in digging a tank in Sheikh Mithia Ghari between the market-place of Patna and its railway station discovered at a

318. *DN*, II, p. 88; *Mahāparinibbāna Suttaṁ*, *op. cit.*, sec. 39, pp. 34-35.

319. Law, *The Magadhas in Ancient India*, p. 39.

320. *YCTI*, II, p. 87; also S. Beal, *op. cit.*, p. 39.

depth of some twelve or fifteen feet below the surface of the ground the remains of a long brick wall with a line of palisades of strong timber running near and almost parallel to it, and slightly inclined towards it. The wooden wall by the which the city was defended, as we learn from Megasthenes and Strabo, was in reality a line of palisades running in front of wall of brick. In the course of this excavation, "In one place there appeared to have been some sort of outlet, for two wooden pillars rising to a height of some 8 or 9 feet above what had evidently been the ancient level of the place, and between which no trace of palisades could be discovered, had all the appearance of door or gate posts. A number of wells and sinks were also found, their mouths being in each case indicated by heaps of fragments of broken mud vessels. From the best-preserved specimens of these, it appeared that their shape must have differed from that of those now in use. One of the wells having been cleared out, it was found to yield capital drinking water, and among the rubbish taken out of it were discovered several iron spear-heads, a fragment of a large vessel, etc." L.A. Waddell had remarked as far back as 1892 that "nearly the whole of the site of the city is intact; much lies below Patna, Bankipur and the E.I. Railway, being buried at a depth of ten to twenty feet. The old city was on the north bank of the old Sone but it waas several miles distanct from the Ganges whch shifted later to the south."

Since 1896 a series of archaeological excavations have been carried out at different sites in the vicinity of modern Patna which formed parts of ancient Pāṭaliputra.

The excavations at Kumrahār by L.A. Waddell in 1896 brought to light the wooden fortification of the city of Candragupta Maurya's time. It also proved the existence of massive 80-pillared hall or eighty stone-columned palace of emperor Aśoka, etc.[321] The archaeological rediscovery of wooden structures at the Maurya capital city confirms the correctness of Megasthenes' statement about it. D.B. Spooner's excavations at the same site in 1912-13 resulted in the discovery of the remains of Aśoka's palace, a "Hall of a Hundred Columns" resembling that of at Persepolis, the structures of the pre-Gupta and early Gupta time, brick built houses of the Gupta period, coins and seals of the period ranging from the third century BC to the Gupta times, including the coins of the Śuṅga period, two copper coins of Kaniṣka and a coin of Candragupta II, earthern pots, the head of an image of Buddha and other antiques.[322] M. Ghosh, while carrying out

321. *Report on the Excavations at Pataliputra* (Calcutta, 1903), pp. 1-35.

322. *ASIAR*, 1912-13, pp. 53-86.

excavations at Bulandībāg (a suburb of Patna) in 1926-27, discovered the remains of defensive wooden palisade of fourteen to fifteen feet height (belonging to the latter part of the fourth century BC) and some other antiquities.[323] During the years 1951-55, the excavations at Kumrahār were carried out under the guidance of A.S. Altekar and V.K. Mishra. The unearthed materials at the site belonged to the Maurya and the post-Maurya times which also include the brick structures of the Kuṣāṇa period. On the basis of the findings it has been established that the habitation at the site began in the age of the Mauryas and continued till about AD 600. It continued to flourish as an urban centre till AD 300, but the period AD 300-600 marks the phase of its decline.[324] The site was also excavated in 1953-54 under the auspices of K.P. Jayaswal Research Institute, Patna.[325] The further excavations were conducted by B.P. Sinha and L.A. Narain in 1955-56 which yielded among other things NBP sherds and a good number of polished sandstone pieces.[326] Some other important archaeological discoveries include the remains of wooden palisades at Lohānīpur, Mahārājgañj and Mangle's tank, punch-marked coins found at Golakpur, Persoionic capital, the railing pillar of the Śuṅga period, coins of Kuṣāṇa and Gupta kings, Buddhist monasteries, Jain temples and other relics and monuments.

Nālandā at a distance of one *yojana* (about 7 miles or 11 km) north-west of Rājagīr and 65 km south-west of Patna was an important town in the mid-Gaṅgā Valley. It was originally a village but it soon developed into a township. It was actually the sixth or fifth century BC which marked the beginning of its transition from a village to a town. It has been frequently referred to in the Buddhist literature.[327] In the Buddha's time, it was a prosperous and thickly populated town.[328] The establishment of a famous Buddhist university there by Kumāragupta I (*c.* AD 414-55) of the imperial Gupta dynasty led to its further growth as a town. As a university town it was as famous in the east as Takṣaśilā in the west. It being the seat of learning and a centre of Buddhist activities contained

---

323. *Ibid.*, 1926-27 (Calcutta, 1929), pp. 135ff; see also M. Wheeler, *op. cit.*, p. 177, Pl. 48.
324. *Report on Kumrahar Excavations* (1951-55), pp. 15-20.
325. *IAR*, 1953-54, pp. 9-10, also 19.
326. *Report on Pataliputra Excavations, 1955-56* (Patna, 1970), pp. 10-11; also *IAR*, 1955-56, pp. 22-23.
327. *DPPN*, II, pp. 56-57.
328. *DN*, I, p. 211; *Sumaṅgalavilāsinī*, I, p. 35; III, p. 873; *JS*, p. 55; *Mahāvastu-avadāna*, III, p. 56; for further details see Law, *Historical Gleanings*, p. 45; "Nalanda in Ancient Literature", 5th Indian Oriental Conference, 1930.

many hundreds of buildings and a number of monasteries. Hiuen-Tsang, who visited the place first in AD 637 and then in 642 and altogether stayed there for about two years, has provided a vivid description of it. According to him, the town was surrounded by a lofty brick wall with one gate. This gate opened into the great college of the university, from where were separated eight other halls standing in the middle of Saṁghārāma (monastery). The university buildings with many storcys were majestic in their dimension and height with richly adorned towers and fairy-like turrets. All the outside courts of these buildings had chambers of the priests. The architecture, sculpture and decorative designs of the buildings were perfect and of exquisite beauty. The whole university area was dotted with beautiful and spacious tanks bearing on their bosoms the blue lotus intermingled with *kanaka* (golden ) flower which enhanced their beauty.[329] I-tsing saw eight halls and three hundred apartments in the university. He gives an account of more than ten water-tanks.[330] Besides these, there was an extensive library consisting of three big buildings one of which was a nine-storeyed buildings full of rare sacred books. This university was of an international fame.

The extensive excavations carried out at the sight by Mr. Spooner (in 1917), Sir John Marshall (in 1917-20) and others also reveal that "the Nalanda University covered an area at least one mile long an half a mile broad. Monastic buildings and *stupa*s attached to them were built according to a pre-conceived plan, thery were all arranged in a row and not huddled together in any haphazard fashion. The central college had seven halls attached to it; besides there were three hundred smaller rooms for lecturing work".[331] The archaeological evidence confirms to a great extent the authenticity of the Chinese accounts of Nālandā.

Nālandā was no doubt a flourishing urban centre as well as a seat of higher learning in both the Gupta and post-Gupta times. It reached the zenith of its progress in the seventh century AD, as indicated by the accounts of the two aforesaid Chinese travellers.

---

329. S. Beal, *op. cit.*, pp. 110-12; *YCTI*, IIL, pp.164-65.

330. See *RBR*; for other details see H.D. Sankalia, *The University of Nalanda* (Madras, 1934); A. Ghosh, *A Guide to Nalanda* (Delhi, 1939).

331. For a report of Nālandā excavations, see *JBORS*, vol. IX, pt. 1.

In the post-Harṣa period its glory as an educational and a religious centre was maintained by those celebrated princes and kings who were patrons of learning and votaries of Buddhism. In one of the epigraphic records (Nālandā inscription of Yaśovarman *c.* AD 725-52)[332] also it is described as a great city and the famous seat of learning. The Nālandā University lost its very existence after its destruction at the hands of the famous Muslim invader, Bakhtiyar Khilji, towards the close of the twelfth century AD.

The ruins of Nālandā bespeak what it was in the past. A. Cunningham has identified some of its ruins with the remains at Baragāon which "consist of numerous masses of brick ruins amongst which the most conspicuous is a row of lofty conical mounds running north and south. These high mounds are the remains of gigantic temples attached to the famous monastery at Nālandā. The great monastery itself can be readily traced by the square patches of cultivation, amongst a long mass of brick ruins, 1600 feet by 400 feet. These open spaces show the positions of the courtyards of the six smaller monasteries which are described by Hwen Thsang as being situated within one enclosure forming altogether eight courts. . . ."[333] There still exists to the south of the ruined monastery a small tank which agrees exactly to the position of the Nālandā tank. There are some other tanks which surround the ruins on all sides. Besides these, the excavated structures, including the crumbling walls of the ancient Nalanda University, can also be seen at the site.

Campā, the capital of the kingdom of Aṅga, was very famous in eastern India. It was one of the largest cities of the mid-Gaṅgā Valley. It was situated on the south or right bank of the Gaṅgā near its confluence with the river Mālinī or Candana. According to the epic and Purāṇic evidence, its oldest name was Mālinī which was later changed to Campā, Campāvatī or Campāpurī after its founder, king Campā.[334] The historicity of this traditional evidence is beyond doubt. In the Buddhist literature also it is mentioned as Campāpurī.[335] In the time of the Buddha, it was one of the most flourishing cities and a great centre of trade and commerce.[336] According to the *Mahāparinibbāna Suttaṁ*, it

---

332. R.K. Chaudhuri, *Select Inscriptions of Bihar*, p. 25.

333. *CAGI*, p. 396.

334. *Mbh.*, Śānti Parva, 5, 6-7; *Mbh. Ko.*, pp. 14-15; *Mts.*, 48, 97; *Vy.*, 99, 105-6; *Vṣṇ.*, IV, 18, 19-20; *Bmd.*, III, 74, 197; *Bhāg.*, IX, 8. 1; *Agn.*, 277, 13-14; *Br.*, XIII, 42-43; *Hv.*, 32, 49; *PK*, p. 166.

335. *Aśokāvadāna*, cf. *SBLN*, p. 8; *Mhv.* (Comm.), pp. 128-29.

336. *DN*, I, p. 111; II, p. 146; *Sumaṅgalavilāsinī*, I, p. 279.

was one of the six great cities of India (the other five being Rājagṛha, Śrāvastī, Sāketa, Kauśāmbī, and Vārāṇasī). It was noted for its internal and external trade which not only contributed to its wealth and prosperity but also gave a boost to its growth as an urban centre. It is said that the traders sailed from her banks with their ships full of merchandise to Suvarṇabhūmi (Lower Burma) and other far distant countries in the trans-Gangetic region for trading purposes.[337] In the early Buddhist period it was a political, religious and commercial centre. The *Mahājanaka Jātaka* (No. 539) informs us that it was a walled city adorned with a gate and watch-tower. The Jain canon also describe it as a well fortified city. It was surrounded by rampart; it had moat and its bastions, gates and arches (*toraṇa*) were lofty. It was divided by roads. As a whole, it was a beautiful and prosperous city.[338] It appears to have been a well-planned city.

The city of Campā went on maintaining its urban character even in Gupta and post-Gupta times as testified to by the accounts of Fa-hian and Hiuen-Tsang. The former, who visited the place in the fifth century AD and stayed there for about three years, did not notice any sign of its decadence. He rather found some monks residing there.[339] The later visited the place called *Chan-p'o* (Campā) in the seventh century AD. According to him, the capital city was more than 40 *li* in circuit. Its brick walls were of great height and the ditch round it was deep and large. He found some ten monasteries mostly in ruins but there were about two to three hundred priests there.[340] The city appears to have partly declined before his visit the reasons of which are not far to discover.

The ancient city of Campā is identical with its ruins at modern Campānagara or Campāpura at a distance of 3 km west of Bhāgalpur in Bihar. The excavations at the site in 1970s brought to light the mud rempart of early NBPW phase and the brick fortifications of its late phase and iron objects, copper coins, punch-marked coins, etc., associated with it; the structures of Kuṣāṇa period and terracotta pieces, ivory objects, stone and glass beads, etc., of the Gupta period.[341]

The excavations have also brought to light two other small towns of the mid-Gaṅgā

---

337. *Jāt.*, VI, p. 34.

338. *Ovāiya Sūtra*, 1; *Uttarādhyayana*, 9, 18, 24; See also Jain *Mahāpurāṇa*, 67, 2; 75, 82; *Padma*, 8, 301; 20 , 15; *Hv.*, 19, 117.

339. Legge, *op. cit.*, p. 100; Giles, p. 65.

340. S. Beal, *op. cit.*, pp. 128-29; *YCTI*, II, p. 181; *BRWW*, II, p. 192.

341. *IAR*, 1969-70, p. 2; 1970-71, pp. 4-5; 1971-72, p. 5; 1972-73, pp. 6-7; 1974-75, pp. 8-9; 1975-76, pp. 7-8; 1976-77, pp. 11-12.; See also B.P. Sinha, *Archaeology and Art of India* (Patna, 1979).

Valley – Chirand in Sāran and Sonpur in Gayā districts of Bihar respectively. The former appears to have come into existence in pre-NBPW phase, i.e., BRW which is assigned to *c*. 1200 BC on the basis of C-14 dating.[342] It had altogether five phases of urban settlement. It was a flourishing urban centre in the Kuṣāṇa period (first-second centuries AD) as testified by the discovery of the brick structures of that period. Its decline began after the third century AD or in the early Gupta period.[343] The latter is associated with NBPW phase of the Gangetic culture. It, however, continued to exist as an urban centre till the end of the Kuṣāṇa period. It was like the former a commercial centre. It became almost decadent in the Gupta period.[344] Buxar (called Vedagarbhapurī in the ancient times) was another important town of the Kuṣāṇa period.

Some towns and cities in Bihar were situated also to the north of the Gaṅgā the most prominent of which was Vaiśālī. It had its own place in the middle Gangetic basin. In pre-Buddhist period, it was popularly known as Viśālapurī after its founder, king Viśāla of the Solar dynasty.[345] At the time of the Buddha, it was rich, prosperous and populous city. It was not only the capital of the Licchavi clan but also the metropolis of the entire Vajjian confederacy. "It had 7,707 storied buildings, 7,707 pinnacled houses, 7,707 pleausre grounds and 7,707 lotus ponds".[346] At that time, it was encompassed by three lofty walls each standing at a distance of one league from the other and at three palaces there ere three gates with watch towers.[347] It was "charming and delightful, crowded with various people, adorned with buildings of various descriptions, storied mansions, buildings and palaces, gateways, triumphal arches, covered courtyards, and charming with beds of flowers in her numerous gardens and groves".[348] It was really a large and beautiful city. It was both an administrative and a commercial centre.

---

342. Sankalia, *PPIP*, p. 557.

343. *IAR*, 1962-63, p. 6; 1964-65, p. 7; 1970-71, p. 7; 1977-78, pp. 17-18.

344. *IAR.*, 1961-62, p. 5; 1964-65, p. 7; 1968-69, p. 6.

345. *Vy.*, 86, 14-17; *Vṣṇ.*, IV. 1, 43-49; *Bmd.*, III, 61, 12-13; *Bhāg.*, IX, 2, 33-34; *PK*, p. 481; *Vāl. Rām.*, Bāla Kāṇḍa, 47, 11-12; also 45, 9-11; *Vāl. Rām. Ko.*, p. 35.

346. *Vinaya Piṭaka (Mahāvagga)*, Vinaya Texts, SBE, II, p. 171, cf. Law, *GEB*, pp. 12-13; *IETBJ*, p. 52; also *Lalitavistara*, ed. S. Lefmann, Ch. III, p. 21.

347. *Jāt.*, I, p. 504; also *GEB*, p. 12.

348. Law, *Geographical Essays*, p. 17; see also *Divyāvadāna*, p. 208; *Mahāvastu*, 1, pp. 253ff; *BI*, p. 41.

The city of Vaiśālī has been identified with moern Basārh (or Basāḍ) with an old ruined fort called Rājā-Viśāla-Kā-garh (or the fort of king Viśāla) at a distance of about 27 miles north-east of Patna.[349] The extensive excavations at the site in the past conducted first by T. Bloch in 1903-4[350] and then by D.B. Spooner in 1911-12,[351] K.P. Jayaswal Research Institute, Patna and A.S. Altekar in 1957-58[352] and B.P. Sinha and S.R. Roy in 1958-62,[353] on the whole, have shown that the ancient city had extended over nearly twenty-four square miles. The discovery of brick-mud rampart (dated second century BC-first century BC to second century AD) in the course of excavations has proved beyond doubt that it was a well-fortified city. The structures of the Kuṣāṇa period, the coins of the kings of pre-Gupta age, monumental *stūpas*, etc., were also exhumed in the excavations. The city had actually assumed an urban character in the early phase of NBPW which continued till the time of the visit of Fa-hian, as he does not make any allusion to it being in ruins.[354] We may infer that the city might have decayed sometime between fifth and seventh centuries. At the time of the visit of Hiuen-Tsang it was almost a ruined city. According to him, "The foundations of the old city Vaiśālī were 60 or 70 *li* in circuit, and the palace city ('that is the walled part of the city') was four or five *li* in circuit, and it had few inhabitants."[355] The Buddhist establishments, of which there were some hundreds, were with the exception of three or four dilapidated and deserted, and the Brethren were very few.[356]

Mithilā, the famous capital of Videha kingdom, also deserves our attention. It was about thirty-five miles north-west from Vaiśālī. It was founded by king Nimi.[357] The capital city of his time has been called Vaijayantapur in the *Rāmāyaṇa*[358] and Jayantapur in the

349. Legge, *op. cit.*, pp. 70-71; CAGI, p. 373; *CASR* (1880-81), XVI, p. 6; E.J. Rapson, *Ancient India from Earliest Times to the First Century AD*, p. 85; also *JRAS*, 1902, pp. 267; *JS*, p. 51.

350. *ASIAR*, 1903-4, pp. 81-122.

351. *Ibid.*, 1913-14, pp. 98ff.

352. *ASIAR*, 1957-58, pp. 10-11.

353. *Vaiśālī Excavations 1958-62* (Patna, 1969), pp. 5-6.

354. Legge, *op. cit.*, p.72; Giles, *op. cit.*, pp. 41-42.

355. *YCTI*, II, p. 63; also S. Beal, *op. cit.*, p. 100.

356. *Ibid.*

357. *Vy.*, 89. 1-3; *Vṣṇ.*, IV, 51; *Bhāg.*, IX, 13.1; *Bmd.*, III, 64, 1-4; *Vāl. Rām.*, Bāla Kāṇḍa, 71, 3.

358. *Vāl. Rām.*, Uttara Kāṇḍa, 55, 4-21.

Purāṇa.[359] During the time of his successor, Janaka I (who was known both as a Videha Janaka and Mithi-Janaka), it was called both Mithilāpurī and Videhapurī.[360] But it was most popularly known as Janakapura after him which now lies just within the border of Nepal.[361] It continued to be the capital of his successors for a considerable period of time. It was obviously an administrative headquarter. According to the *Mahājanaka Jātaka*, the city was laid out by architects with parapets or walls and gates and battlements traversed by streets on every side.[362] It was only seven leagues (about 50 miles) in extent.[363] It has been repeatedly mentioned in the Buddhist literature as the capital of the kingdom of Videha.[364] As a capital city it had no doubt reached the pinnacle of its glory much before the rise of Buddhism. But as a centre of trade and commerce, which gave fillip to its growth as an urban centre, it really flourished at the time of the Buddha. According to the commentatorial tradition of the Buddhist, it was an important centre of internal trade at that time.[365] It is *Mahā-Ummaga Jātaka* which relates that there were four market towns near the four gateways of the city.[366] In the Jain canon it is described as one of the ten capital cities of India. Kālidāsa[367] also mentions it as a city. We do not have any other details with us either of its further growth or of its decline. However, it may be undoubtedly included in the list of ancient cities of north Bihar.

Of all the ancient towns and cities of Bengal, mention may first be made of Mahāsthāna or Mahāsthānagarh, the capital of Puṇḍravarddhanabhukti, about seven miles north of the modern town of Bogra in Bangladesh (erstwhile east Bengal). It has been included in the list of *nagara* and *mahānagara* of Pāṇini (IV, 2, 142; VI, 2, 89 respectively).[368] M.

---

359. *Vy.*, 89, 1-3.

360. *Vy.*, 89, 3-6; *Vṣṇ.*, IV, 5, 20-23; *Bmd.*, III, 64, 4-6; *Bhāg*; IX, 13. 13; *Br.*, 17, 19 & 28; *PK*, p. 424; *Vāl. Rām.*, Bāla Kāṇḍa, 13, 21; 48, 9-10; 71, 3-4; also *Vāl. Rām. Ko.*, p. 239; S.C. De, *op. cit.*, p. 38.

361. See also *CASR*, XVI, p. 34.

362. *Jāt.*, VI, p. 30.

363. *Ibid.*, pp. 160, 246; also III, p. 322, 365; IV, p. 315.

364. *DN*, II, p. 235; *Mhv.* (comm.) pp. 125, 128-29; *Mahāvastu*, III, p. 172; *Divyāvadāna*, p. 424; *Bodhisattvāvadāna Kalpalatā*, 83 Pallava, p. 9.

365. *Paramatthadipanī* (comm. on the *Theragāthā*) by Dhammapāla, ed. F.L. Woodward, pp. 277-78.

366. *Jāt.*, VI, pp. 330-31.

367. *Raghuvaṁśa*, XI, 35-57.

368. *IP*, pp, 65 and 74.

Wheeler has also mentioned it as one of the cities of eastern India.[369] The earliest reference to its identification with Puṇḍranagara occur in the *Kāśikā* (VI, 2, 89), a commentary on Pāṇini's *Aṣṭādhyayī*.[370] This identification finds confirmation in a Mauryan Brāhmī inscription (*c.* third century BC) discovered at Mahāsthāna which refers to it as Puṇḍanagala,[371] and support in the statement of Cunningham.[372] It was one of the most important cities of the Maurya age. It continued to be an urban centre in Gupta and post-Gupta times. It was not only the seat of power but also a religious and commercial centre. According to Hiuen-Tsang, who visited it in the seventh century AD, the capital of Puṇḍravarddhana called *Pun-na-fa-tan-na* was more than thirty *li* in circuit. He further relates that the country had a flourishing population and crops were abundant. There were twenty Buddhist monasteries with above 3000 monks. The temples were 100 in number and there were followers of the various sects including of Digambaras and Nirgranthas.[373] The excvavations at the site by K.N. Dikshita in 1928-29 reveal "that the city site was in full occupation from early Gupta times and must have been founded several centuries earlier; that massive birck temples were built in the late Gupta period at the Govinda Bhita site; that the construction of the present surrounding walls of the city and many of the structures lying near the surface within and outside the city must be attributed to the early Pāla period; that the proportion of secular buildings appears to have dwindled down after the town of the late Gupta period fell into ruins".[374]

Tāmralipti, identical with modern Tamluk situated on the western bank of the river Rūpanārāyaṇa 12 miles above its junction with the Hooghly in the Midnāpur district of West Bengal, was one of the famous port towns of ancient India.[375] It was known to the

---

369. *Op. cit.*, pp. 134-36; *Five Thousand Years of Pakistan*, pp, 101-2.
370. *IP*, p. 75.
371. D.R. Bhandarkar, "Mauryan Brāhmī Inscription of Mahāsthān", *Ep. Ind.*, XXI (1931-32) p. 85; also Barua, *IHQ*, 1934, pp. 57ff; See also M. Wheeler, *EIP*, p. 136, pl. 52.
372. *ASIAR*, 1928-29, p. 88; See also Ranjusri Ghosh, "Pundravardhana in the first phase of urbanization (4th century BC-3rd century AD) — A Study", *PIHC*, 57th Session, Madras, 1996 (Calcutta, 1997), pp. 199-206.
373. *YCTI*, II, p. 184; S. Beal, *op. cit.*, p. 131.
374. *ASIAR*, 1928-29, p. 88.
375. See *CAGI*, p. 425; N.L. Dey, *op. cit.*, p. 203; *Étude*, pp. 271ff.

Buddhists as a Tāmalitti[376] or Tāmalittiya.[377] Ptolemy describes it as Tamalites[378] which is said to have been one of the chief nineteen towns of India.[379] It was a noted commercial centre. It is said that "This place, in ancient times, was the great emporium of the trade between the Ganges and Ceylon."[380] The trial excavations at Tamulk have brought to light the burnt floor, richly decorated terracotta figurines and cast copper coins of late NBPW phase (third-second centuries BC). The substantive urban settlements began here in or around the third century BC or in the Maurya period. The settlements of the Śuṅga and Kuṣāṇa phases (second century BC-third century AD) are marked by the discovery of Śuṅga bowls, rouletted ware, etc.[381] It was visited by both Fa-hian and Hiuen-Tsang. The former simply refers to it as sea-port "50 yojanas east of Champa".[382] The latter mentions it as *Tan-mo-lih-ti* which apparently corresponds to Tāmralipti. According to him, "This country was about 1400 *li* in the circuit; its capital, above ten *li* in circuit, was near an inlet of the sea (the Bay of Bengal). There were above ten Buddhist monasteries and more than 1000 monks. There were more than 50 temples, and the non-Buddhists lived together. The immense quantity of rare and precious merchandise was brought to it by land and sea routes, and so its inhabitants were generally prosperous".[383] On the basis of this account we can draw a plausible conclusion that Tāmralipti continued to flourish as an urban centre from the Maurya age till the time of his visit. There is not even the slightest evidence of its ruin either in Gupta period or in post-Gupta times.

Candraketugarh, identical with present-day Berachampa and the adjoining areas in Norh 24-Paraganas at a distance of about 24 miles north-east of Calcutta, was one of the famous towns in ancient times. The archaeological excavations at the site in late 1950s and 1960s have revealed that the habitation started here in the early phase of NBPW.

---

376. *Sāmantapāsadikā*, pp. 96-97.
377. *Mhv*., p. 93; *Dip*., p. 28; also *HPL*, II, pp. 553-54.
378. *AIT*, p. 169, see also G.E. Gerini, *RTGEA*, pp. 527, note 3.
379. E.H. Warmington, *The Commerce between in the Roman Empire and India*, p. 117.
380. *AIT*, p. 170.
381. *IAR*, 1954-55, pp. 19-20; 1973-74, p. 33; also M. Wheeler, *EIP*, pp. 135-36; *Five Thousand Years of Pakistan*, pp. 102-3, 142.
382. Giles, *op. cit*., p. 65; Legge, *op. cit*., p. 100.
383. *YCTI*, II, pp. 189-90.

NBP sherds were found with silver-copper punch-marked coins and stone and terracotta beads. The burnt bricks belong to the late phase of NBPW. The other important discoveries include the remains of house cemplexes, ring-wells, ivory objects, etc., of the Śuṅga-Kuṣāṇa phase; brick temple with miniature shrines on the sides of the Gupta period and the religious structures of post-Gupta times.[384] G.S. De of Howrah, while excavating a tank at Hadipur near Candraketugarh, discovered a large number of seals, pots and plaques bearing inscriptions in Kharoṣṭhi and in the mixed script (Kharoṣṭhi-Brāhmī) which, according to B.N. Mukherjee, are palaeographically datable to a period from the last quarter of the first century AD to the first quarter of the fifth century AD, and their language is north-western Prākr̥t. He is of the view that certain influential communities from the north-west migrated to lower West Bangal in the early centuries of the Christian era and settled in the flourishing cities of Candraketugarh (which also included De-Gaṅgā) and Tāmralipti for trading purposes.[385] The trade and commerce promoted the urban growth of these two early towns of Bengal and contributed to the economic prosperity of their inhabitants. The period from the third to the sixth century AD marks a distinct phase of urban development of Candraketugarh. It declined in the post-Pāla period.

Bānagarh in Dīnājpur district was another ancient town of Bengal. The site was occupied sometime during the period of NBPW. It developed as an administrative, commerical and religious centre. It remained throughout an urban centre in the pre-Kuṣāṇa, Kuṣāṇa, Gupta and post-Gupta times. Karṇasuvarṇa, the capital of Gauḍa, has been identified with Raṅgamatī, 12 miles south of Murśidābād.

Śiśupālgarh, situated near Dhauli (Purī district) not far distant from Bhuvaneśvara in Orissa (Oḍradeśa of ancient times) was a well-planned and fortified town. Though it represents the early phase of NBPW, its urban origin may be ascribed to *c.* 300 BC which represents the Maurya times. The archaeological excavations carried out at the site during April-June 1948 under the direction of B.B. Lal have conclusively proved that its defensive walls (i.e., a massive clay rampart) was erected in the early phase or about *c.* 200 BC. Later in phase II a (*c.* 200 BC-AD 100), thick layer of laterite gravel was added to

384. For details see *IAR*, 1956-57, p. 30; Report of K.G. Goswami, *ibid.*, 1959-60, pp. 50-51; 1960-61, p. 55; also his "Chandraketugarh and its Archaeological Importance", *Indian Museum Bulletin*, no. 1, pp. 42-46; *IAR*, 1962-63, p. 46; 1965-66, pp. 59-60; 1966-67, p. 48.

385. "The Traders and Rulers from the North-West Remote Precursors of the British in Bengal", *Herald*, vol. III, No. 5 (Delhi, May 1995), pp. 1-2.

it. These were further strengthened by two thick brick walls, and provided with gates in phase III (*c.* AD 200-350). It had 8 large gateways two on each side. In the course of excavations, NBP wares, iron objects, punch-marked coins, the western gateway, the monolithic pillars, tower, door sockets, guard room, main hall and all other remains of a fortified town, etc., were unearthed.[386] It was both and administrative and a commercial centre. Here all the evidence of urbanism up to *c.* AD 350 have been found. It might have declined possibly in the late Gupta period. Jaugarh in Gañjam district of Orissa was a small fortified town. The excavations at the site in 1956-57 have brought to light its earthen rampart 25 feet high, etc.[387] It was basically a commercial centre. It remained an urban centre up to the times of Kuṣāṇas. It saw its desertion in the Gupta period.

Rādhānagar was one of the three early historical cities or urban centres of Orissa (the other two being Śiśupālgarh and Jaugaḍa). This site, which is in Jājpur district at a distance of about 90 km from Bhuvaneśvara, was first located by Prof. K.S. Behera in 1980s while exploring areas near it. He found the site surrounded by several Buddhist sites and monasteries. Later, J. Mishra, an archaeologist, discovered from the site "a fortified wall, measuring 1,200 metres on each side, a rouletted and knobbed ware, terracotta earlobe and ceramic shreds decorated with a lotus wheel". The findings proved that it was inhabited by artisans, craftsmen, traders and monks in the early Christian era. Thirty Buddhist sites of different periods have so far been traced near the site within the radius of 20 km. The discovery of several Buddhist relics resembling those at Udaygiri, Lalitgiri and Ratnagiri revealed that the place had been a Buddhist centre and a "centre of gateway" for trade. The site needs to be excavted on a large scale so as to throw a new light on early phase of urbanisation or trends of urban revolution in Orissa.

Ratnagiri in particular attained an urban status late in the Gupta period which remained intact in post-Gupta times. It developed as an urban centre only on religious ground.

One of the cities of great eminence in the north-eastern part of India in ancient and early medieval periods was Prāgjyotiṣapura, the capital of Prāgjyotiṣa or Kāmrūpa kingdom. The capital city is identical with modern Gauhati on the south bank of the Brahmaputra (the Lauhitya of ancient Indian literary texts). Its foundation is traditionally ascribed to Amūrtarāja, the son of Kuśa. But it has not yet been confirmed by any

---

386. B.B. Lal, "Śiśupālgarh 1948; An Early Historical Fort in Eastern India", *AI*, no. 5 (1949), pp. 62-105; also M. Wheeler, *EIP*, pp. 134-35, and pls. 29 & 30.

387. *IAR*, 1956-57, pp. 30-31.

reliable evidence. We do not have any details of the layout of the city. However, we do have some information about its extent or size. According to the *Rāmāyaṇa* of Vālmīki, this golden city was situated near the Varāha mountain, which was sixty-four *yojana* in extent and it belonged to Narakāsura.[388] The site appears to have been occupied in the pre-Bhārata war period. It is clearly stated in some of the Purāṇas that this was one of the most beautiful city of the east. It was the capital of king Naraka. It flourished under his sovereignty. It was enclosed by a fence for its defence against the attacks of enemies. The present Kāmākhyā was situated in the heart of the city.[389] It further thrived on as a capital of Naraka's immediate successors, Bhagadatta (who took part in the Great Bhārata battle) and Vajradatta, as we learn from the *Mahābhārata*.[390] Kālidāsa also refers to this city as a capital of Kāmarūpa kingdom.[391] This shows his "familiartiy with the urban tradition of north-eastern India".[392] Prāgjyotiṣapura continued to be the capital of the rulers of various dynasties who ruled the said kingdom during the period concerned. According to Hiuen-Tsang, the capital city of *Ka-Mo-Lu-po* (Kāmarūpa), where he stayed for seven days as a guest of king Bhāskaravarma, the contemporary of Harṣa, was "above thirty *li*".[393] It was a principal city. It is not distinguished by any other remarkable feature. A systematic and an extensive excavation of the site is still awaited.

Ambari, which now lies in the heart of Gauhati, was another ancient city of Assam. It evolved as an urban centre in the Kuṣāṇa period and remained so in Gupta and post-Gupta times. It was a major commercial centre of ancient Kāmarūpa. It flourished also as a religious centre and as a seat of art and culture. It was inhabited by artisans, craftsmen, traders, merchants and others. It was a populous, prosperous and gorgeous city as it appears from its ruins discovered in the archaeological excavations at the site conducted by T.C. Sharma in 1970-71 and then again in 1987-89. The most impressive finds from the site are the large varieties of pottery — both indigenous and foreign of some distinctive features. A unique type of pottery which have been found in huge

388. Kiṣkindhā Kāṇḍa, 42, 30-31; also *Vāl. Rām. Ko.*, p. 188.

389. *Mts.*, 163, 81; *Bhāg.*, X, 59, 2-5; *Vṣṇ.*, V, 29, 8, 14, 16-17; *Vmn.*, 114, 45; *PK*, p. 340; *Kālikā Purāṇa*, ed. by Viśvanārāyaṇa Śastrī, Chs. 38 & 39; also ed. with Hindi tr. by Chamanlal Gautam, 1, pp. 470-81; II, pp. 37-39; See also *JRAS*, 1900, p. 25.

390. Sabhā Parva, 31, 9-10; also 23, 17-18; Āśvamedhika Parva, 74, 1-2, 75, 1.

391. *Raghuvaṁśa*, IV, 81-84; also S.C. Banerji, *op. cit.*, p. 29.

392. V.K. Thakur, "Town in Kalidasa: A Note", *PIHC*, 57th Session, Madras, 1996, p. 160.

393. *YCTI*, II, pp. 185-86.

quantity is the Kaolin wares of extremely fine quality. "Among the foreign varieties are the Chinese Celadon ware and perhaps local imitations of Roman arretine and rouletted wares, suggesting evidence of Indo-Roman and Indo-Chinese trade routes through the Brahmaputra valley, since the early part of the Christian era".[394] The other important finds include the beautiful pieces of terracotta art — all made of Kaoliln, a large number of heads of semi-precious stone, terracotta beads and bangles and a terracotta sealings. There are some evidences to show the trade contacts of ancient Kāmarūpa with central India and China.[395] The Radio-Carbon date of the site of a charcoal sample collected from a depth of 1.2 m. is 1030 ± AD 105. This layer has yielded a large number of icons of deities of Hindu pantheon, sculptures and other antiquities. In addition to these, a huge quantity of dressed and decorated stone architectural block of granite and gneiss, among which the rare piece consists of lattice work of black basal, an imported variety of rock, decorated with exquisitely carved lotus motif recalling the Gupta or the Post-Gupta style of art,[396] were also discoverd from the site. On the basis of the archaeological discovery of this city a new chapter on urbanisation can be included in the ancient history of Assam.

### Central India

The towns and cities also flourished in central India (present Madhya Pradesh).

The city of Ujjayinī or Ujjain on the river Śiprā was the capital of the northern part of the kingdom of Avantī (western Mālwā). It was also called Avantīpur. According to the Purāṇic evidence, it was adorned with magnificent buildings, festoons, strong boundary walls, entrance gates, market-complex and trade centres. It was inhabited by the brāhmaṇas, kṣatriyas, vaiśyas and śūdras and other groups including artists, musicians and learned men.[397] It was one of the seven sacred cities of ancient India. It was the most flourishing city at the time of the Buddha.[398] The importance of this city has been highlighted also in the Jain Purāṇas.[399] Pāṇini also refers to this city (*Gaṇa-Pāṭha*, IV, 2,

394. T.C. Sharma, "Excavation at Ambari", *PNEIHA*, 10th Session (Shillong, 1989), p. 23.
395. *Ibid.*, p. 24.
396. *Ibid.*, p. 23.
397. *Br.*, 43, 24-35; see also V.S. Agrawala, "Brahma Purāṇa mein Ujjayini", in *Itihāsa-Darśana* (collection of his papers), ed. by P.K. Agarwala, pp. 157-60.
398. *Sutta-Nipāta*, pp. 18, 86, 192 and 194; *Niddesa*, II, pp. 4-5, cf. *HPL*, II, p. 663; also *Bodhisattvā-vadāna Kalpalatā*, 76th Pallava, p. 10.
399. *Mahāpurāṇa*, 70, 280; *Padma*, 33, 74; *Harivaṁśa*, 20, 3.

82; IV, 2, 127).[400] Kālidāsa calls it a large city.[401] It is supposed to have been his native place and capital of his well-known patron, Vikramāditya. Owing to its position it became a great commercial centre. It was the meeting point of three routes, from the western coast with its sea-ports Surpāraka (Sopārā) and Bhr̥gukaccha (Broach), from the Deccan, and from Śrāvastī in Kośala. In fact, it had its importance as an administrative, commercial and religious centre, and also as a centre of learning. This city was known to the Greeks as "Ozene".[402] A number of coins were found from Ujjain, Besnagar (Vidiśā) and other towns by Cunningham. The earliest coins bear inscription "Ujeniya" in Brāhmī character of probably the second century BC. He calls Ujjain the "noblest city".[403] These coins, however, do not afford sufficient data to allow of any satisfactory chronological arragement.

Ujjain, the capital of Avantī, was excavated by N.R. Banerjee in 1956-58. This city became developed after coming under the impact of iron-using culture of the Gangetic Valley. The archaeological discoveries include great clay ramparts (*c.* 700-500 BC), pottery of black and red ware, two sherds of painted ware, large quantity of NBPW later than 500 BC, stone and baked brick structures associated with iron, etc.[404] On the basis of the fragmentary evidence we can affirm that the organised urban life began here with the introduction of iron shortly after the middle of the first millennium BC. It was in a very thriving position during the days of Mauryas, the Kuṣāṇas and the Guptas. From all points of view it was the most prosperous city during the Gupta period. It retained its urban status even in post-Gupta times, as it appears from its description in the *Kādambarī* of Bāṇa. Hiuen-Tsang describes the capital of *U-she-yen-na* (Ujjayinī) as 30 *li* (or 5 miles) in circuit, which is only a little less than its size at the present day. At the time of his visit, "it had a rich and flourishing population. There were some tens of Buddhist monasteries, of which the majority were in ruins and only three or four were in a state of preservation . . . there were some tens of Deva-Temples, and the non-Buddhists lived

---

400. *IP*, p. 62.

401. See *Raghuvaṁśa*, VI, 32-36; *Meghadūta*, ed. with Eng. tr. and the commentary (*Saṁjīvanī*) of Mallinātha by M.R. Kale, I, 28 , also 30-33, pp. 52-60 and notes.

402. *Periplus*, pp. 42, 187, 270; *AIT*, pp. 38, 102, 154, 373, note.

403. *Co. Anc. Ind.*, Pl. X, 2, 7-8; Pl. XI, 15, 18, *JASB*, 1, 1890, p. 218; V.A. Smith, *CCIM*, I, pp. 145-46, 152-55; Rapson, *Ind. Co.*, p. 14, Pl. IV, 5.

404. *IAR*, 1956-57, pp. 19-21; 1957-58, pp. 34f, 50; See also M. Wheeler, *EIP*, pp. 142ff.

pell-mell. The king was of the brahmin caste. . . ."[405] It appears to have been partly declined. However, it remained further in existence. It was no doubt one of the greatest cities of ancient India. Wilson has aptly remarked that "Few cities perhaps can boast of a more continuous reputation, as it has been a place of great note from the earliest period of Hindu tradition down to the present day".

Māhiṣmati or Māhiṣmatīpura on the river Narmadā between the Vindhya and the Ṛkṣa (Satpurā) ranges was another premier city. It was the capital of the southern part of Avantī. It is said to have been founded by a noted king Mahiṣmāna, the son of Sahajita of the Haihaya dynasty of Yadu's line.[406] It was fortified city. According to the epics[407] and the Purāṇas,[408] this city prospered under the rule of the Haihayas of the south Mālwā. It had been the original capital of Avantī kingdom much before the rise of Buddhism. Its antiquity is as high as that of Mohenjo-Dāro and Harappā. It was known to the Buddhists as Māhissati which along with Ujjain and Vidiśā are described in their literature as great cities.[409] This city also finds mention in the Jain Purāṇas.[410] Kālidāsa refers to its palace and ramparts.[411] It has rightly been identified with Maheśvara or Maheśvarapura on the north bank of the Narmadā (Nīmar district), 40 miles south of Indore.[412] Some scholars have identified it with Māndhātā on the south bank of the Narmadā.[413] But the validity of this identification is doubtful in view of the fact that it lay to the south of Pāriyātra mountain (western Vindhyas), whereas Māhiṣmatī lay to the north of Vindhya

405. *YCTI*, II, p. 250; *BRWW*, II, pp. 270-71.

406. *Vṣṇ.*, IV, 11, 8-9; *Vy.*, 94, 5; see also *Vy.*, 88, 71-72; *Mts.*, 12, 34-35; *Hv.*, 1, 30.

407. *Vāl. Rām.*, Uttara Kāṇḍa, 31, 7-10; *Vāl. Rām. Ko.*, p. 28; *Mbh.*, Sabhā Parva, 28, 17 & 24; also Udyoga Parva, 19, 23.

408. For details see *Vy*; 94, 5-26; *Vṣṇ.*, IV, II, 19; *Mts.*, 43, 8-29; *Bhāg.*, IX, 15, 22; X, 79. 21; *Pdm.*, Bhumikhaṇḍa, 92, 33; Uttarakhaṇḍa, 220. 17; *Bmd.*, 3, 38, 2; 3,46, 11; *PK*, pp. 421-22.

409. *DN*, II, p. 235; *Sutta-Nipāta*, pp. 18, 86, 192, 194; *Sutta-Nipāta Comm.*, II, p. 583; *Niddesa*, II, pp. 4-5; also *HPL*, II, pp. 654, 663.

410. *Mahāpurāṇa*, 16, 152; 71, 208; *Harivaṁśa*, 17, 21; *Padma*, 10, 65.

411. *Raghuvaṁśa*, VI, 43.

412. Sankalia, "Mahismati and Maheswar", in S.P. Gupta and K.S. Ramachandran (ed.), *AIHA*, pp. 215-27; see also *Ind. Ant.*, 1875, pp. 346ff; Wilford, *As. Res.*, IX (1809), p. 105; S.K. Dikshit, *PIHC*, Calcutta Session, 1939, p. 141, note 24; Diskalkar, *PIHC*, Patna Session, 1946, pp. 61ff; Pandey, *JGRS*, VIII (1940), pp. 135-38.

413. Fleet, *JRAS*, 1910, pp. 444-47; *Ind. Ant.*, 1876, p. 53, Law, *HGAI*, p. 174.

and to the south of the Ṛkṣa. The laws of transcription also do not permit us to approve this identification. Its identification with the old town of Maṇḍala on the south or right bank of the Narmadā[414] may, however, be accepted on the ground that like Maheśvara it was a fortified city. The inhabited part extended over two miles along the river. The city in ancient times may have covered the areas on both banks of the Narmadā in the present Nīmar district. Excavations at Maheśvara were carried out in 1952-53 under the guidence of H.D. Sankalia and other.[415] The excavations have brought to light silver and copper punch-marked coins associated with the "NBP and the black-and-red megalithic lilke pottery" of the fourth century BC, etc.[416] According to the eye-witness account of Hiuen-Tsang, *Mo-hi-ssū-fa-lo-pu-lo* (Maheśvarapura) was above 30 *li* (or more than 5 miles) in circuit. The people were non-Buddhists and there were a few temples, and the majority were the followers of the Pāśupata cult. "The king was a brahmin and was not a believer in Buddhism."[417] From his account it is quite evident that the city had not declined at all till the time of his visit.

Vidiśā on the river Vetravatī (modern Betwā) was the capital of the Daśārṇa country (eastern Mālwā region). This ancient city identified with modern Bhilsā in the Gwalior state was situated at a distance of about 26 miles north-east of Bhopal. B.C. Law holds that Vidiśā is the old name of Besnagara,[418] a ruined city situated in the fork between the converging rivers Betwā and Beś at a distance of 2 miles north-west of Bhilsā.[419] The city of Vidiśā rose into prominence as a centre of Buddhism during the time of Aśoka. It is mentioned in the Buddhist literature as a great city.[420] It is said that its inhabitants belonged to the family of the Śākyas.[421] It further thrived during the Śuṅga period. It was a centre of not only Buddhism but also of Vaiṣṇava cult of Hinduism. Both the schools of religion flourished here side by side. The Greek ambassador, Heliodorus, who was converted to Vaiṣṇavism, set-up a pillar in honour of Viṣṇu near this city. Its

414. *CAGI*, p. 412; see also *JASB*, 1837, p. 622.

415. Sankalia, *PPIP*, p. 557; *Indian Archaeology Today*, p. 83.

416. Sankalia, "Coins and Glass Seal from Maheswar Excavations — 1953", in S.P. Gupta and K.S. Ramachandran (ed.), *op. cit.*, pp. 144-49.

417. *YCTI*, II, p. 251.

418. *JGRI*, vol. IX, pt. 1 (1951), pp. 1-10; *HGAI*, p. 336.

419. *ASIAR*, 1913-14, p. 186.

420. *Sutta-Nipāta*, pp. 86, 192, 194; *Niddesa*, II, pp. 4-5 cf. *HPL*, II, p. 663.

421. *Mahābodhivaṁsa*, pp. 98-99.

importance was also due to its central position on the lines of communication between the sea-ports of the western coast and Pāṭaliputra and between Pratiṣṭhāna and Śrāvastī. The city flourished as an administrative, religious and commercial centre. Kālidāsa mentions it not only as a capital city of Daśārṇa country[422] but also as a commercial centre. It is said that it was frequented by a caravan of merchants[423] which is one of its important attributes. It is mentioned in the Purāṇas as Vaidiśāpuram.[424] It is further said that it was full of wealth and happiness. It contained various big mansions and palaces. It was prosperous and pompous.[425] It was also one of the capitals of the rulers of Nāga dynasty in the Śuṅga and the post-Śuṅga periods.

The Besnagar inscription of Heliodorous bears witness to the fact that "At the time when Greek kings were ruling in north-west, and Taxila was the foremost city of the region, the plateau of central India north of the Vindhya range was dominated by the powerful city of Vidisa, now a mere waste of desolate mounds near the modern Bhilsa".[426] The site was excavated in 1965-66. The C-14 date of its NBPW phase is 295 ± 100 BC.[427] It was in a very flourishing state during the Kuṣāṇa period. There was no change in its urban character either in the Gupta period or in post-Gupta times.

Sūktimatī on the river of the same name extending to the banks of the Narmadā originally belonged to the Yādavas. It later became famous as the capital city of the Cedi kingdom,[428] which corresponded roughly to the region along the south bank of the Yamunā, modern Bundelkhaṇḍ and the adjoining tracks, and was continuous to that of the Kurus. Pargiter places the city in the neighbourhood of Bāndā.[429] The Jain Purāṇa refers to the city as Sūktimatīnagar,[430] which is identical with Sotthivati-nagara of the

---

422. *Meghadūta*, *op. cit.*, I, 24 & 25, pp. 45-48; see also *Raghuvaṁśa*, XV, 36.
423. *Mālavikāgnimitram*, ed. with Eng. tr. by M.R. Kale, revd. by J.L. Dave and S.A. Upādhyāya, Act V, pp. 182-83.
424. *Mts.*, 100, 14; *Vṣṇ.*, III, 18, 65.
425. *Grd.*, VII, 34-35.
426. *ASIAR*, 1913-14, pt. 1, p. 17; see also *Mhv.*, (tr. Geiger), 88, note 4.
427. *IAR*, 1965-66, p. 17.
428. *Mbh.*, Aśvamedha Parva, 84, 1-4; *Mbh. Ko.*, p. 29; *Br.*, 15, 15.
429. *Mārkaṇḍeya Purāṇa*, Eng. tr., p. 359; *JASB*, 1895, p. 255.
430. *Mahāpurāṇa*, 29, 55.

*Chetiya-Jātaka*.[431] It was also known as Sūktipurī. It archaeologically represents mixed BRW and PGW cultures.[432] But it is a fact to reckon with that it attained an urban status in the early phase of NBPW which reached to the full bloom during the Kuṣāṇa period.

Tripurī also called Cedinagarī was another important city which finds mention in both the *Mahābhārata*[433] and the Purāṇa.[434] There is also a numismatic evidence to confirm the existence of this ancient city. There are some coins which bear this name in Brāhmī characters of probably the third century BC.[435] It may undoubtedly be identified with modern Tewar, about 6 miles from Jabalpur.[436] Its urban origin goes as far back as the NBPW period. It was both political and commercial centre. It was a flourishing city even in post-Gupta times. In the early medieval period it became famous as a capital of the Cedi kingdom. In fact, the ancient capital of the kingdom was supplanted by it.

Sāñcī, about 45 km north-east of Bhopal, was one of the famous Buddhist centres of ancient India. This place acquired importance during the time of the great Maurya emperor, Aśoka, who was the first to build here *stūpa*s, monolithic pillars and monastery in the third century BC. The first big *stūpa* originally constructed by him was enlarged to nearly twice its size during the Śuṅga period (second century BC). Its wooden railing was replaced by stone railing. The four gateways or *toraṇa*s around the great *stūpa* were built towards the end of the first century BC by the Sātavāhana rulers which are richly engraved with sculptures. These are among the finest specimens of Buddhist art. These Buddhist monuments proved to be stepping-stone of its urban growth. Several *stūpa*s were further built in the early centuries of the Christian era. Four idols of the Buddha were installed at the four gates during the Gupta period. Some Buddhist temples and monasteries were constructed during the seventh century AD and later. The place became crowded with several Buddhist monuments which gave a urban look to it. It was not only a seat of Buddhist religion, art and culture but also a centre of trade and learning. The archaeological discovery of a number of Hindu plaques of Viṣṇu and Gaṇeśa dated AD 13 attests to the fact that Hinduism co-existed with the Buddhism here to some extent during the period. The place continued to flourish as an urban centre from its

431. No. 422.
432. *IAR*, 1958-59, p. 26; 1961-62, p. 98.
433. Sabhā Parva, 28, 37-38.
434. *Pdm.*, Svargakhaṇḍa, 14, 9.
435. Rapson, *Ind. Co.*, p. 14; also *JRAS*, 1894, p. 553,Pl. 15.
436. See *CASR*, IX, p. 54.

NBPW phase down to the end of the early medieval period. The ruins discovered during 1913-18 by John Marshall[437] and others include the remnants of pillars, relics and other antiquities.

The town, Daśapura, mentioned by Kālidāsa has been identified with modern Dasor of Mandasor on the north bank of the Sivanā in the western Mālwā.[438] "It must have been an important city in ancient times as it is mentioned in the *Mahābhārata*, the Nasik inscription and the Gupta inscriptions."[439] The another town called Devagiri by him has been identified with Devagarh, situated south of the Cambal in the central Mālwā.[440] The other towns of note include Eran which was principally a commercial centre. It continued to exist as an urban centre till the end of the Gupta rule. It was deserted in the post-Gupta period.

Kāntipura or Kāntipurī of the Purāṇas,[441] Kuntipura or Kuntalpura of the *Mahābhārata*[442] or Kuntī or Pāṇini, (IV, 1, 175)[443] was one of the important cities of central India in ancient times. In pre-Bhārata war period, it was one of the chief seats of power of the Bhojas of Yadu dynasty. In the later period, it was one of the main capitals of nine Nāga kings, as described particularly in the Purāṇas.[444] They ruled between the second and the fourth century AD. The city mentioned above has been identified with modern Kutwar village (Morenā district), about 40 km north of Gwalior. Cunningham was the first archaeologist to discover the remains of buildings, stone temples, etc., at this site in 1864-65. According to archaeological report of 1927-28 of Gwalior state, more than one thousand Nāga coins were discovered there by different archaeologists. The officials of the Bhopal circle of the Archaeological Survey of India started an excavations of the site in 1994 but it remained incomplete. After a gap of two or three years fresh excavation were undertaken at the site by the archaeologists, including A.K. Sinha. They found high mounds at the site sprawling over an area of about 2.5 sq km. They

437. For details see his *A Guide to Sanchi* (Calcutta, 1918); F.C. Maisey, *Sanchi and its Remains* (London, 1892).

438. *Meghadūta*, *op. cit.*, I, 50, pp. 85-86.

439. *Ibid.*, p. 86.

440. *Ibid.*, I, 45. pp. 77-78.

441. *Vy.*, 99, 382-83; *Bmd.*, 3, 74, 194, 197.

442. Bhīṣma Parva, 10, 37-42.

443. *IP*, p. 62.

444. *Vy.*, 99, 382-83; *Bmd.*, 3, 74, 194, 197; *Vṣṇ.*, IV, 24, 63; *Vṣṇ*; Eng. trans. H.H. Wilson, p. 385.

discovered at several places remains of walls, huts, kitchens, smelting furnaces and ceramic units at the site. The traces of black and red wares indicate that the first phase of settlements might have begun here in the pre-PGW period. The excavation has unearthed painted grey ware dating back to *c.* 1100-800 BC which, according to excavators, show the settlement of the *Mahābhārata* period. The antiquity of the settlement at the site can be determined only after obtaining the Carnon-14 date of samples collected from there. The structures built of stone slabs with mud as binding material and some other artefacts have also been discovered. According to Mr. Sinha, the site could also be associated with one of the main capital cities of the nine Nāga kings during the fourth-fifth century AD. He has identified the site with that of ancient Kāntipurī, as mentioned in the Purāṇas. The archaeological discoveries of the ruins at the site have proved beyond doubt the existence of the city mentioned in the said literary texts.

### Western India

There were both small and large towns or cities in western India.

Dvārakā on the Arabian Sea in Gujarat (ancient Ānarttadeśa) was one of the largest cities of ancient India. It has a hoary antiquity. It was founded in the pre-Bhārata war period. The history of its foundation is too long to be covered here. However, suffice it to say that the city of Mathurā was under the constant attacks of Jarāsandha, a king of Magadha, and the existence of the Yādavas was in jeopardy. Kṛṣṇa, therefore, got the Yādava capital shifted from Mathurā in the north to Dvārakā in the west which not only constituted a watershed in the politico-cultural history of Yādavas but also proved to be a significant landmark in the history of urbanisation in early India.

There are copious references to Dvārakā city in the *Mahābhārata* and Purāṇas. The evidences recorded in them show that Kṛṣṇa along with the Yādavas moved to the west and founded a new city of Dvārakā exactly at the old site of Kuśasthalī, the earliest capital of Ānarttadeśa, originally built by Śaryāti's son, Ānartta, near Raivatagiri (i.e., Jūnāgarh, ancient Girinār or Girinagara) not far off the sea-coast and destroyed by Puṇyajana *rākṣasas*. The city was also called Dvāravatī (city of many gates), Ānarttapurī, Dvārakāpurī and Vṛṣṇyadhakapurī. It was one of the seven important cities of ancient India. It was the second capital of the Yādavas. It was inhabited by the Andhakas, Vṛṣṇīs, Bhojas Sātvatas, Madhus, Arbudas, Māthurakas, Śūrasenas, Visarjanas, Kukuras, Kuntis, Akrūra, Dasārha and others.[445] It seems to have been a densely populated city.

445. For details see Āraṇyaka Parva, 16, 1-4, 19; *Mts.*, 12, 21-22; 13, 38; 69, 9; *Vy*; 86, 24-28; 88, 199; →

Dvārakā was well-planned and fortified city. It was adorned with palatial buildings with domes and minarets, temples, gardens full of trees, lakes full of lotuses, fort-walls, gates, spacious roades, streets, market-complex, the assembly hall of the Yādavas, etc. It was guarded by soldiers well-equipped with arms and weapons. The dramatists, musicians and other artists formed very important sections of the population of the city.[446] It was administrative, religious and commercial centre. It is also believed that it was a proto-historic port city. It had a beautiful urban setting. It was undoubtedly a magnificent city. Its architectural design was very attractive. V.S. Agrawala, while comparing Dvārakā city with Acropolis city of Greece, has observed that the former was more wider and stronger than the city-states of Greece.[447]

The length and breadth of Dvārakā city vary from text to text. In some of the Purāṇas it has been described as a *mahānagarī* (large city) having an area of 12 *yojana* (i.e., about 96 miles),[448] whereas, on the other hand, it is said that the total area covered by it was 100 *yojana*,[449] which is apparently an exaggeration. According to one of the Purāṇas, its length was 10 *yojana* and breadth 5 *yojana*.[450] According to the *Padma Purāṇa*, it covered an area of 2 *yojana*.[451] In the same Purāṇa it is also 30 *yojana*.[452] But, according to the *Mahābhārata*, its length was merely 2 *yojana* and breadth 1 *yojana*.[453] However, on the

---

→ 96, 46, 57-61, 62-66, 83-93, 111-42, up to 258; *Vṣṇ*., IV, 1, 62-64 & 91; V, 23, 9-15; V, 24, 5-7; V, 33, 10; V. 37, 22-39, 42-63; V, 38, 34-35; *Hv*. (Viṣṇu Parva), 34, 1-22; 35, 1-111; 36, 1-40; 39, 10-32; 56, 7, 35; 58, 3-56; *Bhāg*., 1, 10, 1-36; I, XI, 11-12; I, 14, 25; IX, 3, 1-2, 27-36; X, 50, 1-19, 23-58; X, 52, 1-17; X, 53,5-22; X, 58, 12; X, 80, 8-12; XI, 30, 4-48; XI, 31, 23-25; *Bmd*., 3, 61, 18-23; 3, 71, 48, 62, 85; *Brh*., 7, 28-32; 14, 53-56; 195, 1-12; 196, 5-15; 210, 56; 212, 9; *Agn*., 273, 12; *Vrh*., 149, 7-78 & 393; *Pdm*., Uttarakhaṇḍa, 246, 40-45; *Bmv* (Uttarakhaṇḍa), 103, 7-33 & 80; *Bhv*., IV, 129, 44f; *Skd*., Prabhāsakhaṇḍa (44 Chs. on Dvārakā), also 4, 52; *Ghaṭa Jātaka* cf. Fausböll (ed.), *Jāt*., vol. IV, pp. 82-85; *IHQ*, vol. X, pp. 541-50; also Junagarh Rock Inscription of Rudradāman (AD. 150) cf. D.C. Sircar (ed.), *SI*, vol. I, p. 178, line-11.

446. Āraṇyaka Parva, 16, 5-18; *Bh. Sv*., vol. 1, pp. 143-44; *Mbh. Ko*., p. 100; *Bhāg*., I, XI, 12-15; *Hv*., 58, 57-66; *Vṣṇ*., V, 23, 14.

447. *Bh. Sv*., vol. I, pp. 206-7.

448. *Hv*., (Viṣṇu Parva), 58, 36; *Bhāg*., X, 48-54; *Vṣṇ*., V, 23, 13; *Brh*., 196, 12-15. Accroding to Jain Purāṇas (*Padma*, 109, 27; *Harivaṁśa*, 1, 99; *Mahāpurāṇa*, 58, 83; 71, 27) also Dvārakā was 12 *yojana* in extent.

449. *Bmv*., 103, 80; *Bhv*. (Kṛṣṇajanmakhaṇḍa, Uttara), ch. 103.

450. *Vrh*., 149, 7-8.

451. Uttarakhaṇḍa, 200, 66.

452. *Ibid*., 246, 41.

453. Sabhā Parva, 13, 49-54.

basis of archaeological excavations and explorations carried out at different parts of the city (the details of which follow here later) a broad consensus has emerged in favour of 12 *yojana* as its extent. It was divided into four sectors, viz., modern Dvārakā situated on the bank of Gomatī stream where it flows into the Arabian Sea; Mūla-Dvārakā on the south-west coast of Saurāṣṭra (Kaṭhiāwāḍ), about 22 miles east of Porabandar (also called Sudāmāpurī) and 5 km away from Prabhāsapaṭṭan (in the Ūnā Tāluka of Jūnāgarh); Bet-Dvārakā situated in the Gulf of Kaccha at a distance of about 30 km north of modern Dvārakā and Prabhāsatīrtha near Somanāth. Modern Dvārakā (also called Gomatī Dvārakā) was not only the seat of government but also a port and an emporium of trade. Mūla-Dvārakā is traditionally believed to be the ancient or original Dvārakā of Kṛṣṇa's time. Bet-Dvārakā had major settlements of the people. It was not only a pleasure-resort of Kṛṣṇa but also a port city. Gomatī Dvārakā (or Dvārakā) and Bet-Dvārakā were politically and culturally connected with each other.[454]

It was exactly thirty-six years after the Great Bhārata battle that a fratricidal strife ensued among the Yādavas in Prabhāsatīrtha in which practically the entire Yādava males were ruined.[455] After the death of Kṛṣṇa in Prabhāsatīrtha itself the whole of Dvārakā city except for his palace sank into the sea because of its waves or rise in its general water level.[456] The Pāṇḍavas in the course of their wanderings beheld the sunken city in the sea with their own eyes.[457] The city remained submerged under the sea-water until its discovery in 1987-88. The city remained deserted for quite sometime. However, in the later period a new phase of urban settlements started in some parts of the city. The archaeological evidence shows different phases of settlements there of both pre- and post-Gupta periods.

H.D. Sankalia on the basis of results obtained from the deep vertical excavation carried out in 1962-63 near the Dvārakādhīśa temple jointly with the Department of Archaeology, Gujarat, has drawn the conclusion that there were six habitations or six Dvārakās, and the foundation of the first city of Dvārakā on the sea or on the site of

---

454. See also A.D. Pusalker, "Dvaraka", in B.C. Law vol. I (Calcutta, 1945), pp. 218-24; Burgess, "Report on the Antiquities of Kathiawad and Kachh" (London, 1876), p. 13; M.H. Shastri's view in *POC*, VII, pp. 1171 73; *Bombay Gazetteers*, vol. VIII, pp. 518-20, 552; A.S. Altekar, "Ancient towns and cities in Gujarat", *Ind. Ant.*, vol. 54 (1925), p. 25.

455. *Mbh., Mausala Parva,* 2, 1-20; 3, 1-22; 4, 33, 36 & 41; ch. 5; 6, 1-15; 7, 9-22; also *Vṣṇ.*, V, 37, 40-50.

456. *Ibid.*, 8, 4-11, 32-47, 58-74; Aśvamedha Parva, 84, 13-16; *Bh. Sv.*, vol. 3, pp. 221-23; *Vṣṇ.*, V, 37, 36, 59; V, 38, 9-10; *Bhāg.*, XI, 7, 3; XIII, 12, 60.

457. *Mbh.*, Mahāprasthānika Parva, 1, 43.

modern Dvārakā goes just before or around the beginning of the Christian era and not much earlier. The different phase of settlements at Dvārakā, according to him, continued up to the seventh-eighth century AD. He further adds that "Dvārakā . . . was twice submerged into the sea and, therefore, the earlier Dvārakā belonged to Shri Krishna . . . the earliest Dvārakā was found at least in the 2nd-1st century BC-AD. . . ."[458] The dates put forward by him about the antiquity of the city can fairly be disputed.

Modern Dvārakā was no doubt built on the ruins of ancient one. S.R. Rao, a well-known marine archaeologist, further conducted excavation in 1979 in the forecourt or precinct of famous Dvārakādhīśa temple. The remains discovered from here, on the whole, belonged to the period ranging from so-called 1500 BC to the ninth century AD. The remains of some ancient temples with their walls and sculptures intact dedicated to Śiva and Viṣṇu, some red polished ware, *kārṣāpaṇas* or the copper coins of the third phase of settlement dated to first century BC, etc., were found. Altogether there were eight phases of settlements at this site. Modern Dvārakā represents the eighth settlement.

A marine archaeological exploration work was further undertaken by a team of marine archaeologists led by S.R. Rao in 1982 at the sea-coast of Dvārakā and Bet-Dvārakā. During 1982-88, altogether six attempts were made by them in this direction. And ultimately in the sixth attempt (November 1987-February 1988) S.R. Rao with the help of this associates succeeded in discovering the remains of Dvārakā city of Kṛṣṇa's time from the Arabian Sea just off the coast of Dvārakā. The remains of inner and outer fort walls and two main gates of the city, and that of pillars of a stone temple and other structures were discovered from deep below the sea-water. The occurrence of smaller three-holed stone anchors of triangular shape weighing 100 to 1400 kg and other 50 stone anchors led Mr. Rao to believe that Dvārakā was one of the largest ports of the second millennium BC on the Indian coast. The archaeological finds from Bet-Dvārakā include the inner and outer forts of the city, nine courses of stone masonry of the massive fort wall, four three-holded stone anchors, various shells bearing the engravings of lotus (*padma*), which were used as seals for various purposes, the remains of the temples and palaces of Kṛṣṇa's time and many other antiquities and monuments. In Bet-Dvārakā there were three settlements of the so-called pre-*Mahābhārata* (before 1500 BC), the *Mahābhārata* (1500-1400 BC) and the the post-*Mahābhārata* (third century

458. "Antiquity of Modern Dwarka in Literature and Archaeology", in *AIHA*, pp. 191-201; also his "Archaeology and Tradition", in *ibid.*, p. 280.

BC onwards) periods. The former two are believed to have been engulfed by the sea. The archaeological rediscovery of a sunken Dvārakā city confirms its existence as a capital of the Yādavas in Kṛṣṇa's time. There are several old sites in Somanāth and Saurāṣṭra peninsula whose remains still lie submerged under the sea-water.[459] Prabhāsapaṭṭan, which is usually called Paṭṭan Somanāth, was a small port town. It continued to flourish as an urban centre till the end of the Gupta rule. In the post-Gupta period, it was almost a deserted city.

Vallabhī in the south-eastern corner of Kāṭhiāwāḍ was another famous city. It was the capital of the kingdom of the same name. It was also one of the ancient cities of Gujarat. It flourished as an urban centre in the Kuṣāṇa period and continued to be so till the end of the Gupta period. It was a great centre of learning. This city, according to Hiuen-Tsang, who visited it approximately in AD 640, was above 30 *li* (or 5 miles) in circuit, and was very rich and prosperous. It had above 100 Buddhist monasteries and hundreds of Hindu temples.[460] According to the native histories and local traditions, the city was attacked and destroyed by Raja Govinda of Baroda copper-plate inscription in about AD 658. And thereafter it wore a look of a deserted city. Its ruins were first discovered by Colonel Tod[461] and then by Nicholson[462] at Wala at a distance of about 18 miles north-west of Bhaunagar.[463] The ruins are still known by the name of Vamilapura which is only a slight transposition of Valabhīpura. "The remains are scattered over a wide extent, but there is nothing remarkable about them except the unusually large size of the bricks".[464] Vallabhī was, in fact, the capital of the kingdom of the same name which comprised the Kāṭhiāwāḍ peninsula and the districts of Broach and Sūrat.

The city of Ānandapura called *A-nan-to-pu-lo* by Hiuen-Tsang was above 20 *li* in circuit.[465] It has been identified with Vaḍnagar.[466] It was also a commercial centre. It was

---

459. For getting full picture of Dvārakā city see G.P. Singh, *Early Indian Historical Tradition and Archaeology*, pp. 66-73.

460. *YCTI*, II, p. 246.

461. *Travels in Western India*, p. 268, cf. *CAGI*, p. 272.

462. *JRAS*, XIII, p. 146.

463. *Arch. SWI*, vol. II, p. 80.

464. *CAGI*, p. 272.

465. *YCTI*, II, pp. 247-48.

466. *Ibid.*, p. 341.

a flourishing urban centre in the Kuṣāṇa, Gupta and post-Gupta times. Hiuen-Tsang calls it a "rich and flourishing" city.[467]

The capital of Suraṭha or Surāṣṭra called *Su-La-cha*[468] by Hiuen-Tsang is said to have been situated about 83 or 87 miles west of Vallabhī at the foot of Mount Ujjanta. Its position has been fixed at Girinagara or Jūnāgarh.[469] According to Hiuen-Tsang, the capital city was above 30 *li* and its inhabitants were rich and flourishing. It is also identified with the old city of Jūnāgarh.[470]

Roruka (or in later times Roruva), the capital of the kingdom of Sovīra (to the north of Kāṭhiāwāḍ), from which the modern name Sūrat is believed to have been derived, was a port city. It was situated on the Gulf of Kaccha somewhere near the modern Kharragoa.[471] It was one of the great cities of the time of Buddha.[472] The *Mahagovinda Suttanta* of the *Dīgha Nikāya* refers to a number of great cities built by Govinda, including Roruka.[473] It was an important centre of coastal trade.[474] The merchants or caravans arrived there from all parts of India, including Magadha.[475] It is said that during the time of Bimbisāra of Magadha a brisk trade between Rājagaha (Rājagṛha) and Roruka was carried on.[476] The trade and commerce led to its growth as an urban centre in and after the time of the Buddha. After its prosperity declined, the modern Bharoch or ancient Bharukaccha came into prominence.

Bhṛgukaccha or Bharukaccha at the mouth of the river Narmadā and close to the sea, identified with the modern Broach, Baroch or Bharoch in the Kāṭhiāwāḍ peninsula, was one of the famous port towns of ancient India. It is mentioned in the *Mahābhārata*[477]

---

467. *YCTI.*, p. 247.
468. *YCTI*, p. 248.
469. *CAGI*, p. 273.
470. *YCTI*, II, pp. 248-49.
471. T.W. Rhys Davids, *BI*, p. 38; see also his Eng. tr. of Milindapañha, SBE, vol. XXXVI, pt. II (Oxford, 1894, rept. Delhi, 1969), p. 269; N.L. Dey, *GDAMI*, p. 183.
472. *Divyāvadāna*, p. 544.
473. *DN*, p. 235 cf. *HPL*, II, p. 654.
474. *DN*, XIX, 36; *Jāt.*, vol. III, p. 470; see also *Milindapañha*, ed. V. Trenckner, p. 29; Law, *HGAI*, p. 296.
475. *Vimānavatthu Aṭṭhakathā* (comm.), p. 370; *Divyāvadāna*, p. 544.
476. *Divyāvadāna*, pp. 544ff; *Jāt.*, vol. III, p. 470.
477. Sabhā Parva, 47, 8.

and Purāṇas[478] as a town. According to Buddhist tradition, it was named after its founder, Bhiru, a minister of king Rudrāyana of Roruka, the capital of Sovīra.[479] According to Brāhmaṇical tradition, the town was so-called because it was founded by the sage Bhṛgu.[480] In one of the Sanskrit Buddhist texts, it is categorically stated that it was a rich, populous and prosperous town.[481] Its importance as a seaport town in connection with trade and commerce has been highlighted in Buddhist literature.[482] It is said that the merchants with their ships laden with merchandise used to sail from that town for different countries for carrying on trade. Some merchants once sailed from there to Suvaṇṇabhūmi[483] which roughly corresponds with lower Burma (Pegu and Moulmein districts). In one of the Jain canonical text, Bharukaccha has been referred to as Doṇamukha where goods were carried by both land and water routes.[484] It was well known for its maritime trade with both the East and West. The trade and commerce fostered its economic prosperity.

Bharukaccha is one of those ancient Indian towns which attracted the attention of a number of classical writers which may be because of its fame as a commercial centre. They have invariably called it Barygaza.[485] Though it came into existence long before Buddha's time, it reached the height of its prosperity during the Kuṣāṇa period. It further continued to thrive as an urban centre. We do not find any evidence of its decline either in the Gupta or post-Gupta period. This town was visited by Hiuen-Tsang. According to him, it was above twenty *li* in circuit. The inhabitants were devoted to maritime traffic. They were supported by sea-borne trade. He found there ten Buddhist monasteries with 300 monks.[486]

---

478. *Mts.*, 114, 50; *Bhāg.*, I, 10, 35; III, 1,24; *Vy.*, 1, 45, 130; *Mkd.*, 57, 51.
479. *Divyāvadāna*, p. 576, for details see pp. 544-586.
480. *Imp. Gaz. Ind.*, vol. IX, p. 30.
481. *Divyāvadāna*, p. 545.
482. *Jāt.*, IV, pp. 86ff; *DPPN*, II, p. 365; *Dip.*, IX, 26; *Bodhisattvāvadāna Kalpalatā* cf. *SBLN*, p. 51; *Milindapañha*, Bk. VII cf. *HPL*, II, p. 367; *Sāmantapāsādikā* cf. *HPL*, II, p. 405.
483. *Sussondi Jāt.*, cf. *Jāt.*, vol. III, pp. 187ff. According to *Sāsanavaṁsa* (p. 10), Suvaṇṇabhūmi is *Sudhammanagara*, i.e., Thaton at the mouth of the river Sittaung.
484. *Bṛhatkalpa Bhāṣya Vṛtti*, 1, 1090 cf. Jain *LAIJC*, p. 360.
485. For details see *AIT*, pp. 38, 40, 49, 77, 152-53 and 343, note; Gerini, *RTGEA*, pp. 382, note, 400, note 2; *Periplus*, pp. 40-42, 180, 193, 196, 287; *CNES*, pp. 115-19; *CAI*, pp. 292, 295, 297-99, 301-6, 308, 311, 373 and 379; *AICL*, pp. 78, 143-44; *AIMA*, p. 145, note; *AIKK*, p. 10, note 18.
486. *YCTI*, II, p. 241.

The town, Kuṇḍinapura, mentioned in the *Mahābhārata*,[487] Purāṇas[488] and in one of the works of Kālidāsa[489] was the earliest capital of the kingdom of Vidarbha. It was very famous during the time of king Bhīṣmaka. It is identified with modern Kuṇḍapura on the western bank of the Vardhā, about 40 miles east of Amarāvatī in Mahārāṣṭra.[490] Bhojakatapura or Bhojakatanagar mentioned in both the *Mahābhārata*[491] and Purāṇas[492] was the later capital of the Vidarbhas. It is said to have been founded by Rukmin (the son of king Bhīṣma) in Kṛṣṇa's time. It is represented by modern Bhat-Kuli in the district of Amaraoti or Amarāvatī.[493]

The city called Pratiṣṭhāna or Pratiṣṭhānapura in one of the Purāṇas[494] has been identified with the modern Paiṭhan on the north bank of the Godāvarī in the Auraṅgābād district of Mahārāṣṭra.[495] It is one of the oldest cities of the Deccan. It is believed to have been the capital of king Śālivāhana. It is identical with Patiṭṭhāna, Poṭana or Poṭanagara of the Buddhists. It was the capital of the kingdom of Aśmaka (called Assaka in the early Pāli texts) in the time of the Buddha.[496] The city was known to the author of the *Periplus* as Paethana[497] and to Ptolemy as Baithana.[498] The name occurs also in the Poona plate of Prabhāvatī Gupta, the Vākāṭaka queen.[499] It further continued to flourish as the capital city of the Sātavāhana kingdom or of the western part of the kingdom of the Āndhras from about the middle of the second century AD till about first quarter of the third century AD. It gradually began to decline after the third century AD.

---

487. Āraṇyaka Parva, 60, 19, 72, 2.
488. *Vṣṇ.*, V, 26, 1; *Bhāg.*, X, 53, 7, 15, 21; X, 54, 19-20; *Bmv.*, 108, 12-13; *Vy.*, 95, 34-36; *Mts.*, 44, 36.
489. *Raghuvaṁśa*, VII, 33.
490. *Ind. Ant.*, vol. III, p. 262.
491. Sabhā Parva, 28, 40.
492. *Bhāg.*, X, 54, 52; *Vṣṇ.*, V, 28, 9.
493. *Ind. Ant.*, vol. III, p. 263.
494. *Pdm.*, Uttarakhaṇḍa, 180, 2-7.
495. Law, *HGAI*, p. 183.
496. *DN*, II, p. 235; *Vimānavatthu Commentary*, pp. 259ff; *Niddesa*, II, pp. 4-5, cf. *HPL*, II, p. 663; *DPPN*, II, p. 127.
497. *Periplus*, sec. 51, p. 195; *CNES*, p. 125; *CAI*, pp. 304, 312, 381.
498. *AIT*, pp. 176-77.
499. *Ep. Ind.*, vol. XV, p. 39.

Śūrpāraka mentioned in the *Mahābhārata*[500] and Purāṇas[501] or Suppāra or Suppāraka referred to in the Pāli chronicles[502] and a commentary[503] was a seaport town. It is identical with the modern Supārā or Sopārā in the district of Ṭhāṇā (or Ṭhāṇe), 37 miles north of Bombay and about 5 miles north-west of Bassein. In one of the Sanskrit Buddhist texts also[504] it is described as a port town. It seems to have been from very early times an important centre of trade and commerce where merchants from different parts of the country used to flock with merchandise. According to the *Apadāna* and *Manoratha Purani*, there was a regular trade between Bharukaccha, Suppāraka and Suvaṇṇabhūmi.[505] It was perhaps the capital of the Koṅkaṇ or the district that lay around it. Suppāra is described in the *Periplus* as one of the market-towns of western India.[506] It was known to Ptolemy both as Soupara[507] and Sippara, identified by Yule with Śūrpāraka.[508] It was in a thriving state during the Kuṣāṇa period. It, however, declined after the third century AD. Among its ruins have been preserved some monuments of historical interest which also attest to its high antiquity. There are fragments of a block of bacalt like the rocks of Girnār, inscribed with edicts of Aśoka, and an old Buddhist *stūpa*.

## Southern India

The towns and cities of southern India also deserve our attention.

The Age of the Sātavāhanas (first century BC-third century AD) witnessed the efflorescence of a number of towns on the river Kṛṣṇā in the present Gunṭūr district of Andhra Pradesh. One of the prosperous towns of this age was Amarāvatī which stood on the south bank of the Kṛṣṇā. It has yielded two sherds of rouletted ware.[509] It is believed to have come into existence as an urban centre in the early phase of NBPW. However, it became very famous in the second century BC — the period which saw the erection of

500. Sabhā Parva, 28, 43.
501. *Vy.*, 1, 45, 128; *Bmd*; 1, 2, 16, 60; *Mkd.*, 57, 49; *Vmn.*, 13, 51; *Vṣn.*, *Dh.*, 2, 17, 22.
502. *Dip.*, IX, 15, 16, p. 55; *Mhv.*, VI, 46, p. 60; also *HPL*, II, pp. 553-54.
503. *Dhammapada Commentary*, II, p. 210.
504. *Divyāvadāna*, pp. 24ff, 42ff.
505. Cf. *DPPN*, II, p. 1223.
506. *Periplus*, sec, 52, p. 43, also p. 197, note; *CNES*, p. 127.
507. *AIT*, pp. 40-41, 345, note.
508. *Ibid.*, pp. 71-72, 354, note.
509. *AI*, no. 2 (July, 1946), p. 49.

a magnificent Buddhist *stūpa*. The sculptures which belong to the Kuṣāṇa period (second-third century AD) are noted for their artistic excellence. This town figures both in Buddhist[510] and Jain[511] sources. The place was known also for its Buddhist institutions which attracted students from many places. The ruins of some of the Buddhist monuments and the outline of the foundations of the town can still be seen at the site.

The another famous town on the Kṛṣṇā was Nāgārjunakoṇḍa built by the Ikṣvākus, the successors of the Sātavāhanas. Here protective burnt-brick walls with gates have been discovered on the river side.[512]

It is significant to note that both Amarāvatī and Nāgārjunakoṇḍa were important seats of Buddhists art and culture during the times of the Sātavāhanas and the Ikṣvākus. Both the towns were mainly inhabited by artisan classes. In fact, the religious, educational and artistic factors — all combined together — led to their growth as towns.

Dhānyakaṭaka, the modern Dhāraṇīkoṭṭa, on the Kṛṣṇā was an extensive town. It was the capital of the eastern part of the kingdom of the Āndhras or Sātavāhanas. The remains of an ancient township about 1½ miles west of Amarāvatī in all probability represents "Dhanakaṭaka" of the inscriptions.

Pliny speaks of thirty walled (fortified) towns of the "Andarae" (Āndhras). These towns, according to him, were defended by walls, towers, etc.[513] Some of the towns representing the settlements of the Sātavāhana period excavated in the modern Telaṅgānā region may be identical with those mentioned by him.

All the above-mentioned ancient towns of Andhra Pradesh began to decline from the third century AD onwards.

Among the ancient towns and cities of Tamil Nadu mention may first be made of Kāveripaṭṭanam (Puhār), situated at the mouth of the Kāverī river (60 miles south of Pondicherry), and near the sea. It was the earliest capital of the Coḷa kingdom. In fact, it was a port town from where they carried on a brisk trade with the outside world. It was an emporium of trade. Kolapaṭṭana mentioned in the *Milindapañha*[514] has been

510. *Dhammapada-Aṭṭhakathā*, vol. I, p. 83; *Mhv. Comm.*, p. 120.

511. *Mahāpurāṇa*, 6, 205.

512. *IAR*, 1956-57, p. 36.

513. *Nat. Hist.*, VI, 22.

514. P. 359.

identified with his town.[515] Its destruction by the sea must have occurred before the close of the third quarter of the second century AD.

After the destruction of Kāveripaṭṭanam the Coḷas built a new capital city which became famous as Uragapura. It was situated on the south bank of the Kāverī. They beautified it with magnificent palaces and temples. The city finds mention also in the *Mahābhārata*[516] and in one of the works of Kālidāsa.[517] It is identical with the modern Uraiyūr (city of habitation), a suburb of Tiruchirapalli or Trichinopoly. It was known to Ptolelmy as Orthoura, one of the eight inland cities belonging to the maritime territory of Coḷas.[518] The author of the *Periplus* refers to it as Argaru, which appears to be a Greek transcript of its Sankrit name Uragapura. It is described as one of "the ancient capitals of the Chola kingdom".[519] It is said that "here the pearls were bought; and from there the muslins were exported."[520] Thus, it was both an administrative and a commercial centre. It was in a very flourishing state in the third century AD.

According to Hiuen-Tsang the capital of the *Chu-li-va* ("Coḷas") was above ten *li* in circuit.[521] But it is very difficult to identify it.

Kāñcī or Kāñcīpura (modern Kanjeevaram) not far distant from Madras was another important town of the Coḷas. It is on the testimony of Patañjali (IV, 2, 104) that it is generally held that it rose into prominence as a town about the middle of the second century BC. It is described in the Purāṇas as one of the ancient cities of south India.[522] It was one of the seven sacred cities of ancient India.[523] The Pallavas occupied this famous city about AD 350 and made it their capital. Some of their inscriptions[524] throw lights on the ancient history of this city. It is said to have been one of the six universities of Buddhist period.[525] In the times of Buddhadatta and Buddhaghoṣa (fifth century AD), it

---

515. Law, *Tribes in Ancient India*, p.188.
516. Sabhā Parva, 24, 18-20.
517. *Raghuvaṁśa*, VI, 59; see also *Ep. Ind.*, X, p. 103.
518. *AIT*, pp. 64-65, 185-86; also *CAI*, p. 381.
519. *Periplus*, sec. 59 pp. 46, 241, note.
520. *Ibid.*, p. 46; see also *CAI*, p. 307.
521. *YCTI*, II, pp. 224-5; *BRWW*, II, p. 227.
522. *Bmd.*, 4, 19, 15; *Bhāg.*, X, 79, 11-15; *Vmn.*, 12, 50.
523. *Ibid.*, 4, 40, 91.
524. *Ep. Ind.*, I, p. 2; VI, p. 84; VIII, p. 24.
525. Dey, *GDAMI*, p. 137.

was one of the three great centres of Pāli learning.[526] It was not only a seat of power but also a religious and educational centre. It further continued to flourish as an urban centre. It is identical with *Kan-chih-pu-lo* of Hiuen-Tsang. He visited it in AD 640. This capital city, according to him, was above thirty *li* in circuit.[527] It is still in excellent state of preservation.

The great city of Madhurā was the capital of the kingdom of the Pāṇḍyas.[528] It has a very high antiquity. The site of ancient Madurā is situated at the distance of about six miles south-east of the modern Madurai on the northern banks of the river Vaigai. The classical writers, notably, Pliny,[529] the author of the *Periplus*,[530] Ptolemy[531] and Arrian[532] have also described Modoura or Modura as a capital of the Pāṇḍyan kingdom. It is said that "Modura has retained its name almost unchanged, being now called Madhura. It is an inland town in the south. . . . The land of Pandion, of which it was the capital, included most of Tinneveli and extended northward as far as the highlands near the Koimbatur gap. On the west it was bounded by the Southern Ghats and on the east by the sea. . . ."[533] This royal city figures in Buddhist literature as Dakṣiṇa Madhurā.[534] It continued to flourish as a city till about the end of the fourth or fifth century AD. Hiuen-Tsang did not personally visit this city. He has, however, left some informtion which he obtained from his Buddhist friend at Kāñcī. We are told that it was in the state of decadence. Many old monasteries were in ruins. Some portions of the walls of the city were preserved. Brāhmaṇism was gaining prominence over other religious faiths. Buddhism had rather fallen lnto disrepute.[535]

The excavations of 1945 at Arikameḍu near Pondicherry have brought to light a brick built commercial town of the first century AD. It is said that "Arikameḍu . . .

---

526. Law, *Geographical Essays*, p. 60.
527. *YCTI*, II, p. 226.
528. R. Sewell, *HISI*, p. 41.
529. *Nat. Hist.*, VI, 23 (26); also cf. *AICL*, p. 112.
530. *Periplus*, sec. 59 pp. 46, 238, note; also *CAI*, p. 379.
531. *AIT*, pp. 60, 183-4, 351-52, note; see also *AICL*, p. 9, note 3.
532. *Indika*, ch. VIII.
533. *AICL*, p. 112, note 3.
534. See *DPPN*, II, p. 439; *Mhv.*, VII, 50, 69, 72.
535. *BRWW*, II, p. 231.

represents the site of a considerable buried town on the Coromandel coast." It seems to have been occupied in the first and second centuries AD. It was not only a seat of various arts, crafts and indigenous industries but also an important centre of Indo-Roman trade in the early centuries of the Christian era. It was mainly the trading activities which led to its transformation into an urban complex.[536]

Gokarṇa, mentioned by Kālidāsa,[537] was a temple town in north Karnataka. It was, according to him, situated "on the shore of the southern ocean". It has been identified with "Gendia, a town about 30 miles south of Goa in the Kumtā Tāluk of North-Kanara district".[538] It is still a famous place of pilgrimage.

Brahmagiri was another ancient town of Karnataka. It was in a flourishing state in the age of the Mauryas. The rouletted ware was discovered at the site in 1947.[539] It was basically a commercial centre. It continued to thrive as an urban centre till the end of the third century AD.

## General Remarks

According to the epic and Purāṇic tradition, the ancient Indian towns and cities were generally named after those kings who founded them, for excamples, Hastināpura was named after its founder, Hastin, Kauśāmbī after Kuśāmba, Vaiśālī after Viśāla, Mithilā after Mithi, Kuśāvatī after Kuśa, Vasumatī after Vasu, Kuśāgrapura after Kuśāgra, Śrāvastī after Śrāvasta, Māhiṣmatī after Mahiṣmān, Madhurā (or Mathurā) after Madhu, Takṣaśilā, after Takṣa and Puṣkalāvatī after Puṣkala. F.E. Pargiter observes : ". . . countries are said sometimes to have been named after kings, such as Gāndhāra, Ānarta, and Sauvira; and similarly towns, such as Śrāvasti, Hastināpura and Vaiśāli from the kings who founded them. To assert that such kings are merely eponymous is to disregard the evidence supplied by many countries and all times. One might equally assert that Alexander, Seleucus and Constantine were merely eponymous heroes of Alexandria, Seleucia and Constantinople; or that Columbas, Tasman and Rhodes were mythical persons invented to account for Columbia, Tasmania and Rhodesia. It has been a universal

536. For details see R.E.M. Wheeler, A. Ghosh and Krishna Deva, "Arikamedu: and Indo-Roman Trading-station on the East Coast of India", *AI*, no. 2, (July 1946), pp. 17ff.

537. *Raghuvaṁśa*, VIII, 33.

538. Banerji, *Kālidāsa-Kośa*, p. 25.

539. *AI*, no. 4, (July 1947-Jan 1948), pp. 180ff.

practice to name countries, towns, mountains and rivers especially in newly developed regions, after discoverers, conquerors, founders and celebrated men, and the same method must have been adopted by the Aryans who conquered North India and founded new kingdoms and towns there".[540]

The existence of about 140 towns or cities in ancient India during the period under review can be proved on the basis of literary and archaeological evidences. It is practically not possible to accommodate all of them within the ambit of this paper. Moreover, each city has more or less its own history. Out of 104 urban sites excavated so far both vertically and horizontally, 30 have been found associated with PGW phase of culture and 74 with NBPW phase of culture.

## Phases of Urban Growth

The latter half of the first millennium BC was admittedly an important phase in the early histoy of urbanisation in India. The intensive use of iron, abundance of NBPW, the use of punch-marked coins, introduction of ringwells, regulated and controlled market economy, etc., gave fillip to the rise and growth of towns during the period. The use of burnt bricks in place of mud or mud-bricks for building houses and other structures led to the flowering of towns and cities not only in the Gangetic valley but also in different other parts of India. The agrarian economy, developed agricultural system, the availability of surplus food, the formation of guilds of artisans and merchants, various arts, specialised crafts, indigenous industries, well-managed markets and trade and commerce resulted in the growth of urban settlements. The use of money, which was one of necessary concomitants for the growth of an urban economy, also proved to be a stimulant factor for the growth of towns. The economic prosperity of high level, rapid development of material culture, the growth of towns and amenities of life led to the increase in urban population.

The Maurya period witnessed the growth and expansion of towns and cities. The Maurya rulers paid speial attention to the administration of big cities. Various officers were appointed and various Boards were set-up for looking after the affairs of towns and cities. The officer designated *paura* was perfect of the capital city. The officer-in-charge of the city has been called *nagaraka* by Kauṭilya. The archaeological excavations have proved that a large number of towns and cities, including Pāṭaliputra, Kauśāmbī, Vaiśālī,

---

540. *AIHT*, p. 137.

Sārnāth, Takṣaśilā, Ujjain, Rājaghāṭ, Virāṭanagar, Bhītā, Candraketugarh and Brahmagiri, flourished during this period.

The post-Maurya times (*c.* 150 BC-AD 300), which cover the Śuṅga, Kuṣāṇa and Sātavāhana periods, represent the most mature phase of urbanisation in early India. The erection of *stūpas*, *caitya* halls, monumental buildings like temples an monasteries, large mansions, forts and fortifications, towers, ramparts, gateways and defensive walls or lofty walls of cities, etc., at various places during the period transformed the character of urbanism to a large extent.

The Kuṣāṇa period proved to be a blooming period so far as the growth of towns and cities is concerned. The growing crafts and commerce and the increasing use of money or monetisation of the economic structure further promoted the growth of towns during this period. Most of the towns flourished in eastern and northern India in the Kuṣāṇa period. The archaeological excavations have revealed that large brick structures belonged to the Kuṣāṇa phase. It was the Kuṣāṇa age which ensured the safety and security of the towns. In fact, urbanisation was at it speak during this period. The towns thrived in the age of the Sātavāhanas in western India, the Deccan and the far south. The towns and cities prospered in the Kuṣāṇa and Sātavāhana periods specially because of thriving trade with the Roman empire as well as with central Asia. The maritime trade of India with the West and other commercial activities during the period transformed the rural-based economy into an urban economy.

The early phase of the Gupta rule also witnessed the progress in the field of urbanisation. The city administration received the attention of also the Gupta rulers. The head of the city administration was known as *purapāla* or *nagara rakṣaka*. A city was governed by a *pariṣada*. A few cities continued to thrive in early Gupta period which include Ayodhyā, Mathurā, Kauśāmbī, Vārāṇasī, Campā, Tāmralipti and Kānyakubja. The travels of Fa-hian bear eloquent testimony to the existence of those towns during the period.

## Causes of Urban Decline

The process of urban decline or deurbanisation began after AD 300. There were various factors responsible for the decline and downfall of the towns and cities in ancient India.

The decline of towns and cities specially in the Gangetic Doāb may largely be attributed to the foreign invasions. We learn from the *Garga Saṁhitā* that the famous

Indo-Greek ruler, Menander (c. 165-144 BC) invaded the Gaṅgā-Yamunā Doāb and destroyed at least seventeen cities which include Sāketa, the capitals of the Pāñcālas, Mathurā and Kusumapura (Pāṭaliputra). The Hūṇas also destroyed a number of cities, including Indraprastha on the Yamunā, Pāṭaliputra of the middle Gangetic plains and Sanghol in the Punjab.

Some towns and cities became victims of the natural forces. Hastināpura of the epic fame was carried away by the floods in the Gaṅgā, and Dvārakā of Kṛṣṇa's time got submerged in the Arabian sea because of the rise in its water level. There are some evidences to show that the cities were rebuilt and new phases of urban settlement began there. Some of the coastal towns were swept away by the tidal waves in the sea.

Some cities fell prey to the invasions of the rulers of neighbouring states the most notable example of which is the destruction of Kapilavastu at the hands of Viḍuḍabha, the son and successor of Prasenajit of Kośala.

The decline of trade also led to the decay of towns. The Indian trade with the western part of the Roman empire ended in the third century AD. The artisans and merchants living in those towns having not found sufficient means to support them flocked to the villages and took to cultivation as a result of which the commercial importance of towns began to dwindle.

Thus, decline in wealth, population and urban settlements gradually led to the decadence of towns.

The decline of towns in Mahārāṣṭra, Andhra Pradesh and Tamil Nadu generally began from the third century AD onwards. Most of the towns and cities in other parts of India declined in Gupta and post-Gupta times,[541] as evidenced by Fa-hian's and Hiuen-Tsang's accounts of the subject. Hiuen-Tsang visited several towns but found them either almost deserted or dilapidated. However, some cities like Ahicchatra, Śṛṅgaverapura, Kānyakubja, Campā, Nālandā, Mahāsthān, Besnagar, Bānagarh, Ambarī,

541. For details see R.S. Sharma, "Decay of Gangetic towns in Gupta and post-Gupta times", *PIHC*, 33rd Session (Muzaffarpur, 1972), pp. 94-104; also *ABORI*, Golden Jubilee vol. (1973), p. 137f; *Urban Decay in India; c. AD 300-1000* (Delhi, 1987), pp. 59ff; V.K. Thakur, *Urbanisation in Ancient India* (Delhi, 1981), pp. 261-330; also his "Regional Patterns of Early Medieval Formation in India: A Study of Gupta Towns", Presedential Address, section 1 Ancient India, IHC, 58th session (Bangalore, 1997), pp. 5-20.

Tripurī, Sāñcī, Ujjain, Vaḍnagar, Broach, Dvārakā and Kāñcīpuram further coninued to survive. It is striking to note that the urban tradition had not completely died down. A large number of towns and cities flourished in early medieval period also,[542] but they do not fall within the scope of this chapter.

542. While at Shimla in Feb. 1992 in connection with my personal work, I had the opportunity to go through Mrs. Renu Thakur's thesis (then unpublished): *Urbanisation in Early Medieval India c. AD 750-1200* (approved for Ph.D. degree of Himachal Pradesh University, Shimla) in which she has proved the existence of 255 towns during the period which invalidates the views held by some scholars that in the post-Harṣa period only a few towns thrived in India.

# 4

# A Fresh Literary Discovery of the Seals of Dvārakā in the Epic Age

## A Supplement to Archaeological Discovery

No accurate historical study of the antiquity, location and identification of Dvārakā city of Śrī Kṛṣṇa's time in general and that of seals which were used by the republican confederate Yādava tribes like Andhaka-Vṛṣṇīs and other dwellers of the city for various purposes during the period under review in particular can be made without placing our reliance on the combined testimony of the epic — *Mahābhārata* — the Purāṇas and the archaeological findings of a distinguished marine archaeologist, Prof. S.R. Rao. The picture of the subject concerned with particular reference to the seals which so far emerges on the basis of archaeological finds from Bet-Dvārakā Sea is neither very graphic nor complete, and hence, it needs to be supplemented with the help of the epic and Purāṇic evidences.

We do acknowledge the contribution made by Prof. Rao to ancient Indian history and culture through his discovery of the sunken city of Śrī Kṛṣṇa and various other remains comprising mainly the seals made of shells from sea in Bet-Dvārakā (an island 30 km north of modern Dvārakā on the western coast of Saurashtra, Gujarat) between November 1987 and February 1988,[1] but still we find a scope to add something more to the archaeological description of particularly the seals with the help of the epic and Purāṇic texts. Before we proceed further to do so, it must be made here clear that this well planned and fortified big city which covered an area of 12 *yojana* (i.e., 12 × 4 = 48 *krosa* or 96 mile)[2] and contained magnificent buildings, temples, gates, market-complex,

---

1. Gunakar Mule, 'Kahāṅ thī Śrī Kṛṣṇa Kī Dvārakā?', *Gaganāñcal* (ed. G.K. Mathur, Bhāratīya Sāṁskṛtika Saṁbandha Pariṣada, Delhi, 1987), 10, 3, pp. 8-15; *The Hindu*, Gurgaon, Sunday, 7 February 1988; *India Express*, 6 March 1988.

2. *Bhāgavata Purāṇa*, X, 50, 48-54; *Vṣn.*, V, 23, 9-13; *Hv.*, Viṣṇu Parva, 58, 36; *Br.*, 196, 12-15.

all sophisticated arms and weapons, etc.[3], was established in the pre-Bhārata war period by the Yādavas — Andhakas, Vṛṣṇīs, Bhojas, Kukuras, etc. — under the leadership of Kṛṣṇa after deserting their former capital Mathurā[4] but was submerged by the sea-water as a sequel to its tidal wave shortly after the destruction of the Yādavas in the fratricidal war which ensued exactly 36 years after the Great War or after Yudhiṣṭhira's installation on the throne of Hastināpura.[5] The other way in which it can be put is that the city was engulfed by the sea sometime in between the death of Kṛṣna and the accession of Parīkṣit which occurred after the war. The city of Dvārakā no doubt had been lying submerged under the Arabian Sea since the time of Parīkṣit who can be ascribed to roughly the fifteenth century BC on the basis of the chronological computation and interpretation of the Purāṇic date.[6] Prof. S.R. Rao also places the settlement at Bet-Dvārakā of the *Mahābhārata* phase between *c.* 1500-1400 BC with emphasis on *c.* 1424 BC as the date of the war.[7] Thus, the very fact that the city was in existence and was submerged by the sea, as stated in the *Mahābhārata* and the Purāṇas, gets confirmation from the archaeological discovery concerned. The city was, in fact, divided into four sectors, viz., Mūla-Dvārakā (on the south-west coast of Saurashtra, about 5 km away from the Prabhāsa in the Ūnā Tāluka of Jūnāgarh district or east of Porabandar or Sudāmāpurī), modern Dvārakā (in ancient Okhamaṇḍal, Kāṭhiāwāḍ or situated on the

---

3. *Mahābhārata*, Āraṇyaka Parva, 16, 5-12, 17-18; also 13, 31; Mausala Parva, 2, 1-20; 3, 1-22; 4, 33, 36-41; 6, 1-15; 7, 9-22; 8, 4-11, 32-47, 58-74; *Bhāgavata*, X, 50, 7-23, 34-57; *Hv*. Viṣṇu Parva, 58, 3-56; *Vṣn*. V, 23, 4-15; V, 24, 5-7; *Br*. 196, 5-15.

4. Ādi Parva, 210, 15-20; 213, 23-55; Sabhā Parva, 13, 5-17, 24-45, 49-55; Mausala Parva, 2, 5-20; 3, 1-22; 4, 33-41; 6, 1-15; 7, 9-22; V.S. Agrawala, *Bhārata Sāvitrī*, vol. 1, pp. 143-44; *Bhāgavata*, 1, 11, 8-14; ix, 3, 1-2, 27-36; X, 36, 33-39; X, 53, 5-22; X, 58, 12; X, 80, 8-12; *Br*., 7, 29-32; 14, 53-56; 195, 1-12; *Vy*., 96, 46-258; *Brahmavaivartta*, Uttara, 103, 7-33 and 80; *Hv*. Viṣṇu Parva, 34, 1-22; 35, 1-111; 36, 1-40; 39, 10-52; 56, 7-35; *Bmd*., iii, 61, 18-23, iii, 71, 48, 62-85.

5. Mausala Parva 2, 1-20 (only this Parva of the *Mahābhārata* makes reference to 36 years); 8, 10; Mahāprasthānika Parva explicitly mentions that after Parīkṣit's accession to Hastināpura (1, 7-9), the Pāṇḍavas in course of their wanderings beheld the sunken city of Dvārakā in the west (1, 43); V.S. Agrawala, *Bhārata Sāvitrī*, 3, pp. 221-23, *Bhāgavata*, XI, 30, 4-25 and 30-37; *Vṣn*. V, 37, 22-36, 39, 42-63.

6. According to the four Purāṇas (*Mts*., 273, 36; *Vy*. 99, 415, *Vṣn*, iv, 24, 104 and *Bmd*., ii, 3, 74, 225-30) Parīkṣit was born about 1050 years before Mahāpadma Nanda. The *Mts*. (272, 18-22) and *Vsn*. (iv, 24, 20-28) assign 100 years to the rule of nine Nandas (for Mahāpadma 88 and +12 for his eight sons = 100). The dynasty came to an end in 322 BC. Thus, 322 + 100 = 422 years will be added to 1050 which will be an equivalent to (1050+422) = 1472 years.

7. Ref. No. 1 (*supra*).

bank of Gomati stream), Bet-Dvārakā (with major settlements) and Prabhāsa Tīrtha (or Somanāth).

As a matter of fact, it was K.P. Jayaswal who first of all in his presidential address to the Seventh All-India Oriental Conference held at Baroda in December 1933 drew the attention of scholars towards a passage in the *Mahābhārata* dealing with seals used in the Dvārakā of hoary antiquity and emphasised the need of making a further historical enquiry into the subject concerned. H.D. Sankalia had focused only on the antiquity, location and identification of different parts of ancient Dvārakā city on the basis of both literary and archaeological evidences.[8]

There are certain questions as to what types of seals were made?; for what purposes they were used?; what circumstances led to their compulsory use?; and what was their utility in the political and economic contexts? which still await answers. The archaeological evidence, of course, ansers the first question but partly and it is completely silent over the rest of the three. The questions concerned can be satisfactorily answered with the help of the evidences available in the *Mahābhārata* and the Purāṇas.

The archaeological finds from Bet-Dvārakā of great historical importance include various shells with lotus or *padma* engraved on them[9] which were used as seals by the dwellers of the city concerned. The following verses from the *Mahābhārata* also bear an eloquent testimony to the fact that in Dvāravatī (i.e., city of gates identified with Dvārakā) seals bearing the representation of *padma* were seen to the utter surprise of the people:

> *tasmiṁstīrthe (dvāravatīṁ) mahābhāga padmalakṣaṇalakṣitāḥ* । *adyāpi mudrā dṛśyante taddabhūtamṛndama* ॥.[10]

Thus, we find that the literary and archaeological evidence regarding the seals concerned goes in perfect harmony with each other. But here are certain evidenes which we find only in the literary sources. The seals bearing the depiction of trident also find mention in the *Mahābhārata*[11] in addition to the above.

The seals were used for various purposes. Politically, their use was determined

---

8. See his "Antiquity of Modern Dwarka or Dwaraka in Literature and Archaeology", in *Aspects of Indian History and Archaeology* (eds. S.P. Gupta and K.S. Ramachandran Delhi, 1977), pp. 191-201.
9. Ref. No. 1 (*supra*).
10. *Āraṇyaka Parva*, 80, 83.
11. *Ibid.*, 80, 84.

according to the emerging situation. We find that Śālva, a king of Marttikavata or Saubhanagara (i.e., Śālvadeśa or Śālvapur corresponding to Bairāt in Jaipur, the earstwhile capital of Matsyas and it extended from Alwar to north Bikāner, Rajasthan), attacked Dvārakā to retaliate the death of his friend Śiśupāla, a king of Cedi, at the hand of Kṛṣṇa and entered into a battle with Andhaka-Vṛṣṇīs but was ultimately killed by Kṛṣṇa.[12] This invasion created a fear-psychosis of insecurity among the inhabitants of the city. In order to defend the city against any possible future invasion and to make distinction between the friends and foes with the help of the seals, a new plan was chalked out. According to a recorded evidence, the singers, dancers, dramatists, etc., were asked to quit the city perhaps to save them from the extinction. Thereafter the city was made equipped with arms and weapons, well guarded by soldiers.[13]

This was the stage at which Kṛṣṇa as a ruler of Dvārakā (also called Vṛṣnī-Andhakapur) had ordered that all citizens while entering or leaving the city should carry their seals (*mudrā*) for showing to the guards, incharge of its security, as a mark of identification. Thus, seals were also used as a security measure in Kṛṣṇa's kingdom. This can be testified to by the following verses from the *Mahābhārata*:

> *na cāmudroabhiniryāti na cāmudraḥ praveśyate* ।
> *vṛṣṇyandhakaṁpure rājaṁstadā saubhsamāgame* ।।[14]

The importance of seals made from marine shells (also called *śaṅkha*) from the economic point of view in general and their market value in particular have been sufficiently highlighted in the *Harivaṁśa*. The evidences adduced in the text give us an impression that the seals concerned were used to regulate and control the market-economy. They were the stabiliser of finance. That is why, the seals have been called as *vitarakṣaka*. They served the purpose of a standard currency because of availability of plenty of shells

---

12. Āraṇyaka Parva, 15, 1-22; 16, 1-4, 13, 16-23; 17, 1-33; 18, 1-24; also Chs. 19-21.

    The *Gopatha Brāhmaṇa* (1, 2, 9) has referred to 'Salva-Matsyesu' conjointly; V.S. Agrawala (*India as known to Pāṇini*, pp. 56-57) has identified Marttikavata or Śālvadeśa with Alwar-Jaipur region; B.C. Law (*Geographical Essays Relating to Ancient Geog. of India*, p. 133) has placed it along the western side of the Arāvallī Hills; Pargiter (*Ancient Indian Historical Tradition*, p. 279) has located it around Mt. Abu; N.L. Dey, (*Geographical Dictionary of Ancient and Medieval India*, p. 132) has fixed it in Marwar; V.S. Agrawala in his *Bhārata Sāvitrī* (1, pp. 206-9) has also dealt with the subject placing Saubhpur in Ānartta, northern Gujarat.

13. Āraṇyaka Parva, 16, 14-18.

14. *Ibid.*, 16, 19.

there. They were the chief means of transaction for the traders in the market. The poverty and richness of the people were greatly determined by these seals. The purchasing capacity of the people largely depended on the possession of their seals. In order to make the city prosperous and improve the economic condition of its Yādava population, Kṛṣṇa greatly encouraged the free flow of such seals in the market. During his time quite a good number of poor people in Dvārakā city became rich through these seals. As a matter of fact, the financial stability of the whole population of the city entirely depended on the possession of the these seals.[15] The *Padma Purāṇa* also contains a passage about the seals concerned.[16] About 1 km away from Kṛṣṇa's palace at Bet-Dvārakā (an island having a circuit of 12 km) there is a place called Śaṅkhodvāratīrtha, where the work of discovering the shells from the sea was carried out by the people at large scale during the period concerned.

A seal made from a shell bearing the image of a three-headed creature with the heads of bull, unicorn and goat has also been discovered by the marine archaeologist from the Bet-Dvārakā sea which despite being uninscribed bears close resemblance to the Indus-type pictographic seals and other smaller rectangular seals with perforated button at the back. The description of this particular seal is conspicuous by its absence in the epic and the Purāṇas.

There can hardly be any doubt about the fact that the literature and archaeology are supplementary to each other in many respects, including the existence and antiquity of Dvārakā city, the use of its seals, etc. The evidences available in the epic *Mahābhārata* and the Purāṇas about the subject concerned also constitute one of the aspects for judging their historical value. The archaeological discovery of lost Dvārakā city of Kṛṣṇa's time also goes to prove the historicity of the details as provided in the *Mahābhārata* and the Purāṇas about the subject concerned.

---

15. *Hv*. 58, 57-66.
16. Svargakhaṇḍa, 24, 14-16.

# 5

## The Emergence, Growth and Decay of Urban Centres in North-West India In the Pre- and Post-Maurya Period as Gleaned from the Classical Sources

THE pre- and post-Maurya period witnessed the emergence, growth and decay of a large number of urban centres (towns or cities) in different parts of Afghanistan, the Punjab, Sindh and Baluchistan (Gedrosia) in north-west India, as it distinctly appears from the classical (Greek and Latin) sources. The information supplied by the celebrated classical (Greek and Roman) historians, geographers and travellers of both the pre- and post-Christian era (as a whole ascribed to the period extending from the sixth century BC to the sixth century AD) about the subject concerned are of inestimable value. In this connection mention may be made of Skylax (*c.* 518-516 BC), Hecataeus (*c.* 549-486 BC), Herodotus (*c.* 485-425 BC), Megasthenes (*c.* 321-297 BC), Eratosthenes (*c.* 276-194 BC), Polybius (*c.* 204-122 BC), Kallisthenes (*c.* 327-325 BC), Aristoboulos (*c.* 327-323 BC), Nearkhos (*c.* 336-313 BC), Onesikritos (*c.* 326-325 BC), Strabo (*c.* 64 BC -AD 21), Pliny (*c.* AD 23-79), a Greek merchant of the first century AD and the author (anonymous) of the *Periplus* (*c.* AD 80-89), Arrian (*c.* AD 96-180), Apollonius of Tyana (about the middle of the first century AD or AD 43-44), Philostratus of Lemnos (*c.* AD 172-230 or 180-250), Ptolemy (*c.* AD 150), Apollodorus (latter half of the second or first century BC), Diodorus Siculus (*c.* 80-21 BC), Quintus Curtius Rufus (first century AD or *c.* AD 41-54), Plutarch (*c.* AD 45-125), Justin (second half of the second century AD), Isidore of Charax (first century AD), Aelian (who flourished about the middle of the second century AD), Solinus (first half of the third century AD), Dionysios Periegetes (third century AD or not later than AD 300), Julius Valerius (an Alexandrian writer of the fourth century AD), Ammianus Marcellinus (*c.* AD 380-400), Nonnos (fifth century AD or about AD 500) and Kosmas Indikopleustes (about the middle of the sixth century AD or AD 547). Here it must be made specifically clear that Nearkhos, Onesikritos, Aristoboulos, and Kallisthenes accompanied Alexander on his Asiatic expeditions and presented an eye-witness accounts of the subject in their respective works. Nearkhos (an Admiral of the Fleet) wrote his famous *Journal of Voyage* after completing his journey in September 325 BC. The fragments of his memoirs are preserved in the works of Arrian (*Anabasis*, Bk. VI, chs. XIX-XXIV; *Indica*, pt. II, chs. XVIII ff.) and Strabo (*Geog*. Bk. XV). Onesikritos also wrote his *Journal of Voyage* and *History of Alexander's Life*. The other two writers in their works on Alexander dealing with the history of his war have also inserted some valuable information about the subject, which constituted the sources of information for the later Greek writers. Diodorus, Arrian, Plutarch, Curtius and Justin — the five well-known Alexander's historians — have also dealt with the subject in their respective works which have been extensively used along with other classical treatises by the present writer for purpose concerned.

The study of the subject is primarily based on the original sources (in the form of translations of the Greek and Latin texts preserving the narratives, extracts and fragments of the works of various classical authors). But just to supplement and support them we have utilised some of those works which are purely based on the non-classical sources. In order to identify the place-names and determine the exact geographical location and position of old and forgotten towns and cities situated in the hills and valleys of Afghanistan, in the plains of the northern, central and southern Punjab, in the upper, middle and lower valley of the Indus and in some parts of Baluchistan with some amount of accuracy and precision, we have placed our reliance on the combined testimony of both classical and non-classical sources. The classical accounts of the subject have also been corroborated and confirmed by the literary sources, the archaeological evidence (coins, inscriptions and remains or ruins of the cities), the Chinese account of Hiuen-Tsang or Yuan Chwang (AD 629-45) and the statements of the explorers and travellers (who discovered the remains of towns or cities described in the classical literature) and some chroniclers and geographers wherever necessary.

It is worthy of remark that the classical authors have presented conflicting, contradictory and divergent accounts of the subject. The accounts are both mythological and historical. Some of them have been assailed with the charges of mendacity, while some have been praised for applying their sound judgement and presenting very trustworthy and intelligible accounts distinguished by their conspicuous merits. However, their authenticity have been examined in the light of the facts recorded in different sources.

The transformation of place-names from the Sanskrit to Persian and then on to the Greek because of the Persian and Greek rule in north-west India for sometime between the sixth and the first century BC, as a whole, has really made our task of identifying them in the geographical setting very difficult. Moreover, the lack of uniformity in the system followed by different scholars for transcribing and transliterating the classical appellations sometimes makes the confusion worse confounded. Thus, all the available evidences have been harmonised together for piercing through the haziness enveloping the subject with particular reference to the identification and geographical locations of the towns and cities concerned.

The four cardinal factors, demographic, political, economic and military, greatly responsible for urbanisation, were conspicuously present in north-western India. From the classical description of the subject it is quite evident that the towns and cities were thickly populated. The small cities contained the population of roughly 5,000 and above, and the bigger ones upwardes of 10,000. The free cities were generally without chief or king. The cities with chiefs were the seats of sovereign power. Each city-state had its own political institutions, including assembly or council, and laws and army. Each citizen owed allegiance to his city. The citizens possessed all real property, exercised all political rights and performed all military duties. Most of the capital cities of the tribal states, which broadly fall within the two categories —monarchical and oligarchical or republican-gradually developed as urban centres. Some of them assumed the character of small city-states. The large, populous and extensive cities were well protected by defensive walls, forts and fortifications and ramparts of formidable strength. They also served as strongholds or acropolis. Many cities were founded for defensive purposes in the sense of offering the stout resistance to the Persian and Macedonian invaders. The people were by and large agricultural communities. Because of having their settlements on the banks of the rivers in different parts of north-western India they enjoyed the irrigational facilities which led to their economic prosperity. Most of the towns and cities were situated along the banks of the rivers Kophen (Kābul = Skt. Kubhā), Khoaspes (Kunār, a tributary of the Kābul), Soastus (Swāt = Skt. Suvāstu) and its tributary Gaurior Panjkora in Afghanistan, the Indus (Skt. Sindhu), and Hydaspes (Jhelum = Skt. Vitastā), Akesines (Cenāb = Skt. Asiknī, later Candrabhāgā), Hydraotes (Rāvī = Skt. Paruṣṇī, later Irāvatī), Hyphasis (Beas = Skt. Vipāśā) and Hesydrus (Sutlej = Skt. Śatadru or Śutudri) in Punjab. The higher agricultural production facilitated the growth of commercial activities. Many towns and cities developed as great emporium of trade. The people with surplus production played an active role in the growth of trade and commerce. Some towns and cities also developed as religious and educational centres. Some of them contained temples with the gods and goddesses. There were some splendid structures of artistic beauty. The architectural style of some of the urban centres, particulary in Gāndhāra region (the Kābul and the Swāt valleys in Afghanistan, and Peśāwar, and Rāwalpiṇḍī district in the northern Punjab), underwent profound changes because of the successive rule of the Persians, Macedonians, Graeco-Bactrians, Śakas and Kuṣāṇas there between the sixth century BC and the first century AD.

In most of the parts of north-western India, the towns and cities belonged to the tribal people. Besides the tribal towns and cities, there were some other urban centres including the Brāhmaṇical cities in the lower Sindh. However, it cannot be denied that some of them were no better than the early urban centres of the Gangetic valley (ascribed to the earlier half of the first millennium BC) with mud huts the circumference of which formed a protective wall of no great height or thickness. Some were, of course, of enormous size which flourished as centres of urban culture. The cities were, on the whole, both large and small. Their construction, location and fortifications give us some idea of the system of town-planning then in vogue.

The classical sources bear an eloquent and glowing testimony to the existence of a large number of towns and cities exceeding one thousand in north-western part of India. This is what it can be substantiated by the evidences adduced by J.W. McCrindle on the basis of his exhaustive study of the data contained in the classical literature.[1] But the entire details are not available because many towns and cities passed into oblivion as a result of their early destruction. Only few of them were explored and discovered which remained the object of attraction for many. Rufinus (*c.* AD 340-420) in one of his Latin works has unravelled a mystery of history by stating that Metrodoros, a Persian by birth, had penetrated to north-west India for the purpose of seeing its various towns and cities which attracted him the most.[2] But the date of his visit is not specified.

Max Duncker has categorically stated that the north-western part of India with numerous towns and cities were known to the Greek writers.[3]

Vasudeva Sharana Agrawala on the basis of his comparative study of Pāṇinian and classical traditions relating to the towns and cities of north-west India has correctly

1. *AICL*, pp. 9ff; *IIA*, pp. 58ff.
2. *Hist. Eccles.*, 1.9, *AICL*, p. 185.
3. *HA*, vol. IV, p. 408.

observed: "That ancient India possessed a large number of flourishing centres of population in the form of cities or towns is also attested to by Greek writers. According to them the Panjab was full of towns, centres of industry and economic prosperity. Many of these figured as forts or centres of defence. . . . Both Pāṇini (a native of Śalātura in Gandhāra or "Lahur, a small town four miles north-west of Ohind in the angle of the river Kābul meeting the Indus) and the Greek geographers depended on a common source of tradition. . . ."[4] It has been further stated that the number of cities — 500 between the Jhelum and the Beas (the Vāhika region) — as recorded by the historians of Alexander's campaign almost tallies with the figures given by Pāṇini in his *Aṣṭādhyāyī* (*Sūtra*s and *Gaṇa-Pāṭha*).[5]

The foundation of most of the cities may reasonably be ascribed to the indigenous people. However, there were some which bore the stamp of Hellenic cities because of being transformed with a new Greek name or enlarged by Alexander effecting the settlements of the native people and the Greeks or Yavaṇas. A few ancient cities of indigenous origin received new names from the Macedonian conqueror. Alexander was not only the destroyer but also the builder of the cities. In pursuance of his policy to secure the permanence of his Indian conquests by founding cities, he built some new cities in north-west India and fortified and garrisoned them with large body of troops to overawe and hold in subjection the tribes in their neighbourhood. He planted colonies in the places concerned with the Greek and Indian settlements. The civil administration was entrusted to native chiefs while the executive and military authority was wielded by Macedonian officials.[6] Some of the large and important towns of native urban communities were converted by him into military and non-military colonies dominated by Greek population in oriental environment. According to Plutarch, seventy Asiatic cities at the least owed their origin to Alexander out of which forty can still be traced.[7] But this cannot be accepted as a well ascertained fact. Grote is of the view that the number is exaggerated, and disparages their importance.[8]

Megasthenes' statement that "the Indians in old times had neither the towns nor temples of the gods. When Dionysos came and had conquered the people, founded the

---

4. *IP*, pp. 75-76.
5. *Ibid.*, pp. 496-97.
6. *IIA*, Introd. pp. 4-5, William Rotertson, *HDAI*, p. 27.
7. *IIA*, p. 5, note I.
8. *History of Greece*, vol. XII, cf. *ibid.*

cities and gave laws to these cities", as quoted by Arrian,[9] cannot be accepted *in toto*. It is a fact to be reckoned with that temples were hardly found in north-west India before the dawn of fourth century BC, as it also appears from Kauṭilya's *Arthaśāstra*, but the towns and cities very much existed there preceding the century which Megasthenes belonged to. Moreover, Dionysos was a legendary figure. His historictiy is yet to be proved. As a matter of fact, some of them had already come into existence before the Persian invasion of the north-west in the sixth century BC. Some of them were founded later. The cities were mostly situated in the Valleys of Kābul, Kunār, Swāt and the Indus, and on the banks of the five rivers of the Punjab. A large number of towns and cities were discovered there by Alexander and his companions or followers in course of the campaign between 327 and 325 BC. Many of them were destroyed during the period concerned. But some were found in existence up to the first century AD and some continued to exist beyond that period. Megasthenes himself refers to the cities that existed in different parts of India including the north-west.

It is undeniable that some Greek writers do not mention temples, palaces and other large buildings of the people of north-west India, but, according to Arrian (who derives his authority from Megasthenes), the towns were too numerous to be reckoned, and they were close to each other. He remarks that the towns situated on the banks of rivers were generally built of wood, because no buildings of brick would have last long owing to the destructive rains, and also the rivers which overflowing their banks cause an inundation over the plains; those cities which stood on lofty eminences were built of brick and mud.[10] He also makes mention of some of the important towns and cities of north-west India.

Pliny, while describing the position, boundaries and physical characteristics of India in his work, also pointed out that "In this country the nations and cities are numberless should one attempt to reckon them all up. It was opened up to our knowledge not only by the arms of Alexander the Great and of the kings who succeeded him, Seleucus and Antiochus, . . . but also by certain Greek authors, who resided with Indian kings, such as Megasthenes, and Dionysius who was sent by Philadelphus, and have thus informed us of the power and resources of the Indian nations. However, there is no room for a

9. *Indika*, pt. I, Ch. VII, cf. *AIMA*, 1st edn., p. 199.
10. *Indika*, pt. I, Ch. X, cf. *AIMA*, p. 204.

careful examination of their statements, they are so diverse and incredible. The companions of Alexander the Great have written that in that tract of India, which he subdued, there were 5,000 towns, non less than cos — that its nations were nine in number. . . ."[11] On the basis of a thorough scrutiny of data available in the classical texts we do not find the number of towns stated above as worthy of our credence.

The first discovery of a city in north-west India is ascribed to Skylax of Karyanda, a Greek sea-captain, who undertook a naval expedition sometime about 517 BC under the direction of the Persian king Darius I (*c.* 522-486 BC) to explore the course of the Indus. He found a city named Kaspatyros in the "Gāndhāra country" somewhere near the upper course of the Indus where he embarked. He set out on his voyage from this city down the Indus towards the east and to the sea as described by him in his own narrative,[12] which became the source of information for the later Greek writers. There has been some controversy among scholars in the past over the exact location of this place. According to A.V. Williams Jackson, "the town may have been situated near the lower end of the Cophen (Kābul) river before it joins the Indus".[13] M.A. Stein, while making an attempt to identify the exact site of Kaspatyros, suggests that this city must have been situated near Jahangira, a place on the left bank of the Kābul river, some six miles above the confluence of the latter with the Indus at Attock from where Skylax and his companions started on their voyage. He refers to many ruined sites near Jahangira, and near Alladher closeby on the Indus.[14] The geographical position assigned to this city by him has also been supported by other scholars.[15]

Hecataeus of Miletus, who derived his authority from Skylax, called this city Kaspapyros. He speaks of it as a city of the Gandaraeans or Gandarians.[16] He has

11. *Natural History*, Bk. VI. c. 17(21); *AICL*, pp. 107-8.
12. Cf. Herodotus, *History*, Bk. IV, 44; tr. G. Rawlinson, vol. III, pp. 589-91; see also *AICL*, p. 4; *AIMA*, Introd. p. 5, note; A.V.W. Jackson, "The Persian Dominion in Northern India Down to the Time of Alexander's Invastion", in E.J. Rapson (ed.), *CHI*, vol. I, *Ancient India*, p. 301; B.N. Puri, *India as Described by Early Greek Writers*, pp. 4-5 and 49.
13. *CHI*, I, p. 301.
14. *MAGK*, p. 12, fn. 2.
15. See *AICL*, pp. 4-5, fn. 2; *CHI*, I, p. 301, fn. 1.
16. Fragm. 179 in C. Muller (ed.), *Fragmenta Historicorum Graecorum* (Paris, 1841), I. p. 12 cf. *CHI*, vol, I, p. 301; *AICL*, p. 2, fn. 2; *AIMA*, Introd. p. 5, note and pp. 152-53, note; E.R. Bevan, "India in Early Greek and Latin Literature", in *CHI*, vol. I, pp. 354-55.

preserved some extracts from the narrative of Skylax in his geographical work, the *Periodos Ges*, which appeared before *c.* 500 BC. Herodotous, borrowing the ideas from his predecessors, placed the city, Kaspatyros, in the land of Pactyiec or Pactyes (Afghanistan).[17] Though Herodotus had very vague and hazy knowledge of the territorial settlements of the people in the towns and cities to the west of Indus as indicated by J. Rennell,[18] we may resonably infer from his statement that the northern Indians who dwelt near the said city and the country of the Pactyes, Paktyike or Pashtus (represented by the ethnic name Pakhtūn or the Paṭhān) were no other than the hill-tribes of the Upper Kabul valley whose mode of life resembled that of the Bactrians. M.A. Stein has made it quite clear that "Kaspatyros or Kaspapyros, whichever form may be more accurate, must have been situated in that territory where the Indus first becomes navigable, i.e., in the ancient Gāndhāra, the present Peshawar Distric".[19]

The author of the *Periplus* refers to this city as "Caspapyra". W.H. Schoff, translator and annotator of this text, has categorically stated that it was from this town that Skylax began his voyage of discovery at the command of the Persian king Darius. It could not have been far above the modern Attock [33⁰ 53'N., 72⁰ 15'E]. In view of the fact that the *Periplus* distinguishes it from Gāndhāra, he prefers to fix its location in that direction.[20]

Ptolemy designates this city as "Kaspeiria", but he has, however, misplaced it. He describes Kaspeiria as situated below the sources of the Bidaspes (Jhelum), the Sandabal (Cenāb) and the Adris (Rāvī).[21] The geographical position assigned to it by Ptolemy in his map would bring Kaspeiria close to the junction of the Hydaspes (Jhelum) and Zaradros (Sutlej), i.e., the neighbourhood of Multān.[22] This is obviously an error in the latitude implied by him to fix its position. However, some scholars have mistakenly identified this city with Kashmir. Masson observes that in the time of Ptolemy Kashmir was the most powerful and extensive kingdom which was watered by Jhelum, Cenāb and Rāvī. It included within it provinces of the lower Himālayan region that lay between Kashmir

---

17. *History*, Bk. III, 102 and also IV, 44; *AICL*, p. 2; see also V. De. St. Martin, *Étude*, pp. 364, 376-78; *Memories de L'Acadèmie des Inscriptions, Sav. e'trang, Ire S'erie*, t.v. pp. 17f, 81-86.
18. *The Geogrphical System of Herodotus*, vol. I, p. 309.
19. *MAGK*, p. 11.
20. *Periplus*, 48, p. 189.
21. *AIT*, VII, i, 42, pp. 108-9, see also pp. 128 and 360, note.
22. See the old map reproduced in *ibid.*

and the Sutlej.[23] Lassen[24] and V. De St. Martin[25] are almost in agreement with each other in suggesting the Ptolemy's statement refers to a period when the power of the dynasty ruling over Kashmir actually extended over the wide territories, as indicated above. J.W. McCrindle also affirm that Kaspeiria of Ptolemy corresponds with Kashmir or the Sanskrit name Kaśyapapur which has been used in different forms by some classical writers by a slight contraction. The sovereigns of this city in Ptolemy's days had extended their rule far beyond the limits of the present kingdom of Kashmir.[26] This identification, however, does not seem to be valid. This city, according to Burnouf, is a contraction of Kaśyapamira which is Kaspapyrus of old geographer Hecatacus and Kaspatyros of Herodotus.[27] M. D'Anville does not support its identification with Kashmir. He rather takes it as a city mentioned by Hecatacus and Herodorus.[28] Stephanus Byzantinus (or Stephanus of Byzantium) in his *Geographical Dictionary* (in which can extract from the work of Hecatacus is preserved) refers to it as a Gandaric city.[29] B.C. Law asserts that Kashmir, the Kaspeiria of Ptolemy, was included in the Gāndhāra kingdom in the dim past.[30] But at the same time he is disposed to accept it as a Kaspapyros city of Gāndhāra.[31] As a matter of fact, it was Ptolemy's Asmirae or Asmiraia which stands for Kashmir, as pointed out by Ammianus Marcellinus,[32] and not Kaspeiria or Kaspiraei. This is also supported by the statement of St. Martin.[33]

Dionysios of Samos or Dionysios Periegetes in his *Bassarika* (a lost poem whose fragment is preserved in the work of Stephenus of Byzantium and first noticed by D'Anville)[34] and Nonnos is his *Dionysiaka* (xxvi, 165)[35] have made incidental notices of

---

23. *Various Journeys*, vol. III, p. 164, cf. *ibid.*
24. *Ind. Alt.*, II, p. 898.
25. *Mémoires de L'Acade'mie des Inscriptions, Sav. e' trang, Ire S'erie*, t.v., p. 330.
26. *AICL*, pp. 2-3, fn. 2, p. 199, fn. 5; *IIA*, p. 194, note. 1; *AIMA*, pp. 152-53, note; *AIT*, p. 108.
27. Cf. *AIT*, p. 108.
28. *Antiquite Geographique de L'Inde*, pp. 21f, 40f.
29. Cf. *MAGK*, p. 11; H.H. Wilson, *HHK*, App. VIII, p. 114.
30. *HGAI*, p. 97.
31. *Tribes in Ancient India*, pp. 9-17.
32. *History*, Bk XXIII, cf. *AIT*, p. 327.
33. *Étude*, p. 414, cf. *AIT*, pp. 300-5.
34. Cf. *MAGK*, p. 10.
35. *AICL*, p. 199.

the people of this city as Kaspeiroi and Caspeiri respectively. They were among the Indian tribes who rose in open revolt against Bacchos in remote past. No clear picture however emerges from their explanations.

E.H. Bunbury is of the firm opinion that Caspapyrus of Hecatacus or Kaspatyros of Herodotus was one of the capital cities of Gāndhāra.[36] A.H.L. Heeren[37] and Mannert[38] place it in the vicinity of Kabul. James Rennell has fixed its location on the upper part of the Indus above Attock from where Scylax set out to explore the Indus.[39] Wilford has identified it with Kashabpur, a modern town near Jhelum,[40] which is merely based on his supposition. Wahl places it with confidence at the fort of Kuttver,[41] which is also hypothetical. It will not be reasonable to entertain such hypothesis.

H.H. Wilson was the first oriental scholar to strongly advocate the identification of Kaspapyrus or Kaspatyrus with Kaśyapapura, a city being named after Kaśyapa, a great sage and the first colononiser of the country. This was, according to him, the original designation of Kashmir which in its palmy days comprehended great part of the Punjab and extended as far as the Indus. In support of this identification he has advanced the argument that no such place as Kaspatyrus has been traced westward of the Indus in Afghanistan. Alexander and his generals met with no such city in that direction.[42] He seems to have been guided by the oriental tradition which still supports the identification of Kashmir with its original name Kaśyapapura. But this should be borne in mind that this city may be distinguished from that of the Greek writers concerned. The philological derivation of Kaśyapapura or Kashmir from Kaspapyros is based on Wilson's fanciful ethymological interpretations of the latter name. It is Curious to note that Alberuni (on

36. *HAG*, vol. I, p. 142.
37. *Historical Researches*, vol. I, *Asiatic Nations*, pp. 280, 293.
38. Cf. H.H. Wilson, *Ar. Ant.*, p. 136.
39. *MMH*, p. 146.
40. Cf. Troyer's *Raja-Tarangini*, vol. II, p. 305.
41. Cf. *Ar. Ant.*, p. 136.
42. *Ar. Ant.*, pp. 136-37, *HHK*, App. VIII, pp. 114-16; *Miscellaneous Essay*, p. 117; see also *AIT*, p. 108.

the authority of an Indian Scholar),[43] A. Foucher,[44] W. Vincent[45] and A. Cunningham[46] have identified Kaśyapapura with Multān, but in the opinion held by Lassen[47] and Humboldt[48] it is taken to be Kashmir which is unworthy of acceptance. V.A. Smith, on the one hand, doubts the connection of the name with Kashmir of the present day, but, on the other hand, seems to be little inclined to associate it with the same assuming that its earlier extension was wider.[49] However, M.A. Stein rejects its identification with Kashmir.[50] The contradictions in the statements of scholars concerned, which are very much apparent here, no doubt, widen the scope of speculation about the identification of the city described by classical writer. But in view of the fact that the knowledge of three early Greek writers, Skylax, Hecatacus and Herodotus, did not advance much beyond the frontiers of the Indus constituting as one of the remotest provinces of the Persian empire towards the east, it will not be reasonable on our part to approve of the identification of this city with ancient Kashmir. This town must have been situated in Gāndhāra region or near Kābul whose sovereigns in all probability by the middle of the second century AD might have extended their rule far beyond the limits of their kingdom to Punjab and Kashmir. We may further assume that as Kashmir formed part of ancient Gāndhāra, the people from the former place settled down in the city which came to be known as Kaspatyros or Kaspapyros. St. Martin (*Étude*, pp. 376-78] has rightly placed the city in the basin of Kabul to the west of the Indus.

Before providing the detailed description of other towns and cities of Afghanistan in northern India, here it will be worthwhile to note that its greater part (Eastern Ariana) beyond the Indus remained in the possession of the Indians for several centuries both anterior and posterior to the Macedonian invasion.

The city called by Pliny Capisa or Capissa[51] and by his copyist, Solinus, Caphusa can

43. E.C. Sachau, *Alberuni's India*, I, p. 298.
44. *L'ancienne Route de L' Inde*, vol. I, pp. 94, 190-94; vol. 2, pp. 195-98, cf. Motichandra, *Sārthavāha*, pp. 47-48.
45. *The Voyage of Nearchus and the Periplus of the Erythrean Sea*, I, p. 12.
46. *Co. Anc. Ind.*, p. 32; *CAGI*, p. 199.
47. *Ind. Alt*, vol. I, p. 142; vol. II, pp. 631, 635.
48. *Asie Centrale*, I, p. 102.
49. *EHI*, 4th rev. edn. by S.M. Edwards, pp. 32, 37-38.
50. *MAGK*, pp. 12-13.
51. *Hist. Nat.*, VI, 23 (25); *AIMA*, p. 108, note.

easily be identified with Pāṇini's Kāpiśī (IV, 2, 99), the ancient capital of the kingdom of Kapiśa, Kapisene of Ptolemy or "*Ka-pi-shih*" of Yuan Chwang.[52] The said kingdom included the whole of modern Kohistan-Kafiristan as well as the two large valleys of Ghorband and Panjshir.[53] Ptolemy places the town of Kapiśa amongst the Paropanisade 2½ degrees to the north of Kabura or Kabul[54] which is nearly 2 degrees in excess of the truth. Arrian (*Indica*, I, 3) has also incidentally referred to the city of Kapiśa. St. Martin,[55] A. Foucher[56] and R.D. Banerji[57] have placed this city in the upper region of the Kophes or Kabul. According to Pliny, this famous city was destroyed by the Achaemenian emperor Cyrus (*c*. 558-530 BC)[58] in the course of his invasion of north-west India. The historical tradition also attributes the destruction of this city to the Persian invader. In the Behistun Rock Inscription (*c*. 520-518 BC) of Darius (*c*. 522-486 BC), king of Persia, Capisa figures as Kāpisa-kāni which signifies merely a stronghold.[59] The Kaspioi of Herodotus (*Hist*., III, 93; VII, 67, 86) were the people of Kapiśa who have been located in the wild tract of Kafiristan to the north of the Kabul river.[60] There are some missing links in the classical accounts of this urban centre in the upper Kabul valley which can be restored with the help of other sources.

The city, Kāpiśī, is identified with modern Begrām, about 50 miles north of Kābul, on the ground of an epigraphic evidence, i.e., a Kharoṣṭhi inscription found there naming the city,[61] the ruins of which are described in a memoir by Charles Masson.[62] A. Cunningham, on the basis of the routes followed by Hiuen-Tsang in the course of his

52. Thomas Watters, *YCTI*, vol. I, p. 122.
53. Thomas, *JRAS*, 1906, pp. 191, note 1, 460-61; E.J. Rapson, *JRAS*, 1905, pp. 783-84; see also R.C. Jain (ed.), *MAIMA*, p. xxxvi.
54. *Geog*,. VI, 18, 4.
55. *Étude*, p. 14 f.
56. *Op. cit*., vol. I, p. 52 cf. Motichandra, *op. cit*., p. 11.
57. *PAHI*, p. 74.
58. *Op. cit*.
59. See *Old Persian Inscriptions* in general, ed. and tr. F.H. Weissbach (Leipzig, 1911), *Bahistān Inscription*, 3, 61; *Bahistān Inscription*, ed. and tr. L.W. King and R.C. Thompson (London, 1907); S. Sen, *Old Persian Inscriptions*, pp. 2 ff; *JAOS*, vol. 72, no. 1 (Jan.-March, 1952), p. 9 f.
60. Thomas, *JRAS*, 1906, p. 191, note 1.
61. Sten Konow, *Ep. Ind*., vol. XXII (1933), p. 111.
62. *JASB*, vol. V, (Jan. 1836), pp. 1-6.

visits to the capital of *Ka-pi-shih* in AD 630 and again fourteen years later in AD 644,[63] has fixed the position of the said capital city at Opian near Begrām.[64] This place was visited by Mr. Masson sometime betweeen 1833 and 1836. He describes it as "distinguished by its huge artificial mounds, from which, at various times, copious antique treasures have been extracted".[65] He further observes that "it possesses many vestiges of anitquity; yet, as they are exclusively of a Sepulchral or religious character, the site of the city, to which they refer, may rather be looked for the actual village of Malik Hupian on the plain below, and near Charikas".[66] Begrām, which is the city *par excellence*, lies about 6 or 7 miles to the "E.N.E. of Charikar and Opian", Opiane of Hekataeus and Stephanus of Byzantium and Opianum of Pliny. According to the traditions of the people, "Begrām was a Greek city, which was overwhelmed by some natural catastrophe".[67] The name of Opian is certainly as old as the fifth century BC, as Hekataeus places a tribe called the Opiai to the west of the upper course of the Indus where there was a royal town or fort.[68] This is what Stephanus has also mentioned in his *In Voce Alexandria*. B.N. Puri's supposition that Opiai do not represent any tribe[69] can very well be disposed of.

The city of Kāpiśi at Begrām near Kabul after being destroyed by Cyrus in the sixth century BC in all likelihood might have been rebuilt bearing the same name either in its neighbourhood or at Opian sometime between the third and the second century BC. Because the professed historians of Alexander do not mention this city. It might have come into existence during the time of Aśoka. In the post-Maurya age it fell under the rule of Eukratides (*c*. 181-160 BC), the Greek ruler of Bactria, after Appollodotus I was deprived of the kingdom of Kapiśa by him. In the age of the Kuṣāṇas, the city gained popularity as a centre of trade and commerce. It is said to have formed part of the Kuṣāna empire of Kaniṣka in the first century AD[70]. The city continued to flourish down to the eighth century AD. In the seventh century AD, Hiuen-Tsang found the kingdom of

63. See V.A. Smith, "The Itinerary of Yuan-Chwang", in Thomas Watters, *op. cit*., vol. II, pp. 333-35, 342-43.
64. *CAGI*, p. 17.
65. *Travels*, iii, p. 126, cf. *CAGI*, pp. 17-18.
66. *Ibid*., iii, p. 161, cf. *CAGI*, p. 18.
67. *Ibid*., iii, p. 159, cf. *CAGI*, p. 25.
68. Hekataeus, *Geog*., Frag., 174-79, Fragm, 175 in C. Muller (ed.), *Fragmenta Historicorum Graecorum* (Paris, 1841), I, 12; see also *AICL*, p. xiv.
69. *Op. cit*., p. 5.
70. R. Girshamana, *Le Kusans* (Paris, 1946), p. 145; *YCTI*, vol. I, p. 124.

Kapiśa in a very flourishing state with towns, temples, etc.[71] The city remained as capital of Afghanistan till AD 792-93 — the year in which it was sacked by the Arbas in their desperate bid to conquer Afghanistan. The city gradually began to decay because of desertion of the people after Kabul took its place as a new capital.

The existence of towns or cities within the confines of the kingdom of Kapisene or Kapiśa can also be proved with the help of evidences available in classical literature.

The city founded by Alexander in 329 BC (two years before his actual campaign) in the land of the Paropamisadai (Kābul) or at the foot of the Paropamisos range or Caucasus (Hindukush) and called after himself Alexandria, as stated by Strabo,[72] Pliny,[73] Arrian,[74] Curtius[75] and Julius Valerius,[76] is identified with the city the vast ruins of which in all probability lay at Opian or Houpian in the nieghbourhood of the village of Charikar situated in the beautiful valley of the Koh-Daman where the three roads leading from Baktra into Afghanistan converged.[77] The city occupied a commanding position in the plain of Koh-Daman, "about forty miles in length by sixteen or eighteen in breadth. It stretches to the very foot of the Hindu-Kush, and gives exit at its northern end to four several routes, by which that chain may be passed."[78] It is believed that Alexander after the conquest of some parts of Afghanistan to commemorate the victory founded in the land of the Paropamisadai a city named Alexandria. The city at the foot of the Kaukasos or Central Hindukush, which forms the northern frontier of Kabul, was more or less a military colony. Pliny's *Alexandrian Opianes*[79] is interpreted by Philemon Holland (who translated his work in AD 1601) as "the city of Alexandria in Opianum".[80] Stephanus also places it in "Opiane"[81] which agrees exactly with the site of the present Opian near

71. *YCTI*, vol. I, pp. 122-29; vol. II, p. 266.
72. *Geog*,. Bk. XV, ch.II, sec. 10, *AICL*, p.90.
73. *Hist. Nat.*, VI, 21. 23.
74. *Anabasis of Alexander and Indica*, Eng. tr. by E.J. Chinnock, *Anab.*, Bk. III, ch. XXVIII; Bk. IV, Ch.XXII; *IIA*, pp. 58 and 331-32, note A.
75. *History of Alexander the Great*, Bk. VII, Ch. 3.
76. *The Itinerary of Alexander the Great*, Ch. 104, *AICL*, p. 150.
77. *AICL*, pp. 87, fn. 4, 90, fn. 2, 150, fn. 1; E.H. Bunbury, *HAG*, vol. I, p. 142, . V.A. Smith, *EHI*, pp. 52-53; *CAGI*, p. 19.
78. Lord, "Account of Koh-daman", *JASB*, vol. VII, p. 521.
79. *Hist. Nat.*, VI, 17.
80. Cf. *CAGI*, p. 18, fn. 3.
81. *In Voce Alexandria*, Cf. *CAGI*, p. 18.

Charikar. According to the measurement recorded by Pliny, the city was situated at 50 Roman miles, or 45.96 English miles distant from the city of Ortospana (or Kabul).[82] According to W.W. Tarn, the city called Alexandria stood on the west bank of the united Panjshir and Ghorband rivers near the confluence facing Kapiśa on the east bank. It is represented by the modern Begrām.[83] In July 1833, Charles Masson left the city of Kabul to explore the districts north of it at the base of the Hindukush with the primary object of identifying the site of "Alexandria and Caucasum", and after his continuous researches of four succeeding years he discovered numerous interesting objects and the ruins of an ancient city of immense extent on the plain now called Beghrām or Begrām, 25 miles N. 15 E. from the modern city of Kabul. In a square plain of nearly six miles in each direction, situated at the north-east point of the level country of the Kohistan, in an angle formed by a ridge of Hindukush, he found fragments of pottery, lumps of iron, and other indications of a numerous population, coins, seals, rings, and other signs of habitation, some few fragments of sculpture, but no vestiges of buildings were discovered, except, at the depth of three or four feet, where lines of cement which seem to be the remains of foundations, and a large unburnt bricks forming mounds of considerable extent, which have been supposed to indicate the walls of the city, were found. He has suggested other localities, of which Perwan might be preferred, as being eight miles north-west of Begrām, and so much nearer to the Caucasus. He has also given indications of extensive sites of anceint cities in the Kohistan and the Koh-Daman. In the valley of the latter, he discovered two very important sites, which unquestionably refer to the capital cities of ancient times. At the second of these, about sixteen miles from Begrām, was found some important structure — a palace or a citadel. Many important vestiges of anitiqutiy are said to be discoverable. The distances would nearly correspond as to Charikar in the plain of Begrām and to Ghorband in the valley of that name. In the course of his investigations between 1833 and 1836, he collected above thirty thousand coins including those of Greek and Indo-Scythic princes.[84] From his discoveries no conclusive opinion can be formed as to a preferable site for so-called Alexandria city. Nor can we draw any postitive conclusion from the statements of two other renowned travellers, A. Burnes[85] and Mr. Vigne,[86] and the celebrated geographer, C. Ritter,[87] with

82. *Hist. Nat.*, VI, 17 (21).

83. *GBI*, p. 462.

84. *JASB*, vol. III (April, 1834), p. 153 f; *JASB*, vol. V (Jan., 1836), pp. 1 f, 5-6; *Travels*, III, pp. 155-65.

85. *Travels In Punjab, Bokhara*, etc., vol. I, p. 184.

86. *Visit to Ghazni, Kabul and Afghanistan*, p. 198 cf. H.H. Wilson, *Ar. Ant.*, p. 180.

87. Quoted by H.H. Wilson, *op. cit.*, p. 180.

regard to the identification of this city with Bamian. Its reputed antiquity and the excavations in its vicinity are some of the chief arguments in its favour. But this fact cannot be lost sight of that it is about eighty-five miles distant from Kabul. Hence Bamian cannot be Alexandria. The same objection may be urged against the place — Sighan, as proposed by M. Court. Although there may be the ruins of a fortress attributed by the natives to Alexander, yet it is still farther beyond the summits of the Caucasus than Bamian.[88]

From the data available to us we can simply deduce that there were some urban centres in and around Opian, Charikar or Begrām, north of Kabul. One of them, which was already in existence near either of the former two places, might have been taken over by Alexander after his advent into India and converted into a city of Greek type or the Yavaṇa colony. It might have been further enlarged with the settlements of the people of the land and the Macedonians. The work of making a city of Greek type was carried through under the supervision of Nicanor, a Macedonian of high rank. The so-called Greek City Alexandria (near Kāpiśī) was capital of the province of the Paropanisadae or upper Kabul valley in Alexander's time.

The another city of Alexandria may be identified with Yavanapur of the *Mahābhārata*,[89] Ālakandaka or Alakṣandraka of Kauṭilya,[90] Alasanda of Buddhists, as mentioned in the *Apadāna*,[91] *Milindapañha*,[92] *Mahāniddesa*[93] and *Mahāvaṁsa*,[94] or Ālisamdaya of the Śvetāmbara Jains, as referred to in the *Bhagavatī* (6, 7) and *Sthānāṅga* (5, 3, 459).[95] Sylvain Levi[96] has discussed in detail the problems relating to the identification of this city with the equivalent words found in ancient Indian literature. The city seems to have developed as an entrepot. In fact, this city or town on the Indus founded by Alexander had commercial importance. It was very famous for coral trade.

---

88. *JASB*, vol. V, p. 390.
89. Sabhā Parva, 28, 49.
90. *Arthaśāstra*, ed. Shamaśāstrī, p. 78; see also *AIT*, pp. 370-71, note.
91. II, p. 359.
92. Ed. V. Trenckner, pp. 82, 327, 331, 359; see also M. Pelliot, *JA*, II, 1914, p. 379 f.
93. Ed. by L.D. Law and E.J. Thomas, vol. I, pp. 154-55; vol. 2, pp. 414-15.
94. Ed. XXIX, 39; tr. by W. Geiger, p. 194, note 3.
95. Cf. A. Weber, *Ind. Stud.*, XVI, 303.
96. "Alexander and Alexandria in Indian Literature" (Originally pub. in French in the *Memores de L' Institute Francais*, vol. IXVII — Me'langes Maspero vol. II), tr. by P.C. Bagchi, *IHQ*, vol. XII (1936), pp. 121-33.

There were other towns at the foot of the Caucasus or in the immediate vicinity of Alexader's city. Pliny has assigned exactly the same position to the town of Cartana (Kartana),[97] which may be identified with Ptolemy's Karsana, placed by him on the right bank of a river that comes from the vicinity of Kapiśa and Niphanda (or Opian), and joins the river of Lokharna or Logarh, nearly opposite Nagara. According to A. Cunningham, it was situated on the right bank of the United Panjshir and Ghorband rivers, immediately at the foot of the Kohistan hills, and within 6 miles of Opian or Alexandria Opiane, which corresponds with the locality of Begrām. He accepts this identification on the ground that Parwan and Kushan (Ptolemly's Baborana and Kapiśa respectively), the two ancient places in the neighbourhood of Opian, are both on the left bank of the Ghorband river.[98] Karsana and Opian, the two distinct places, like London and Westminster are said to have "approached each other as they increased in size, until at last they virtually became one large city". The coins of the earlier Greek kings of Ariana-Euthydemus, Demetrius and Eukratides — bear the monograms of both cities, "but after the time of Eukratides, that of Opaina disappears altogether, while that of Karsana is common to most of the later princes. The contemporary occurrence of these mint monograms proves that the two cities were existing at the same time; while the sudden disuse of the name of Opian may serve to show that during the latter period of Greek occupation, the city of Alexandria had been temporarily supplanted by Karsana".[99]

Cartana was a walled town, noted for its rectangular precision. The city called Cadrusi or Cadrusia is placed both by Pliny and Solinus close to the Caucasus or in close proximity to Alexandria.[100] Philemon Holland, the translator of Pliny's work, renders the passage concerned thus: "Upon the hill Caucasus Standeth the town Cadrusi, built likewise by the said Alexander".[101] But according to the commentators, Pliny's Cadrusi was the name of a people whose city was called Alexandria.[102] It has been rightly pointed out that "As a general rule, the Greeks . . . designated the various peoples whom they encountered

97. *Hist. Nat.*, VI, 23.

98. *CAGI*, p. 23.

99. *Ibid.*, pp. 24-25.

100. Pliny, *Hist. Nat.*, VI. 25, Solinus, IVII.

101. Cf. *CAGI*, p. 27.

102. Cellarius, III, 22, p. 514, cf. *CAGI*, pp. 26-27.

by the names of their principal towns". Like "Kabura (Kabul) and the Kabolitae, Drepsa and the Drepsiani, Taxila and the Taxili or Taxiles, Kaspeira and the Kaspeirae, . . . there was most probably also a town named Cadrusia, whose inhabitants were called Cadrusi".[103] Cunningham seem to be disposed to identify the city of Cadrusi with the old site of Koratas, which Masson discovered under the hills of Kohistan, 6 miles to the north-east of Begrām, and on the north bank of the Panjshir river. There are the usual remains of an old city, consisting of mounds covered with fragments of pottery, amongst which old coins are frequently found. There are also remains of masonry works about the hills, which the people call Kafir-kot or the Kafir's fort.[104.]

Alexandria, Cartana and Cadrusi became famous as three Greek towns. Both Curtius[105] and Diodorus[106] are in perfect agreement with each other about the settlements of 7000 of the people of the land in the new towns as their citizens with those of Alexander's mercenaries who established themselves in the region 2800 miles away from their old home. Plutarch's[107] categorical statement, that there were Hellenic cities in the neighbourhood of Kaukasos, goes as a corroboration of the assertion of Diodorus, that Alexander built other cities, each distant a day's journey from Alexandria.

The few other cities of Kapisene has received the notice of only Ptolemy. The names of peoples as well as their towns are recorded by him. His Parsioi, Parsii or Parsyetai were the people of the Panjhir or Panjshir Valley. And their two towns Parsia and Parsiana are identified with capital of Parsii called Farzah and Panjhir respectively.[108] A town named Panjhir is also mentioned by the early Arab geographers.

Ptolemy in his *Geography* has supplied a long list of towns. The towns not already noticed are Barzaura in the north and Drastoka and Naulibis in the south.[109] The first of these may be Bazarak, a large town in Panjshir valley, the second was most probably a town in one of the daras or valleys or the Koh-Daman, and the last may be Nilab of Ghorband.[110]

---

103. *CAGI*, p. 27.
104. Masson, *Travels*, II, p. 166 cf. *CAGI*, p. 27.
105. *Hist. of Alex.*, VII, 3, 23.
106. *Bibliotheca Historica*, XVII, 83.
107. *Oration*, I 5, *AICL*, p. 207 and fn.2.
108. *Geog.*, VI, 18, 4, *AIT*, pp. 311-13.
109. *Ibid.*
110. *CAGI*, p. 27.

The towns and cities situated within the boundaries of Aria, Arachosia and Paropanisadae to the west of the Indus in Afghanistan are also worthy of our notice. These three formed important parts of Ariane or Ariana, which, according to Megasthenes and Pliny,[111] belonged to India (i.e., Greater India). Their inhabitants in common have been called in the classics Areitanians of Ariainoi.

From Strabo's and Ptolemy's description of the extent of the boundaries of different parts of Ariana it appears that Aria was bounded by Baktriana on the north, by Drangiana on the south, and by Paropamisadai on the west.[112] According to Strabo, Aria was two thousand Stadia (two hundred and twenty-nine miles) in length, and only three hundred Stadia (or little more than thirty-four miles) in breadth in the level country.[113] If these measurements be correct, Aria will be restricted to the tract from about Meshed to the neighbourhood of Heral[114] — a position well enough reconcilable with what Strabo relates of Aria. Ptolemy has enumerated no fewer than thirty-five towns belonging to the small province of Areia[115] (Arii of Herodotus, *Hist*, Bk. VII, 61-62). It is not possible to verify his long list of cities because of absence of details thereof and for want of authentic data in regard to their identifications. However, a number of small towns, as H.H. Wilson[116] points out, existed on the road from Meshed to Herat and thence towards Kandahār or Kabul. The Aria, Arii, Arioi or Areia of the classical authors is believed to be the ancient capital city called by oriental writers Hera or Heri [= *Harōiva* in the *Avesta* = *Haraiva* in the old Persian inscriptions = Skt. *Sarova* = mod. Herāt] situated on the river Arius or Arias [= R̥gvedic Sarayū = mod. Hari Rūd] in north-western Afghanisthan. In the Elamite version of the Behistun inscription it is called Arriya. According to the local tradition, as recorded by Wilson, "Herat unites the claims of the ancient capital and the city built or rather repaired by Alexander".[117] It is said that "Hari was founded by Lohrasp, extended

111. *AIMA*, 1st edn. pp. 45-49; Pliny, *Hist. Nat.*, VI, 23.
112. Strabo, *Geog.*, Bk. XV. Ch. II, Sec. 9, *AICL*, p. 89; Ptolemy, *Geog.*, VI, 17, Sec. I, *AIT*, pp. 305-6.
113. Every 10 Stadia = approximately 1-1/6 miles.
114. *Ar. Ant.*, p. 150; Rawlinson, *Ind. Ant.*, vol. V, pp. 329-30. The distance from Meshed to Herat is about 232 milels, according to Conolly, *Travels,* vol. I, p. 414; by a different route it is 279 miles, cf. *Ar. Ant.*, p. 150, fn. 3. According to Fraser, it is either 221 or 238 miles, *Travels in Khorasan*, App. p. 118 Cf. *ibid.*, pp. 171-72, fn. 5.
115. *AIT*, pp. 307-10.
116. *Ar. Ant.*, p. 151.
117. *Ibid.*, p. 151 and fn. 4.

by Gushtasp, improved by Bahman, and completed by Alexander".[118] The capital of Aria, according to Strabo[119] and Arrian,[120] was Artakoana (also read Artakakana), the identity of which with Herat on the west or its immediate vicinity cannot be ruled out. Strabo specifies as other cities, Alexandria[121] and Akhaia.[122] The cities mentioned by Isidore of Charax include Artakauna and Alexandria.[123] Ptolemy not only mentions Areia or Hera, but two other cities, Artakaudna and Alexandria.[124] Ammianus Marcellinus says: "Aria possesses a great many towns, of which the most distinguished are Bitaxa (or Bitana), Sarmatina, Sotera, and Nisibis and Alexandria".[125] We do not have any source-material at our disposal to identify them except for the last one. According to Strabo, Alexander after having reduced to his authority the people called Arianians founded a city in their country — Arioi, which he called Alexandria,[126] which is reasonably taken as Herat.[127] Strabo quoting from the *Geog.* of Eratosthenes (xi, 48) gives the distance from Alexandria in Ariis to Bactria at 3870 stadia (387 English miles).[128] Further, Strabo in his incidental notices of India (XI, viii, 9), quoting Eratosthenes, assigns the distance from the Kaspian Gates to Alexandreia in the country of the Arioi (identified with Herat) at 4,530 stadia (518 miles).[129] The total distance from the Kaspian Gates to Alexandria in Ariis is reckoned at six thousand four hundred stadia or seven hundred and thirty-one miles. Alexandria in Ariis, according to another source, is said to be situated at six thousand stadia from the Kaspian, or above six hundred and eighty miles, which is as nearly as possible the distance of Herat from Asterabad.[130] The distance from the Kaspian Gates to Alexandria

---

118. Letters from Mohun Lall, *JASB*, Jan. 1834, p. 9, cited in *Ar. Ant.*, p. 151 and fn. 5.
119. Cf. *AIT*, p. 309; *Ar. Ant.*, p. 151.
120. *Anab.*, III. XXVII.
121. *Geog.*, XV, ii, 8, *AICL*, p. 87.
122. Cf. *Ar. Ant.*, p. 151.
123. *Ibid.*
124. *AIT*, pp. 307-10.
125. *History*, Bk. XXIII, Ch. VI, *AICL*, p. 93 and *AIT*, p. 328.
126. *Geog.*, XV, i, 26; XV, ii, 8, *AICL*, pp. 31 and note 1, 87 and note 3.
127. *AICL*, p. 87, note 3.
128. Bunbury, *HAG*, vol. I, pp. 486-87.
129. *AICL*, pp. 88, note 2, 100 and note 2 (culled from Falconer's Version); see Eng. tr. of Strabo's *Geographica* by H.C. Hamilton and W. Falconer, vol. III; see also Pliny *Hist. Nat.*, VI, 17; VI, 21.
130. *Ar. Ant.*, p. 149, see also p. 171.

is in favour of the identification of that city with Herat, and its traditional attribution to Alexander may not be wholly unfounded. Artakoana could not, however, have been very distant from it. According to Barbie de Bocage, it was situated at a place called Fusheng,[131] the Busheng or Pusheng of Ibn Haukil, one stage from Herat, on the borders of Heri river. M. Court proposes to place it at Obeh or Oba, ten farsangs from Herat. He refers to a town called Ardekoun, which is valuable testimony for the genuineness of the appellation Artakoana.[132] According to Pliny, the river flowed by Artakoana, which will apply either to Herat or Pusheng. Ptolemy places Artakaudna on the banks of the Areian or Arian lake, about two-thirds of a degree north-west of his Alexandria.[133] M. Jacquet seems to have attached weight to the postition of the latter, as assigned by Ptolemy.[134] In Heeren's estimation, Alexandria and Artakoana are almost identical. His statement, "that Arrian does not inform us of the foundation by Alexander of any new city in this country. . . . Several ancient cities received new names from the Macedonian conquerors",[135] seems to be absolutely justified. This also confirms the traditon. "It seems not unlikely that Artakoana, Alexandria, and Aria are aggregated in Herat".[136]

The people of Aria called Arioi (or Arii), according to Strabo, were situated beside the Drangai (the people of Drangiane or Drangiana) both on the north and on the west, and nearly encompassed them[137] because of their contiguity or geographical proximity to each other. The metropolis or ancient capital of Drangiana, according to Strabo,[138]

---

131. *Ar. Ant.*, p. 150.
132. *Ibid.*
133. *AIT*, pp. 307-10.
134. Notes by M. Jacquet on M. Court's *Conjectures Sur les Marches d'Alexandre*, *JA*, October 1837.
135. *Historical Researches.*, vol. I (*Asiatic Nations*), p. 256.
136. *Ar. Ant.*, p. 152.
137. *Geog.*, XV, ii, 9, *AICL*, p. 89.

    Drangiane of the ancients corresponds in general with the province now called Seistan on the frontier of Afghanistan. It was actually adjacent to southern Afghanistan. Some part of the Drangiana are included in modern Baluchistan and some in northern part of Iran. In ancient times, some portion of it formed part of India, as it transpires from the accounts of classical scholars. It was well known for its urban culture. The inhabitants were called variously Drangai, Zarangae and Sarangaei (of Herodotus). Its another name Zarang, according to Burnouf, was derived from the Zend word, Zarayo, a lake, a word still retained in the name of the lake in Seistan Zarah. In fact, Śakasthāna (abode of the Śakas), which formed southern part of Baluchistan, was later called Seistan (Drangiana of classical writers).
138. *Geog.*, XV, ii, 8, *AICL*, p. 87.

Pliny[139] and Ammianus Marcellinus,[140] was Prophthasia called by Isidore of Charax Phra,[141] which is identified with much probability with modern Furrah or Farah (in Afghanistan), one hundred and thirty miles south of Herat, and generally accepted as the northern capital of the province now called Seistan,[142] "There can be no reasonable doubt', says Bunbury, "that Phra, which is described by Isidore of Charax as the largest town in the district immediately north of Drangiana, is the same name with the modern Furrah, and we are distinctly told by Stephanus of Byzantium, on the authority of the historian of Charax, that Phrada was the name of the city which was called by Alexander Prophthasia. . . ."[143] But, according to Plutarch, Alexander founded the city, or at least converted an insignificant village into a town of note. Prophthasia, a city of Drangiana, has been mistakenly placed by him in Sogdiana.[144] The ancient capital Prophthasia (the Persian Peshawaran), according to Eratosthenes, as quoted by Strabo (*Geog.*, XI, viii, 9, p. 514), was 1,600 stadia (183 miles) distant from Alexandria in Aria (Herat),[145] which considerably exceeds the actual distance from Herat to Furrat, but he himself adds that others only give it as 1500 stadia. D'Anville proposed Parra or Phurrah for the site of Alexandria which is not convincing at all. It is not supported by any evidence either. Pliny, in one place, calls Prophthasia the capital of the Zariaspae.[146] Arrian refers to the royal city of the Zarangaei (Drangae), which is recognised in Zarang, an ancient name for the capital of Seistan.[147] It is worthy of note that up to seventh century AD Drangiana's capital, situated between the river Helmund and the lake Zarah, still retained the name of Zaranj. Dushak, the capital of Seistan, is supposed to be Zaranj or Zarang, and in this name the Zarangae of antiquity is unquestionably preserved. In the neighbourhood of Dushak the remains of several ancient cities were seen by Captain Christie. About half-way between Dushak and Furrah he found the relics of a very large city named

139. *Hist. Nat.*, VI, 21.

140. *History*, XXIII, vi, *AICL*, p. 94.

141. *Mansiones Parthicae*, ed. C. Muller, *Geographi Graeci Minores* (Paris, 1855), I, 244-56; ed. and tr., W.H. Schoff, *Parthian Stations of Isidore of Charax* (Philadelphia, 1914), Section 16; also *AIT*, pp. 307-10.

142. *AICL*, p. 87, note 6, p. 100, note 3; *Ar. Ant.*, pp. 153-54; *AIT*, pp. 307-10.

143. *HAG*, vol. I, pp. 486-87; *AICL*, p. 87 note 6.

144. *Oration*, 1.5, *AICL*, p. 207.

145. *AICL*, p. 88, note 2, p. 100.

146. *Hist. Nat.*, VI, 25.

147. *Anab.*, III, xxviii.

Peshawarun, about twenty-seven miles north of the former, as pointed out by H.H. Wilson.[148] Ibn Haukil has mentioned the city of Zaranj as Ram-Shehristan, a curious compound of Indian and Persian appellatives.[149] Ammianus Marcellinus has categorically stated that besides other cities, the Drangiani, who lived in close vicinity to the hills contiguous to Aria, had "two of which they proudly boast, Prophthasia and Ariaspe, on account of their opulence and renown".[150] Ptolemy calls Ariaspa the second city of Drangiana. The people of this city called Ariaspae or Aryaspae represented, according to Wilson, the Indian "Aryaśva" — "the rearers or riders of excellent horses".[151]

The Arachotoi or Arachotus or Eratosthenes,[152] Arachotoi of Strabo,[153] Arachotae of Pliny,[154] Arachotia or Arachosia of Arrian,[155] Curtius,[156] Dionysios,[157] Polybios,[158] Ammianus Marcellinus[159] and an unknown writer who follows the geographies of Eratosthenes and Ptolemy (*Anonymi Geographiae Expositio Compendiaria*),[160] Arachotes of Megasthenes[161] and Nonnos[162] or Ptolemy's Arakhosia or Arakhotes[163] represents the city as well as the province.

Arachosia extended westward beyond the meridian of Kandahār. It was bounded on the north by the Paropanisos mountain (the western section of the Hindukush), on the

148. *Ar. Ant.*, p. 154.
149. Cf. *Ibid.*
150. *Hist.*, XXIII, vi, AICL, p. 94.
151. *Ar. Ant.*, pp. 155, 177.
152. Quoted by Strabo, *Geog.*, XI, viii, 9, *AICL*, p. 88, note 2 and p. 100.
153. *Geog.*, XV, ii, 8-9. 10, *AICL*, pp. 88-89.
154. *Hist. Nat.*, VI, 23; also VI, 21, 8-23 inserted in *AIMA*, 1st edn. Frag. LVI, p. 151. Pliny borrowed or derived his information from Megasthenes' *Indika*; also *AIMA*, p. 108, note.
155. *Anab.*, III, xxviii; VI, 15; *Indika*, II, 1.7.
156. *Hist. Alex.*, VII, 3.
157. *Bassarika*, LI, 1080-1165, *AICL*, p. 188.
158. *History*, XI, 34, *AICL*, p. 210.
159. *History*, XXVIII, vi, *AICL*, p. 94.
160. *Geog.*, VI, 24, *AICL*, p. 212.
161. *Frangments of the Indika Megasthenes*, ed. E.A. Schwanbeck (Bonn, 1846), Bk. 1, Fragms. III and IV, pp. 12, no. 6. 29-30, no. 24; *AIMA*, 1st edn. p. 108, note and Frag. LVI, p. 151 and note.
162. *Dionysiaka*, XXVI, pp. 206-9; *AICL*, p. 199; see also G.P. Singh, "The *Dionysiaka*: A Classical (Greek) Source of History of Ancient India", *Shodhak*, JHR, vol. XXVIII, pt. A, sr. 82, 1999, p. 1.
163. *Geog.*, VII, 1, *AIT*, pp. 33-34.

east by the Indus, on the west by Drangiana, and on the south by Gedrosia. It was situated to the south of Paropanisadai. It was a rich and populous province (or kingdom) and acquired early importance as one of the main routes by which Persia communicated with India. It was watered by the Helmund and its tributaries. The river Urghundab or Arkandab passed through it. It comprised the greater part of south-western Afghanistan and a considerable portion of Eastern Afghanistan.[164] Its Zend name (as give in the *Avesta*) was *Harahvaiti*[165] and its old Persian name (as recorded in the inscriptions) *Hara(h)-uvati*.[166]

The city called by Ptolemy Kandaroi[167] and by Isidore of Charax Kandake[168] can be identified with modern Kandahār, which was probably one of the capitals of Arachosia. The people called "Arachosii" in the *Periplus*, according to W.H. Schoff, "occupied the country around the modern Kandahār".[169] The identification of Arachosia itself or its capital with Kandahār (in south-eastern Afghanistan) has been generally accepted by the scholars.[170] The claims of Kandahār to antiquity has been doubted by H.H. Wilson.[171] But in the light of the references to it in classical literature under different denominations, such doubt can be dissipated. The distance from Prophthasia to the "city Arachotoi" or "Arachotus", as given by Eratosthenes, was 4,120 stadia (about 469 miles),[172] which, in a direct line, would bring us to the Indus. The measurement given here supports Rawlinson's identification of Arachotos with a site at Ulan-Robat, where there are ruins

164. Strabo, *Geog.*, XV, ii, 9; *AICL*, pp. 88 and note 1, 89, 199, note 2; *AIT*, pp. 341-42, note.

165. See *Avesta*, Eng. tr. J. Darmesteter, SBE, vol. IV, (Oxford, 1887, rept. Delhi, 1974), p. 2f.

166. See *Behistun, Persepolis and Naqsh-i-Rustam Inscriptions* of Darius (*c.* 522-486 BC) and Persepolis Insc. of Xerxes (*c.* 486-465 BC) in D.C. Sircar (ed.), *SI*, vol. I, pp. 5-14; also *JAOS*, vol. 72, no. I (Jan-March, 1952), pp. 9 ff (the word has been called variously Haraquaiti, Harakhuvati, etc.).

167. *Geog.*, VI, 12, 4, *AIT*, p. 276, see also p. 281; Bunbury, *HAG*, vol. II, pp. 641-42. Ptolemy has distinguished Kandaroi or Kandahār (VI, 12, 4) from Gandarai or Gāndhāra (VII, 1, 44). But he has erroneously placed the former in Sogdiana. Such mistakes are found in his work. The tribe of Sogdiana has been separately mentioned by him as Kandari, who cannot be confounded with that of modern Kandahār.

168. Cf. *Ar. Ant.*, p. 151.

169. *Periplus*, 47, p. 183.

170. *AIMA*, 1st edn. pp. 151-52, note; *AIT*, p. 34; *CHI*, vol. I, pp. 388, 489; V.A. Smith, *EHI*, Append. F, pp. 158-60.

171. *Ar. Ant.*, p. 175.

172. Strabo, *Geog.*, XI, viii, 9, *AICL*, p. 100.

of a city of a very remarkable character.[173] Keeping in view the distance of Arachotus city from Ortospana (Kabul), which was, according to Eratosthenes, two thousand stadia,[174] or about two hundred and twenty-eight miles, Wilson has identified the city of the Arachoti with a small town — Arkandab or Urghundab situated on the river of the same name, which is said to be two hundred and twenty miles from Kabul.[175] Placing his reliance more on the recent measurements, as given by different perambulators, which have placed the city of Kandahār on the south-west at the distace of three hundred and nine miles[176] or three hundred and thirteen miles from Kabul[177] than on the ancient measurements, as recorded by the classical writers, he has rejected the identification of Arachosia directly with Kandahār.[178] There may be some inaccuracies in the classical measurements derived by Eratosthenes, Strabo and Pliny from the itineraries of Alexander's marches based on the details of his two surveyors, Diognetes and Baiton, and its is also true that their exactitude cannot be ascertained because of being taken by different routes, however, the identification of the city of the Arachosians with Kandahār cannot be denied.

The Arachotus is also celebrated as the site of a city said to have been founded by Semiramis (the far-famed Assyrian Queen, who appears to have flourished in the eighth century BC),[179] the remains of which, M. Court says, are to be seen on the Arghasan river, four farsangs from Kandahār, on the road to Shikarpur. This appears somewhat incompatible with the Arachotus being the Urghundab.[180] The Arachotus being the chief city is considered to be the capital of Arachosia.[181] The aforesaid name of the capital is preserved in Arokhaj or Rokhaj (also called Roh-Kaj) of the Arab geographers (who derived the term possibly from the Greek), as pointed out by J. Rennell,[182] H. Rawlinson[183] and Wilford.[184] H.H. Wilson, getting clues from the *itineraries* of Ibn Haukil (tr. by Sir

173. *AICL*, p. 100, fn. 4.
174. Strabo, XI, viii, 9, *AICL*, p. 100.
175. *AR. Ant.*, p. 175.
176. *Ibid.*
177. *CHI*, vol. I, p. 490.
178. *Op. cit.*, p. 175.
179. Pliny, *Hist. Nat.*, VI, 25.
180. Cf. *Ar. Ant.*, p. 157.
181. *Ibid.*, AIT, p. 34; H. Rawlinson, *JGIS*, vol. XII, p. 113.
182. *MMH* (London, 1793), p. 169; D'Anville, *Geographie Anc. tom.*, ii, p. 291.
183. *Ind. Ant.*, vol. V, pp. 329-30.
184. *As. Res.*, vol. VIII, p. 336.

William Ouseley),[185] and *Geography* of Al-Edrisi,[186] places Arachotus somewhere to the north of Rokhaj (fifty-six miles distant from Bost on the Helmund, at the confluence of the Urghundab) and south of Ghazni in Afghanistan.[187] We find some discrepancies in Wilson's statements, for in one place he has placed the people called Arachoti near Kandahār had the Arkandab river.[188]

A. Cunningham[189] and M.de St. Martin[190] have identified one of the two capitals of the Arachosia of classical writers with modern Ghazni. But the validity of this identification can be questioned on the basis of the distance of the latter from Kabul, which is only eighty-eight miles, which falls short of the distance of the former from Kabul, i.e., two hundred and twenty-eight miles, as given by the classical geographers. St. Martin has identified Arachosia with Kandahār too.[191] But Cunningham has identified the other capital with *Guzar* or *Guzaristan*, which is the chief town on the Helmand of the present day, and with *Ozola* of Ptolemy, which he places in the north-west of Arachosia, the position of which is reconcilable with *Guzaristan*.[192]

Dionysios in his *Bassarika* (a poem in hexameter verse which contains a *Description of the whole world*) and Nonnos in his *Dionysiaka* (a Greek epic poem in hexameter verse) refer pointedly to the impregnability of a place called *Gaza*. Dionysios calls it: "As stern in war as if it was made of brass"[193] and Nonnos observes: "They fortified, with a net-like enclosure of interlacing works, Gazos, on immovable bulwark of Ares, and never has any armed enemy breached its compact foundations".[194] Stephanus of Byzantium has also quoted the *Bassarika* of Dionysios as his authority for this Indian town. The evidence recorded in these two classical works pertaining to the place concerned seems to have prompted Cunningham to identify the Arachosian capital with Ghazni. But it is

---

185. Ouseley, *Oriental Gerography*, pp. 209, 210 cf. *Ar. Ant.*, p. 174.
186. *Geography of Al-Edrisi* : Preface to Ibn Haukil, p. xvii, cf. *Ibid.*
187. *Op. cit.*, p. 174.
188. *Op. cit.*, p. 178.
189. *CAGI*, pp. 33-35.
190. *Étude*, pp. 14ff, cf. *AIMA*, 1st edn. p. 108, note.
191. *Ibid.*
192. *CAGI*, p. 34.
193. Quoted in *ibid.*, p. 35.
194. *Dionysiaka*, XXVI. 30.

very difficult to determine as to how far the appelation *Gazos* or Ptolemy's Gazaka (which has been misplaced amongst the Paropamisadae to the north of Kabul, instead of to the south of it) corresponds with modern town of Ghazni. The statement of Stephanus of Byzantium, that "the town cities named Arakhosia and Arakhoti were near the country of the Massagetae or near Sakastene — the country of Sakas, who were of the same race as Massagetae",[195] is wholly inadmissible.

Ammianus Marcellinus has expressly stated that "Among the cities of the country, Arachosia, the most important are Alexandria and Arbaca and Choaspa".[196] The identification of the said cities except the first one is uncertain. Alexandria also figures in the list of towns enumerated by Ptolemy. Alexander, after subduing the Indians bordering on Arachosia in the southern part of Afghanistan, constructed a city after the manner of the Yavaṇas at a point commanding the roads which marked the celebration of his victory. The Macedonians and some thousands of the native people settled side by side in the newly built city. The city called "Alexandria — among — the — Archosians" is usually considered to be Kandahār.[197] In fact, like many other cities this too was given the name of the conqueror. "It was only one of the chain of cities which marked the track of conquering Hellenism."[198]

The people called by Strabo Paropamisadai are more correctly denominated by Ptolemy the Paropanisadai. They are exactly the same whom Ammianus Marcellinus calls the Paropanisatae. They, according to these three authorities, were bounded on the west by Aria, on the north by Bactria, on the east by the Indus and on the south by Arachosia. The tribes comprehended under this name were located along the southern and eastern sides of Paropamisos or Paropanisus range[199] (Avestan Upāirisaena) or the Central Hindukush (Avestan US-Hindava), and thus occupied Kabulistan and a considerble part of Afghanistan. They belonged to the province of the same name called by Pliny Paropamisadae[200] and by an unknown writer (who follows Eratosthenes and Ptolemy)

---

195. Cf. A. Cunningham, *CISSK*, pp. 32-33, *Geog. Jour.*, vol. XII, p. 13.

196. *History*, XXIII, vi, *AICL*, p. 94.

197. H.H. Wilson, *op. cit.*, p. 157; *CHI*, vol. I, p. 311; Paul Masson Oursel *et al.*, *AIIC*, p. 30.

198. *CHI*, vol. I, p. 311.

199. Strabo, *Geog.*, XV, i, 8; XV, ii, 8, 9, 10; *AICL*, pp. 14, note 3, 87-89; *AIT*, VI, 18, 4, pp. 310-12; A. Marcellinus, *Hist.*, XXIII, vi, *AICL*, p. 93.

200. *Hist. Nat.*, VI. 23.

Paropanisadae,[201] which comprised the Kabul valley (east Afghanistan) and the country north of the Kabul river now known as Laghmān or Lamghān (= Skt. Lampaka), Kohistan and Kafiristan (Kapiśa).

The existence of Kabul in the second century AD as the capital of the province or "country" (Afghanistan) can be testified to by the evidence of Ptolemy. He calls it Karura (Karoura) or Kabura (Kaboura) which, according to him, was situated on the Lokharna or Logarh river[202] whose ruins are still available on the right bank of the same river. This was one of the principal cities of the Paropanisadi. The inhabitants of the city has been called by him Kabolitae. The same city has been called by him,[203] Strabo,[204] Pliny,[205] Eratosthenes[206]and Ammianus Marcellinus[207] Ortospana, which Cunningham has identifed with "the ancient city of Kabul and its citadel or high fort, the Bala Hisar".[208] The distance from the city of Arachotus to Ortospana on the three roads from Bactra, according to Eratosthenes (Strabo, XI, viii, 9) was 2,000 stadia (228 miles), as has been already stated. The said three roads, which include "the north-east road, by the Panjshir valley and over the Khawak pass to Anderab", "the west road, by the Kushan valley, and over the Hindukush pass to Ghori" and "the south-west road, up the Ghorband valley, and over the Hajiyak pass to Bamian", diverged at Opian near Charikar. Ortospana or Pliny's Orthospanum because of being on the high road to Bactria has been conjecturally equated by H.H. Wilson with Orthostana (= the Sanskrit Ūrddhasthāna or Ūrdhvasthāna), i.e., high place or lofty city. This also applies to the elevated plain on which Kabul was situated.[209] Foucher (one of the most reliable French authorities on the subject) is also of the opinion that both Kabura and Ortospana stand for Kabul, and perhaps Ortospana was situated in the immediate vicinity of Kabul.[210]

It is significant to note that after the destruction of Kāpiśī, the first capital of

---

201. *Geog.*, VI, 24 cf. *AICL*, p. 212.
202. *Geog.*, VII, I; VI, 18, 4, *AIT*, pp. 34 and 311-12; see aslo *IIA*, p. 58, note 4; *Ar. Ant.*, pp. 160, 176.
203. *Ibid.*
204. *Geog.*, XV, ii, 8, *AICL*, p. 87.
205. *Hist. Nat.*, VI, 17, 21.
206. Cf. Strabo, XI, viii, 9, *AICL*, p. 100 and note 5.
207. *Op. cit.*
208. *CAGI*, pp. 19, 30.
209. *Op. cit.*, p. 176.
210. *Op. cit.*, vol. 2, pp. 213-14, cf. Motichandra, *op. cit.*, p. 91.

Afghanistan, by Cyrus, Kabul shot into prominence as its second capital, which was also known as Ortospana. By the seventh century AD its popularity as the capital seems to have declined. Because Hiuen-Tsang in place of the city of Kabul mentions *Hu-pi-na* (Opian or modern Hupian, situated to the north of Charikar) as the capital,[211] which, according to V.A. Smith, was that of the Kabul territory.[212] Cunningham's view that Kabul was included within the territories of Opiai[213] is no longer tenable in view of the fact that both Kabul and Opian near Charikar were two different urban centres with their respective territory at the distance of about 50 miles from each other. Further, in ancient times Kabul remained in existence as the city at its original place (at Logarh river) till its occupation by the Saffarid ya'qub ibn Laith in H. 256 = AD 870-71. After the Arab conquest of the place the new city of Kabul came into being in the early medieval period which was situated on the Kabul-Rūda. It continued to exist as a chief city. Besides the chief city of Kabura or Ortospana, some towns were also located in the territories of the Paropanisadae along the Kophes or Kabul river. The most notable of these is Naulibis or Naulibus, as mentioned by both Ptolemy[214] and Ammianus Marcellinus.[215] The name bears a closer affinity to Nilab, an important town situated to the south of the Kophes or on the Ghor, and affluent of the Kabul river. This may be the probable site of this town. We have no data for determining the locations of either Agazaca or Marcellinus[216] or Arguda or Argandi of Ptolemy[217] which is almost identical with Argante of Hekataeus who has mentioned it in his *Geography* as the Indian city juxtaposed to Gandarii (the people of Gāndhāra).[218] The town of Bagarda, as mentioned by Ptolemy, has been placed in the valley of Wardak or Logarh valley in the province of Kabul, inhabited by the Wardak tribe of Afghans.[219]

Strabo has rightly pointed out that in the country of Paropamisadae the towns were numerous, well supplied with everything, except oil.[220]

---

211. *YCTI*, vol. II, pp. 266-67.
212. "The Itinerary of Yuan-Chwang", in *ibid.*, pp. 342-43.
213. *CAGI*, p. 30.
214. *AIT*, pp. 311-12.
215. *Op. cit.*
216. *Op. cit.*
217. *AIT*, pp. 311-12.
218. *AICL*, Introd., xiv, Bunbury, *HAG*, vol. I, p. 142.
219. *CAGI*, p. 32; M. Elphinstone, *An Account of the Kingdom of Kabul*, vol. I, p. 160.
220. *Geog.*, XV, ii, 10.

Here it may be added that Aria, Arachosia and Paropanisadae (with their respective capitals at Herāt, Kandahār and Kābul) remained in the possession of Persians from about the middle of the sixth century BC to the time of Alexander's invasion. The latter wrested them from the former and established in them colonies of his own. But, subsequently, Seleukos Nikator ceded them to Sandrokottos (Candragupta Maurya) following a treaty of peace ratified in 305 or 303 BC.[221] And, consequently, they fromed parts of Maurya empire, and remained as integral parts of northern India till about the end of the ninth century AD.

The Bactria or Baktriana (= Skt. Bāhlīka = Avestic Bakhdhi = Old Persian Bakhtri = mod. Balkh), a principal part of Ariana or in the words of Apollodoros "the ornament of all Ariana",[222] is placed on the Oxus (Skt. = river Vaṁkṣu) in the northern part of Afghanistan. Strabo observes: "Baktriane is coterminous on the north both with Aria and the Propamisadai".[223] Both Pliny[224] and Ptolemy[225] place it at the back of Mount Paropanisus, but the latter erroneously places the city of "Bactra" in Sogdiana.[226] G.E. Gerini (a distinguished authority on Ptolemy's *Geography*) has also mistakenly placed it in Arakhosia.[227] Both the views are quite inconsistent with the information recorded by the historians of Alexander. As a matter of fact, this city has been lying since time immemorial between the Oxus and the Hindukush.

Ptolemy in a very unequivocal manner refers to "Bactra" as "one of the oldest cities in the world".[228] Strabo also speaks of its great fertility and wealth which enabled the Grecian rulers to become powerful and to extend their sovereignty to other countries. Arrian (*Anab*., iii, 29) mentions it as one of the two chief cities of the Bactrians.

Heeren, while dwelling upon the subject at length, has also admitted that the city of

221. For details see Strabo *Geog*., XV, i, 10; XV, ii, 9; Pliny *Hist. Nat*., VI, 20; Plutarch, *Life of Alexander*, Ch. LXII; Justin, *Historiae Philippicae*, XV, 4; *Periplus*; p. 189; R.C. Jain (ed.), *MAIMA*, pp. xii-xiii; V.A. Smith, *EHI*, App. F. pp. 158-60; Lassen, *DPI*, p. 42.

222. Cf. Strabo, *Geog*., XI, xi, 1, *AICL*, pp. 100-1.

223. *Ibid*., XV, ii, 9, *AICL*, p. 89.

224. *Hist. Nat*., VI, 16 (18).

225. *AIT*, VI, 11, 1-9, pp. 267-74.

226. *Ibid*.

227. *RTGEA*, p. 40, note 3.

228. *AIT*, VI, 11, 9, p. 271; H.G. Rawlinson has also described Bactria as one of the great cities of ancient times. According to him, it was in a flourishing state between the sixth century BC and the sixth century AD. It was the great commercial entrepot of the East (*Bactria*), pp. 10-18, 23.

Bactria was the chief seat of the manufactures of India and commerce between the east and west of Asia. He says: "It was destined by nature to be the first place of exchange for the productions of India, which it purchased with those of its own climate. . . . The city of Bactra must be regarded as the commercial entrepot of Eastern Asia. . . . Not only does Bactra constantly appear as a city of wealth and importance in every age of the Persian empire, but it is continually interwoven in the traditions of the East with the accounts of Semiramis and other conquerors. . . . In this part of the world the human race made its first advance in Civilisation. . . ."[229]

Strabo has mentioned Adrapsa or Darapsa as a principal Baktrian city where Alexander, according to him, reached on the fifteenth day after leaving the city Alexandria he had founded at the foot of Kaukasos. He first crossed over the summits of the mountains and then marching through the territory of the Paropamisadae entered into Baktriana.[230] The same city has been mentioned by Pliny,[231] Arrian[232] and Ptolemy[233] with a slight change of name, i.e., Zariaspa, Drapsaca, Drepsa, etc. According to Arrian, it was one of the first cities taken by Alexander after crossing the mountains. It has been identified with Anderab of the present day, but it is said that "this identification rests on very slender ground". Further, its identity has been established with Kunduz[234] which is probably more correct. Ptolemy has mentioned various cities of Bactria including those founded and destroyed by the Macedonian conqueror (between 329 and 327 BC — the period during which he was occupied in reducing that province) but no satisfactory indication has been offered about their locations. Hence, I refrain from entering into further details.

Despite the fact that the Persians, the Greeks, the Indo-Scythians and the Kuṣāṇas — all ruled over Bactria between the sixth century BC and first century AD as a whole — the site of the capital remained unchanged and the city continued to flourish. In the seventh century AD, the capital was known as "Little Rājagr̥ha City", as revealed by Hiuen-Tsang.[235]

The geographical transformation in the frontiers of Bhāratavarṣa from the times of

229. *Op. cit.*, vol. I, pp. 424 f; vol. II, pp. 211, 297; vol. III, p. 387.

230. *Geog.*, XI, xi, 2; XV, ii, 10; see also Bunbury *HAG*, vol. I, pp. 425ff.

231. *Hist. Nat.*, VI, 18.

232. *Anab.*, III, 29; IV, 1, 7, 15.

233. *AIT*, pp. 268-69.

234. *AICL*, p. 90, note 4.

235. *YCTI*, vol. I, p. 108.

the Persian invasion to the fourth century BC sometimes creates difficulty in our way in fixing their limits. However, the elucidation of the subject in the contemporary geographical setting is a guiding factor in ascertaining the exact position of the towns and cities situated within the boundaries of India which successively fell under the occupation of foreign powers.

From the accounts of classical authorities it transpires that the towns and cities lying between the great mountain ranges of the Hindukush (called Paropanisos), the northern frontier towards the west (in the north-east of Kabul), and the Indus — so-called eastern frontier, were all Indian at the time of Alexander's invasion.

An old Indian city transformed with a new Greek name, Nicaea, Nikaea or Nikaia, was situated somewhere between Alexandria and the Kabul river. According to Arrian, Alexander from this city advanced towards the Kophen or Kabul.[236] Julius Valerius, while clarifying the position of this city, has fairly stated that Alexander marching from Bactra forthwith recrossed Caucasus or mountain rampart and reached Alexandria. "After passing through the country of the Parapapisamides (Paropanisadae) he directed his march towards the Indus by way of the city of Nicaea and the river Cophoen (Kabul)".[237] In the course of the march many tribes were put to the sword, and their towns captured. According to Nonnos (*Dionysiaka*, xvi, last three lines), Bacchus built a stone city, named Nikaia, near a lake which he also called *Indophon* in remembrance of his victory over the Indians on this spot. The conspicuous absence of authentic details of this city in the Classical texts sparked off a lot of controversy among scholars in the past over its exact geographical position and identification. According to Wilson, "the Greek name does not imply a Greek city, and it was probably a translation of some such appellation as Jayapur, "the city of Victory"".[238] Elphinstone during his Kabul mission in 1808 found tribes speaking language closely allied to Sanskrit and not Greek. One such village-tribe was Nisa similar to Nikaia. General Abbott identified the city with Nangnihar — five miles west of modern Jalalabad.[239] H.G. Raverty,[240] Burnes,[241] V.A. Smith[242] and J. Hutchinson and J. Ph. Vogel[243]

236. *Anab.*, IV, 22, 6; *IIA*, p. 59.
237. *The Itinerary of Alex, the Great*, Ch. 104, *AICL*, pp. 150-51.
238. *Ar. Ant.*, p. 183.
239. *IIA*, Appendices, Note B, pp. 332-33.
240. *NAB*, pp. 48-51.
241. *Op. cit.*, vol. III, pp. 186-90.
242. *EHI*, p. 53.
243. *History of the Panjab Hill States*, vol. II, p. 666.

have also located the city of the west of Jalalabad. Wilson has fixed its location on the plain of Begrām at a spot with ruins about 18 miles distant from Houpian[244] which is also favoured by Bunbury.[245] Thirlwall supposes that Nikaea was a new name given to the city otherwise called Ortospana or Kabura, the site of the modern Kabul.[246] This can also be corroborated by statement of Cunningham.[247] Ritter, Droysen[248] and T.H. Holdich[249] also put it at Kabul. M. Jacquet infers that it was situated at some distance from the Kophen.[250] The evidence adduced, particularly by Arrian, that Alexander proceeded to that river from the city of Nikaea, invalidates the assumptions with regard to its location at Kabul. Foucher discovered the ruins of this city on the spot where the roads to Mandarāvara and Cārabāga diverged.[251]

After having a deeper insight into the classical sources we find that between the Kophen or Kabul river and the Indus there were a large number of towns and cities. There stood also the famous ancient Indian city of Nysa. The earliest reference to this city occurs in Homer's *Iliad* (Bk. VI, 130-40). But the description thereof is more fictional than historical. However, the city was not a fiction of the poet but a historical reality. The existence of this city in pre-Alexandrian period can be proved by the evidences furnished in both the classical and non-classical sources. Megasthenes,[252] Pliny,[253] Strabo,[254] Arrian,[255] Curtius,[256] Justin,[257] Plutarch[258] and others have also mentioned this

---

244. *Op. cit.*, p. 183.
245. *HAG*, vol. I, p. 439, note.
246. *History of Greece*, vol, VII, p. 5.
247. *CAGI*, p. 30.
248. *IIA*, Note B, pp. 332-33.
249. *The Gates of India*, pp. 85-88; see also *CHI*, vol. I, p. 312, note 3.
250. *JA*, October 1837, p. 379, note.
251. *Op. cit.*, vol, II, p. 205.
252. *Indika*, Bk. IV, Fragm. XLVI, and Fragm. LVI, cf. *AIMA*, 1st edn, pp. 110 and 152; *Ind. Ant.*, vol. V, p. 89.
253. *Hist. Nat.*, VI, 21, 8; VI, 23, 11.
254. *Geog.*, XV, i, 8 and 27, *AICL*, pp. 12-13, 32-33; see also Hamilton and Falconer, *op. cit.*, vol. IIII, p. 76; *AIMA*, p. 110.
255. *Anab.*, Bk. V, Ch. I, *IIA*, pp. 79-80; *Indika*, pt. I, Chs. I & V, cf. *AIMA*, 1st edn, pp. 179-80 and 195; see also Chinnock, *op. cit.*, p. 399.
256. *History of Alexander the Great*, VIII, 10, *IIA*, pp. 192-94.
257. *Historiae Philippicae*, XII. 7, IIA, p. 321.
258. *Life of Alexander*, Ch. LVIII, *IIA*, p. 305.

city with some variations in their presentation of accounts of the subject. The foundation of this city has been ascribed to a mythical hero, Dionysos, by both Megasthenes[259] and Arrian[260] on fabulous ground and under the erroneous impression that in the most primitive times the people of India were living in the villages, and they had neither the towns nor cities. It was Dionysos who came along with other Greeks at the head of the considerable army and conquered the country, settled therein and converted the villages into large cities and gave laws to them. One of the cities named Nysa or Nyssa was founded by him at the foot of the mountain called Meros. Arrian says "the city of Nysa is no mean monument with Mount Meros".[261] The Nysaeans or Nysaioi, according to them, were not an Indian race but the descendants of the Greeks. Diodorus has also narrated more or less the same story.[262] The evidence relating to Dionysos has been partly quoted by Strabo.[263] Diodorus in particular ascribes the foundation of the city to another mythical figure, the Greek Bacchus. He is said to have built many cities in India one of which he called Nysa in memory of that (Nysa ) in Egypt where he was brought up. At this Nysa in India he is believed to have planted ivy which continues to grow here. Besides many other marks of his visit left there, he got his statue carved as lasting monument of his expedition.[264] About the middle of the first century AD Apollonius with his fellow-traveller, Damis of Assyria, after crossing the Kophen (the Kabul river) entered the city of Nysa ruled by a king (Akouphis), and "saw the peaked summit of Mount Nysa, where was a circular space fenced with a hedge of laurels, vine and ivy planted by the hands of Bacchus himself, whose statue in white stone adorned the centre of this rustic temple". This can be confirmed by Philostratos' statements recorded in his biographical work, *Life of Apollonius of Tyana*.[265] The sense underlying the narratives or legendary accounts of the classical writers concerned leads us to warrant the belief that this city was founded by the Greek colonists long before the invasion of Alexander. It is, however, very difficult to ascertain the truth contained in their statements. Alexander personally saw many towns and cities between the Kabul and the Indus Doāb. According to Curtius (VIII, 10), he visited the flourishing city of Nysa too. He attacked it and, consequently, the Nysaeans

259. *AIMA*, 1st edn. p. 110.
260. *Ibid.*, pp. 179-80.
261. *Ibid.*, p. 195.
262. *Bibliotheca Historica*, III, 63 and 72.
263. *Geog.*, XV, I, 8, *AICL*, p. 13.
264. *Bib. Hist.*, tr. by Booth, Bk. I, ii, 12, *AICL*, p. 204.
265. *AICL*, p. 192.

offered their submission to him. The city was eventually claimed to be the Greek or Ionian colony.[266] This city is generally placed near Mount Meros on the opposite bank of the river Kabul or in the valley of Kabul.

According to St. Martin[267] and Bellew,[268] the existing Nysatta village situated near thc northern bank of the river Kabul, six miles below Hashtnagar or Puṣkalāvatī preserves the vestige of the ancient city of Nysa. The city was actually situated to the west of the Indus (above Attock) in the Swāt valley. Holdich, whose knowledge of the Indian frontier is unsurpassable, has fixed its location on the lower spurse of the three-peaked Koh-i-Mor,[269] which is also supported by Smith.[270] The Nysaeans have been placed on the "well-watered slopes of those mountains which crown the uplands of Swat and Bajour, where they cultivated the vine for generations". The city called Nagara by Ptolemy in his *Geography* [VII, I, 43] is identified with Nagarahāra, an ancient capital of a kingdom of the same name, the ruins of which have been traced four or five miles to the west of Jalālābād.[271] St. Martin states that Udayanapura was an old name of Nagarahāra.[272] The popular tradition also affirms it. Cunningham has fixed the position of the said capital at Begrām, about two miles to the west of Jalālābād. He also admits that Nagara was situated midway between Kabura (Kabul) and the Indus.[273] In the beginning of the fifth century AD this city was called *Na-kie* or Nagara by Fa-hien. It was then and independent state governed by its own king.[274] The same city was called by Hiuen-Tsang *Na-ka-lo-ho* (Nagara or Nagarahāra), when he visited it in AD 630. It was then without a king, and subject to Kapisene or Kapiśa with its dependency city of Hi-lo or Hidda, situated near

---

266. See J.E. Schwartzberg (ed.), *HASA*, pp. 169 ff; Heeren, *Historical Researches*, vol. I, p. 294.

267. Cf. *IIA*, Note G, p. 339; *AIMA*, p. 180, note.

268. *Ethnography of Afghanistan*, pp. 64-76.

269. *The Indian Borderland*, pp. 270-342; *The Gates of India*, pp. 122-24; see also *Ar. Ant.*, p. 193.

270. *EHI*, pp. 56-57. R.C. Jain (*MAIMA*, XXXVII, App. 3) has mistakenly placed the city between the Kaukasos and the Pamir or Meru mountain.

271. *AICL*, p. 13, note 1; *IIA*, Note G, p. 338; *CAGI*, p. 39; *AIT*, pp. 113-14; *JRAS*, vol. XIII, pp. 183- 207. Many places bore the name of Nysa. The Indian Nysa did not become known to the Greeks till Alexander's expedition. In the cosmogonic geography of the *Zend-Avesta* it figure as a part of Ancient Iran, See A.D. Humboldt (ed.), *Central Asia* (1843), I, pp. 116 ff.

272. Cf. M. Julien, *Hiouen Thsang*, iii, p. 305, see also *IIA*, p. 338, note; *AIT*, p. 113.

273. *CAGI*, pp. 38-39.

274. H.A. Giles, *RBK*, pp. 12, 15.

Peśāwar south of Udayana.[275] The mention of this city by the Chinese pilgrims not only testifies to its existence but also strengthenes the classical evidence. In the post-seventh century AD this city probably followed the fortunes of the sovereign state, and became successively a part of the brāhmaṇa kingdom of Kabul and of the Mohammedan empire of Ghazni. It may be noted here that the city of Nysa is often confounded with Nagara of Ptolemy. But the fact remains that both were two different cities and not the same as held by some scholars.

Strabo makes a mention of small town, Plemyrion. He adds that the river Khoaspes (Kunār) falls into the Kophes (the Kābul river) near it after passing by another city, "Gorys" (the city of Gauraeans or Gauraioi situated on the bank of the river "Guraeus" or Gauri, modern Panjkora).[276] "Plemyrion must have been situated at or near where Jalālābād now stands".[277] The city called "Gorys" is identified with "Gorydale"[278] on the eastern bank of the Khoes (the Kunār or Kameh river) or in the valley of the Kābul river which was also taken by the Macedonians.

The towns and cities situated in the region between two rivers, the Khoaspes or Kunār (a tributary of the Kophes or the Kābul river) and the Indus received the notices of not only the professed historians of Alexander but other classical writers too.

The town called by Arrian Arigaion[279] or Arigacum,[280] which is absolutely identical with Argacum of Julius Valerius,[281] was situated to the east of the river Khoaspes. It was one of the walled towns. According to Arrian, it was fortified by double wall. The weight of the evidence is in favour of its identification with Bajour or Bagawar, the capital of the province of the same name.[282] According to some other evidence, it is represented by Naoghi or Nawagai, a village in the modern province of Bajour.[283] It is further suggested

275. *YCTI*, vol. I, pp. 182-89.

276. *Geog.*, XV, i, 26, *AICL*, p. 31.

277. *AICL*, p. 31, note 3.

278. Thirlwall's *History of Greece*, vol. VII, p. 7.

279. *Anab.*, IV, 24, *IIA*, p. 64.

280. *Indika*, tr. Chinnock, *op. cit.*, pp. 230-31.

281. *The Itinerary of Alex.*, Ch. 105, *AICL*, p. 151 and note 3.

282. *IIA*, p. 64, note 1; *Ar. Ant.*, p. 189; B.C. Sinha, *Studies in Alexander's Campaigns*, p. 26; J.F.C. Fuller, *The Generalship of Alexander the Great*, pp. 126, 245.

283. *IIA*, p. 64, note 1; Fuller, *op. cit.*, p. 126.

that "Arigaeum may be found in Arichand",[284] but since this is on the east of the Landai river, the validity of this identification may be doubted. However, in this direction besides the town of Bajour, there are several ruins, and some of these may be the relics of Arigaeum. The name of the place is apparently Indian — "Arijaya" or "Arinjaya", "the foe-vanquishing city"[285] which is comparable with "Ārjunāva" of the *Kāśikā* on Pāṇini (IV, 2, 69).[286] The town mentioned by the Greeks is said to have "commanded the road between the Kunār and the Panjkora valley".[287] This capital town belonged the Aspasians or Aspasioi[288] (Sanskrit Aśvakas = Āśvāyana of Pāṇini, *sūtra* IV, 1, 110,[289] or Cavaliers) of Alishang-Kunār or Chitral-Bajour valley. They were the eastern branch of the Aśvakas — the indigenous hill-tribes that occupied the mountainous regions to the north of the Kābul river. They are represented by the Pashtus, probably the ancestors of the modern Afghans. The said town was very populous, opulent and prosperous.

The Aspasians, on perceiving Alexander's approach after he had crossed the Kunār river to subjugate them, set their town on fire having thought it hopeless to save from his onslaught, abandoned it and retired to an inaccessible mountains. But the latter took care to have rebuilt on account of its commanding position or because of its advantageous site.[290] It was recolonised by a number of the native people and the war-worn Greeks. The strength of the inhabitants of the town from the demographic point of view is strikingly illustrated by the fact that 40,000 of them were taken captive in course of their pitched battles with Alexander.[291] The Aspasians besides the principal city, Arigaeum, had another town called Andaka by Arrian[292] and Akadera by Curtius.[293] Alexander took possession of this town and then garrisoned. It is identified with the

---

284. M. Court, "Alexander's Exploits on the West of the Indus", in *JASB*, April 1839, pp. 307-9.
285. *Ar. Ant.*, p. 189.
286. *IP*, p. 457.
287. *CHI*, vol. I, p. 317.
288. Arrian (*Anab.*, IV. 24-25) and Ourtius (*Hist. Alex*, VIII, 10) mention them as Aspasians, whereas, on the other hand, Aristoboulos (quoted by Strabo, *Geog.*, XV, i, 17, *AICL*, p. 22; refers to them as Aspasioi). Strabo mentions them both as Aspasioi and Hippasii or Hippasioi (*Geog.* XV, i, 27, *AICL*, p. 33; also *MSS*, XV, 691, 698, cf. *CHI*, vol. I, p. 316, note 1).
289. *IP*, pp. 456-57.
290. Arrian, *Anab.*, IV, 24-25, *IIA*, pp. 63-66; Valerius, *The Itinerary of Alex.*, Ch. 105, *AICL*, p. 151.
291. Arrian, *Anab.*, IV, 25, *IIA*, pp. 65-66.
292. *Anab.*, IV, 23, *IIA*, pp. 60-62; *Indika*, tr. Chinnock, *op. cit.*, pp. 230-31.
293. *Hist. Alex.*, VIII, 10, *IIA*, pp. 192-93, also p. 64, note 1.

present town named Adrek, not far from the confluence of the Alishang with the Kabul river.[294] Here it is to be added that the name of Apasians' chief is not mentioned by any classical writer. There were many other walled cities belonging to the Aśvaka tribes.

The towns and cities situated within the Gandharic territory lying on both sides of the Kābul river, immediately above its confluence with the Indus at Ohind (mod. Peśāwar dist.) about 16 miles north of Attock, also deserve our notice. The ancient name of Ohind was Udabhāṇḍapur, the place of transhipment of goods across the Sindh. It is equivalent to Hiuen-Tsang's *U-to-kia-han-cha*, which is transcribed as Utakhaṇḍa.

A city called by the classic authors variously Massaga, Massaka, Mazaga, and Masoga was situated on the bank of the river Souastos or Swāt or near the Guraeus or Panjkora river. This celebrated city, which was strongly fortified, was the capital of the kingdom of the Assakenians, Assakenos or Assakenoi (the Aśva-senīs, "those fighting on horeseback") of the valleys of Swāt and Buner. It was very large, populous and prosperous city. It had great defensive walls and magnificent gates.[295] Strabo in his faithful account of the subject calls it "the chief city of the country (the realm of the Assakanos) and the royal residence'.[296] According to Curtius, it occupied a very strong position was surrounded by a wall of stone and sun-dried brick thirty-five stadia in circumference. Thirty-eight thousand infantry were deployed to defend the city against Alexander's invasion.[297] Valerius, while adding to this information, has revealed that the walls of the towns of

294. *Ar. Ant.*, p. 187.

295. Arrian, *Anab.*, IV, 26, *IIA*, pp. 66-68; *Indika*, pt. I, Ch. I, *AIMA*, 1st edn. p. 180 and note; Chinnock, *op. cit.*, pp. 230-31; Curtius, *Hist. Alex.*, VIII, 10, 22-5, *IIA*, pp. 191-94; Diodoros, *Bib. Hist.*, XVII, 84, *IIA*, pp. 269-70; Justin, *Hist. Phil.*, XII, 7, *IIA*, p. 322 and note 2; Plutarch, *Lif. Alex.*, Ch. 58, *IIA*, p. 305; Strabo, *Geog.*, XV, i, 27, *AICL*, p. 33; J. Valerius, *The Itin. of Alex.*, Ch. 106, *AICL*, p. 151; see also *CAI*, pp. 11-13, 162, 215; B.N. Puri, *op. cit.*, p. 54; Bunbury, *HAG*, vol. I, pp. 425-29, 442-43; Heeren, *Historical Researches*, vol. I, pp. 294-95; *HASA*, pp. 169 ff; Duncker, *HA*, vol. IV, Ch, IV; "The Nations and Princes of the Land of the Indus", p. 393; J.T Wheeler, *India from the Earliest Ages*, vol. III, pp. 156, 160-61; "Greek and Roman India", in *The History of India from the Earliest Ages*, 1st edn. (London, 1881), rept. in *Ancient India* (Delhi, 1983), pp. 99, 102-3; W.W. Tarn, *Alexander the Great*, vol. I, p. 89; Holdich, *The Gates of India*, p. 128; Raverty, *NAB*, pp. 200, 234; Enriquez, *The Pathanm Borderland*, p. 37; Deane, *JRAS*, 1896, p. 655; Aurel Stein, *On Alexander's Track to the Indus*, pp. 43-44; "Alexander's Campaign on the Indian North-West Frontier", *Geog. Journ*, *JRGS*, no. 70 (1927), pp. 417-39; "An Archaeological Tour in Upper Swat and Adjacent Hill Tracts", *MASI*, no. 42 (Calcutta, 1930); *Archaeological Tour in Buner* (Lahore, 1898), p. 53.

296. *Geog.*, XV, I, 27, *AICL*, p. 33.

297. *Hist. Alex*, VIII, 10, 22-5, *IIA*, pp. 194-95.

the Accae (Assakenian) tribes were of "most formidable strength and equipped with every means of defence . . . the town was protected by a double ring of remparts".[298] The city of Massaga was the citadel for the hill-people and was impregnable because of a fortress which stood on a precipitous mountain. Arrian (*Anab.*, IV, 26) says that Massaga was the greatest city in the dominions of the Assakenians.

The exact location of the city called Massaga or Massaka has not yet been ascertained in a conclusive manner. However, there was a town called Mashanagar (as mentioned by Babur in his Memoir) on the river of Swāt.[299] with which the identity of this city can, incontrovertibly be established. Rennell also identified Massaga of Alexander's historians with this city.[300] M. Court states that at a distance of twenty-four miles from the town of Bajour a ruined site of ancient city exists which is called Massangar (Massanagar) or Mashkine.[301] He further holds that the ancient remains of the city called Maha-gram or Ma-gram are observable near a hill called Mount Maram.[302] Pāṇini identified the warlike people called Assakenoi with the Āśvakāyanas (*Naḍādi-gaṇa*, IV, 1, 99) of the Swāt valley (Suvāstu, IV, 2, 77 = ancient Uddiyāna = Udayana of the Buddhist literature) and their capital with Maśakāvatī which is mentioned in the *Mahābhāṣya* as the name of the river (IV, 2, 71), which denotes that portion of the river Swāt in its lower reaches where the town of the same name in Gāndhāra or Massaga or Massanagar was situated on it.[303] Aurel Stein also located it in the lower Swāt valley.[304] St. Martin in his map of the basin of the Kophes has placed it near the river of Swāt in 34°40'N. Lat.[305] Some traces of its name are still to be found in the regions which must have been subject to the authority of its sovereign. The Sanskrit name of the city must have been Maśaka. In the *Mahābhārata* exactly the same name figures as one of the four important towns of the north-west.[306] This proves the remote antiquity of the urban settlement in this region.

---

298. *The Itine. of Alex.*, Ch. 106, *AICL*, p. 151.
299. Cf. *IIA*, Note D, pp. 334-35.
300. *MMH*, pp. 120-21.
301. "On Alexander's exploits on the West of the Indus", *JASB*, April 1839; also *IIA*, Note D, pp. 334-35; *AICL*, p. 33, note 2; *Ar. Ant.*, pp. 189-90.
302. *Ar. Ant.*, pp. 189-90.
303. *IP*, pp. 43, 75, 456-57, 489; also *Bh. Sāv.*, vol. I, p. 207; Lassen, *Ind. Alt.*, vol. II, pp. 136-38, St. Martin, *Étude*, pp. 35-36.
304. *On Alexander's Track to the Indus*, p. 44.
305. Cf. *AICL*, p. 33, note 2.
306. Bhīṣma Parva, 12, 33-34; see also *Bh. Sāv.*, vol. 2, pp. 130-31; *Mbh. Ko.*, pp. 667, 512.

→

M. Elphinstone is of the firm opinion that the names of the towns and cities of north-west India can be found in the Sanskrit sources.[307] Olaf Caroe proposes the Katgala site for Massaga of the Greek historians.[308] G. Tucci has located it somewhere near Chakdarra in the Swāt region.[309] Holdich connects it with a place called Matkanai near the Malakand Pass situated on the south bank of the Swāt.[310] This is also called a "Pakhtoon city".[311] This was perhaps one of the greatest cities of Gāndhāra in eastern Afghanistan or the largest among the tribal cities that belonged to the Aśvakas of that region. Plutarch has rightly called Massaga a city of the Gandridai (Gandarians).[312] The river Swāt (Souastene of Ptolemy, VII, 1, 42) with its western tributary, the Gauri, flowed through Gāndhāra the basins of which were inhabited by them. This capital city of the tribal kingdom was apparently in the territory of Kabul. The Assakenians were the western branch of the Aspasians or the Aśvakas.[313] They were separated from each other by the territory of the Guraeans. They were ethnically connected. It is because of their propinquity that they are considered the kindered tribes. They relied for their defence on the fortifications of their towns. The Assakenians dominion seems to have been "encompassed by the Swāt on the north, the Landai on the west and the Kabul on the south".[314] The Massaga city was besieged and razed to the ground during the operation of Alexander. The reigning

→ In the aforesaid Parvan of the *Mbh.*, the town has been confounded with the people of the same name inhabiting the Śaka-dvīpa or Śakasthān called by the ancient historians of Greece Massagetae who had ethnic affinities with the Śakas or Indo-Scythians.

The Hanskāyana of the *Mbh.* (Sabhā Parva, 48, 13) in all probability represents the Aśvakāyana or Assakenoi because it finds mention along with other tribes of the north-west.

307. *The History of India*, ed. E.B. Cowell, 9th edn., pp. 331, 36.

308. *The Pathans*, p. 53.

309. *East and West* (New Series), vol. XIV, nos. 1-2, p. 27.

310. *Op. cit.*, p. 105 and Map facing p. 94; see also *EHI*, p. 57; L.J. Trotter and W.H. Hutton, *History of India from the Earliest times to the present day*, p. 29.

311. R.C. Jain, *MAIMA*, App. 3.

312. *Oration* I. *Concerning the Fortune of Alexander*, 2, *AICL*, p. 206, note 1.

313. For details about the Aspasians and Assakenians with special reference to the Aśvakas see *AIMA*, 1st edn, pp. 152-53, note; *IIA*, Note C, pp. 333-34; *AICL*, p. 22, note 1; *CHI*, p. 316, note 1; St. Martin, *Étude*; pp. 376-78; A.A. Macdonell, *HSL* (Oxford, 1936), pp. 412 ff; Lassen, *Ind. Alt.* vol. II, p. 129; *HA*, vol. IV, Ch. IV, p. 386; *IP*, pp. 456-57; Tucci, "The tombs of the Asvakayana Assakenoi", in *East and West*, vol. XIV, nos. 1-2, pp. 27-28; R.N. Saletore, *EIC*, vol. I, pp. 126, 128, 139; B.C. Law, *HGAI*, pp. 66-67; *Tribes in Ancient India*, p. 180; *IETBJ*, p. 107; S.M. Ali, *The Geography of the Purāṇas*, pp. 171-72; Varāhamihira's *Br. Sam.*, XIV, 22 (described as Aśmaka).

314. S.B. Chaudhari, *ESAI*, p. 52.

king at the time called Assakenos was slain in the course of its siege by the troops of Alexander. The latter after sometimes found the walls of the city deserted and the city burned down by its inhabitants, who had dispersed in quest of safer hiding-places.[315] This city seems to have been the seat of sovereign power which controlled the whole realm. The wife of the deceased king, Queen Kleophes (Justin, XII, 7, 10-11), mistakently called the mother by Curtius (VIII, 10, 35), was restored to the throne and ruled for sometime over her own kingdom comprising many towns and cities.

We have also some archaeological evidence to prove the close commercial relations of the said tribal people of the Swāt region with Taxila as well as their settlements in this region sometime between the fourth century BC and the second century BC. A few inscribed copper coins of the Aśvaka tribe bearing the legends in early Brāhmī characters were discovered by Cunningham in the neighbourhood of Taxila. One of these coins (No. 13) bears the legend "Vataśvaka",[316] which both V.A. Smith[317] and Buhler[318] have taken as equivalent to Sanskrit Aśvaka. It may be identified with the Aśvakas of Indian literature and the Assakenoi of the classical literature. The legend may be interpreted as meaning Aśvakānāmvataḥ = Vataśvakaḥ. The coin has been assigned to 350 BC by Smith.[319] Whereas, on the other hand, Rapson[320] and J. Allan[321] have assigned the coins in general to the third century BC and the early second century BC respectively. Whatever may be the fact, the possibility of the shifting of the Assakenians from the Swāt valley to Taxila region because of their territorial proximity after the occupation of their towns and cities by Alexander as well as in the later period cannot be precluded. The archaeological discoveries made in the Saidu Sharif region (Swāt State) by Italian archaeological mission also help us establish the age-old conneciton of the Aśvakas of the Swāt valley as well as those of the Taxila coins with the horse.[322]

The territory of the Assakenians, besides its metropolis (Massaga), was adorned

---

315. Arrian, *Anab.*, IV, 26, 27, *IIA*, pp. 66-70; Curtius, *Hist Alex.*, VIII, 10, *IIA*, pp. 194-96; Valerius, *Itin. Alex.*, Chs. 106 and 109, *AICL*, pp. 151-52.
316. *Co. Anc. Ind.*, p. 61, Pl. 11, 17.
317. *CCIM*, vol. I, pp. 147, 157.
318. *Indian Studies* (Wien, 1895), no. III, p. 46.
319. *Op. cit.*, p. 147 (in p. 157 he has suggested third century BC).
320. *Indian Coins*, p. 14.
321. *CCBM*, pp. cxlvi-cxlvii.
322. See the views of C. Silvi Antonini and G. Tucci, *East and West*, vol. XIV, nos. 1-2, pp. 16-17, 27-28.

with two other small fortified towns, which have been called by Arrian Bazira and Ora,[323] by Curtius Beira and Ora[324] and by Julius Valerius Baziphara and Hora.[325] The former also finds mention in the Buddhist literature as a city of Uttarāpatha. In the Pāli Chronicle, *Dipavaṁsa* (p. 27), and the text, *Buddhavaṁsa* (XXVIII, 8), it figures as Vajirā and in the Sanskrit Buddhist text, *Bodhisattvāvadāna Kalpalatā* (p. 4), as Vajrāvatī. In one of the epigraphic records (the Sanskrit inscription discovered in Barikoṭ in upper Swāt valley ascribed to an illustrious ruler of Kabul of Shahi dynasty, Jaipal Deva, who ascended the throne in AD 960) also it figures as Vajirā or Vajirāsthāna.[326] Aurel Stein, who undertook an archaeological exploration of North-West Frontier of India in 1926, identified Bazira with the ancient stronghold marked by the ruins of Bir-Koṭ hill — the castle of Bir (called Beira by Curtius, VIII, X, 22) in the Swāt Valley now represented by Barikoṭ.[327] M. Court has identified it with a place named Bāzār, situated on the southern face of the Koh-Ganga mountain, where are very extensive ruins.[328] Cunningham relying upon the traditional belief identified the site of the original town of Bazira with Bāzār, a large village situated on the bank of the Kalpan or Kālī-pānī river, and quite close to the town of Rustam, built on a very extensive old mound.[329] The position is said to be an important one, as it stands just midway between the Swāt and the Indus rivers. It was apparently a market-town and great centre of trade. It has been "from time immemorial the entrepot of trade between the rich valley of Swāt and the large towns on the Indus and the Kabul rivers".[330] Judging by the importance of the place, Curtius (VIII, 10) called it an opulent city. Rennell conjecturally identified it with Bajour, which lies midway between the river of Kunār and Landai.[331] But there is nothing beyond the similarity of the two names to subscribe to this view.

The town of Ora has been placed by Stein farther up the Swāt valley and identified

---

323. *Anab.*, IV, 27, 28, *IIA*, pp. 68-71.

324. *Hist. Alex*, VIII, 10, *ibid.*, p. 194.

325. *Itin. Alex.*, Ch. 107, *AICL*, p. 152; See also Smith, *EHI*, pp. 59-60; *HASA*, pp. 169 ff; Bunbury, *HAG*, vol. I, pp. 442-43; *HA*, vol. IV, Ch. IV, p. 395; *CAI*, pp. 13-15; B.C. Sinha, *op. cit.*, pp. 27-28; Fuller, *op.* cit., pp. 126, 246-47; Heeren, *Historical Researches*, vol. I, pp. 294-95.

326. *Ep. Ind.*, vol. XXI, p. 301.

327. *Alexander's Track to the Indus*, pp. 46, 59-60.

328. Cf. *Ar. Ant.*, p. 191.

329. *CAGI*, p. 56.

330. *Ibid.*, *IIA*, Note E, p. 335; *Ar. Ant.*, p. 191.

331. *MMH* (Section III, corrected and enlarged in 1791), p. 121.

with Ude-gram situated at a distance of seven or eight miles north of Bīr-koṭ.[332] M. Court has identified it with a town called Oora that still exists in the districts of Buner.[333]

Both the towns mentioned above were besieged, stormed and ultimately captured by the generals of Alexander. Thereafter, those who survived fled out of their cities in the dead of night to a strongly fortified rock called Aornos for safety. The information supplied by Arrian[334] and Valerius[335] in this regard are almost identical. As a matter of fact, after the fall of Massaga, Bazira and Ora in the hills of Swāt and Buner the inhabitants deserted their towns and took shelter in a mountainous fortress on the left bank of the Indus. Valerius has categorically stated that Alexander "on coming to that locality, seized a great many cities".[336] This locality was near the fort of Aornos (Varaṇā of Pāṇini, IV, 2, 82) in the domain of the Āśvakāyaṇas. The identification of this celebrated hill fort has been one of the most perplexing problems of Indian archaeology. The accounts of Arrian,[337] Strabo,[338] Diodorus,[339] Justin,[340] Philostratus[341] and Valerius[342] are discrepant. The other views are equally conflicting. However, Strabo has given an indication that the foot of Aornos was washed by the Indus near its source,[343] which according to the ancient belief was at a distance of some 70 miles above Attak or Attock. Court was the first man to suggest that ". . . it is probably the castle which was opposite Attak, and the vestiges of which we see upon the summit of the mountain". Its foundation is attributed to Raja Hodi.[344] Cunningham relying chiefly on the classical accounts of the subject took it as Varnos and placed it in the country of the Varni. He has identified it with the fort of Raja Vara, whose name, according to him, is till attached to all the ruined strongholds between Hashtnagar (Puṣkalāvatī) and Ohind (Udbhāṇḍa). The old hill-fort and the city of Takht-

332. *Op. cit.*, pp. 59-60.
333. *JASB*, April, 1839, p. 309.
334. *Anab.*, IV. 27-28, *IIA*, pp. 68-71.
335. *Itin. Alex.*, Ch. 107, *AICL*, p. 152.
336. *Ibid.*, Ch. 108, AICL, p. 152.
337. *Anab.*, IV. 28-30, *IIA*, pp. 70-76.
338. *Geog.*, XV, i, 8, *AICL*, p. 13.
339. *Bib. Hist.*, XVII, 85, *IIA*, pp. 271-72.
340. *Hist. Phil.*, XII. 7, *ibid.*, p. 322.
341. *The Life of Apollonius of Tyana*, ii, 10.
342. *Itin. Alex.*, Ch. 108, *AICL*, p. 152.
343. *Geog.*, XV, i, 8, *AICL*, pp. 13-14; see also Curtius, *Hist. Alex.*, VIII, 11, *IIA*, pp. 197-200.
344. *JASB*, 1836, p. 395.

i-Bahai, 15 miles to the north-east of Hashtnagar is said to have been the residence of Raja Vara. Some ruins of his fort at the foot of the hill are called Raja Vara's stables. He has also connected it with the ruined fortress of Rānī-gat situated immediately above the small village of Nogrām, about 16 miles to the north of Ohind.[345] General Abbott identified the "Aornos of history' as the Mahāban hill on the western bank of the Indus,[346] which concurs with Arrians view.[347] Bellew in his work, *Ethnography of Afghanistan*, suggests that the Greek name Aornos is a transformation of the native word *Aranai* (a common Hindi name for hill-ridges in that part of the country), adding that there is an *aranai* spur of Mahāban, near Charorai in the Chumla valley. He seems to identify the rock wth the modern Malka near the summit of Mahāban.[348] Aurel Stein in the course of his tour in the Upper Swāt District in 1926 located the site of this mountain fortress on the left bank of the Indus. He later identified it with old remains at Pir-sae in the Swāt valley.[349] It was the refuge of all the neighbouring tribes. Valerius, while highlighting the importance of this place, has asserted that "a thousand peasantry had full scope for their industry".[350] This stronghold was assaulted and captured by Alexander.[351] While elaborating on the subject, Arrian has candidly stated that he also built a fort there and placed it under the command of the Indian chief (king of Gāndhāra region) named Sisikottos (Śaśigupta).[352] In a different context, he has pointed out that "he placed a garrison in the castle of Aornos".[353]

A small town in the realm of Assakenians called by Arrian Dyrta, lying to the north of Aornos or Mahāban, was also occupied by Alexander.[354] It has been identified with Dhyr (Dir).[355] However, the information available about this town is too meagre to present a clear picture of it.

---

345. *CAGI*, pp. 51-52; *JASB*, 1848, p. 103.
346. *JASB*, 1854, p. 309; 1863, p. 409; see also *IIA*, Note F, pp. 335-37; *AICL*, p. 13, note 2; Grote's *History of India*, vol. VIII, pp. 437-38, cf. *AIMA*, 1st edn. pp. 110-11.
347. *Anab.*, IV, 28.
348. *AICL*, p. 13, note 2.
349. *Geog. Jour.*, no. 70 (1927), pp. 417-39; *Alexander's Track to the Indus*, pp. 118-19, 143-48, 154.
350. *Itin. Alex.*, Ch. 108; *AICL*, p. 152.
351. Arrian, *Anab.*, IV, 29, *IIA*, pp. 73-74; Strabo, *Geog.*, XV, i, 8, *AICL*, p. 13.
352. *Anab.*, IV, 30; *IIA*, pp. 75-76.
353. *Ibid.*, IV, 29.
354. Arrian, *Anab.*, IV, 30; *IIA*, p. 76 and note 3.
355. *Ar. Ant.*, p. 192.

Another small town called Embolima by Arrian,[356] Ptolemy[357] and Curtius[358] was not far from Aornos. Arrian relates that Alexander after taking possession of Peukelaotis (which I have described here later quite separately) captured other small towns on the river Kophen, and arrived at last at Embolima, a city seated not far from the rock Aornos.[359] Curtius' statement vindicates the truth that when he had finished his campaign the west of the Indus by the capture of Aornos, he proceeded towards Embolima.[360] Ptolemy has fixed its position near the junction of the Kābul river with the Indus.[361] It represents the combination of two neighbouring places, i.e., Amb-Balimah. Abbott has identified the town with these two on the Indus, 8 miles to the east of Mahāban or Aornos,[362] which exactly corresponds with what Arrian says: "Aornos was only one day's march from Embolima" (*Anab.*, IV, 28). Cunningham has identified it with modern Ambar-Ohind at a distance of two miles from each other.[363] Court proposes Ambar, a town not far from the west bank of the Indus, for Embolima,[364] or it may be Amb, higher up. This identification seems to be incontestable. The two forts of Amb and Balimah are now in ruins on the spur of the Mahāban, which preserve to this day the traditions of the inhabitants of these two urban centres.[365] Ritter takes Embolima opposite Attock.[366] It is said to be about 60 miles above Attak or Attock.[367] Many small towns situated on the western bank of the Indus along with it were occupied by the said invader. The town of Orobatis (perhaps Oroppa) west of Puṣkalāvatī was fortified and garrisoned by Alexander's generals.[368] We do not have any concrete evidence about its identification.

Elphinstone has correctly observed that an extensive tract comprehending the valleys of Kunār, Kabul, Panjkora, Swāt, Buner, and Chumla were occupied by various divisions

356. *Anab.*, IV, 28; *IIA*, p. 72.
357. *AIT*, p. 142.
358. *Hist. Alex.*, VIII, 12; *IIA*, p. 200.
359. *Anab.*, IV, 28; *IIA*, pp. 72-73.
360. VIII, 12.
361. *AIT*, pp. 142-43.
362. *JASB*, 1854, p. 309; also *IIA*, pp. 72, notes 3 and 5, 337, Note F.
363. *CAGI*, p. 48.
364. *Ar. Ant.*, p. 191
365. *IIA*, p. 72, note 5; George MacMunn, *MRI*, pp. 22-23; *AIT*, pp. 142-43.
366. *Ibid.*
367. *AIT*, pp. 142-43.
368. *IIA*, p. 72, note 1; *EHI*, p. 60.

of the Yusuf-Zai tribe of Afghans, "in which there are some considerable towns, and in many places of which there are extensive vestiges of ancient population and prosperiy".[369]

It is striking to note that the towns and the surrounding places after being occupied by Alexander were abandoned by the inhabitants, who were mainly the hill-tribes. They crossed the Indus and took refuge in Abhisāra country in the hills between the upper Jhelum and Cenāb.

One of the two chief cities of Gāndhāra has been called by Strabo Peukolaitis,[370] by Pliny Peucolaitis or Peucolaitae,[371] by Arrian Peukelaotis, Peukelaitis or Peukelas,[372] by Ptolemy Proklais[373] and by an anonymous author of the *Periplus* Poclais[374] or Proklais,[375] which is a transliteration of Pukkalaoti, the Pāli form of the Sanskrit Puṣkarāvatī or Puṣkalāvatī. It was the western capital of the kingdom of Gāndhāra (Gandarioi of Herodotus, Bk, iii, C, xci; Gandaritis of Strabo, XV, i, 26; Gandarai of Ptolemy or Gandaraei of *Periplus*, sec. 47). The people inhabiting the city have been called Peukalensians or Peukalei (transcript of Pāli Pukkala) by Dionysios Periegetes.[376] According to Arrian, it was a fortified, very large, populous and prosperous city, seated not far from the river Indus.[377] It was indeed a splendid structure of magnificent size. In early times it was a great emporium of commerce.[378] It was also a centre of Buddhism. At the time of Alexander's expedition it was the capital of a chief or king named Astes (Hāsti).[379] This city was also named after him Hāstinagara or Hashtnagar. As stated by Arrian, the city was captured after a siege of thirty days by Hephaestion and its chief was killed in the

369. *An Account of Kabul*, vol. 1, p. 328, cf. *Ar. Ant.*, p. 188.
370. *Geog.*, XV, i. 27, *AICL*, p. 33 and note 3.
371. *Hist. Nat.*, VI, 21.
372. *Anab.*, IV, 22; *IIA*, p. 59, IV, 28; *IIA*, p. 72; *Indika*. I, I, *AIMA*, 1st edn., p. 180 and note; Chonnock, *op. cit.*, pp. 228, 403; aslo Lassen, *Ind. Alt.*, vol. II, p. 858.
373. *AIT*, VII, I, 44, pp. 115-17, 362, note.
374. *Periplus*, *tr.* by Schoff, Sec. 47, pp. 183-84.
375. *Periplus*, cf *CNES*, p. 121 with comments of C. Muller.
376. *Bassarika*, LI, 1080-1165, *AICL*, p. 189.
377. *Indika*, I, I; *IIA*, p. 180
378. *Periplus*, tr. Schoff, p. 183; *IIA*, p. 59, note 5.
379. Arrian, *Anab.*, IV, 22; *IIA*, p. 60.

defence of one of his storngholds. His successor Sangaeus (Skt. Sañjay) was then allowed by Alexander to become governor (Hyparch) of the city.[380]

The Peucolaitae of Megasthenes (*Indika*, Fragm. LVI, *AIMA*, 1st edn., p. 151) probably stands for the dwellers of Puṣkalāvatī city.

The city, Peukolaitis, belonged to the people called Astakenians or Astakenoi[381] (Hāstināyana of Pāṇini, *sūtra* VI, 4, 174).[382] They along with other indigenous tribes of Gāndhāra like Aspasioi, Assakanos, etc., have been placed by both Arrian[383] and Strabo[384] in the regions between the river Kophes and the Indus. Ptolemy has correctly fixed the position of the city on the eastern bank of the river of Suastene or Swāt.[385] According to archaeological and other evidence, modern Parang and Chārasadda, situated 17 miles to the north-east or north-west of Peśāwar (Purūṣapura) near the junction of the river Swāt with the Kābul, preserve the vestiges of the ancient city of Puṣkalāvatī.[386] The two large towns of Parang and Chārasadda are said to have formed part of Aṣṭanagar or eight cities, that are seated close together on the eastern bank of the lower Swāt river now called the Landai. The other six towns are Tangi, Shirpao, Umrzai, Turangzai, Usmanzai and Rajur[387] for which we do not have equivalent words in the classical sources. The rulers of all the eight cities together inclusive of Astes were called Aṣṭakarāja. Puṣkala is still represented by the modern Pakholi in the neighbourhood of Peśāwar. The remains of Puṣkalāvatī city in the vicinity of above-mentioned two large towns constitute the mute evidence to its glorious past.

Court placed the fort of Hisār standing on a mound above the ruins of the old town of Hashtnagar opposite Rajur.[388] "All the suburbs", he says, "are scattered over with vast

380. *Periplus*, IV, 22; *IIA*, p. 60, note 1; also Curtius *Hist. Alex.*, VIII, 12, 13; *HA*, vol. IV, Ch. IV, pp. 392-93.

381. Strabo, *Geog.*, XV, i, 27, *AICL*, p. 33, note 1.

382. *IP*, p. 456.

383. *Indika*, I, I; *AIMA*, 1st edn. p. 180.

384. *Geog.*, XV, i, 27.

385. *AIT*, pp. 115-17.

386. *CASR*, vol.II (1871), pp. 90 ff; vol. XIX (1885), pp. 96-110; *ASIAR*, 1902-3 (by John Marshall), pp. 41 ff, 140-54; *AIMA*, pp. 180-81, note; *Periplus*, tr. Schoff, p. 184; *IIA*, pp. 59, note 5, 72, note 3.

387. A Foucher, "Notes Sur La geographie ancienne du Ganhara", in *Bulletin de L' E'cole francaise d'Extreme-Orient*, Hanoi, October 1901, tr. into English by H. Hargreaves, *Notes on the Ancient Geography of Gandhara* (Vārāṇasī, 1974), pp. 10-11; *CAGI*, pp. 42-43; see also Cunningham, *Co. Anc. Ind.*, p. 32; B.N. Puri, op. cit., p. 55; *IIA*, pp. 59, note 5, 181, note.

388. *JASB*, 1836, p. 479.

ruins".[389] The archaeological excavation carried out at Chārasadda in 1958-59 under the guidance of Sir Mortimer Wheeler also testifies to the existence of a group of small towns there. Bala-Hisar (high fort) was first occupied by the Persian in the latter half of the sixth century BC. The site is said to be a memorial to the Pax-Persica. To the east of it a line of rampart was unearthed, which represents the part of the town besieged by the troops of Alexander. The excavations at the different site of Gāndhāra have brought to light a radical change in the town-planning in the second century BC after the establishment of the rule of the Indo or Bactrian Greeks. They abandoned the old site (Bala-Hisar) and rebuilt a new city as Shaikhan (at Puṣkalāvatī) in conformity with the Graeco-Parthian plan.[390] However, the popularity of the ancient city of Puṣkalāvatī did not decline till the dawn of the seventh century. Hiuen-Tsang found this city, which he calls *Pu-se-ka-lo-fa-ti*, in a flourishing condition. It was about fourteen or fifteen *li* (1 *yojana* = 8 miles or 4 *krosa*s - 40 *li*) in circuit, well peopled and decorated with gates, temples, etc.[391] Whereas, on the other hand, in *Pu-lu-sha-pu-lo* (Purūṣapura) he found that the royal family was extinct, the towns were desolate and the inhabitants were very few.[392] Puṣkalāvatī had all the characteristic features of an urban centre in the latter half of the first millennium BC or in NBPW phase. It was an administrative, religious and commercial centre which led to its growth as a city. It remained an urban centre till the end of the Gupta rule. It began to decline from about the middle of the seventh century AD onwards.

Various small towns or the lower Kabul valley or those lying between Puṣkalāvatī and the Indus were occupied by Alexander with the help of two local chiefs named Kophaios (or Cophaeus) and Assagetes (Aśvajit).[393] The former was the king of the region about Puṣkala near the Kophen and the latter the king of the Assakenoi (successor of the king killed in Massaga).[394]

In very early times the frontiers of the kingdom of Gāndhāra extended even to the country east of the Indus, where was situated its famous eastern capital called by the

389. *JASB.*, 1836, p. 394.

390. M. Wheeler, *Charasada*, Summary facing p. 1; *EIP*, p. 172 and Pl. 54; see also John Marshall, *Taxila*, vol. I, p. 4.

391. *YCTI*, vol. I, p. 214.

392. *Ibid.*, p. 199.

393. Arrian, *Anab.*, IV, 28.

394. A.E. Anspach, *De Alexandri Magni Expeditione Indica* (London, 1903), p. 65, note 200, cf. *CHI*, p. 319, note 1.

Greeks Taxila (Skt. Takṣaśilā = Pāli Takkasilā, or Takhasilā, as found in a copper-plate inscription[395] = Tākṣaśila of Pāṇini, iv, 3, 93). This great capital was, no doubt, one of the most ancient cities of India. It was built of the material like most other cities of India. Accordng to the Purāṇic evidence (*Vy.*, 88. 188-91) it was named after Takṣa, the son of Bharat. The name of the city is generally taken to mean either "the Rock of the Takkas", the tribes, or "the Rock of Takṣaka", the great Nāga king. It also means the hewn stone or cut rock. Pomponius Mela in his *Compendium of Geography* (iii, 7), written about AD 42, had rightly pointed out that various legends were invented to account for the name. It is stated that "The Takkas, a Turanian race, the earliest inhabitants of Rawalpindi District gave their name to the town of Takshaśilā or Taxila".[396]

The classical writers are unanimous in their accounts of the position, size and wealth of Taxila. Aristoboulos (who accompanied Alexander on his eastern expedition and wrote a history of his wars) was the first to mention it as "the great city".[397] Megasthenes was the next to state that Taxila was a famous city of the Taxillae (*Indika*, Fragm LVI), which was visited by Alexander the Great. According to Strabo, "Taxila, a large city between the Indus and the Hydaspes, was governed by good laws. The surrounding country was densely populated and extremely fertile".[398] Arrian describes it as the most populous, wealthy and flourishing city. It was, according to him, the capital of Taxiles. He further adds that it was the greatest of all Indian cities, which lay between the Indus and the Hydaspes.[399] As a city it was indisputably unequalled in whole north-western India. Plutarch observes: "Taxiles ruled over a part of India (Taxila) which was as large as Egypt".[400] But Strabo says that according to some, it "was larger than Egypt".[401] Pliny calls it "a famous city" of Amanda (Gāndhāra), which, according to him, was situated in

---

395. Obtained by Roberts, deciphered by J. Downson in *JRAS*, vol. XX, p. 221; see also notes on the same inscripition in *JASB*, 1863, p. 139.

396. W.W. Hunter, "The Greeks in India", in *The indian Empire : Its Peoples, History and Products*, 3rd edn. (London, 1882), rept. in *Ancient India* (Delhli, 1983), p. 87, note 6; see also *JRAS*, vol. XX, p. 343.

397. Quoted by Strabo, *Geog.*, XV, i, 17, *AICL*, p. 22.

398. *Ibid.*, XV, i, 28, *AICL*, pp. 33-34; also Hamilton and Falconer's tr. *op. cit.*, vol. III, p. 90.

399. *Anab.*, V, 3 and 8; *IIA*, pp. 83 and 92; see also Henry Baveridge, *Com. Hist. Ind.*, vol. I, p. 31; F. Annie Steel, *IPPH*, p. 37; Holdich, *Gates of India*, pp. 99, 114, 179, 185; Smith, *EHI*, pp. 50-54.

400. *Lif. Alex.*, Ch. 59, *IIA*, p. 305.

401. *Geog.*, XV, i, 28, *AICL*, p. 34.

a level country where the hills unite with the plains.[402] According to Diodorus, the region, which was well watered by rivers and highly renowned for its prosperous and happy condition, contained along with many other kingdoms the realm subject to Taxiles.[403] Julius Valerius has also recorded that Taxiles held sway over the vast dominions situated between the Indus and the Hydaspes.[404] The inhabitants of the city were known as "Taxilans", as stated by Dionysios.[405] And the dynastic title of the ruling class was Taxiles. Ptolemy has fixed the position of the city called "Taxiala" at $125^0$ 32· 15′ between the Indus and the Bidespes (Hydaspes).[406] Pliny, citing Diognetos and Baeton, the perambulators or measurers of Alexander's marches, recorded that Taxila to the east of the Indus was only 60 Roman, or 55 English, miles distant from Peucolaitis or Hashtnagar to the west of the Indus, which would fix its site somewhere on the Haro river to the west of Hasan Abdal (in the Attock Dist.) or at just two days march from the Indus.[407] The actual distance between Puṣkalāvatī and Taxila, the two famous capital cities of the Gāndhāra kingdom, according to A. Cunningham, was 74 miles (English), 19 in excess of Pliny's estimate. But according to the recent measurements, the distance from Chārasadda (the site of the ruins of Puṣkalāvatī) to Shāh-ḍherī (the site of Taxila's ruins) is 80 miles.

The great city of Taxila has a chequered history. In order to get a very graphic picture of this city within a chronological framework, we have combined the classical and archaeological evidence together. It is worthy of remark that the site has been extensively excavated by several excavators between 1913 and 1950. These excavations have brought to light the existence of a number of ancient cities built at or near Taxila between the sixth century BC and the first century AD. Sir John Marshall has presented an illustrative account of archaeological excavations carried out at the site for over two decades at regular interval between 1913 and 1934. The vast ruins of Taxila bespeak its past glory as a city.

Cunningham was the first archaeologist to discover the ruins of the city Taxila, described by the classical writers concerned. He found the ruins of this ancient city in the vicinity of Shāh-ḍherī, just one mile to the north-east of a town called Kāla-kā-Sarāi

402. *Hist. Nat.*, VI, 23.

403. *Bibliothéké*, XVIII, 6, *AICL*, p. 201.

404. *Itin. Alex.*, Ch. 104, *ibid.*, p. 150 and note 4.

405. *Bassarika*, LI, 1080-1165, *AICL*, p. 189.

406. *AIT*, pp. 118-21.

407. *Hist. Nat.*, VI, 21; *AIMA*, 1st edn. Frag, LVI, p. 150, note; *AICL*, pp. 17-18, note 1.

(between Attock and Rāwalpiṇḍī), or at the distance of a three-days' journey to the east of the Indus. The extensive ruins of a fortified city abounding with *stūpas*, monasteries, temples, etc., are scattered over a wide space extending about 3 miles from north to south, and 2 miles from east to west. They lie about eight miles to the south-east of Hasan Abdal and about twenty-two miles north-west of Rāwalpiṇḍī in northern Punjab.[408] The discovery of these ruins and their identification as those of Taxila is one of the great services which Cunningham has rendered to the cause of Indian archaeology. Excavations have shown that the Bhir mound on the west side towards the rock-seated village of Shāh-ḍherī was the most ancient of all the urban sites at Taxila. In fact, it stands for a small village of Bir or Bhir which stands on the great mound. Through the midst of the ruins flows a stream called the Tabrā or Tamrā Nālā, which is identical with a river called variously in different MSS of the *Pseudo-Kallisthenes* the Tiberoboam, Tibernābon, etc. Here we have some idea of town-planning in ancient India. According to Cunningham, "The remains of the walls can be traced only in a few places both on the east and west sides; but the whole surface is covered with broken stones and fragments of bricks and pottery".[409] Haitāl — a strong fortified position — is immediately to the north-east of the Bhir Mound. Sir John Marshall, one of the excavators of the site, says that till 326 BC "the town had no architecture worthy of the name. With rare exceptions its buildings were a rambling conglomeration of ill-aligned and ill-built walls of plastered rubble resembling rather the slum of a poverty-stricken sub-urb than the central lay-out of a capital city. The only architectural feature . . . is the occasional use of untidy stone pedestals designed to carry wooden roof-posts".[410] The general culture of the city was of the same inferior order. Only at the end of the fourth century or shortly after the arrival of Alexander there was spectacular improvement. He further observes that before the arrival of the Indo-Greeks in the second century BC the layout of the first city was irregular and haphazard. There were streets and lanes ". . . for the convenience of the

---

408. *CASR*, vol. II (1871), pp. 112, 125; vol. V (1875), p. 66; *CAGI*, pp. 88-89, 94 f; A. Foucher, *op. cit.*, p. 38 note 4; see also Delmerick's "Notes on the Archaeological Remains at Shah-Ki-Dheri and the site of Taxila", *JASB*, 1870, p. 89; *ASIAR* (by John Marshall), 1912-13, Pt. I, pp. 1-5, 8-16; 1915-16, pt. I, pp. 10-12; Aurel Stein, *ARNWI*, p. 11; Robert Shafer, *EAI*, p. 129; N.L. Dey, *GDAMI*, pp. 200-2; V.A. Smith, *The Oxford History of India*, rev. by H.G. Rawlinson, pp. 48-49; *AIMA*, pp. 150-51, note; *IIA*, p. 342, note I.

409. *CAGI*, pp. 94-95.

410. *Taxila*, vol. I, p. 20; see also M. Wheeler, *EIP*, pp. 173-74, pls. 50, 51.

traffic and other purposes, small open squares were provided. Further, to protect the corners of houses from damage by passing carts and chariots wheel-guards were set up by erecting rough stone pillars at the corners of building.[411] The houses were also irregular in plan, the principle underlying their design was of an open court with rooms on one or more sides. There were two such courts in well-to-do houses and they had probably more than one storey. The rooms were about fifteen to twenty in number. Their walls were mud-plastered and white-washed with lime and provided with wooden balconies and flat roofs".[412] There was also drainage system for the city. The earliest urban settlement at Bhir mound was little earlier than the invasion of the Persian king, Darius I (*c.* 522-486 BC). After the end of the Achaemenian rule over Taxila it probably attained independence. Between the fifth and second century BC this city was thrice destroyed and thrice rebuilt at higher levels. This was the site where the palace of the Taxiles was located. Beneath the Bhir mound lies the ruins of the old city which Alexander visited in 326 BC.[413]

At the time of the Macedonian invasion, Taxila (the site of Bhir Mound) was a very rich and flourishing city, and it continued to be so for many centuries thereafter. The material prosperity of its people was reflected in the presents received by Alexander in 326 BC from the king Ambhi called Omphis by Curtius[414] and Mophis by Diodorus.[415] According to the former, "Taxiles presented Alexander and all his friends with golden crowns, together with eighty talents of coined silver, while Alexander not only returned to Taxiles the presents he had given, but added a thousand talents with many banqueting vessels of gold and silver, a vast quantity of Persian drapery. . . ."[416] According to Arrian, the present sent by Taxiles to him consisted of 200 talents of silver.[417] We learn from Plutarch that it was Alexander who gave 1000 talents in coined money to Omphis. The archaeological discovery of several bent-bar silver coins of about 300 BC from Bhir

---

411. *Taxila*, vol. I, p. 89.
412. *Taxila*, pp. 92 f.
413. *Ibid.*, pp. 3, 12 f, 20.
414. *Hist. Alex.*, VIII, 12, 14, *IIA*, pp. 200-3.
415. *Bib. Hist.*, XVII. 86, *ibid.*, pp. 272-73; see also Sylvain Levi, *JA*, vol. XV, Series, 8, 1890, p. 234.
416. *Hist. Alex.*, VIII. 12, *AICL*, p. 34, note 1.
417. *Anab.*, V. 3, *IIA*, p. 83.

Mound[418] lends credence to the classical description of the subject. There is a striking similarity between the two. While establishing the link between the two, Allan has emphatically asserted that the presents consisted of silver bar coins, found in the Bhir Mound at Taxila.[419] Kallisthenes, who accompanied Alexander, has also remarked that Taxila was very populous and possessed of incredible wealth.[420] The king called Taxiles surrendered himself and his kingdom with its capital at Taxila unreservedly to the great conqueror in 326 BC. In the third century BC, it formed the part of the Maurya empire. The great Aśoka made it his place of residence while he held the vice-royalty of the Punjab during the lifetime of his father, Bindusāra (*c.* 298-273 BC). After the death of Aśoka, the great king Subhagasena (*c.* 227-202 BC) called Sophagasenus by Polybios[421] established his sway over Taxila. He has been wrongly identified with Jaloka (one of the Aśoka's sons)[422] or Samprati (Aśoka's grandson in the line of Kuṇāla).[423] He was most probably the descendant of Vīrasena of Gāndhāra who was the great grandson of Aśoka.[424] The importance of this city as an emporium of trade in the age of the Mauryas has been highlighted in the *Periplus*.[425] Its reputation as a centre of trade and as a seat of learning had already been established between the sixth and the fourth century BC. It was also the seat of the government. These were the three primary factors which led to its growth as an urban centre in north-west India.

In the early part of the second century BC, Taxila became a province of the Graeco-Bactrian monarchy. The Bactrian Greeks laid the foundation of a new city at a site called Sirkap, which successively remained in occupation of the Greeks, the Scythians (Sacae or Śakas), the Parthians or Pahalavas and the Kuṣāṇas altogether for nearly three centuries during their rule. The new city of Sirkap was well fortified. It was

---

418. Wheeler, *EIP*, p. 174, pl. 53; Allan, *CCBM*, pp. xvi, 1, 2, pl. 1; Smith, *CCIM*. p. 136; *MASI*, no. 59 (Delhli, 1939), pp. 1, 3,100, pl. IV; G.M. Young, "A New Hoard from Taxila (Bhir Mound)", *AI*, no. 1 (1946), pp. 27-36; see also *IPPH*, p. 37; *JNSI*, vol. IV, pt. I, p. 61.

419. *Op. cit.*, p. xvii.

420. *IIA*, pp. 342-43, note I.

421. *History*, XI, 34 (2), *AICL*, p. 209.

422. Lessen, *Ind. Alt.*, vol. II, p. 273.

423. *JIH*, vol. LVI, pt. I, (1978), p. 48.

424. W.W. Tarn, *GBI*, p. 130 and note 2; *JASB*, 1920, pp. 305, 310.

425. *Periplus*, tr. Schoff, p. 270.

defended on all sides — by the lofty citadel of Hatiāl on the south, by the Tanra Nālā on the west, and by the Gau-Nālā on the east and north sides. The streets and buildings were laid out by the Hellenistic town-planner on the typical Greek Chess-board pattern. Kacha-koṭ or the mud fort lies to the north of Sirkap.[426] The coins of the Greek rulers of Taxila[427] bear witness to thier rule during the period concerned. In 126 BC, this city was wrested from the Greeks by the Indo-Scythian Sus or Abars with whom it remained for about three quarters of a century. They in thier turn were dispossessed of it by another branch of the Śakas, Maues (Moa or Moga), who sometime between 20 BC and AD 22 established his sway over both Puṣkalāvatī and Takṣaśilā to the west and the east of the Indus respectively. His name figures in the Taxila copper-plate grant[428] as well as in the coins.[429] The Greek city originally built sometime between 183 and 175 BC lay buried under the mound of Sirkap which has been thoroughly excavated but very little has been discovered from here. The city of Sirkap was remodelled by the Śaka-Pārthians.

By the middle of the first century AD the rebuilt city of Sirkap reached the pinnacle of glory. It was a well-planned city. This is the city which Apollonius of Tyana and his Assyrian companion, Damis, visited during the reign of the Pārthian Gondopharnes or Bardanes (AD 42-45). After having crossed the river Indus they reached Taxila and stayed there for three days. They saw a city about the size of Nineveh (the great Assyrian capital city of by-gone ages), walled like a Greek town (Athens), and the residence of a sovereign (who ruled over what had foremerly been the kingdom of Poros). Outside the walls they found a beautiful temple of shell marble with a shrine and many columns. Round the shrine were hung pictures on copper tablets representing the feats of Alexander and Poros. The various figures were protrayed in a mosaic of Orichalcum, silver, gold and oxydised copper, but the weapons in iron. The metals were so ingeniously worked into one another that the pictures which they formed were comparable to the productions of the most famous Greek artists. Apollonius waited in this temple till he was invited by the king, whose name was Phrotes (a Pārthian ruler), to enter the gates of the city and present himself at the palace. There he was received by the king (who spoke Greek).

426. Marshall, *op. cit.*, vol. I, pp. 4, 12 f, 21 f, 113; *CAGI*, pp. 97-98.

427. E.J. Rapson, *Indian Coins*, pp. 5-6, 14.

428. Sten Konow, *CII*, vol. II, pt. I, no. XIII, pp. 23-29; see aslo *JIH*, vol. XIV (1935), pp. 328-38.

429. Rapson, *op. cit.*, pp. 7-8, 14; Cunningham, *Co. Anc. Ind.* p. 60, pl. II, III; *CASR*. XIV, p. 16, pl. x.

They were taken to the palace, which was considerably large and well built. "It was no less magnificent and architecture and the male chamber and the porticos and the whole of the vestitute was very chaste in style." "The palace was, however, no distinguished by any superior splendour from the residence of the wealthier citizens, and within its precincts there were no trace of courtly pomp, no sentinels, no guards, and but very few attendants." They found the city divided by narrow streets and well arranged. It reminded Apollonius of Athenes. The houses were so connected that from outside they appeared to be a single storied but there were underground rooms euqal in length to the chambers above. The large buildings and other dwelling houses pleased the travellers more than all the pomp of Babylon. They also saw the temple of the sun, which stood outside the walls of the city, and in it statues of Alexander and Poros, the one of gold and other of bronze. Its walls were of red marble, but glittering with gold, and the image of the god was of pearls. They also saw a temple in front of the wall about 100 ft in length and built of steel like stone. The above description of the city is based on the eye-witness accounts of the travellers, as recorded by Philostratos in his biographical work.[430] The said work is primarily based on the narrative of the journey preserved in the *Journal* of Damis, which is a trustworthy record of their visit to this city. The classical account of this city can be partly corroborated and supplemented by an archaeological evidence. John Marshall in the course of his excavation at the site also discovered some remains of almost identical nature. According to him also, the city was well-planned. The buildings were like that of the modern city of the Near and Middle East. There were streets with a row of shops. The private dwelling-houses of the citizens were small and single-storey structures. The large houses belonged to the rich. The royal palace was planned on a bigger scale and with more spacious courts and rooms. It was decorated with gates. Near the palace the houses were rather carefully planned and furnished with layer courts. There were separate houses for the governing classes living with attendants and slaves. There were houses for the soldiers who guarded the ramparts. He found it a walled city. It was adorned with shrines, temples and various other religious structures.[431] Some other monuments and antiquities of great historical and archaeological importance were also discovered by him. We find that a Kuṣāṇa king, identified with Wima Kadphises, occupied this city in AD 77 or 78.

430. *The Life of Apollonius of Tyana*, Eng. tr. by F.C. Conybeare, Bk. II, Chs. 20, 22 and 25; *AICL*, pp. 191-93; B.N. Puri, *op. cit.*, pp. 146-49; *CAI*, pp. 388-89; see also *CAGI*, p. 91; *IIA*, p. 344, note I; G.P. Singh, "Early History of North-West India as Described by the Greek and Assyrian Travellers", JIH (Platinum Jubilee Volume), pp. 45-48.

431. *Taxila*, vol. I, pp. 140-41; see also S. Piggott, *Some cities* of *Ancient India* (Oxford, 1945).

In the first century AD, probably after AD 78, the celebrated Buddhist king Kaniṣka built another city at Taxila, which is at present represented by the remains of Sir-Suk or Sir-Sukh. It remained under the sway of the Kuṣāṇas till the early third century AD. It was also a fortified city. But very little has been explored at this site. Cunningham, while providing the detailed description of Taxila, has concluded that each city built there including that of Sirkap and Sir-Suk was "nearly as large as Shah Jahan's imperial city of Delhi".[432] Some ruins of the city of Taxila especially massive walls of stone have also been found in the vicinity of Mānikyāla[433] at a distance of eight days journey from Hashtnagar or few miles away from Shāh-ḍherī. Bhir Mound, Sirkap and Sir-Sukh, the three important sites of urban settlements, formed parts of a large Taxila city. The city remained in existence from NBPW phase till its fall in early Gupta period.

The Taxila city was visited by the Chinese pilgrims Fa-hian in AD 400[434] and Hiuen-Tsang in 630 and afterwards in 643. According to latter, the district of *Ta-cha-shi-lo* (Takṣaśilā or Taxila) was 2000 *li* (or 333 miles) in circuit and its capital above ten *li* in circuit. He did not find the city in a flourishing condition. The inhabitants were very few. The royal family had become extinguished.[435] It appears that between the sixth century BC and the third century AD at least four to six cities were built here. Like Bāhlika, Kāpiśī, Kabul and Bamian or Bāmanpur this city also underwent metamorphosis. The history of north-west India is replete with several examples of destruction and construction of the cities at or near these sites. After the seventh century AD the city, Taxila, disappears altogether from history, and we know neither how nor when its ruin was accomplished. However, we have every reason to believe that this city might have been destroyed by the Hūṇas in the fifth or sixth century AD, and was never re-built. The extensive ruins of this great city comprising all its different parts built at different periods of history now cover an area of more than six square miles.

H.D. Sankalia, while dealing with evolution of urban culture and antiquity of some towns and cities in north-west India, has expressed the view that both the cities, Takṣaśilā and Puruṣapura, had come into existence about 2300 years before from now.[436] But in absence of any corroborative evidence we can neither confirm nor deny it. Cunningham's

432. *CAGI*, p. 100.

433. M.A. Court, "Memoir of a Map of the Provinces of Peucelaotis and Taxila", *JASB*, vol. V (1836), p. 468.

434. H.A. Giles, *The Travels of Fa-hsien* or *RBK*, p. 12.

435. *YCTI*, vol. I, pp. 240-41.

436. *Akhaṇḍa Bhārata Mein Saṁskṛti Kā Uṣaḥ Kāla*, p. 9.

statement that the mounds of ruins found in all directions in Afghanistan constitute the mute evidence of the existence of a number of flourishing towns there in ancient past[437] seems to be reliable. The impact of Persian and Hellenic urban tradition on the planning, patterns and designs of the towns and cities of the indigenous people of particularly Gāndhāra region during their contacts with them cannot be denied.

We would also like to examine the relevance of an identical statement of the two classical authors, Appllodoros (author of the *History of Parthia*)[438] and Justin.[439] According to them, Eukratides (one of the most powerful Greek monarchs of Bactria) conquered India and became "lord of a thousand cities, which acknowledged his authority." It is true that he occupied Bactria, the Kabul valley, Ariana (Arachosia and Aria), Kapiśa, Nicaea, Gāndhāra with its eastern capital at Taxila, and some other parts of western Punjab sometime between *c.* 181 or 175 BC and 160 BC. But we are not in a position to ascertain the exact number of cities, which were in his possession. We very often come across such exaggerated statement in the classical sources.

The classical notices of Sangala, one of the principal cities in northern Punjab, are confined to the two historical accounts of Arrian and Curtius, and a passing mention by Diodorus. Curtius simply calls it "a great city defended not only by a wall but also by a swamp".[440] Arrian, while describing the city, observes that it was strong both by art and nature, being protected by brick walls and covered by the lake. It was adorned with the gates, rampart etc. There was a low hill close to the city walls,[411] which was possibly the abandoned mound of earlier cities. Diodorus has incidentally referred to the city without providing a description thereof.[442] This fortified city, according to them, was the capital of the Kathaians or Kathaeans (Skt. Kaṭhas), who belonged to the warrior class or kṣatriya tribe. They were one of the independent tribes of Punjab. They inhabited the regions lying to the east of the Hydraotes. Some writers, however, as Strabo informs us, have placed the "Kathaia" in the tract between the two rivers, the Hydaspes and the Akesines,[443] but this view is manifestly wrong. According to the narrative of Arrian,

---

437. *CASR*, vol. 5, 1875 (report for the year 1872-73), pp. 4-5.
438. Quoted by Strabo, *Geog.*, XV, i, 3, *AICL*, pp. 8-9.
439. *Hist. Phil.*, XII. 6.
440. *Hist. Alex.*, IX, I; *IIA*, p. 217.
441. *Anab.*, V, 22, 4; *ibid.*, p. 115.
442. *Bib. Hist.*, XVII, 91.3; *ibid.*, pp. 279-80.
443. *Geog.*, XV, I, 30; *AICL*, pp. 36, 37, note 1; see also Hamilton and Falconer, *op. cit.*, vol. III, p. 92.

their capital, Sangala, was situated between the Hydraotes and the Hyphasis, which is absolutely correct. It is on this basis that some authorities have placed this city in the Gurdāspur district (about 50 miles N.E. from Amritsar) not far from Fathgarh[444] and some at Jaṇḍiālā to the east of Amritsar.[445] It is generally placed either near Lahore or between Lahore and Multān or in the Amritsar district.[446] It has not yet been ascertained where this city actually stood. But the Kathaians must have been situated to the east of the river Rāvī and may probably have been nearly if not altogether co-extensive with what we now call the districts of Lahore and Amritsar. C. Masson has proposed "Haripa" (Harappā), which was quite close to the Rāvī, as the site of Sangala.[441] The topographical features of the place, the hill or rising ground and a swamp with the remains of a brick fort suit very well with the description of Arrian. It is said to have been the site of a very extensive and ancient town. It is very difficult to determine the exact location of the city which was attacked and destroyed by Alexander's troops. At the time of Alexander's invasion, it was, no doubt, a large city with more than 12,000 population. The administration of the city was controlled by them and not by any king or chief. According to Arrian, 17,000 Kathaeans defended their city, while it was stormed by the Macedonians. They all lost their lives and the city was razed to the ground.[448]

Pāṇini's Sāṅkala (*Gaṇa-Pāṭha*, IV, 2, 75),[449] according to the laws of transcription, has been identified with Sangala of the Greeks.[450]

The Sagala of Ptolemy's *Geography* (VII, 1, 46)[451] corresponds exactly with the Sanskrit Śākala (as mentioned in the *Mahābhārata* and the Purāṇas) and the Pāli Sāgala, a city of great note in ancient times. It was situated between the rivers Hydraotes and the Akesines. It occupied the district of Siālkoṭ, Saint Martin takes it as royal city in the

444. *IGI*, vol. XII, p. 393; C.A. Smith, *JRAS*, 1903, p. 687; *EHI*, p. 81.

445. *CHI*, vol. I, p. 332, note 7.

446. For details see Rennell, *MMH*, sec. iii, pp. 122-23; HA, vol. IV, Ch. IV, pp. 400-2; H. Baveridge, *Com. Hist. Ind.*, vol. I, pp. 35-36; A. Steel, *IPPH*, p. 40; Bunbury, *HAG*, vol. I, pp. 444-45 and 505, note Hh; Heeren, *MAHA*, p. 218 f; R.D. Banerji, *PAHI*, p. 79; J.T. Wheeler, *India from the Earliest Ages*, vol. III, p. 165; "Greek and Roman India" in *op. cit.*, p. 105, W.W. Hunter, "The Greeks in India" in *op. cit.*, p. 88; Burnes, *op. cit.*, vol. III, p. 182.

447. "Extracts from Notes of a journey from Lahore to Kerachee", *JASB*, vol. VI, p. 57.

448. *Anab.*, V, 23; V, 24, 5; *IIA*, pp. 117-21; see also *CAI*, pp. 47-51.

449. *IP*, p. 73.

450. Sylvain Levi, *JA*, vol. XV, Series 8 (1890), pp. 237-39; *AIT*, p. 365, note.

451. *AIT*, pp. 122-24, 157, 169 and also 365-66, note; see also M.R. Singh, GDEP, pp. 155-56.

north of India.[452] Here it must be made specifically clear that it was situated to the west of the Hydraotes,[453] and Sangala on the east bank of that river.[454] Some Savants regardless of the laws of transcription have attempted to establish the identity of both,[455] but the fact remains that they were two different cities in two different directions of two different periods.

Cunningham has also mistakenly taken Sangala of the classical writers and Śākala of the *Brāhmaṇas*, Sāgala of the Buddhists or Sagala of Ptolemy as identical.[456] But his theory is no longer tenable, as there are some reasons, mainly philological, which go against his hypothesis. He found a site for the the city concerned at Sangalawala-Tiba, a small rocky hill or Sangala Hill (in the Jhang district) with ruins upon it and a large swamp at its base, situated between the Rāvī and the Cenāb at a distance of about sixty miles to the west of the former river or Lahore. On the north-eastern side of the hill he found the remains of two large buildings. He found the plain on the north and west sides of the hill strewn with broken pottery and fragments of brick gathering the impression that the town once must have extended in both of those directions. The remains covered an area of about 1½ miles.[457] However, this could not have been the site of the Grecian Sangala, because all the historians place that city between the Rāvī and the "Beas". It was probably the site of Śākala or Sāgala[458] in Central Punjab. As regards the settlement of this important site, question has lately been considerably advanced by the researches undertaken by the Punjab Government at Sanglawaia-Tiba with the positive result of showing that no such large fortified city as Sangala could have ever existed there.

Ptolemy's Sagala, Pāli Sāgala or Śākala of Sanskrit writers roughly corresponds to the modern Siālkoṭ and the surrounding regions between the Rāvī and the Cenāb. It was situated to the west of the Hydraotes or Rāvī at a distance of about sixty miles from Lahore. It was the capital of the Madras.[459] It is believed that the city passed under the

452. *Étude*, p. 326.

453. See Lassen, *Pent. Ind*., p. 65, V, 16; *AIT*, p. 365, note.

454. *Ibid*., p. 20; *AIT*, p. 365, note.

455. Wilson, *Ar. Ant*., pp. 196-97; see also *As. Res*., vol. XV, p. 108; Bunbury, *HAG*, vol. 1, pp. 444-45.

456. *CAGI*, p. 151.

457. *Ibid*., pp. 153-55, 160; are also Wilford, *As. Res*., vols. V, p. 282; VI, p. 520; IX, p. 53.

458. *IIA*, note M, pp. 347-48; *AICL*, p. 37, note 1; see also C.J. Rodgers, *Report on Sangala Tibba*, News Press, Lahore, 1906, *PASB*, 1896.

459. *AICL*, p. 200, note 2; B.C. Law, *HAGI*, pp. 105, 122; *AIT*, pp. 365-66, note; Fleet, *PIOC*, 14th Session (Algiers, 1905), I, pp. 164 ff; see also *CASR*, XIV, pp. 44-46.

sway of Alexander in 326 BC, who placed it under the Satrap of the adjacent territory between the Jhelum and the Cenāb. One of the Greek kings, Euthydemos (*c.* 220-190 BC), the founder of the greatness of the Baktrian kingdom, held eastern Punjab with its capital at Śākala (Siālkoṭ), and the city was thereafter named after him as Euthydemia. This is the city called by Nonnos "Euthydimeia".[460] We do not have any positive evidence to prove the historical authenticity of the conventional statement that his son Demetrios (*c.* 190-165 BC) rebuilt the city, having been destroyed by the Macedonians, and called it Euthydemia in honour of his father Euthydemos.[461] It has also been rejected by Tarn on both historical and textual grounds.[462] But we have positive proof to show that it became the capital of the most famous Indo-Greek ruler, Menander or Milinda (165-145 BC).[463] This city, situated in a delightful country, well watered and hilly, abounding in parks and gardens, groves and lakes, tanks, well-laid out streets, cross-roads and market-complex, wore a beautiful look. It was adorned with splendid and magnificent buildings, various strong towers and ramparts, defensive walls, superb gates, entrance archways and with the royal citadel in its midst, white-walled and deeply moated. It was crowded with peoples of all castes, brāhmaṇas, kṣatriyas or nobles, vaiśyas or traders and śūdras or servants, and the leading men of each of the different sects. It was a great centre of trade end commerce. The shops were filled with innumerable sorts of costly merchandise. There were some shops for the sale of Benares muslin, other clothes of various kinds, jewels and other costly articles. The guilds of traders displayed their goods in the bazaars. The city was full of money, and of gold and silverware, of copper and stoneware, indicating its wealth and prosperity.[464] Later, in the early part of the sixth century AD, it became the capital of the Hūṇa conqueror, Mihirakula, who not only destroyed it but also subdued all the neighbouring provinces. In AD 630, Hiuen-Tsang found the walls of the city called *She-kie-lo* (Śākala) completely ruined, but their foundations still remained, showing a circuit of about 20 *li* or 3½ miles. In the midst of the ruins he saw a small portion of an inhabited old city, which was only 6 or 7 *li* or just one mile in circuit. He also found the other neighbouring rowns in dilapidated condition.[465] After having investigated all the

460. *Dionysiaka*, Bk. XXVI, *AICL*, p. 200 and note 2.
461. Saint Martin, *Étude*; pp. 103-8; *Ind. Ant.*, 1884, p. 350; *AICL*, p. 200, note 2.
462. *GBI*, pp. 247-48, 486-87.
463. B.C. Law, *HPL*, vol. II, p. 356; Rāula Sānkṛtyāyana, *Pāli Sāhitya Kā Itihāsa*, p. 183.
464. *Milinda-pañha*, ed. V. Trenckner, pp. 1-3; Rāhula Sānkṛtyāyana, *op. cit.*, pp. 183-84.
465. *YCTL*, vol. I, 288-90.

available sources we find that the Greek writers' Sangala identical with Sāṅkala of Pāṇini was different from Śākala or Sāgala. The former was situated between the Rāvi and the "Beas" and the latter between Rāvī and the Cenāb. The former was situated to the east and the latter of the west of the Rāvī.

The city of Pimprama, situated on the eastern side of the Hydraotes, according to Arrian,[466] Diodorus[467] and Justin,[468] belonged to Adraistai called by Ptolemy Adraistoi or Adeisathra[469] (Āraṭṭas, Adhṛṣṭas, or Aristas of Pāṇini, VI, 2, 100; *Gaṇa-Pāṭha*, IV, 2, 80) who were independent tribes not being subject to authority of any king. The city was located in sub-urban area, which was not well-equipped with all necessary paraphernalia of urbanism. It was eight leagues or *yojana* distant from Lahore towards the south-east. After it was captured by Alexander, the inhabitants deserted it which gradually led to its decadence. Some more important towns or cities of northern Punjab are described below.

Strabo affirms that the dominions of the great Porus confined between the Hydaspes and Akesines — an extensive and fertile tract (not more than forty miles in width) — contained about 300 cities.[470] Their exact number cannot be determined with any amount of certainty. However, it cannot be denied that at the time of Alexander's invasion numerous towns existed within the limits of the kingdom of Porus the details of which are, of course, wanting in the classics with few exceptions. In other sources as well the details of only a few towns of the contemporary peroid are available.

One of the principal towns called the town of Jhelum is said to have been "situated on the west bank of that river, 30 miles to the north-east of modern Jalālpur, and exactly 100 miles to the north-west of Lahor. The remains of the old towns consist of a large ruined mound to the west of the present city, about 1300 feet square and 30 feet high, which is surrounded by fields covered with broken bricks and pottery".[471] The city remained in existence even later than the first century BC. The ancient Girjak or Girivraja,

---

466. *Anab.*, V, 2. *IIA*, pp. 115, 116 and note.
467. *Bib. Hist.*, XVII, 91, *ibid.*, pp. 279-80.
468. *Hist. Phil.*, XII, 8, *ibid.*, p. 323; see also Orosius, *History*, III, 19 (for Adraestae); B.C. Law, *HGAI*, p. 63 (for identification of Adraistai).
469. *AIT*, p. 377, note.
470. *Geog.*, XV, I, 29, *AICL*, p. 35; Hamilton and Falconer, *op. cit.*, vol. III, p. 91.
471. *CAGI*, pp. 135-36.

the capital of Kekaya kingdom, which very much formed the part of the dominion of Porus, can also be taken as one of the cities of that time. This name remained in use until the time of Akbar when it was changed to Jalālpur. This town is situated on the west bank of the Jhelum at the point where the Kandar ravine joins the old bed of the river. Cunningham has observed that "the town might formerly have been about three or four times its present size".[472] He has identified Girjak with the remains of walls on the top of the Mangal-De hill, which rises 1100 feet above Jalālpur. He says that "there is no doubt that the city did once extend to the westward for some considerable distance, as the ground on that side is thickly strewn with broken pottery for about half a mile. Its antiquity is undoubted, as the coins which it yields reach back to the times of Alexander's successors. But . . . it is much older; as its favourable position at the south-east end of the lower road would certainly have led to its occupation at a very early period".[473]

The ruined city near Dārāpur (ancient Udamnagar or Udinagar) is said to have been situated on the west bank of the river, 20 miles below Jhelum, and 10 miles above Jalālpur.[474] Court, while including these ruins under that of Gagirakhi (Gir-Jhāk or Girjak), described that they extended along the banks "of the Hydaspes from near Jalalpur to Darapur".[475] According to this account, the ruins covered and area of not less than 6 or 7 miles in length. Cunningham identified Girjhāk with an old ruined fort on the top of the hill to the north of Jalālpur, about 8 miles from Dārāpur.[476] Burnes also describes the old city as extending "for three or four miles".[477] It is said that "the ruins consist of two large mounds just half a mile apart, with two smaller mounds about midway between them". On the south mound Dilāwar (Udinagar) is situated and on the north mound old Dārāpur stands. Between these mounds the fields are covered with broken bricks and pottery, and the whole place is said to be the ruins of a single city.[478] Many old coins including that Indo-Scythians have been collected from the site, which must have been reoccupied in the post-Alexandrian period as early as the second century before the

472. *CAGI*, p. 137.
473. *Ibid.*, p. 138.
474. Burnes, *op. cit.*, vol. II, p. 51; Court, *JASB*, 1836, pp. 472-73.
475. *Op. cit.*
476. *CAGI*, p. 136.
477. *Op. cit.*
478. *CAGI*, p. 137.

Christian era. The headquarters of Porus must have been about Muhābatpur, 4 miles to the south-west of present town of Mong and 3 miles to the south-west of modern Jalālpur.

We learn from Strabo,[479] Arrian,[480] Megasthenes and Pliny,[481] Diodorus,[482] Justin[483] and Plutarch[484] that Alexander after having crowned himself with victory in the battle with Porus built two memorable cities — one called Boukephala, Boukephalia or Boukephalas and the other Nikaea or Nikaia a "city of victory". The former was built on the western bank of the Hydaspes in memory of his horse and the latter on its eastern bank, the site of the battle, in commemoration of his victory. According to some reliable evidences, either Jalālpur or Dilāwar at the distance of 10 miles from each other was the site of the first city. Jalālpur is said to be 30 miles higher up the river Jhelum. The second city is now represented by Mong (founded by Rājā Moga), 6 miles to the east of Jalāpur or at the same distance to the south of Dilāwar. If the two cities were built on the same plan, which is not improbable, then Dilāwar would have the preferable claim to represent the first city, as its ruined mound is of the same size and height as that of Mong. It may be added here that the battlefield was near Pakral, about 3 miles to the north of Sukchenpur.[485] The absence of details of the monolithic structure of the said two cities in the classics raises doubts in our mind about their construction by Alexander himself. The original sites of the cities of indigenous origin might have received new names in a Hellenised form which was not very unusual at the time of Alexander's invasion. Some rudimentary walls were, of course, erected on the Hydaspes by his army to mark the new cities. The possibility that Bugiād or Bugiāl, the name of the district in which Dilāwar is situated, might have been transformed with new Greek name, Boukephala, cannot be precluded. This Greek city can also be identified without much

479. *Geog.*, XV, I, 29, *AICL*, pp. 35-36 and note 4.

480. *Anab.*, V, 19; *IIA*, p. 110; Chinnock, op. cit., p. 296, note 4.

481. *Hist. Nat.*, VI, 21, 8-23, cf. *AIMA*, 1st edn., Frag. LVI, pp. 149-50.

482. *Bib. Hist.*, XVII, 89; *IIA*, pp. 276-77.

483. *Hist. Phil.*, XII, 8; *IIA*, p. 323.

484. *Lif. Alex.*, Ch. LXI, *IIA*, p. 309; also *Oration*, I, 5, *AICL*, p. 207.

485. For details see *CAGI*, pp. 149-50; *CASR*, vols. II, pp. 174-75; XIV, pp. 41-42; *AICL*, pp. 35-36, note 4; *IIA*, p. 110, note 3; *AIMA*, p. 150, note; Aurel Stein, *ARNWI*, p. 32; "The Site of Alexander's passage of the Hydaspes and the battle with Paris", *Geog. Jour.* (JRGS), no. 8 (1932), pp. 31-46; Baveridge, *Comp. Hist. Ind.*, vol. I. pp. 34-35; A.K. Majumdar, *EHIDS* (1st pub. Dacca, 1917, rept. Delhi, 1981), vol. II, p. 508; J.T. Wheeler, *India from the Earliest Ages*, vol. III, p. 163; W.W. Hunter, "The Greeks in India", in *op. cit.*, pp. 88, 90; Elphinstone, *Kabul*, vol. I, p. 109; Burnes, *op. cit.*, vol. II, p. 49; Court, *JASB*, 1836, pp. 472-73; Abbott, *JASB*, Pt. 2 (1848), p. 619; *AIT*, pp. 124, 366, note.

hesitation with the modern town of Jhelum. The new cities however rose into prominence and seem to have flourished for centuries.

The author of the *Periplus* refers to the first city as Bucephalus Alexandria (sec. 47). Schoff, the translator and annotator of the text, has correctly stated that "Its position is marked by an extensive mound west of the present settlements. The mound is known as Pindi, "the town", and yields large ancient bricks and numerous Graeco-Bactrian coins. Its position at a ferry on the high-road from the west to the Indian interior gave it great commercial importance".[486] Here have been found some old coins, but not earlier than those of the Indo-Scythian period, and three iron tripods of Greek firms. Ptolemy in his *Geography* (VII, I, 46) has also located it at the Jhelum (Bidespes) and highlighted its importance.

Nonnos has also mentioned Nicaea[487] as a city founded by Alexander. According to Pliny (VI, 21), it was the "chief of three cities which belonged to the Asini" (or Asene, one of the Indian tribes).

The total urban population of the dominions of Poros on the basis of available indications could be estimated not less than fifty thouasnd. From the accounts of Arrian (*Anab.*, V, 18) and Diodorus (*Bib. Hist.*, XVII, 89) it appears that more than twenty thousand people lost their lives in the battle of Porus with Alexander.

An older native town on the bank of Akesines was rebuilt and fortified on Hellenic principles (Arrian, *Anab.*, V, 29, 3) where Wazīrābād now stands from where one road goes to Jalālpur and other to Jhelum. It is known as sixth Alexandria.[488]

According to Arrian, a large tract lying to the west of the Akesines and coterminous with the dominion of Porus included as many as thirty-seven towns, "the smallest of which contained not fewer than 5,000 inhabitants while many contained upwards of 10,000".[489] These belonged to the free tribe called Glaukanikoi by Arrian and Aristoboulos and Glausai by Ptolemy. They have been identified with Glaucukāyanakas of the *Kāśikā*

---

486. *Periplus*; p. 184; see also *CNES*, p. 121 with note by C. Muller.

487. *Dionysiaka*, Bk. XXVI, *AICL*, p. 198 and note 5.

488. *IIA*, p. 129, note 2; Lassen, *Ind. Alt.*, vol. II, p. 165 note.

489. *Anab.*, V, 20; *IIA*, p. 112; Chinnock, *op. cit.*, p. 276; see also *HA*, vol. IV, p. 400; *Comp. Hist. Ind.*, vol. 1, p. 35.

on Pāṇini (IV, 3, 99).[490] It is said that their territories were situated in the fertile and densely populated regions lying in the south of Kāśmir (the Bhimber and Rajauri districts) between the upper courses of Jhelum and the Cenāb and the Rāvī.[491] From the statement of Arrian it is quite evident that the towns were both small and large. He says (*Anab.*, V, 20, 21) that Alexander took them and handed over to Porus thereby adding much to what he had before possessed.

Strabo deriving his authority from previous writers (names not mentioned) has categorically stated that "the Macedonians conquered nine nations situated between the Hydaspes and Hypanis (generally called in the classics the Hyphasis), and possessed 5,000 cities not one of which was less than Kos Meropis (or simply Kos) and that Alexander after having reduced all this country delievered it over to Poros".[492] But Strabo himself says that "the number seems to be exaggerated".[493] Pliny's statement based on the writings of the companions of Alexander the Great exactly tallies with that of Strabo with regard to the number of nations and thier towns, which were subdued by the Macedonians.[494] Apollodorus states that there were 1500 cities between the Hydaspes and Hypanis.[495] Arrian has also postulated that seven nations in all (seven territorial units of the Punjab) conquered by Alexander contained more than 2,000 (two thousand) towns.[496] V.A. Smith has supported this number without assigning any valid reason therefor.[497] Plutarch refers to 5,000 cities.[498] These figures are obviously imaginative, fabricated and factually incorrect. The number of towns, i.e., "5,000", as specified by Strabo, Pliny and Plutarch, is evidently a mistake for "500", which can be authenticated by the statment of McCrindle.[499]

It is worthy of remark that the historians of Alexander presented a distorted and

490. *IP*, pp. 75-76, 496.
491. *IIA*, pp. 111, note 2, 112, also 113-15.
492. *Geog.*, XV, I, 3; XV, I, 33, *AICL*, pp. 9 and 39-40 (respectively).
493. *Geog.*, XV, I, 33; *ibid.*, p. 40.
494. *Hist. Nat.*, VI, 17 (21), *AICL*, p. 108.
495. Cf. M. Elphinstone, "The Greek Accoounts of India", in his *The History of India*, ed. by E.B. Cowell, 9th edn. (London, 1911), rept. in *Ancient India* (Delhi, 1983), Ch. III, p. 28.
496. *Anab.*, VI, 2; *IIA*, p. 133.
497. *EHI*, p. 93.
498. *Lif. Alex.*, Ch. IX; *IIA*, p. 309.
499. *IIA*, p. 112, note 1.

magnified ficture of the subject with reference to the number of towns or cities in Punjab only to glorify his deeds. Bunbury has also pointed out that "the Greeks were misled ny the exaggerated reports so common with all orientalists, and so greedily swallowed by the historians of Alexander with a view of magnifying the exploits of the great conqueror".[500] However, it is a fact to be reckoned with that the so-called seven or nine nations (territorial units) lying between Hydaspes and Hyphasis contained some considerable cities whatever thier number may be. Alexander after having subjugated all the territories concerned returned them along with the towns to Porus in presence of all the ambassadors or representative of the people who assembled after his defeat, and thus he not only reinstated him in his kingdom but also added a large province to it in honour of his valour he displayed. As a matter of fact the vanquished Porus was restored to his sovereignty through the clemency of Victorious Alexander. The above statement can be confirmed by the unanimous testimony of Plutarch (*Life of Alex*. Ch. LX), Justin (*Hist. Phil*., XII, 8), Arrian (*Anab*., VI, 2) and Onesikritos.

Here it must be made clear that the towns, which are said to have been delivered by Alexander to Porus, not only included those of lying between the Jhelum and the "Beas", and between the Jhelum and the Cenāb (the territory of Porus), but also those which belonged to the Kathaioi, Glausai and other independent tribes of northern Punjab. These towns seem to have flourished for centuries as centres or urban culture. The period and causes of their decay are not known to us. Many other flourishing and prosperous villages which were no less populous than the towns are also included in the figures shown above. The towns enumerated, particularly by the Greek writers, actually comprise both the urban and semi-urban areas. And sometimes it becomes difficult to distinguish between the two. In fact, the classical concept of a town or city was totally different from that of modern time.

The capital of Sophites, Sopeithes or Sophytes (Saubhūta of Pāṇini, *Gaṇa Pāṭha*, IV, 2, 67 and 75, or Saubhūti), one of the petty kings of the western Pubjab, according to Arrian, was situated on the left or eastern bank of the Hydaspes or on its opposite bank,[501] which Cunningham has identified with an ancient city whose ruins in the form of an extensive mound lay in the neighbourhood of Ahmedabad or at Jobnāthanagar at some distance from Nikaea or Mong where Alexander defeated Porus.[502] Thus, it was

500. *HAG*, vol. 1, p. 453.

501. *Anab*., VI, 2, 2; *IIA*, p. 133; see also *AICL*, p. 37, note 1.

502. *CAGI*, pp. 130-31, 142.

very close to the kingdom of Porus. It was a semi-urban centre. Strabo has placed his dominion in the tract between the two rivers, the Hydaspes and Akesines.[503] But Curtius has located it on the west of the Hyphasis.[504] It seems that there is no agreement among the classical authors with regard to the position of the kingdom and its capital, which belonged to an independent sovereign called Sopeithes. However, we learn from Diodorus[505] and Curtius[506] that his cities were governed by the good laws in highest degree with admirable political system. He struck coins in *c.* 305 BC with his name in Hellenised form, "Sophutes" or "Sophutou", which is a transliteration of Saubhūta.[507] The inscribed silver coins concerned, according to R.B. Whitehead,[508] do not belong to him. But his view is not acceptable. It may be added here that the capital city remained in excellent state of preservation till much later date. We do not have any definite information about its destruction.

The two another ancient cities in the northern Punjab were "Labokla" and "Amakatis" or "Amakapis", as mentioned by Ptolemy.[509] The identification of the first one (also known as Lohawar) with the great city of Lahore was first made in Kiepert's *Map of India*, as stated by Lassen.[510] It has since been confirmed by the researches of T.H. Thornton, the author of the *History and Antiquities of Lahor*. This is the city which has been the capital of the Western Punjab for nearly one thousand years. The second one has been placed by Ptolemy himself to the west of the Hydraotes of Rāvī, and in the immediate neighbourhood of Labokla or Lahore.

The town called Ambakapi or Amakatis is actually represented by the two ruined mounds known as Amba and Kapi. The mound of Amba lies upwards of 9 miles to the south of Shekohpura. It is said to be "900 feet-square, and from 25 to 30 feet in height;

503. *Geog.*, XV, I, 30, *AICL*, pp. 36-37; Hamilton and Falconer, *op. cit.*, vol. III, p. 93.

504. *Hist. Alex.*, IX, I, *IIA*, p. 219; see also *AICL*, pp. 37, note 1, 46, note 3; *IIA*, pp. 133, note 2, 411; Bunbury, *HAG*, vol. I, p. 455; *MMH*, p. 123 (for different views about the location).

505. *Bib. Hist.*, XVII, 91, 92; *IIA*, pp. 279-80.

506. *Hist. Alex.*, IX, I; *IIA*, pp. 219-20; see also *AICL*, p. 57, note 3.

507. V.A. Smith, *CCIM*, vol. I, pp. 7, 8, pl. I. 1; Rapson, *Indian Coins*, p. 3, pl. I.8; also his Remarks in *N. Chr.*, 1904, p. 323; D.C. Sircar, *SI*, vol. I, p. 83 and note 2; *CHI*, vol. I, p. 348 and pl. I, 17; *AICL*, p. 37, note 1.

508. *N. Chr.*, 1943, pp. 60-72 cf. *JNSI*, vol. VII, pp. 23-26. Sylvain Levi (*JA*, XV, 8, 1890, p. 237 f) has correctly identified Sophytes with Saubhūti.

509. *AIT*, pp. 125-26.

510. *Ind. Alt.*, vol. III, p. 152; see also *Ar. Ant.*, p. 99.

but as the whole of the surrounding fields, for a breadth of about 600 feet, are covered with broken pottery, the full extent of the ancient town may be taken at not less than 8000 feet, or upwards of 3 miles in circuit. The mound itself is covered with broken bricks of large size", amongst which Cunningham discovered several pieces of carved brick. He also found one piece of grey sandstone, and piece of speckled iron ore, similar to that of Sangala.[511] The distance of the mounds from Lahore is about 25 miles. According to the local tradition, the town was founded by Raja Amba about two thousand years ago or just about the beginning of the Christian era which synchronises with the rule of the Indo-Scythians and the Pārthians or Pahalavas in the Pubjab. The small mound of Kapi is 2½ miles to the east of Amba on the old high-road to Lahore. Ptolemy's Daidala can be identified with Depālpur, which was on the Sutlej to the south of Labokla and Amakatis.

The Sibi (Skt. Śivis) called by the Megasthenes[512] and Ptolemy[513] Sibae, by Arrian,[514] Strabo,[515] Dionysios Periegetes[516] and Nonnos[517] Sibai, by Curtius[518] Sobii and Diodorus[519] and Justin[520] Siboi, inhabited a district between the Hydaspes and the Indus and their capital stood at a distance of about thirty miles from the former river, and as appears from Diodorus, at some distance above its confluence with the Akesines.[521] According to Curtius, they occupied the region between the Hydaspes and Akesines. Arrian locates them between the Indus and the Akesines. Their territories were actually situated to the west of the Cenāb below its junction with the Jhelum. They were free tribes numbering about fifty to sixty thousand. According to an epigraphic evidence, they were the inhabitants of Shorkot region in the Jhang district lying between the Rāvī and the Cenāb in the central Punjab, and the ancient name of their capital was Śibipura,[522]

511. *CAGI*, pp. 164, 166; see also *AIT*, p. 127.
512. *AIMA*, 1st edn., p. 111 and note.
513. *AIT*, p. 290.
514. *Indika*, pt. I, V (12), *AIMA*, p. 196; see also R.C. Jain (ed.), *MAIMA*, p. XV.
515. *Geog*., XV, I, 8 and 33, *AICL*, pp. 14 and note 2, and 40 (respectively).
516. *Bassarika*, LI, 1080-1165, *AICL*, p. 189.
517. *Dionysiaka*, Bk. XXVI, *AICL*, pp. 199-200, note 11.
518. *Hist. Alex*., IX. 4, *IIA*, pp. 232-33.
519. *Bib. Hist*., XVII. 96, *ibid*., pp. 285-86.
520. *Hist. Phil*., XII. 9, *ibid*., p. 324.
521. *IIA*, note Ee, p. 366.
522. "Shorkot Inscriptions", J. Ph. Vogel, *Ep. Ind*., vol. XVI (1921), p. 16; see also B.C. Law, *HGAI*, pp. 66, 127-28.

which is identical with Śivapur of Patañjal (*Mahābhāṣya*, IV, 2, 2). Aritṣṭapura of Pāṇini (*Sūtra*, VI, 2, 100),[523] Pāli Ariṭṭhapura or Aristobothra of Ptolemy may be another city.

A huge mound of ruins of Shorkot marks the site of the chief city or town called Śibipura. It was visited by Burnes, who describes the place as "a mound of earth, surrounded by a brick wall, and so high as to be seen for a circuit of six or eight miles".[524] He adds that it is much larger than Sehwan (a city of Sindh, which I have described here separately along with other cities of that region). According to the measurement of De la Hoste, "it is 1200 feet long, by 750 feet broad".[525] The presence of a wall of large-sized bricks, irrefutably, proves the high antiquity of the urban settlement at this place. It is much smaller but loftier than Harappā. Burnes assigns its downfall to Alexander himself. But we find that it was enlarged and strengthened by Philip whom Alexander left behind as governor of the Oxudrakae and Malli. Shorkot was in the direct line of Alexander's route, from the junction of the Hydaspes and Akesines to the capital of the Malli. Shorkot may be the "Alexanderia Soriane" of Stephans Byzantinus. The antiquity of Shorkot may be ascertained approximately by the coins which have been found in its ruins. A single copper piece of Apollodotus was obtained by Burnes. It leads us to warrant the belief that the town must have been reoccupied by the Greek kings of Ariana and the Punjab. It was in the flourishing state during the sway of the Indo-Scythians which can by evidenced from the discovery of their copper coins in large numbers. It continued to thirve from 126 BC down to AD 250, or perhaps later. The local tradition relates that his town had been destroyed by some king of the westward, about 1400 years ago. We can, thus, attribute its destruction to the White Hūṇas who must have entered the Punjab from the westward during the sixth century AD. But the discovery of some coins of the brāhmaṇa kings of the Kabul valley and the Punjab leads us to Surmise that the place was either deserted thereafter or remained in a very decayed state for sometime and it was again occupied by one of these brāhmaṇa kings in the tenth century.

One of the free tribes called by the historians of Alexander the Malli or Malloi (Mālavas) occupied an extensive territory situated between the lower Hydraotes and the Akesines. Their territories as a whole not only comprehended the modern Doāb of the Rāvī and Cenāb but also extended to the junction of the Indus and the Akesines. They occupied the fertile valley of the lower Hydraotes on both sides of the river. They also

523. *IP*, p. 73, also pp. 54, 66.

524. *Op. cit.*, vol. I, p. 113.

525. *JASB*, 1840, p. 913.

inhabited the lower reaches of the Indus. Thus, their dominions comprised the greater part of the modern Multān district and some parts of the Montgomery and Jhang districts. They had in their possession several fortified towns besides their capital city, and they were all densely populated. Their towns were mostly situated on the north of the confluence of the Hydraotes and Akesines and the capital to its south.[526] Their towns or cities were situated both along the Cenāb and the Rāvī in the central and southern Punjab.

Here mention may first be made of those towns which were located in the central Punjab. Their first city according to Arrian, was 400 stadia (or 46 miles) distant from the Akesines. He described it as a walled city with a castle or citadel which was captured by assault by Alexander in his campaign against the Malli.[527] Curtius (*Hist. of Alex.*, IX, 4, 10) places it at 250 stadia, or 28¾ miles from the junction of the Hydaspes and Akesines. It is identified with Koṭ Kamāliā, a small but ancient town situated on an isolated mound on the right or northern bank of the Rāvī. It is 44 miles to the south-east of the junction of the Hydaspes and Akesines, and 35 miles to the east or south-east of Shorkot. It possesses an ancient mound of burnt brick ruins. It owes it origin to the Malli tribe which still exists in this part of the country.[528]

Arrian relates that there was "another city of Malli, into which a great body of Indians had fied for safety".[529] When Alexander despatched perdik as to blockade the city, its inhabitants deserted the place and took refuge in the neighbouring marshes near the Rāvī. This town has been identified with Harappā, which is situated 16 miles to the east-south-east of Koṭ Kamāliā, and on the opposite high bank of the Rāvī.[530] "The great mass of ruins is on the western side, where the mound rises to 60 feet in height in the centre. At this point there are several massive walls built of large bricks, which are,

526. For details see Arrian, *Anab.*, VI. 4-9; *IIA*, pp. 137-46; *Indika*, pt. I, Ch. IV; *AIMA*, 1st edn., pp. 190-91, note; Curtius, *Hist Alex.*, IX, 4-7; *IIA*, pp. 234-46; Diodorus, *Bib. Hist.*, XVII, 98-99, *IIA*, pp. 287-89; Plutarch, *Lif. Alex.*, Ch. 63, *IIA*, pp. 311-12; Justin, *Hist. Phil*; XII, 9, *IIA*, pp. 324-25; *IIA*, note P, pp. 350-51, note Q. pp. 351-52; Smith, *EHI*, pp. 98-100; Raverty, *op. cit.*, p. 364; *Ind. Ant.*, vol. V, pp. 87-96, 333; also the views of R.L. Raikes and R.H. Dyson, *Ancient Cities of the Indus*, ed. by G.L. Possehl, pp. 225 f, 230 f, 230f; B.C. Law, *HGAI*, pp. 110-11; *HA*, vol. IV, p. 403 f; *Comp. Hist. Ind.*, vol. I, p. 37; J.T. Wheeler, *India from the Earliest Ages*, vol. III, p. 165; *AIIC*, p. 33; *AICL*, p. 40, note 1; Gerini (*RTGEA*, p. 535) calls the people "Malla".

527. *Anab.*, VI, 7, *IIA*, pp. 142-44.

528. *CAGI*, p. 175; *IIA*, p. 141, note 1.

529. *Anab.*,VI, 6, *IIA*, pp. 140-41.

530. *CAGI*, p. 177; *ibid.*, pp. 141-42, note 2.

no doubt, the remains of some extensive building".[531] Burnes estimated the extent of the ruins as "about three miles in circumference. . . ."[532] But this comprises only the remains of the walled town. Masson relying on the tradition recorded theat Harappā once extended on the west as far as Chichawatni, a distance of 12 miles, which confirms the belief of the people as to the former site and importance of their town.[533] Saint Martin's identification of the "Mallian capital" with Harappā[534] seems to be absolutely baseless. Tradition attributes the destruction of both Koṭ Kamāliā and Harappā to the western king of the sixth century, i.e., the White Hūṇas who overthrew Shorkot. The coins found in the ruins of Harappā are similar to those discovered at Shorkot. Thus, all these towns must have experienced the same fortune. Harappā remained uninhabited for several centuries.

Arrian refers to a "town well fortified both by the art and nature" (*Anab.*, VI, 3), the art being the brick walls, and the nature, the enormous mounds of earthen ramparts. This is the town which he perhaps includes into the "strongest cities" (*ibid.*, VI, 4). Curtius" account that on the bank of the Rāvī there was a strong fort (*Hist. of Alex.* IX, 4, 10) agrees with that of Arrian. It was one of the towns of the Malli which was captured by Alexander. This town was first identified by Rennell with the present town of Toulumba or Tulamba (in the southern Punjab). He adds that it was on the opposite side of the Cenāb in the neighbourhood of the Malloi.[535] Cunningham has also identified it with the same town which, according to him, is situated on the left bank of the Rāvī, at a distance of about 52 miles to the north-east of Multān. He says, "The antiquity of Tulamba is vouched for by tradition, and by the large size of the bricks, which are similar to the oldest in the walls and ruins of Multān. . . ."[536] Masson has suggested that it represents either "the capital of the Malli" or the fort held by Brāhmaṇs, whose defence was so obstinate and so fatal to themselves, and which was evidently contiguous to the capital of the Malli".[537]

---

531. *CAGI*, p. 178.
532. *Op. cit.*, vol. I, p. 117.
533. *Travels*, vol. I, p. 453; *JASB*, vol. VI, p. 57.
534. Cf. *IIA*, note Q, pp. 351-52.
535. *MMH*, Sec. III, p. 128.
536. *CAGI*, pp. 189-90; se also *IIA*, p. 142, note 1.
537. *Travels*, vol. I, p. 456.

Arrian (*Anab.*, VI, 7) specifically makes a mention of the strongly fortified "city of the Brachmans (brāhmaṇas)" in the territory of the Malloi, which was captured by Alexander in his campaign against the latter. The Garrison "abandoned the city and fled to the castle" which being stormed they set fire to thier houses, and perished in the flames. Several thousand of the brāhmaṇa population lost their lives. Cutrisus (*Hist. of Alex.*, IX, 4) and Diodorus (*Bib. Hist.*, XVII, 98-99) have also presented very faithful accounts of the city of the brāhmaṇas with special referece to the loss of the human lives. It is said that there were two towns of the brāhmaṇas near the Rāvī, which were taken by Alexander, and some of the occupants burnt themselves out of panic and consternation.[538] Arrian's city of the brāhmaṇas has been identified with the old ruined town and fort of Atari (in the southern Punjab) which is situated at the distance of 20 miles to the west-south-west of Tulamba and 34 miles to the north-east of Multān. "The remains consist of a strong citadel 750 feet square and 35 feet high with a ditch all round it, and a tower in the centre 50 feet high. On two sides are the remains of the town forming a mound 20 feet high, and 1200 feet square, the whole being a mass of ruin 1800 feet in length, and 1200 feet in breadth".[539] The large size of the bricks points to the high antiquity of the place.

Arrian quite separately refers to "the capital city of the Malli" where "many of the inhabitants of other cities had fled for their better security". He adds that it had the greatest number of defenders, 50,000, and it was the largest city, situated on the south of the confluence of the Hydraotes and the Akesines. Alexander after having captured and destroyed several towns, north and south of the Rāvī, came to this city.[540] It was not only the largest but also the "Strongest city".[541] Julius Valerius, while providing a picturesque description of this place, observes: "There was a city in India into which many had fled for refuge — one that was of immense size and of impregnable strength".[542] This is the city which Alexander besieged and brought its whole population to subjection. Strabo

538. Rennell, *MMH*, Sec. III, pp. 126-27; Orme's *Indostan*, vol. II, p. 225, cf. *ibid.*, p. 127, fn.

539. *CAGI*, pp. 192-93; *IIA*, p. 143, note 1 and note Q, p. 352.

540. *Anab.*, VI, 8, *IIA*, pp. 144-45.

541. *Ibid.*, VI, 4, *ibid.*, p. 137.

542. *The Iti. of Alex.*, Ch. 115, *AICL*, p. 1543.

calls it "a small town of the Malloi in the capture of which Alexander received a wound".[543] From the narrative of Arrian (based on the account of Aristoboulos and the materials supplied by Ptolemy, who accompanied Alexander) also it is quite evident that this "city belonged to the Malli".[544] Plutarch calls the inhabitants of the city both the Mallotes and the Malloi.[545] They also figure in the *Journal of Voyage* of Nearkhos, as described by Arrian in his *Indika* (pt. II, Chs. XVIII f).[546]

The famous metropolis of the Malloi has been identified with the ancient Mūlasthānapura or modern Multān (the capital of the southern Punjab), which in Alexander's time was situated at the distance of fifteen miles above the confluence of the Rāvī and the Cenāb. And now it is about thirty miles below the junction of that rivers, and about 34 miles from the brāhmaṇa city of Atari. In the first half of the second century AD it was situated on the bank of the Rāvī, but now on the Cenāb perhaps because of the change of the course of the rivers concerned. Multān comprises nearly the same territories as those occupied by the Malloi of the Greek historians. This city owes its name to the Malloi.[547] Burnes, one of the chief protagonists of its identification with this place, has revealed that it is still called by the native people "Mallithān, the place of the Malli".[548] V.A. Smith does not accept this identification. He is of the view that this place has no etymological connection with the name Malloi. Their stronghold or the chief city, according to him, was "situated somewhere near the boundary of the Jhang and Motgomery Districts, 80 or 90 miles to the north-east of Multān".[549] But there are many other considerations in favour of its identification with the place shown above.

Cunningham, while firmly establishing the link of the Mallian capital with Multān, has stated that ". . . it consists of walled city and a strong fortress, situated on opposite

543. *Geog.*, XV, I, 33, *AICL*, p. 40.

544. *Anab.*, VI, 11, *IIA*, p. 149.

545. *Oration*, I, 2; II, 9. *AICL*, pp. 206-7.

546. *CNES*, p. 171 and note 13.

547. For details see *AICL*, pp. 40, note 1, 154, note 4, 206, note 1; *IIA*, note Q, p. 352; *CNES*, p. 171, note 13; Rennell, *MMH*, Sec. III, pp. 123, 125-26; Baveridge, *Comp. Hist. Ind.*, vol. I, p. 37. Bunbury, *HAG*, vol. I, pp. 450-51; Robertson, *HDAI*, p. 20; Burnes, *op. cit.*, vol. III, p. 114; Gustav Oppert, *OIB* (Delhi, 1972), pp. 20, 82; W.W. Hunter, "The Greeks in India", in *op. cit.*, pp. 88-89; *CAGI*, pp. 186, 198-201.

548. *Op. cit.*

549. *EHI*, p. 100.

banks of an old bed of the Rāvī. . . . The original site consisted of two low mounds not more than 8 or 10 feet high. . . . It had 46 towers or bastions, including the two flanking towers at each of the four gates. The walled city, which envelops the citadel for more than two-thirds of the curve, is 4200 in feet length, and 2400 feet in breadth. . . . Altogether the walled circuit of Multān, including both city and citadel, is 15,000 feet or very nearly 3 miles, and the whole circuit of the place, including its suburbs, is 4½ miles".[550] Thirlwall has also pointed out that the Malloi had numerous towns and cities with ramparts and fortresses.[551]

The capture of the capital of the Malloi at the hands of Alexander and his army[552] compelled its inhabitants to desert it and take refuge in the neighbouring area. It really marked the beginning of the decline of their city. According to Hiuen-Tsang, this place called "*Mou-lo-san-pu-lu*" (Mūlasthānapura) was 4000 *li* (or 667 miles) and its capital above 30 *li* (or just 5 miles) in circuit.[553] His evidence attests to the fact that the ancient name of the city remained in use till the first half of the seventh century. A few years after his visit, probably in the middle of that century, it was invaded and captured by brāhmaṇa *rājā* of Sindh named Chach. Subsequently, it was occupied by Muhammad bin Kasim in AD 713. The decline and fall of many towns and cities may be assigned to the Arabs who overran the whole of the lower Punjab.

Arrian not only refers to the cities of the Malloi but also to that of the Oxydrakai[554] (Kṣudrakas of Pāṇini, *Gaṇa-Pāṭha*, IV, 2, 45,[555] Pāli Khuddakas). Their name in the classics appears in various forms.[556] Arrian (*Indika*, pt. I, Ch. IV) places them on the

550. *CAGI*, pp. 194-95.

551. *History of Greece*, vol. VII. Ch. 54.

552. Arrian, *Anab.*, VI, 9-11, *IIA*, pp. 146-49; Curtius, *Hist. Alex.*, IX, 4-6, *ibid.*, pp. 234-44; Diodorus, *Bib. Hist.*, XVII, 98-99, *ibid.*, pp. 287-89; Justin, *Hist. Phil.*, XII, 9, *ibid.*, pp. 324-25; Plutarch, *Lif. Alex.*, Ch. 63, *ibid.*, pp. 311-12; *The Itinerarium Alexandri*, Ch. 115; *Pseudo-Kallisthenes*, III, IV.

553. *YCTI*, vol. II, p. 254; Julien, *Hiouen Thsang*, vol. III, p. 410.

554. *Anab.*, VI, 14, *IIA*, p. 154.

555. *IP*, pp. 76, 455.

556. Arrian informs us that Megasthenes' Oxydrakai (*AIMA*, 1st edn., pp. 110 and 190) is absolutely correct form. Strabo calls them both Hydrakai (*Geog.*, XV, I, 6, *AICL*, p. 12) and Oxydrakai (*ibid.*, XV, I, 8 and 33, *AICL*, pp. 13, 40); they are called by Diodorus Syrakousai (*Bib. Hist.*, XVII, 98, *IIA*, pp. 287-88), by Curtius Sudracae (*Hist. Alex.*, IX, 4, *ibid.*, p. 234) and by Pliny Sydracae (*Hist. Nat.*, VI, XII, 6); in the *Romance History of Alexander*, falsely ascribed to Kallisthenes →

Hydaspes above its confluence with the Akesines, and if this was their real position they must have been situated to the north of the Malloi. The same author places them (in other source, *Anab.*, VI, 4) between the Hydraotes and the Hyphasis. Bunbury has made it clear that a trace of third name may be found in that of Ooch, a principal city situated just below the junction of the Sutlej with the Cenāb. "Very little reliance can be placed on this etymology, but the position thus suggested would accord well with the narrative of Arrian, and on the whole it seems not improbable that the Oxydracae may have occupied the district of Ooch together with the adjoining province of Bahawulpoor".[557]

The capital of the Oxydrakae (one of the free nations or tribes) has been identified with modern Uchh in the southern Punjab. "This old town", says Cunningham, "is situated on the eastern bank of the Panjnad (Pañcanada or confluence of the five rivers), 70 miles to the south-south-west of Multān, and 45 miles to the north-east of the present confluence with the Indus ant Mithānkot".[558] "Its favourable position at the old confluence of the Punjab rivers must have made it a place of importance from the earliest times". In the time of Alexander it must have been a very populous city. There is another Uchh on a mound to the west of the confluence of the Cenāb and Jhelum; and a third Uchh is also situated on a mound. Wilson has identified it with "Ooch, a town on the left bank of the Akesines."[559] In Alexander's time this river (Cenāb) joined the Indus near this town, but now the point of junction is lower down near Mithānkoṭ,[560] probably at the distance of forty miles. St. Martin has identified it with "Chuchpur" or an ancient fort standing on the eastern bank of the Indus right opposite Mithānkoṭ.[561] According to Burnes, Uchh is formed of three distinct towns, a few hundred yards apart from each other, and each encompassed by a brick wall, now in ruins. The mound was formed of the ruins of houses caused by the inundation of the Cenāb.[562] Masson mentions only two separate towns, and adds that Uchh is chiefly "distinguished by the ruins of the former towns,

---

→ (*"Pseueo-Kallisthenes"*) they are also called Oxydrakai; in the Latin version of Julius Valerius it is recorded that Alexander lived in their country with brāhmaṇas (*AICL*, pp. 177-78); see also *Ancient Cities of the Indus*, p. 230; *IIA*, note P, pp. 350-51.

557. *AICL*, p. 12, note 1; IIA, Note P, pp. 350-51.

558. *CAGI*, p. 204; see N.L. Dey, *GDAMI*, p. 195; also *IIA*, p. 156, note 3.

559. *Ar. Ant.*, pp. 200-1.

560. *AICL*, p. 23, note 2.

561. *Étude*, pp. 124-25 cf. *IIA*, p. 156, note 3.

562. *Op. cit.*, vol. I, p. 79.

which are very extensive and attest the pristine prosperity of the locality".[563] Rennell identifies it with "Outch" of the Greek historians.[564] The popular belief and the old tradition also confirm that there were once seven different towns bearing the same name Uchchanagar.

We learn from Arrian (*Anab.*, VI, 15) that Alexander "ordered a city to be built at the confluence of the two rivers (Cenāb and the Indus), imagining that by the advantage of such a situation it would become rich and populous". This place bore the name of Alexandria Uchh[565] which corresponds with Askaland-Usah, one of its later names. This city was the capital of one of the four principalities of Sindh under Ayand who reigned after Alexander. It was captured by Chach on his expedition against Multān. The "Iskandar" of the *Chach-nāmah* must be the Alexandria or Uchh.[566] At a later period, it formed part of the independent kingdom or province of Multān. This ancient city has been repeatedly destroyed and rebuilt the details of which do not fall within the purview of the treatment of the present subject.

Sankalia's statement that in the whole Punjab the urban culture flourished seems to be perfectly correct.[567]

Both Megasthenes and Pliny mention twelve tribes each possessing two cities. The tribes include the Sibarae, Abaortae, Sarabhan, Sarophages, Sorgae, Baraomatae, Umbrittae, Aseni etc. The Aseni had altogether three cities, including the capital Bucephala which was so named because it was built where Alexander's famous horse was buried.[568] The tribes enumerated must have occupied a tract of country lying above the confluence of the Indus with the streams of the combined rivers of the Punjab. The Sibarae represent Sauviras who were not far from the banks of the Indus with their capital Roruka. The Aseni were situated to the east of the river. The Umbrittae are definitely the Abastanoi (Skt. Ambaṣṭhas) of the historians of Alexander who dwelt in the neigbourhood of the lower Akesines. The other obscure tribes cannot be identified with any certainty. The details of thier cities are not available either.

---

563. *Travels*, vol. I, p. 22.

564. *MMH*, p. 123.

565. W.W. Hunter, *op. cit.*, pp. 89-90.

566. *JASB*, 1838, p. 94.

567. *Op. cit.*, p. 9.

568. *AIMA*, 1st edn. p. 149 and note; Pliny, *Hist. Nat.*, VI, 21 (23), cf. *ibid.*

Before we proceed further to describe some of the important towns and cities of Sindh in the west, it will be quite in the fitness of things to make it clear here that in ancient times it comprised the whole valley of the Indus from the Punjab to the sea, including the Delta and the island of Kacch.

The towns situated in the Indus valley and its neighbourhood numbering about firty-one have been divided by Ptolemy into the following six groups. The towns of the first group (five in number) belonged to the upper part of the valley and were situated near its junction with the Kophes. The towns of the second group are indicated by their relative positions they held. They were successive stages on the great caravan route which ran parallel with the western bank of the river all the way from its junction with the Kophes downwards to the coast. The third group consists of the towns which were the chief marts of commerce in the Delta. The towns of the fourth group were successive stages on another caravan route which on the eastern side of the river traversed the country from the great confluence with the combined rivers of the Punjab downward to Delta. The towns of the fifth group (seven in number) were situated towards the eastern side of the Delta. The towns of the sixth group were included in the territory of the "Khattriaioi" (kṣatriya tribes or warriors) which extended on both sides of the river from the confluence with the Punjab rivers as far as the Delta.[569] St. Martin's statement that none of them can be identified[570] is no longer tenable. The towns identified have been placed in the relevant places.

Here we will begin with the towns situated in Upper Sindh. The royal city or the capital of a king called Musikanus or Mousikanos by Strabo,[571] Diodorus[572] Arrian[573] and Julius Valerius,[574] or Sousikana or Musikana of Ptolemy[575] or of the people called Musicani by Curtius[576] has been identified with Alor,[577] which remained the metropolis of the rich,

569. *AIT*, pp. 136-58.

570. *Étude*, pp. 234 ff.

571. *Geog.*, XV, I, 21, 22, 33 and 34, *AICL*, pp. 26-27, 40-41; Hamilton and Falconer, *op. cit.*, vol. III, p. 96.

572. *Bib. Hist.*, XVII, 102, *IIA*, pp. 292-93.

573. *Anab.*, VI, 15, *ibid.*, pp. 157-58.

574. *Itin. Alex.*, Ch. 112, *AICL*, p. 153.

575. *AIT*, p. 145.

576. *Hist. Alex.*, IX, 8.

577. *AICL*, p. 26, note 4, p. 41, note 2; M'Murdo, *JRAS*, vol. I, p. 33; *CAGI*, pp. 216-18; Raverty, *op. cit.*, pp. 566-70, 663.

poweful and flourishing kingdom of Upper Sindh for many ages. It figures conspicuously in the records of the Macedonian invasion. We learn from Arrian that this kingdom in Alexander's time was "the richest and most populous throughout all India". Onesikritos while speaking of its opulence and economic prosperity noted that "the country produced everything in abundance" as we learn from Strabo.[578] That the territory of its ancient capital Alor or Aror was very rich and fertile is a well ascertained fact. Arrian relates that Alexander "ordered Kraterus to build a castle in the city. . . ." It was no doubt a large fortified city. It was visited by Hiuen-Tsang in AD 641.[579] This celebrated city was situated on the west bank of the Indus, near Bhakar, the ruins of which are still traceable five miles to the south-east of modern Rohri or Ruhri in Sukkur district. In ancient times it was about 150 miles distant from Debal (mod. Karachi). The said capital city, Alor, continued to flourish till its destruction by the Indus partly before AD 680 and completely after AD 712. The inundations of the Indus made an Eden of all the lands they overspread. It is also asserted by the Mohammedan chroniclers of the conquest of Sindh that this city was deserted in consequence of the alteration of the course of the Indus.

Both Arrian (*Anab.*, VI, 16) and Curtius (*Hist. of Alex.*, IX, 8, 26) mention those two principal cities, which were situated within the dominion of the king Oxykanus (Portikanos of Strabo, *Geog.*, XV, 1, 33) on the west of the Indus adjoining those of Musikanus or lying to the south-east of Alor. Curtius' description of the two towers of the citadel of the chief city, perhaps the capital, point to the fact that it was the lofty town or *porta-gām*. It was perhaps one of the five towns called *Pentagramma* by Ptolemy. The said capital was captured by Alexander after a siege of three days. Another city also met the same fate. The capital has been identified with Mahorta (Mahāvarddha-grāma or the great lofty city) situated on the bank of the Ghār river, 10 miles north-west of Larkāna.[580] Masson describes it as "the remains of an ancient fortress, on a huge mound, named Maihota".[581] It was "one of the most flourishing places in Sindh". "The site of Mahorta must always have been a position of great importrance, both commercially and politically, as it commanded the high-road from Sindh, via Kachh-Gandāva, to Kandahār".[582] In the

578. *Geog.*, XV, I, 34, *AICL*, p. 41.
579. *YCTI*, vol. II, p. 253.
580. *CAGI*, pp. 219-20; see also *IIA*, p. 158, note 1.
581. *Travels*, vol. I, p. 461.
582. *CAGI*, p. 220.

time of Alexander, when the Indus flowed down the bed of the Nāra, the nearest point of the stream was Alor, from which Mahorta was distant 45 miles to the south of west, but at present the latter place is within a few miles of the river Indus.

Ptolemy's Binagara, placed on the Indus to the eastward of Oskana (Oxykanus),[583] has been identified by Cunningham with Alor.[584] But more correctly it can be connected with Mahorta. The early Arab geographers also mention a town of identical name, Bania, but they place it in lower Sindh, situated at the distance of a single journey below Mansura.[585]

Ptolemy's "Boudaia"[586] has been identified by Arab geographers or chroniclers of the conquest of Upper Sindh with the town of "Bodhpur" situated between Alor and Mittankoṭ (or Mithānkoṭ) or to the west of the Indus.[587] One of the largest and populous towns to the west of the Indus called by Ptolemy "Banagara", lay on the line of communication between Kabul and the Indus,[588] which was visited by both Fa-hian and Hiuen-Tsang.

Ptolemy places a town called "Musarna" on a small affluent of the Indus to the north of the "Askana" rivulet. This town belonged to the people called by him Musarnei (the Massanae of Diodorus or the "Masūrakarṇa" of the *Gaṇa-Pāṭha* on Pāṇini, II, 4, 49; IV, 1, 112) whose name still exists in the district of Muzarka to the west of the Indus below Mithānkoṭ in Upper Sindh. Musarna may be the town of Shahpur.

We learn from Arrian (*Anab*., VI, 15) and Diodorus (*Bib. Hist*., XVII, 102) that Alexander founded a city or town in the realm of the people called the Sogdi by the former and the Sodrae by the latter which was named after him Alexandria. This can also be supported by the statement of Curtius (*Hist. of Alex*., IX, 8). On the basis of Diodorus' testimony it can be established that Alexander "placed 10,000 inhabitants" in the new city, built on the opposite banks of the Indus (probably to the northward of Alor). It is said that he founded this city, "marking out docks again for the commerce which he foresaw under Greek initiative in the new Age".[589] As a matter of fact, the capital city of the Sogdi or the

583 *AIT*, p. 152.

584. *CAGI*, p. 218.

585. *AIT*, p. 145.

586. *Ibid*., p. 151.

587. *Ibid*.

588. *Ibid*., pp. 140-41.

589. *CHI*, p. 338.

Sodrae, the free tribe of Upper Sindh, had already come into existence before the arrival of Alexander there. The latter might have constructed his own city or erected a citadel near the former one with the settlements of the Greek and native population in conformity with his usual practice. The site might have later developed as one of the urban centres in Sindh. The narrative preserved by Arrian (*Anab.*, VI, 15) is very much in favour of the identification of the old site, Seorai, near Fazilpur with the town of the Sogdi. Here Masson heard that there was formerly a considerable town.[590] "About 8 miles to the north-east of Sabjalkot there is a village named Sirwahi, which may possibly represent the Seorai of Sindhian history. It is 96 miles in a direct line below Uchh, and 85 miles below Alor, or very nearly midway between them".[591] The native historians as well as the early Arab geographers place a strong fort, named Bhatia, between Multān and Alor, which from its position has a good claim to be identified with the city which Alexander is said to have built amongst the Sogdi. However, it is very difficult to say how far these identifications are satisfactory. Bhatia, defended by a lofty wall and a deep broad ditch, was taken by assault in AD 1003 by Mahmud of Ghazni.

The ancient city of Sindomana or Sindimana distinctly figures in the accounts of Strabo,[592] Arrian[593] and Plutarch[594] as the capital of the king called Sambos, Sambus or Sabos (Sambhu) whose principality was situated in Middle Sindh. Curtius (*Hist Alex.*, IX, 8) without naming his (Sabus) capital states that Alexander after having received the "submission of several towns, captured the raja's strongest city by mining", Diodorus (*Bib. Hist.*, XVII, 102) mention only the name of the king and not his capital. The said capital city has been satisfactorily identified with Sehwan, which stands on a site of very high antiquity that is the vicinity of the Lakki mountains. It preserves many vestiges of antiquity, especially the great mound, which was once the citadel or castle, which, according to Burnes, "is in all probability as old as the ages of the Greeks".[595] Its early occupation is admitted by all inquirers. M'Mudrdo says "Sehwan is undoubtedly a place

590. *Travels*, vol. I, p. 382.
591. *CAGI*, p. 215.
592. *Geog.*, XV. I, 33, *AICL*, p. 40 and note 2.
593. *Anab.*, VI, 16, *IIA*, p. 159.
594. *Lif. Alex.*, Ch. 64, *ibid.*, pp. 313-14.
595. *Op. cit.*, vol. III, p. 37.

of vast antiquity, perhaps more so than either Alor or Bāhmana".[596] It is also stated by Cunningham that "The favourable position of Sehwan, on a lofty isolated rock, near a large lake; with food and water in abundance would certainly have attracted the notice of the first inhabitants of Sindh".[597] In all the old maps it is placed on a western branch of the Indus. In Alexander's time, however, the river pursued a course from which Sindomana lay at a considerable distance to westward. It is said that "when the river flowed down the eastern channel of the Nara, Sehwan was not less than 65 miles distant from its nearest point at Jakrao".[598] The Greek name Sindomana corresponds with *Saindhava-vanam* or *Saindhuwān* meaning the "abode of the Saindhavas". Wilson is of the opinion that "Sindomana is readily recognisable in a very allowable Sanskrit compound, Sindhu-mān (the possessor of the capital or Rāja of Sindh) with which Sindhu-vān is synonymous, and the latter may have been softened in common speech to the modern Seh-wan".[599] The early Arab geographers mention the capital differently as Sadustān or Sadusān. It is mentioned in native histories of Sindh as one of the towns captured by Muhammad bin Kasim in AD 711. It was again captured by Mahmud of Ghazni in the beginning of the eleventh century. It remained for several centuries as one of the most flourishing urban centre in Sindh. But now it is in a very much decadent position.

Ptolemy's "Pesipeda",[600] which can be identified with little plausibility with "Besmeid" of the early Arab geographers, appears to be a town of considerable importance, which lay to the east of the Indus on the route form Mansura to Multan. Cunningham has identified it with Sehwan,[601] but I see no reason to do so. I rather find fair scope to raise the objection to their identity.

---

596. *JRAS*, vol. I, p. 30.
597. *CAGI*, pp. 223-24.
598. *Ibid.*, p. 223.
599. *Ar. Ant.*, p. 205; also *IIA*, note S, p. 355.
600. *AIT*, pp. 142-44.
601. *CAGI*, p. 224.

Alexander's historians — Arrian,[602] Curtius,[603] Diodorus[604] and Plutarch[605] — have also taken notice of a large city or town of the Brachmans (brāhmaṇas) of the Indus valley. Diodorus in particular calls this city *Harmatelia* (*Brāhmathala* or Brāhmaṇa-sthala — an honorific denomination) and adds that it was the "last town of the Brāhmaṇas on the river".[606] This town has been placed by them near Sindomana in Middle Sindh, but after having thoroughly investigated the data available to us and carefully analysed them we find that it was situated in the territory of Musikanus. His dominions must have embraced the whole of the valley of the Indus down the head of the Delta (Patala). In fact, it was the capital city which belonged to the whole brāhmaṇa population inhabiting the Upper, Middle and Lower valley of the Indus. It can be certainly identified with the ancient city of Brāhmaṇābād, Bahmanwā or Bahmanābād of the early Arab geographers and historians. It was originally called Bāmiwān and afterwards Brāhmaṇābād. It corresponds both in name and position with the city called Brahmana. According to an age-old tradition of the Sindhians too, it was known as Bāmiwān. The greek historians call the country of the brāhmaṇas. Brachmanoi or Brahmanoi and its capital Brahmana. The same place has been called Brāmaṇaka by both Pāṇini (*Sūtra*, V, 2, 71),[607] and Patañjali (*Mahābhāṣya*, IV, 2, 104).[608] The *Kāśikā* on Pāṇini describes it as "the land of brāhmaṇas" who were *āyudhajīvins* or followers of military art. It is to be noted that even Rājaśekhara in his *Kāvyamīmāṁsā* (ninth century AD) mentions "Brāhmanavaha" ("abode of the brāhmaṇas") as one of the *janapadas* of the west.

The Brāhmaṇic capital appears to have been one of the magnificent cities in Sindh. It was defended by a brick-wall and adorned with gates. It was stormed and captured by Alexander the account of which has been provided by Plutarch on the basis of former's letters. After a gap of several centuries the city of the brāhmaṇas was occupied by Muhammad bin Kasim in AD 712. According to the native histories and traditions of the people, Brāhmanābād was destroyed by an earthquake. Its destruction may be tentatively assigned to the latter half of the tenth century. Several legendary accounts are there

602. *Anab.*, VI, 16, 5, *IIA*, p. 159.
603. *Hist. Alex.*, IX, 8.
604. *Bib. Hist.*, XVII, 102 and 103, *IIA*, pp. 293-94.
605. *Lif. Alex.*, Ch. 59, *IIA*, p. 306.
606. *Bib. Hist.*, XVII, 103, *IIA*, p. 294 and Note T, pp. 355-56; see also Vincent, *The Voyage of Nearchus*, p. 136.
607. *IP*, p. 51; also *Bh. Sāv.*, vol. I, pp. 169-72.
608. B. N. Puri, *India in the Time of Patañjali*, p. 74.

about the destruction of all the old cities in the Punjab as well as of those in Sindh. However, it is no use dwelling upon them further. We are very much indebted to M. Bellasis for the discovery of the ruins of a large city at Bambhra-ka-thūl in 1854 which was in the occupation of the brāhmaṇas at the time of Alexander's invasion as well as in the later period. The ruins are situated near an old bed of the Indus at a distance of 47 miles to the north-east of Haidarabad, 28 miles to the east of Hāla, and 20 miles to the west of the eastern Nara. The broken brick tower still stands on the place. His excavations which include even extensive pre-historic remains have proved conclusively that the city was destroyed by some terrible convulsion of nature.[609] It is probable that most of the inhabitants who escaped the great catastrophe would have returned to the ruined city and many of them again reared their houses on the old sites. But the walls of the city were fallen and the place had become decayed so much so that it remained uninhabited for sometime. According to another evidence, it was Bāhmana, 8 miles east of Shehdādpur.[610]

If the city of the brāhmaṇas taken by Alexander was near Sindomana, as indicated by his historians, we may rather look for it in the position of Amree, eighteen miles below Sehwan, which, although now an insignificant village, is said to have been once a large city and the favourite residence of former kings.[611]

The Delta of the Indus called Patalene or Pattalene received its name from the city of Patala or Pattala, which was its capital. Strabo has very categorically stated that Patalene contained "a considerable city Patala", which give its name to the island.[612] Arrian says that in the time of Alexander it was not only fortified but also greatest city in the parts of the country about the mouths of the Indus.[613] Diodorus calls it "a city of great note".[614] Nearkhos in his *Journal of Voyage* has also described it as a town of considerable importance.[615] It also figures in Ptolemy's *Geography* (VII, 1, 59).[616] Arrian

609. For details see *JBBRAS*, vol. V, pp. 413-17; see also *IIA*, note T, p. 355 and *CAGI*, pp. 225-32 for correct identification of brāhmaṇa city.

610. R.D. Banerji, *PAHI*, p. 81.

611. Burnes, *op. cit.*, vol. III, p. 59.

612. *Geog.*, XV, I. 33, *AICL*, p. 40, see also XV, I, 13, *ibid.*, p. 19 and note 6.

613. *Anab.*, VI, 17, 18 and 20, *IIA*, pp. 160-62, 165; see also his *Indika*, pt. I, Ch. 2, *AIMA*, 1st edn., p. 183 and note 1.

614. *Bib. Hist.*, XVII, 104, *IIA*, p. 296.

615. Cf. Arrian *Indika*, pt. II, Chs. XVII ff, in *CNES*, p. 156.

616. *AIT*, pp. 146-48; see also J. Ph. Vogel, "Notes on Ptolemy", in *BSOAS*, vol. XIV, pt. I, p. 84; Law, *HGAI*, p. 117.

on the authority of Nearkhos says, "this river also forms a delta by its two mouths, no way inferior to that Egypt, which, in the Indian language, is called Pattala".[617] Dionysios periegetes also supports the view that it was "called in the tongue of the natives, Patalene"[618] Pliny quoting Onesikritos and Nearkhos as his two chief authorities clearly mentions "Patala, a celebrated port".[619] He further says that it lies at the mouth of the Indus triangular in shape 220 miles in breadth.[620] Nonnos has only made a passing reference to it.[621]

The ancient city of Patala in Lower Sindh also known as Pāṭalpur or Potalpurī seems to have derived its name from the Sanskrit word Poṭala, i.e., the "harbour" or "a station for ships". It was obviously a port town. It is definitely Pāṭṭana of the *Gaṇa-Pāṭha* on Pāṇini (IV, 1, 14) and Pāṭṭanaprastha of Patañjali (V, 2, 104) and Patasila or Pitasila of Hiuen-Tsang. It is curious to note that the name "Poṭala" has been consistenly applied to a city in the Delta of the Indus in the Buddhist writings of Tibet.

The absence of any concrete evidence in the classics about the geographical position of the city of Patala sparked off different kinds of speculation about its identification. The only clue which we can from the narratives of Arrian (*Anab.*, VI, 17) and Curtius (*Hist. of Alex.*, IX, 8) is that it was not very far from Brāhmaṇa, the city of the brāhmaṇas. This very indication provided solid ground for some writers to identify it with Brāhmaṇābād or modern Bahmanābād, four miles south-west from Thatha, or with the latter itself.[622] But this does not appear to be very much convincing because of the fact that the city of Patala was either at or near the head of the Delta, which may not be the position of either of them. This city in Alexander's time stood where the river Indus bifurcated. And hence, Major General Haig's supposition that it was not far from a spot which lies 35 miles south-east of Haidarabad[623] may be taken as tenable to some extent. Its identification with ancient Pāṭalpur is absolutely correct, but its identification with

---

617. *Indika*, Pt. II.
618. *Bassarika*, LI. 1080-1165, *AICL*, p. 188.
619. *Hist. Nat.*, Bk. II. Ch. 73 (75), *AICL*, p. 109.
620. *Ibid.*, VI, 21 (23) cf. Megasthenes, *Indika*, Frag. LVI, *AIMA*, 1st edn., p. 153, see also p. 141, note.
621. *Dionysiaka*, Bk. XXVI, *AICL*, p. 198.
622. Rennell, *MMH*, pp. 129-31; Vincent, *Voyage of Nearchus*, pp. 144 ff; Burnes, *op. cit.*, vol. III, p. 81; M'Murdo, *JRAS*, vol. I, p. 24; Wilson, *Ar. Ant.*, pp. 207-8; *HA*, p. 406, Baveridge, *Comp. Hist. Ind.*, vol. I, pp. 37-38; *AIIC*, p. 33; see also C. Speir, *Phases of Indian Civilization*, pp. 211-12.
623. See his *The Indus Delta Country*, p. 19.

modern Haidarabad (the native capital of Sind), 47 miles to the south-west of the ruined city of Brāhmaṇābād, and 85 miles from Laribandar (or ancient Debal, a site between Karachi and Thatha)[624] is not beyond question . The identity of Haidarabad and Nirankoṭ of the Arab historians and geographers is a well-established fact. In fact, the city of Patala in Alexander's time was the capital of Lower Sindh. It was at a distance of 30 miles from Haidarabad or near the very ancient site of Brahmana or Brāhmaṇābād. The distance between the two ancient cities, Brāhmana and Patala, was about 17 miles.

In support of the identification of Patala with the site near Brāhmaṇābād we feel necessary to add that the base of the Delta was reckoned by Aristoboulos at 1000 stadia (or 115 miles); by Nearkhos at 1800 stadia and by Onesikritos at 2000 stadia, as quoted by Strabo.[625] Onesikritos mistakenly compares it in size with the Egyptian Delta, which has a base of 1300 stadia or 160 miles. The distance of Patala from the sea may be taken at from 1000 stadia or 115 miles up to 125 miles. Now, the distance of Haidarabad from the Ghāra, or western mouth of the Indis is 110 miles, and from the Kori or eastern mouth 135 miles. Thus, this city can unhesitatingly be identified with the site at some distance from present Haidarabad.

The local tradition recorded in the Sanskrit books of the *Brāhmaṇas* of Sehwan also confirms it that the ancient name of Patala city near the city of the brāhmaṇas quite far from Haidarabad was Pāṭalipurī, of Kabul Chichapalapur and of Multān Prahlādapur.[626] Strabo records that Patalene was reduced by Alexander.[627] Most of the ancient towns and cities in Sindh were re-designated by the brāhmaṇas as well as the Mohammedans.

It has been rightly observed that ". . . the Punjab and Sindh republics were studded with numerous and prosperous cities".[628]

In the time of the author of the *Periplus* (the last quarter of the first century AD), the capital of Lower Sindh was Minnagara, "City of the Min", which was the Hindu name for the Indo-Scythians or the Śakas and Yueh-chi. It was called so because of its occupation by the Pārthians (Dahae Scythians from the Oxus) who gave the name of Indo-Scythia (Śakasthāna) to the lower valley of the Indus. That is why this city has been mentioned

624. For detail's see *CAGI*, pp. 235-40; St. Martin, *Étude*, pp. 180 ff; *IIA*, note U, pp. 356-57; W.W. Hunter, *op. cit.*, pp. 89-90; *AIT*, pp. 146-47, 369-70, note.

625. *Geog.*, XV, I, 33, *AICL*, p. 40.

626. J. Wilson, *JBBRAS*, vol. III (1850), p. 77.

627. *Op. cit.*

628. A.S. Altekar, *State and Government in Ancient India*, p. 136.

as "the metropolis of Scythia".[629] In the list of Isidor of Charax (or Kharax) also it figures as one of the cities of Sakastene, or Sejistan. Mr. Schoff, the translator and annotator of the text (*Periplus*), says : "Minnagara was a name given temporarily to several cities in India during the period of the occupation by the Scyths. After the collapse of the Indo-Scythian power these cities resumed their former names with their autonomy".[630]

He has identified it with the Patala — "the capital of the delta country".[631] The author of the text himself saw here some of the antiquities such as "ancient shrines, walls of forts", etc., of Alexander's time.[632] It was a market-town where the foreign merchants reached by ascending the river from another port-town in the maritime region to the north of Patala. This port-town has been called Barbaricum in the *Periplus*,[633] which is Barbarei of Ptolemy's *Geography* (VII, 1, 59)[634] and perhaps the Barce of Justin.[635] It stood at the mouth of the Indus river, and was a famous emporium of trade. From the *Periplus* it appears that the both Minnagara and Barbaricum were well-connected with each other through trade. It is said that the merchant vessels anchored at Barbaricum, where all their cargos were unloaded and carried up to metropolis (Minnagara) by the river, to the king.[636] The former place has been distinctly mentioned by the author as the "market-town". It is said that Barbaricum is the Hellenised form of the Hindu word —- "Bandar, port or possibly some name such as Bahardipur, which survives in the modern Delta".[637] It may be Shah-bander (Royal port) which now lies far inland to the east of the present main channel of the Indus. The frequent references to this place in the *Periplus* as an important centre of trade and commerce creates an impression that it must have been one of the flourishing urban centres in the Lower Indus Valley during the period concerned. Both the towns mentioned above were abandoned at a much later period.

Cunningham has judiciously identified Minnagara with the city of Thatha, situated

---

629. *Periplus*, sec. 38, p. 37.
630. *Ibid.*, p. 165.
631. *Ibid.*, p. 166.
632. *Ibid.*, Sec. 41, p. 39.
633. *Ibid.*, Secs. 38-39, pp. 37, 165.
634. *AIT*, p. 146.
635. *Hist.*, XII. 10.
636. *Periplus*, Sec. 39, pp. 37-38.
637. *Ibid.*, Sec. 38, p. 165.

at the distance of 3 miles from the western bank of the Indus, or 2 days' journey from Laribandar. Minnagara, according to him, is Manhābari of the Arab geographers, which is placed on the western bank of the Indus at 2 days' journey from Debal. In modern times the ships anchored at Laribandar from where the merchants carried their goods to Thatha either by land or by water.[638] This reminds us of position of Minnagara and Barbaricum in the first century AD. Vincent has wrongly placed the former at the distance of about 60 miles above Thatha.[639] M'Murdo places it on the Lohāna river, not far from Brāhmaṇa, and he identifies it with Bi-nagara or Agri-nagara of Ptolemy.[640] But this proposition is very confusing. Bi-nagara, as mentioned earlier, appears to be completely different city from Minnagara position wise. Agri-nagar was, of course, the later appellation of Minnagara. It was in the possession of a chief by caste an Agri, which is believed to have descended from Alexander. It is compatible with our supposition that it must have been a city bearing this name in the first half of the second century AD Barbaricum is generally identified with the "ruined town of Bhampura, situated at the head of the Ghāra creck, which is supposed by the natives to be the site of the most ancient seaport in Sindh".[641] The importance of Minnagara and Barbaricum as two chief centres of trade and commerce in the lower valley of the Indus has been acknowledged by all those scholars who made little investigation into the subject.

Curtius (*Hist. of Alex.*, IX, 10) says that Alexander himself founded several towns during his long stay in Lower Sind, probablly before his departure from India in early 325 BC. But the details thereof are not yet available. I, therefore, dismiss it as a blatant lie.

Pliny, quoting Megasthenes, makes a mention of 300 cities that belonged to the people adjoining the island of Patale.[642] There seems to be palpable exaggeration in his statement with regard to the number of cities. These cities in all probability include the villages also. However the people who are said to be in possession of the cities belonged to different areas. They include the tribes who occupied the territories between Śikārpur and Mithānkoṭ on the western bank of the Indus. The other tribes to whom the cities belonged are Syrieni or Suriyanis occupying the territories near the Indus in the

638. *CAGI*, pp. 243-44.

639. *Periplus*, p. 349.

640. *JRAS*, vol. I, p. 31; see also *AIT*, pp. 152, 156, 372, note.

641. *CAGI*, p. 247.

642. *Hist. Nat.*, VI, 21 (23) cf. Megasthenes, Frag, LVI, *AIMA*, 1st edn., pp. 147-48 and note.

neighbourhood of Bhakar or Bakkar; Darangae or Jhadejas of Kacch; Kokaris now settled on the banks of lower Sutlej; Nharonis of Baluchistan with ancestral seat in regions to the east of the Indus; and Godiarei, Nereae, Olostae, etc., of Baluchisatan.[643]

The towns situated to the west of the lower Indus within the geographical imits of India are also worthy of our notice. One of the famous port towns of ancient times has been called by Nearkhos Krokala or Krokola, where he himself stayed for twenty-four-days in the course of the voyage. He found its harbour so large and commodious that he dignified it with the great conqueror's name, as stated by Arrian.[644] This town, which is identical with the Kolaka of Ptolemy, can undountedly be identified with modern Karachi.[645] This identification does not rest on the slender ground. It is rather confirmed by the fact that "the district in which Karachi is situated is called Karkalla to this day".[646] According to Nearkhos, this island town was situated oppostie the river Arbis at a distance of 70 stadia. This is the river on the eastern bank of which the territory of the people of the maritime region immediately adjoining the Indus called Arabitae (the tribesmen of the Dravidian stock, popularly known as Arava), was situated. The said town was "150 stadia, or 17¼ miles, from the western mouth of the Indus, which agrees exactly with the relative position of Karachi and the mouth of the Ghāra river".[647] Pliny, quoting from the *Journal of the Voyage* of Onesikritos and Nearkhos, states that "the town of Arbis" was founded by the latter in the course of the voyage. He further adds on their authorities that a city, "Xylenopolis" was founded by Alexander.[648] The town of Arbis perhaps corresponds in position with that of Aroba or Arba at the mouth of the river of the said name, which belonged to the Arabitae.[649] Pliny's statement, that it was built by Nearkhos, is probably based on his misunderstanding. It is also not sufficiently explained where and near what river Xylinopolis was founded. It is perhaps a Greek compound meaning either "Timber-town" or "Wooden-town", which was situated, no doubt, on the western bank of the western arm of the Indus, and probably near the island of Krokola.

The Oritae or Horitae (Another Draviḍian tribe represented by the modern Brahui)

643. *Hist. Nat.*, see also James Tod, *AAR*, vol. I, p. 86.

644. *Indika*, pt. II, Ch. 21.

645. See M'Murdo, *JRAS*, vol. I, p. 42.

646. Burnes, *op. cit.*, vol. I, p. 10.

647. *CAGI*, p. 258.

648. *Hist. Nat.*, VI, 23 (26), *AICL*, pp. 110-11.

649. See Heeren, *Historical Researches*, vol. I, p. 297.

occupied an extensive territory on the western bank of the Arbis. The region inhabited by them was known as Ora. Their capital called Rhambakia, according to an unanimous testimony of Arrian,[650] Curtius[651] and Diodorus,[652] was originally a large village, but later it was converted by Alexander into a city. He, hoping that it would rise to be a rich and populous city, got it colonised and provided all necessary infrastructure required for the purpose concerned. The foundation of thc city was laid by Alexander and its superstructure was later raised by Leonnatus, who was left behind to complete it. The latter was entrusted with the responsibility to look after the peopling of the new city. Its new population comprised largerly the people from the Pashtu country (Arachosians), which has been hinted at by Curtius.[653] The native people and the Greeks had already occupied the place which roose to be a city of great importance. Diodorus reveals that "it was built on a very favourable site near the sea but above the reach of the highest tides". There was gradual increase in the urban population. The new city was named after Alexander as Alexandria. This is not only recorded by the former's historians, but also by his two famous companions, Onesikritos and Nearkhos, whom quoting Pliny says: "Alexandria was built by Leonnatus by Alexander's order in the territories of this people (Horitae)".[654] Pliny has himself described it as a "fine city defended by marshes..."[655]. It appears in the *Periplus* as "Rhambacia",[656] and in Ptolemy's *Geography* as "Rhambakia", the capital city of the Rhamnai (the Ramaṇas of the *Mahābhārata* and the Ramaṭhas of the Purāṇas) whose early seat was in the land of the "Oreitai" before they settled in Gedrosia (Baluchistan),[657] west of modern Karachi. It is said to have been at no great distance from the modern Las Bela. According to Holdich, its whole neighbourhood is full of evidences of early occupation,[658] but the exact site is undetermined. Cunningham has placed it at the western boundary of the Oritae at a place called Malana "to the east of Rās Mālān or Cape Mālān of the present day, about twenty miles to the west of the

650. *Anab.*, VI, 21, 22; *Indika*, pt. II, Ch. 23.

651. *Hist. Alex.*, IX, 10, 34.

652. *Bib. Hist.*, XVII, 104, 8.

653. *Hist. Alex.*, IX, 10, 7.

654. *Hist. Nat.*, VI, 23 (26), *AICL*, p. 111.

655. *Ibid.*, VI, 20.

656. Sec. 37, pp. 161-63.

657. *AIT*, pp. 159, 319-22, 375-76, note; see also Banerji, *PAHI*, pp. 81-82.

658. *Gates of India*, pp. 320, 372.

Aghor river".[659] But his identification of the city with "Rāmbāgh"[660] seems to be a mere deduction or fanciful notion.

The city, Rhambakia, has been described by Stephanus or Byzantium in his *In Voce Alexandria* as the "sixteenth Alexandria", near the bay of Melane. It is worthy of remark that Alexander during his nineteen months' stay in India built new cities, ports and roads on the lines of his marches, which became radiating points of Hellenism. It has been correctly stated that his military and non-military colonies, both large and small, in India were far numerous. All of these had previously been in the occupation of native urban communities, and some of them were large and important towns. Many cities were founded by him with Greek population, including his disabled soldiers, in oriental environment. His colonisation marked the opening of a new era in the economic life of the ancient world. "The new and momentous feature of it was the transformation of the oriental marts into business centres of a type hitherto unknown to the East. Most of his colonies were undoubtedly Greek city-states not only from the political and social but also from the economic point of view".[661]

The towns or cities of ancient Gedrosia (Baluchistan), a dependency of Sindh, received the notices of only few classical writers. Arrian on the authority of Aristoboulos calls the capital of Gedrosia "Poura".[662] Strabo refers to it as the "royal city of the Gedrosioi", visited by Alexander.[663] It is identified with a town called Puhra, which is probably Banpur (in western Baluchistan) of the present day.[664] Ammianus Marcellinus says, "Gedrosia too has its cities. . . . The cities which are considered superior to the others are Sedratyra and Gynaeconlimen".[665] But these two unfortunately have not yet been identified. The

659. *CAGI*, p. 260.

660. *CAGI*, p. 261.

661. For details see M. Rostovtzeff, *SEHHW*, vol. I, pp. 131-33; see also H.A. Devies, *An Outline History of the World*, p. 147; Robertson, *HDAI*, p. 27.

662. *Anab*., VI, 22.

663. *Geog*., XV, II, 7, *AICL*, p. 86.

664. Heeren, *Historcal Researches*, vol. I, p. 270; Bunbury, *HAG*, vol. I, pp. 519-20; *AICL*, p. 86, note 3; see also A. Stein, "On Alexander's Route to Gedrosia", *Goeg. Jour*., vol. 102, nos. 5-6 (1943), pp. 193-227; "Notes on Explorations in Makran and other Parts of Southern Baluchistan", *Ind. Ant*., vol. 58 (1929), pp. 211-12; "An Archaeological Tour in Gedrosia", *MASI*, no. 43, Calcutta, 1931 (for its ancient boundary); *IIA*, note 5, pp. 357-58.

665. *History*, Bk. XXIII, Ch. 6, *AICL*, p. 94.

"Killouta" of Onesikritos and Nearkhos corresponds as nearly as possible with the town of Kilāt or Kalāt in modern Baluchistan.

The existence of towns and cities in different parts of north-west India testifies to the material prosperity of the people concerned. We find that several factors were responsible for the decline and fall of the towns and cities in north-western India as a whole. It is undeniable that in pre-Alexandrian period some cities in eastern Afghanistan were razed to the ground by the Persians. But the greater responsibility for their destruction can undoubtedly be assigned to Alexander and his mercenaries. In the course of their campaigns a large number of tribal people were put to sword and their towns and cities were assaulted, stormed, captured, damaged and destroyed. The survivors including the populace and potentates fled away to seek refuge in nearby safer places. Some towns and cities were set ablaze by their inhabitants themselves having lost all hopes to defend them. Some towns were deserted by the people out of fear and sheer frustration. A large section of the tribal people abandoned their respective original place, dispersed in different groups and took refuge in the neighbouring as well as far distant areas, which resulted in the decrease of the urban population and decline of the towns and cities. More or less the same story was repeated in the Punjab. This particular fact is well attested by the statements of the classical authors themselves. Both Julius Valerius[666] and Aelian[667] have attributed the destruction of the tribal cities in general to the Macedonians. The Brāhmaṇic cities in the Punjab and Sindh met the same fate. Here this fact should not be lost sight of that Alexander not only destroyed but also built the cities. Somewere re-built by his successors as well as by the indigenous population. However, some towns in the Punjab in particular were demolished by the White Hūṇas in the early part of the sixth century AD. An evidence to this effect has been furnished particularly by Kosmas Indikopleustes. The indication given by him show that they sacked and captured some Indian cities including "one that was surrounded by water and was thus protected from assault".[668] The inundation of the areas inhabited by the urban communities in the Punjab, which may be attributed to the flood waters of its rivers, particularly the Hydraotes and Akesines, also resulted in the decline of some towns there. And so is the case with some towns of Sindh which were devastated by the river Indus. It has been remarked that "for ages the Indus has been pushing its bed

666. *The Itinerary of Alexander the Great*, Chs. 104-16, *AICL*, pp. 151-55.

667. *On the Peculiarities of Animals*, Bk XV, Ch. XXI, *AICL*, p. 145.

668. *The Christian Topography*, Bk. XI, *AICL*, pp. 163-64.

across the valley from east to west, generally by the gradual process of erosion, which effectually wipes out every trace of town and village on its banks; but at times also by a more or less sudden shifting of its water into entirely new channel; leaving large tracts of country to go to waste, and forcing the inhabitants of many a populous place to abandon their old homes, and follow the river in search of new settlements".[669]

Both Nearkhos and Aristoboulos, as quoted by Strabo, speak of the rising of the rivers in the Punjab and Sindh and the following inundations of the plains. They concur also in stating that "the cities built upon mounds become islands, as in Egypt and Ethiopia and that the inundation ceases after the setting of Arcturus when the waters subside",[670] Aristoboulus says that "when he was sent on some business, he saw a tract of land deserted which contained more than a thousand cities with their villages, for the Indus, having forsaken its proper channel, truned itself into another on the left much deeper into which it burst like a cataract . . . for this had been raised by the inundations. . . . ."[671]

The convulsion of the nature, particularly the earthquakes, also resulted in the destruction of some cities. The remains of the ancient cities in the Punjab and Sindh constitute the mute evidence to the urban settlements there. Most of the towns and cities in general had eclipsed by the seventh century AD. However, some towns in Sindh fell under the occupation of the Arabs between AD 711 and 713. The glory and glamour of the old cities thereafter diminished. Some continued to exist even beyond that period. Some in spite of being occupied by the rulers of several dynasties continued to flourish for centuries, and they are still found in excellent state of preservation. The extensive ruins of ancient cities (as described in the classical sources) found in different parts of north-western India constitute the distinguishing hallmark of the past urban life of the people concerned.

669. *JRAS* (New Series), vol. XVI, p. 281.
670. Strabo, *Geog.*, XV, 1, 18, *AICL*, p. 23.
671. *Ibid.*, XV, 1, 19, *ibid.*, p. 25.

# General Bibliography

## Original Sources: Texts, Translations and Commentaries

### Literary Sources


THE VEDAS

*Atharvaveda Saṁhitā*, ed. with Sāyaṇa's comm. by S.P. Pandit, Bombay, 1895-98; trans. with comm. by R.T.H. Griffith (*The Hymns of the Atharvaveda*), 2 vols. Vārāṇasī, 1896-97, rept. 1968; trans. by W.D. Whitney (*On the Vedas*), HOS, Cambridge, 1905, 2nd Indian rept., Delhi 1971, Calcutta, 1972; text with Hindi trans. and comm. by Dayānanda Sarasvatī, Dayānanda Saṁsthān, Delhi, vs 2032; ed. with Hindi trans. and Sāyaṇa's comm. by R. Sharma Ācārya, 2 vols. Bareli, 1973, 1975.

*Ṛgveda Saṁhitā*, ed. with Sāyaṇa's comm. by F. Max Müller, 2nd edn., London, 1890-92; trans. by R.T.H. Griffith, Benares, 1896-97; trans. by H.H. Wilson, 6 vols., London, 1866-88; ed. with Hindi trans. and Sāyaṇa's comm. by R. Sharma Ācārya, 4 vols., Bareli, 1974-75.

*Yajurveda, Taittirīya Saṁhitā*, ed. by A. Weber, *Ind. Stud.*, XI and XII, Berlin, 1871-72; ed. with the comm. of Mādhava, Calcutta, 1854-99; trans. by A.B. Keith (*The Veda of the Black Yajus School*), HOS, XVIII and XIX, 1914, rept. Delhi, 1967.

THE BRĀHMAṆAS

*Aitareya Brāhmaṇa*, ed. and trans. by M. Haug, Vārāṇasī, 1976-77; trans. by A.B. Keith, HOS, vol. XXV, Cambridge, Mass., 1920, rept. Delhi, 1971.

*Gopatha Brāhmaṇa*, ed. by R.L. Mitra and H. Vidyābhūṣaṇa, Calcutta, 1872.

*Śatapatha Brāhmaṇa*, ed. by A. Chinnaswami Śāstrī, P. Śāstrī and R.N. Dikshita, 2nd edn., Vārāṇasī, 1984.

THE ĀRAṆYAKA

*Taittirīya Āraṇyaka*, ed by H.N. Apte, Poona, 1898.

THE DHARMA-ŚĀSTRA

*Manu-Smṛti*, ed. with the *Manvartha-Muktāvalī* comm. of Kullūka Bhaṭṭa and the *Maṇiprabhā* Hindi comm. of H.G. Śāstrī by G.S. Nene, Vārāṇasī, 1970.

THE EPICS

*Mahābhārata*, ed. with Hindi trans. by S. Dāmodar Sātavalekar and Śrutiśīla Śarmā, Pāradi (Gujarat):

*Ādi Parva*, 1968.

*Anuśāsana Parva*, 1978.

*Āraṇyaka Parva*, 2 vols., 1969.

*Āśramavāsika Parva*, 1977.

*Āśvamedhika Parva*, 1977.

*Bhīṣma Parva*, 1972.

*Droṇa Parva*, 1975.

*Karṇa Parva*, 1973.

*Mahāprasthānika Parva*, 1977.

*Mausala Parva*, 1977.

*Sabhā Parva*, 1982.

*Śalya Parva*, 1973.

*Śānti Parva*, 2 vols., 1979-80.

*Svargārohaṇa Parva*, 1977.

*Udyoga Parva*, 1969.

*Virāṭa Parva*, 1969.

*Vālmikī-Rāmāyaṇa*, ed. by D.R. Mankad, Oriental Research Institute, Baroda, 1965; trans. by R.T.H. Griffith, London, 1870.

*Ayodhyā Kāṇḍa*, ed. with Hindi trans. by Akhilānanda, Amritsar, vs 2019.

*Bāla Kāṇḍa*, ed. with Hindi trans. of Yudhiṣṭhira Mīmāṁsaka by Akhilānanda, Amritsar, vs 2025.

*Kiṣkindhā Kāṇḍa*, ed. with Hindi trans. by Akhilānanda, Amritsar, vs 2021.

*Uttara Kāṇḍa*, cf. *Vālmikī-Rāmāyaṇa Kośa* by R.K. Rai, Vārāṇasī, 1965.

*Yuddha (Laṅkā) Kāṇḍa*, text with Hindi trans. of Vijayapāpla, Bahālagarh, vs 2029.

## PURĀṆAS

*Agni Purāṇa*, ed. by R.L. Mitra, Calcutta, 1873-79; trans. by M.N. Dutt, 2 vols. Cacutta, 1903-04; text with Hindi trans. of T. Jha and G.S. Tripāṭhī, Prayāg, 1986.

*Bhāgavata Purāṇa*, text with Hindi trans. and annotation, 2 vols., 8th edn., Gorakhpur, Samvat, 2040; ed. with Eng. trans. by C.L. Goswami, 2 pts., 2nd edn., Gorakhpur, 1982.

*Bhaviṣya Purāṇa*, Veṅkaṭeśvara Press, Bombay, 1910; ed. with Hindi trans. by R. Sharma Ācārya, 2 vols., Bareli, 1978.

*Brahma Purāṇa*, ed. by H.N. Apte, Ānandāśrama Skt. Series, Poona, 1895; text with Hindi trans. of T. Jha, Prayāg, 1976.

*Brahmāṇḍa Purāṇa*, Veṅkaṭeśvara Press, Bombay, 1913.

*Brahmavaivartta Purāṇa*, ed. with Hindi trans. by T. Jha, Allahabad, 1985.

*Garuḍa Purāṇa*, Eng. trans. by M.N. Dutt, Calcutta, 1908, rept. Delhi, 1983.

*Harivaṁśa Purāṇa*, ed. by N. Mukhopādhyāya, ASB, Calcutta, 1858; R. Kinjawadekar, Poona, 1936; text with Hindi trans. and comm., 4th edn., Gorakhpur, Samvat, 2044.

*Kālikā Purāṇa*, ed. by V.N. Śāstrī, Vārāṇasī, 1972; ed. with Hindi trans. by Chamanlal Gautam, 2 vols. Bareli, 1973.

*Kūrma Purāṇa*, ed. with Hindi trans. of Shree Chaudhari Shree Nārāyaṇa Singh by Ānandasvarūpa Gupta, Vārāṇasī, 1972.

*Liṅga Purāṇa*, Veṅkaṭeśvara Press, Bombay, 1927.

*Mārkaṇḍeya Purāṇa*, ed. by K.M. Banerjee, BIS, ASB, Calcutta, 1862; ed with Hindi trans. by Dharmendra Nath Śāstrī, Meerut, 1983; trans. by F.E. Pargiter, BIS, ASB, Calcutta, 1904.

*Matsya Purāṇa,* Ānandāśrama Skt. Series, Poona, 1907; text with Hindi trans., 2 vols., Gorakhpur, 1985; ed. with trans. of various oriental scholars and notes of B.C. Majumdar, S.C. Vasu, H.H. Wilson, Bentley, Wilford and others by J.D. Akhtar, vol. I, SBA, Delhi, 1972.

*Padma Purāṇa*, ed. by V.N. Mandalika, Ānandāśrama Skt. Series, Poona, 1893-94; *Svargakhaṇḍa*, ed. by Aśoka Chatterjee Śāstrī, Vārāṇasī, 1972.

*Skanda Purāṇa*, ed. by Vāsudeva Śāstrī, 3 pts., Ānandāśrama Skt. Series, Poona, 1893.

*Vāmana Purāṇa*, ed. with Hindi trans. of G.C. Vedānta Śāstrī, Shree Chaudhari Shree Nārāyaṇa Singh and G.S. Rai by Ānandasvarūpa Gupta, Vārāṇasī, 1968.

*Varāha Purāṇa*, ed. by P.H. Śāstrī, BIS, ASB, Calcutta, 1893.

*Vāyu Purāṇa*, Ānandāśrama Skt. Series, Poona, 1905; ed. by R.L. Mitra, 2 vols. BIS, ASB, Calcutta, 1880-88; text with Hindi trans of R.P. Tripāṭhī Śāstrī, Prayāg, 1987.

*Viṣṇu Purāṇa*, ed. by J. Vidyāsāgara, Calcutta, 1882; text with Hindi trans. of Muni Lal Gupta, 9th edn., Gorakhpur, Samvat, 2041; trans. by M.N. Dutt, Calcutta, 1894, and H.H. Wilson, Calcutta, 1961.

*Viṣṇudharmottara Mahāpurāṇa*, Veṅkaṭeśvara Press, Bombay, 1912.

## OTHER LITERARY WORKS

*Abhijñāna-Śakuntalā* of Kālidāsa, ed. with Rāghavabhaṭṭ's comm. by N.B. Godabole and K.P. Parab, Bombay, 1883; Eng. trans. by W. Jones, London, 1790.

*Amarakośa* of Amara Siṁha, text with the *Maṇiprabhā* Hindi comm. of H.G. Śāstrī, Vārāṇasī, 1957.

*Arthaśāstra* of Kauṭilya, ed. by R. Shamaśāstrī, Mysore, 1909; trans. by R. Shamaśāstrī, Bangalore, 1915; ed. with Hindi trans. by Vachaspati Gairola, Vārāṇasī, 1984.

*Aṣṭādhyāyī* of Pāṇini, ed. with German trans. by Von Otto Bohtlingk (Pāṇini's *Grammatik*, Leipzig, 1887; ed. by B.M. Sharma, Vārāṇasī, 1948; ed. with Eng. trans. by S.C. Vasu, 7 vols., Allahabad, 1891-98, rept. 1929; ed. with comm. by Brahmadatta Jijñāsu, pt. I, 1st edn. Amritsar, vs 2021, pt. II, 2nd edn. Amritsar, vs 2031.

*Bṛhat Saṁhitā* of Varāhamihira, ed. by H. Kern, BIS, ASB, Calcutta, 1865; ed. with Hindi trans. and comm. by B.P. Mishra, Bombay, 1952.

*Daśakumāracarita* of Daṇḍin, ed. by P. Banerji, Calcutta, 1888; ed. with Eng. trans. by M.R. Kale, 4th edn. Delhi, 1966.

*Kāśikā* (comm. on the *Aṣṭādhyāyī* of Pāṇini) by Paṇḍita Vāmana and Jayāditya, ed. by Bāla Śāstrī, Vārāṇasī, 1898.

*Kāvyamīmāṁsā* of Rajaśekhara, ed. with *Prakāśa* Hindi comm. by G.S. Rai, Vārāṇasī, 1964.

*Mahābhāṣya* of Patañjali, ed. by F. Kielhorn, 3 vols., Bombay Skt Series, Bombay 1880-85.

*Mālavikāgnimitra* of Kālidāsa, ed. by K.P. Parab, Bombay, 1915; Eng. trans. by C.H. Tawney, Calcutta

1875 and 1891; text with the comm. of Kāṭayavema and Eng. trans. of M.R. Kale, revd. by J.L. Dave and S.A. Upādhyāya, Delhi, 1985.

*Meghadūta* of Kālidāsa, ed. with Eng. trans and the comm. *Saṁjīvanī* of Mallinātha by M.R. Kale, Delhi 1969.

*Mudrārākṣasa* of Viśākhadatta, ed. with the *Śaśikalā* Sanskrit and Hindi comms. by S.V. Singh, Vārāṇasī, 1973.

*Nirukta* of Yāska, ed. with Hindi trans by Uma Shankar Sharma, Vārāṇasī, 1966.

*Raghuvaṁśa* of Kālidāsa, ed. with the comm. *Sañjivanī* of Mallinātha by K.M. Joglekar, Bombay 1916; ed. with Eng. trans. and Mallinātha's comm. by M.R. Kale (Cantos I-V), Delhi, 1972.

*Rājataraṅgiṇī* of Kalhaṇa, trans. by M.A. Stein, vol. I, Delhi, 1960.

BUDDHIST WORKS

*Aṅguttara Nikāya*, ed. by R. Morris and E. Hardy, 5 vols. PTS, London, 1885-1900; comm. or *aṭṭhakathā* (*Manorathapūranī*, by Buddhaghoṣa), ed. by M. Walleser and H. Knopp, 4 vols., London, 1924-40.

*Apadāna* (part of the *Khuddaka Nikāya*), not yet edited.

*Aśokāvadāna*, ed. by S.K. Mukhopadhyaya, Delhi, 1963.

*Atthasālin* (comms. on the *Abhidhamma Piṭaka*, by Buddhaghoṣa ed. by E. Müller, PTS, London, 1897; trans. by P. Maung Tin, 2 vols., PTS, nos. 8-9, London, 1920-21.

*Avadānaśataka*, ed. by J.S. Speyer, 2 vols., St. Petersburg, 1906.

*Bodhisattvāvadāna-Kalpalatā*, cf. *Sanskrit Buddhist Literature of Nepal*, by R.L. Mitra, Calcutta, 1882.

*Buddhavaṁsa* (part of the *Khuddaka Nikāya*), ed. by R. Morris, PTS, London, 1882; trans. by B.C. Law, PTS, London, 1938.

*Cūḷavaṁsa*, by Dhammakitti, Sumaṅgala and others, ed. by W. Geiger, 2 vols., PTS, London, 1925-27; trans. by W. Geiger, 2 vols., Colombo, 1953.

*Dhammapada* (part of the *Khuddaka Nikāya*) ed. by S.S. Thera, PTS, London, 1914; trans. from Pāli by F. Max Müller, SBE, vol. X, pt. I, Oxford, 1881, rept. Delhi, 1973; ed. with Sanskrit and Hindi trans. by Rāhul Saṅkṛtyāyana, Sāranātha, 1933, 2nd edn., Lucknow, 1957; comm. (*Dhammapada-aṭṭhakathā* by Buddhaghoṣa), ed. by H.C. Norman and L.S. Tailang, 5 vols. in 6 pts., PTS, London, 1906-15.

*Dīgha Nikāya*, ed. by T.W. Rhys Davids and J.E. Carpenter, 3 vols., PTS, London, 1890-1911, rept. 1947-60; trans. by T.W. and C.A.F. Rhys Davids (*The Dialogues of the Buddha*), 3 vols., PTS, London, 1899-1921, rept. 1959; comm. (*Sumaṅgalavilāsinī*, by Buddhaghoṣa), ed. by Rhys Davids and J.E. Carpenter, 3 vols., PTS, London, 1886-1932.

*Dīpavaṁsa* (a chronicle of Ceylon), ed. and trans. by H. Oldenberg, London, 1879, rept. Delhi, 1982.

*Divyāvadāna*, ed. by E.B. Cowell and R.A. Neil, Cambridge, 1886, rept. 1976, ed. by P.L. Vaidya, Delhi, 1959.

*Jātaka* (part of the *Khuddaka Nikāya*), ed. by V. Fausböll, 6 vols., London, 1877-97; trans. by various scholars under the editorship of E.B. Cowell, 7 vols., Cambridge, 1895-1913.

*Kalpadruma-avadāna*, cf. R.L. Mitra, *op. cit.*

*Kathāvatthu*, by Buddhaghoṣa, ed. Minayev, JPTS, London, 1889.

## *Coins and Inscriptions*

Allan, J., *A Catalogue of the Indian Coins in the British Museum, Ancient India*, London, 1936.

Bhandarkar, D.R., *Inscriptions of Aśoka*, Calcutta, 1920.

Chaudhuri, R.K., *Select Inscriptions of Bihar*, Patna, 1958.

Cunningham, A., *Coins of Ancient India from the earliest times down to the seventh century* AD, London, 1891, rept. Vārāṇasī, 1971.

———, *Coins of the Indo-Scythians, Śakas, and Kushans*, London, 1888, rept. Vārāṇasī, 1971.

———, *Coins of Medieval India*, London, 1893.

Fleet, J.F., *Corpus Inscriptionum Indicarum*, vol. III, *Inscriptions of the Early Gupta Kings*, Calcutta, 1888.

Gardner, P., *The Coins of the Greek and Scythic Kings of Bactria and India*, London, 1886.

King, L.W. and Thompson, R.C. (ed. & tr.), *The Sculptures and Inscription of Darius the Great on the Rock of Behistūn in Persia*, London, 1907.

Konow, S., *Corpus Inscriptionum Indicarum*, vol. II, Delhi, 1929.

Rapson, E.J., *Indian Coins,* Vārāṇasī, 1969.

Sewell, R. and Aiyangar, K., *The Historical Inscriptions of Southern India*, Madras University Historical Seris, No. V, 1932.

Sircar, D.C., (ed.), *Select Inscriptions Bearing on Indian History and Civilization*, vol. I (from the sixth century BC to the sixth century AD), Calcutta, 1965. Apart from other inscriptions, this work also contains old Persian inscriptions, *Behistūn*, *Persepolis* and *Naqsh-i-Rustam inscription* of Darius, and *Persepolis inscriptions* of Xerxes (pp. 4-14). Some of these inscriptions are also in *JAOS*, vol. 72, no. 1, Jan-March 1952, pp. 9 ff.

Smith, V.A., *Catalogue of the Coins in the Indian Museum*, Calcutta, vol. I, *Coins of Ancient India*, Oxford, 1906, rept. Vārāṇasī, 1972.

Whitehead, R.B., *Catalogue of the Coins in the Punjab Museum,* Lahore, vol. I, *Indo-Greek Coins*, Oxford, 1914.

## *Modern Works*

Abbott, E., *History of Antiquity*, trans. from the German of Max Duncker, London, 1880.

Adams, R., *The Evolution of Urban Society*, London, 1966.

Agrawal, D.P. and Ghosh, A. (ed.), *Radiocarbon and Indian Archaeology*, Bombay, 1973.

Agrawala, P.K. (ed.), *Itihāsa-Darśana* (collection of papers of the late V.S. Agrawala), Vārāṇasī, 1978.

Agrawala, V.S., *India as Known to Pāṇini* (A Study of the Cultural Material in the *Aṣṭādhyāyī*), Vārāṇasī, 1963.

———, *Bhārata Sāvitrī* (an indepth historical study of the *Mahābhārata*), vols. I and 2, 2nd edn. Delhi, 1977, vol. 3, 1st edn. Delhi, 1968.

———, *India as Described by Manu,* Vārāṇasī, 1970.

Ali, S.M., *The Geography of the Purāṇas*, Delhi, 1983.

Altekar, A.S., *State and Government in Ancient India*, Delhi, 1977.

———, "Ancient Towns and Cities in Gujarat," *Ind. Ant.*, vol. 54, 1925, p. 25f.

——— and Majumdar, R.C. (ed.), *The Age of the Vākāṭakas and the Guptas*, Delhi, 1954.

Allchin, B.R., *The Birth of Indian Civilization — India and Pakistan before 500 BC*, Harmondsworth, 1968.

———, *The Rise of Civilization in India and Pakistan*, Cambridge, 1982.

Anspach, A.E., *De Alexand'ri Magni Expeditione Indica*, London, 1903.

Anville, M.D., *Antiquite Geographique de l Inde*, Paris, 1775.

Bagchi, P.C., *Pre-Aryan and Pre-Dravidian in India* (Eng. trans. of original French articles by Sylvain Levi, J. Parzyluski & C.), Calcutta, 1929.

Banerji, N.R., *The Iron Age in India*, Delhi, 1965.

Banerji, R.D., *Prehistoric Ancient and Hindu India*, Calcutta, 1934, rept. 1950.

Banerji, S.C., *Kālidāsa-Kośa*, Vārāṇasī, 1968.

Baveridge, H., *A Compreshensive History of India*, vol. I, 1st edn. London, 1862, rept. 4th edn. Delhi, 1982.

Bellew, *Ethnography of Afghanistan*, Woking, 1891.

Bhandarkar, D.R., *Some Aspects of Ancient Indian Polity*, Banares, 1929.

———, *Carmichael Lectures on the Ancient History of India*, 1918, Calcutta, 1919.

———, *Commemorative Essays*, persented to Sri R.G. Bhandarkar, BORI, Poona, 1917.

Bhatt, J. (ed.), *Aśoka ke Dharmalekha*, Delhi, 1957.

Budge, E.A.W., *The Life and Exploits of Alexander the Great*, Cambridge, 1889.

Bunbury, E.H., *History of Ancient Geography Among the Greeks and Romans from the Earliest Ages till the Fall of the Roman Empire,* 2 vols., 1st edn. London, 1879, 2nd edn. New York, 1959.

Burnes, A., *Travels in Punjab, Bokhara*, etc., vol. I, 2nd edn. London, 1835.

Bury, J.B., *A History of Greece to the Death of Alexander the Great*, London, 1959.

Chakrabarti, D.K., "Concept of Urban Revolution in the Indian Context," *Purātattva*, No. 6, 1972-73, pp. 27-32.

———, "Beginning of Iron and Social Change in India," *Indian Studies: Past and persent,* Calcutta, vol. XIV, no. 4, 1973, pp. 329-38.

———, "The Beginning of Iron in India," *Antiquity*, vol. 50, 1976, pp. 114-24.

———, "Iron in Early Indian Literature," *JRAS*, no. 1, 1979, pp. 22-28.

Chakraborty, S.K., *A Study of Ancient Indian Numismatics*, Mymensing, 1931.

Chattopadhyaya, D.P. (ed.), *History and Society,* Calcutta, 1978.

Chattopadhyaya, S., *Racial Affinities of Early North Indian Tribes*, Delhi, 1973.

Childe, V. Gordon, "The Urban Revolution," *Town Planning Review*, Liverpool, vol. XXI, no. 1, 1950, pp. 3-17.

———, *What Happened in History*, Harmondsworth, 1942, rept. 1985.

———, *Man Makes Himself*, London, 1965.

———, "Civilisation, Cities and Towns," *Antiquity*, vol. XXXI, 1957, pp. 36-37.

Choudhuri, S.B., *Ethnic Settlements in Ancient India*, Calcutta, 1955.

Cowell, E.B. (ed.), *The History of India*, by M. Elphinstone, 9th edn. London, 1911.

Cunningham, A., *The Ancient Geography of India*, 1st edn. London, 1871, rept. Vārāṇasī, 1979.

Das, A.C., *Ṛgvedic India — Cultural History of India as depicted in the Ṛgveda*, Calcutta, 1921.

De, S.C., *Historicity of Rāmāyaṇa and the Indo-Aryan Society in India and Ceylon*, Delhi, 1976.

Devies, H.A., *An Outline History of the World*, Oxford, 1964.

Dutt, B.B., *Town Planning in Ancient India*, Calcutta, 1925.

Eck, D.L., *Banaras: City of Light*, London, 1983.

Elephinstone, M., "The Greek Accounts of India", reptd. from his *The History of India*, in *Ancient India* (a collection of writings of some authors reptd. from their respective original works), Delhi, 1983, pp. 11-33.

———, *An Account of the Kingdom of Kabul*, vol. I, 2nd edn. London, 1839.

Fairservis, W.A., *The Roots of Anceint India*, New York, 1971.

Feer, M.L., *A Study of the Jātakas*, Delhi, 1984.

Fick, R., *The Social Organisation in North-East India in Buddha's time*, trans. by S.K. Maitra, Calcutta, 1920.

Führer, A., *Monumental Antiquities and Inscriptions of North-Western Provinces and Oudh*, London, 1891.

Fuller, J.F.C., *The Generalship of Alexander the Great*, Dehradun, 1977.

Gerini, G.E., *Researches on Ptolemy's Geography of Eastern Asia*, London, 1909, 2nd edn. Delhi, 1974.

Ghosh, A., *The City in Early Historical India*, Simla, 1973.

Ghoshal, U.N., *A History of Indian Political Ideas*, Bombay, 1959.

Gupta, P., *Geographical Names in Ancient Indian Inscriptions (up to AD 650)*, Delhi, 1977.

Gupta S.P. and Ramachandran, K.S., (ed.), *Aspects of Indian History and Archaeology* (a collection of papers of H.D. Sankalia), Delhi, 1977.

Gupta S.P., "Two Urbanisation in India," *Purātattva*, no. 7, 1974, pp. 53-60.

Haig, M.R., *The Indus Delta Country — A Memoir Chiefly on its Ancient Geography and History*, 1st edn. London, 1894, rept. Gurgaon, 1974.

Hauser, Philip M. and Schnore, L.F., (ed.), *The Study of Urbanization*, London, 1965.

Heeren, A.H.L., *Historical Researches into the Politics, Intercourse and Trade of the Principal Nations of Antiquity*, vol. I, *Asiatic Nations*, Oxford, 1833.

———, *Manual of Ancient History: The Constitutions, the Commerce and the Colonies of the States of Antiquity*, Oxford, 1833.

Holdich, T.H., *The Gates of India*, London, 1910.

———, *The Indian Borderland*, Methuen, 1901.

Hopkins, E.W., *Great Epic of India*, 1st edn. New York, 1901, rept. Calcutta, 1969.

Humboldt, A.D. (ed.), *Central Asia*, vol. I, New York, 1843.

Hunter, W.W., "The Greeks in India," reptd. from his *The Indian Empire: Its Peoples, History and Products*, 3rd edn. London, 1882, in *Ancient India (supra)*, Delhi, 1983, pp. 86-96.

Hutchinson, J. and Vogel, J. Ph., *History of the Punjab Hill States*, 1st edn. Lahore, 1933, rept. Simla, 1982.

Jain, J.C., *Life in Ancient India as depicted in the Jaina Canon and Commentaries* (6th century BC to 17th century AD), Delhi, 1984.

Jain, K.P., *Some Historical Jaina Kings and Heroes*, Delhi, 1941.

Jayaswal, K.P., *Hindu Polity: A Constitutional History of India in Hindu Times*, pts. I & II, Bangalore, 1981.

——, "Places and Peoples in Aśoka's Inscriptions bearing on the Identification and Location of the Republics mentioned in his proclamations," *Ind. Ant.*, vol. LXII, 1933, pp. 121-33.

Kane, P.V., *Dharmaśāstra Kā Itihāsa*, vol. II, Lucknow, 1982.

——, "Ancient Cities and Towns mentioned in the *Mahābhāṣya*," *JBBRAS*, vol. XXVII, pt. 1, 1951, pp. 38-42.

Kennedy, J., "Some Notes on the *Periplus of the Erythraean Sea*," *JRAS*, 1916.

Kosambi, D.D., "The Beginning of the Iron Age in India," *Journal of the Economic and Social History of the Orient*, vol. VI, pt. 3, 1963, pp. 309-18.

——, *The Culture and Civilization of Ancient India in Historical Outline*, Delhi, 1972.

Lal, B.B., "Excavations at Hastināpur and Other Explorations in the Upper Gaṅgā and Sutlej Basins," *AI*, nos. 10 & 11, 1954-55, pp. 5 ff.

Lal, B.B. and Gupta, S.P. (ed.), *Frontiers of the Indus Civilization*, Delhi, 1984.

Lal, M., *Settlement, History and Rise of Civilization in Gaṅgā-Yamunā Doab from 1500 BC-300 AD*, Delhi, 1984.

Lassen, Chr., *Indische Alterthumskunde* (A German work on the History and Antiquities of India), 4 vols., 1st edn. Leipzig, 1847-62, vols. I & II, 2nd edn. Leipzig, 1867-74.

——, *De Pentapotamia Indica* (Ancient Geography and History of North-Western India based on Greek and Latin Sources), Bonn, 1827.

Law, B.C., *Historical Gleanings*, Vārāṇasī, 1976.

——, *India as Described in Early Texts of Buddhism and Jainism*, Delhi, 1980.

——, *Geography of Early Buddhism*, Vārāṇasī, 1973.

——, *Geographical Essays Relating to Ancient Geography of India*, Delhi, 1976.

——, *Kṣatriya Clans in Buddhist India*, Calcutta, 1922.

——, *Some Kṣatriya Tribes of Ancient India*, Calcutta, 1923, rept. Delhi, 1979.

——, *Ancient Mid-Indian Kṣatriya Tribes*, Calcutta, 1924.

——, *Tribes in Ancient India*, Bhandarkar Oriental Series, no. 4, Poona, 1943.

——, *Historical Geography of Ancient India*, 1st edn. Paris, 1954, rept. Delhi, 1976.

——, *The Magadhas in Ancient India*, Vārāṇasī, 1976.

——, *A History of Pāli Literature*, 2 vols., Delhi, 1983.

——, *Geographical Aspect of Kālidāsa's Works*, Delhi, 1976.

Macdonell, A.A., *History of Sanskrit Literature*, Oxford, 1936.

Macdonell, A.A. and Keith, A.B., *Vedic Index of Names and Subjects*, 2 vols., 1st edn. London, 1912, rept. 3rd edn. Indian Texts Series, Delhi, 1967.

MacMunn, G., *Martial Races of India*, Delhi, 1979.

Majumdar, A.K., *Early Hindu India: A Dynastic Study*, vol. I, Dhaka, 1917, rept. Delhi, 1981.

Majumdar, B.P., "Political Theory and Practices in the Mālava and Yaudheya Republics," *JIH*, vol. 47, pt.2, p. 306.

Majumdar, R.C., *Corporate Life in Ancient India*, Calcutta, 1920.

Malik, S.C., *Indian Civilization: The Formative Period*, Simla, 1968.

Marshall, John, *Taxila*, vol. I, 1st edn. Cambridge, 1951, 1st Indian rept. Vārāṇasī, 1975.

Masson-Oursel, P.&C., *Ancient India and Indian Civilization*, trans. from the French by M.R. Dobie, London, 1934, rept. 1951.

Martin, M.V., de st., *E'tude Sur La Geographie Grecque et Latine de l' Inde* (Geography of India as Derived from the Greek and Latin Sources), Paris, 1858.

Max Müller, F., *The Vedas* (collections of his lectures and Writings pub. in his various works), Vārāṇasī, 1969.

Mishra, D.P., *Studies in the Proto-History of India*, Delhi, 1971.

Motichandra, *Sārthavāha*, Patna, 1966.

———, *Geographical and Economic Studies in the Mahābhārata*, Lucknow, 1945.

Mukherjee, B.N., "Some Interesting Yaudheya Coins," *JAS*, vol. XX, nos. 1-4, 1978, pp. 36-37.

Mumford, L., *The City in History: Its Origin, Its Transformation and Its Prospects*, London, 1961.

Oppert, G., *Original Inhabitants of Bhāratavarṣa*, Delhi, 1972.

Pande, S.N., *Geographical Horizon of the Mahābhārata*, Vārāṇasī, 1980.

Pandey, R.B., *Bharatiya Itihāsa Kā Paricaya*, Vārāṇasī, 1963.

Pargiter, F.E., *Ancient Indian Historical Tradition*, 1st edn. London, 1922, rpt. Delhi, 1972.

———, *The Purāṇa Text of the Dynasties of the Kali Age,* Oxford, 1913, rept. Vārāṇasī, 1962.

Pearson, C., "Alexander, Porus and the Punjab," *Ind. Ant.,* vol. XXXIV, 1905, pp. 253 ff.

Piggott, S., *Some Cities of Ancient India*, Oxford, 1945.

Possehl, G.L. (ed.), *Ancient Cities of the Indus*, Delhi, 1979.

Prasad, Beni, *The State in Ancient India,* Allahabad, 1928.

Prinsep. J., *Essays on Indian Antiquities*, ed. by E. Thomas, London, 1858.

Puri, B.N., *India in the time of Patañjali*, Bombay, 1968.

———, *Cities of Ancient India*, Delhi, 1966.

———, *India as Described by Early Greek Writers,* Vārāṇasī, 1971.

Rai, R.K., *Vālmīki-Rāmāyaṇa Kośa* (Descriptive Index to the Names and Subjects of *Rāmāyaṇa*), Vārāṇasī, 1965.

———, *Mahābhārata Kośa* (A Descriptive Index to the Names and Subjects in the *Mahābhārata*), Vārāṇasī, 1982.

Rai, U.N., *Prācīn Bhārata Mein Nagara tathā Nāgarika Jīvana*, Allahabad, 1965.

Rapson, E.J. (ed.), *The Cambridge History of India*, vol. I, *Ancient India*, Cambridge, 1922, rept. Delhi, 1962.

———, *Ancient India from the Earliest Times to the first century* AD, Cambridge 1914, rept. Vārāṇasī, 1981.

Raverty, G.H., *Notes on Afghanistan and part of Baluchistan*, London, 1883.

Rawlinson, H.G., *Bactria from the Earliest Times to the Extinction of Bactrio-Greek Rule in the Punjab*, Delhi, 1978.

———, *Intercourse Between India and the Western World from the Earliest Times to the Fall of Rome*, Delhi, 1977.

Raychaudhuri, H.C., *Political History of Ancient India*, 6th edn., Calcutta, 1953.

Ray, N.R., "Technology and Social Change in Early Indian History — A Note posing a Theoretical Question," *Purātattva*, no. 8, 1975-76, pp. 132-38.

Redman, Charles L., *The Rise of Civilization*, New York, 1978.

Renou, L., *Vedic India*, trans. From the French by Philip Spratt, *Classical India*, vol. III, Vārāṇasī, 1971.

Rennell, J., *Memoir of a Map of Hindoostan* (based on M.D. Anville's Maps of Asia and India pub. in 1751-52), London, 1788, with section III corrected and enlarged in 1791 and then pub., London, 1793, 1798.

———, *The Geographical System of Herodotus*, 2nd revd. edn., London, 1830.

Reu, V.N., *Ṛgveda Par Ek Aitihāsik Dṛṣṭi*, Delhi, 1967.

Rhys Davids, T.W., *Buddhist India*, Delhi, 1971.

Robertson, W., *An Historical Disquisition Concerning Ancient India*, 1st edn. Edinburgh, 1818, rept. Delhi, 1981.

Rockhill, W.W., *The Life of the Buddha*, London, 1907.

Rose, H.A., *Glossary of the Tribes and Castes of the Punjab and North-West Flontier Province,* 3 vols., Lahore, 1919.

Rostovtzeff, M., *Social and Economic History of the Hellenistic World*, vol. I, Oxford, 1972.

Roy, B.P., *Political Ideas and Institutions in the Mahābhārata*, Calcutta, 1975.

Roy, T.N., *The Ganges Civilization*, Delhi, 1983.

Ruben, W., "The Development of the Town in Ancient India," in *History and Society*, ed. by D.P. Chattopadhyaya, Calcutta, 1978, pp. 229-30.

Sankalia, H.D., *Prehistory and Protohistory of India and Pakistan*, Poona, 1974.

———, *Indian Archaeology Today*, Bombay, 1962.

———, *Akhaṇḍa Bhārata Mein Saṁskṛti Kā Uṣāḥ Kāla*, Vārāṇasī, 1981.

Sāṅkṛtyāyana, R., *Pāli Sāhitya Kā Itihāsa*, Lucknow, 1973.

———, *Ṛgvedic Āryans*, Allahabad, 1957.

———, *Purātattva Nibandhāvali*, Allahabad, 1939.

———, *Buddhacaryā*, Vārāṇasī, 1952.

Śāstrī, A.M., *India as seen in the Bṛhat Saṁhitā of Varāhamihira*, Vārāṇasī, 1969.

Schoff, W.H., "The Name of the Erythrean Sea," *JAOS*, New Haven, vol. XXXIII, 1913, pp. 349-62.

Schwartzberg, J.E. (ed.), *Historical Atlas of South Asia*, Chicago, 1978.

Sen, Chitrabhanu, *Ancient Peoples of the Punjab* (Eng. trans. of two articles of J. Przyluski, originally pub. in French in the *Journal Asitique*, Paris, 1926, and 1929, rept. *Indian Studies: Past and Present*, Calcutta, 1960.

Shafer, R., *Ethnography of Ancient India*, Wiesbaden, 1954.

Sharma, G.R., *The Excavations at Kauśāmbī*, 1957-59, Allahabad, 1960.

Sharma, R.P., *Paurāṇic Kośa*, Vārāṇasī, VS 2028.

Sharma, R.S., *Aspects of Political Ideas and Institutions in Ancient India*, Delhi, 1968.

———, "Decay of Gangetic Towns in Gupta and post-Gupta Times," PIHC, 33rd session, Muzaffarpur, 1972, pp. 94-104.

———, "Iron and Urbanization in the Gaṅgā Basin," *IIHR*, vol. I, no. 1, 1974, pp. 98-103.

———, "Class Formation and its material Basis in the upper Gangetic Basin (*c*. 1000-500 BC)," *IHR*, vol. II, no. 1, 1975, p. 2f.

———, "The Later Vedic Phase and the Painted Grey Ware," *Purātattva*, no. 8, 1975-76, pp. 63-68.

———, *Urban Decay in India, c. AD 300-1000*, Delhi, 1987.

Singh, G.P., *Political Thought in Ancient India*, Delhi, 1993.

———, *Early Indian Historical Tradition and Archaeology*, Delhi, 1994.

———, "The Role of the Brāhmaṇas in Anti-Alexander Movement in North-West India *c*. 326-325 BC," *SHC*, vol. 3, no. 1, March 1995, pp. 1-7.

———, "The Dionysiaka: A Classical (Greek) Source of History of Ancient India," *Shodhak*, JHR, vol. 28, pt. A, Sr.82, 1999, pp. 1-3.

———, "Early History of North-West India as Described by the Greek and Assyrian Travellers," *JIH* (Platinum Jubilee Volume), pp. 41-52.

Singh, M.R., *A Critical Study of the Geographical Data in the Early Purāṇas*, Calcutta, 1972.

Sinha, B.C., *Studies in Alexander's Campaigns*, Vārāṇasī, 1973.

Sinha, B.P. (ed.), *Potteries in Ancient India*, Patna, 1969.

———, *Archaeology and Art of India*, Patna, 1979.

Sircar, D.C., *Studies in the Geography of Ancient and Medieval India*, Delhi, 1971.

Sircar, S.C., *Some Aspects of the Earlier Social Life of India*, London, 1928.

Sjoberg, G., *The Preindustrial City of Past and Present,* New York, 1960.

Smith, V.A., *The Early History of India from 600 BC to the Muhammadan Conquest*, revd. by S.M. Edwards, 4th edn. London, 1967.

———, "The position of the Autonomous Tribes of the Punjab Conquered by Alexander the Great," *JRAS*, 1903, p. 685 f.

———, *The Oxford History of India*, revd. by H.G. Rawlinson, Oxford, 1908, 3rd Indian rept. Delhi, 1981.

Speir, C., *Phases of Indian Civilization,* Delhi, 1973.

Steel, F.A., *India Through the Ages: A Popular and Picturesque History of Hindustan*, Delhi, 1976.

Stein, M.A., *Memoir on Maps Illustrating the Ancient Geography of Kashmir*, ASB, Calcutta, 1899 (reptd. from *JASB*, vol. LXVIII, pt. I, extra no. 2, 1899), Patna, 1977.

———, *Archaeological Reconnaissances in North-Western India and South-Eastern Iran*, London, 1937.

———, *On Alexander's Track to the Indus*, London, 1929.

———, "Alexander's Campaign on the Indian North-West Frontier," *Geog. Jour.*, no. 70, 1927, pp. 417-39.

———, "An Archaeological Tour in Upper Swat and Adjacent Hill Tracts," MASI, no. 42, 1930.

——, "The site of Alexander's Passage of the Hydespes and the Battle with Porus," *Geog. Jour.*, no. 8, 1932, pp. 31-46.

——, "An Archaeological Tour in Gedrosia," *MASI*, no. 43, 1931.

——, "On Alexander's Route to Gedrosia," *Geog. Jour.*, vol. 102, nos. 5-6, 1943, pp. 193-227.

Tarn, W.W., *The Greeks in Bactria and India*, Cambridge, 1938.

——, *Alexander the Great*, 2 vols., Cambridge, 1950.

Thakur, V.K., *Urbanisation in Ancient India*, Delhi, 1981.

——, "Role of Iron in the Origin of second Urbanisation in India: A Resurvey of Evidence," PIHC, Bodh Gaya session, 1981, pp. 61-69.

——, "Town in Kālidāsa: A Note," PIHC, 57th session, Madras, 1996, pp. 159-69.

——, "Regional Patterns of Early Medieval Formation in India: A Study of Gupta Towns," Presidential Address, section I, Ancient India, IHC, 58th session, Bangalore, 1997.

Thapar, R., *A Hsitory of India*, vol. I, Penguin Books, Baltimore, 1966.

——, *The Past and Prejudice*, Delhi, 1975.

——, *From Lineage to State: Social Formations in the Mid First Millennium BC in the Gaṅgā Valley*, Bombat, 1984.

Tod, J., *Annals and Antiquities of Rajasthan*, vol. I, London, 1829, rept. Delhi, 1971.

Toynbee, A. (ed.), *Cities in Destiny*, London, 1967.

Tozer, H.F., *A History of Ancient Geography,* Oxford, 1897, rept. 2nd edn. Delhi, 1975.

Tripathi, R.S., *History of Ancient India*, Delhi, 1985.

Tripathi, V., *The Painted Grey Ware: An Iron Age Culture of Northern India*, Delhi, 1976.

Trotter, L.J. and Hutton, W.H., *History of India from the Earliest Times to the Present Day*, Delhi, 1975.

Upādhyāya, B.S., *India in Kālidāsa*, Delhi, 1968.

Vedavācaspati, A.P., *Vedon Ke Rājanitika Siddhānta* (A Study in Vedic Polity), Delhi, 1983.

Vogel, J.Ph., "Notes on Ptolemy," *BSOAS*, vol. XIV, pt. I, p. 84.

Waddell, L.A., *Report on the Excavations at Pāṭaliputra*, Calcutta, 1903.

Warmington, E.H., *The Commerce Between the Roman Empire and India*, Cambridge, 1928.

Weber, A., *History of Indian Literature*, Eng. trans. from the second German edn. by J. Mann and Th. Zachariae, London, 1882, rept. Delhi, 1981.

Wheeler, J.T., *India from the Earliest Ages* (Hindu, Buddhist and Brahmanical Revival), vol. III of *The History of India*, Delhi, 1973.

——, "Greek and Roman India," reptd. from his *The History of India from the Earliest Ages,* London, 1881, in *Ancient India, (supra)*, Delhi, 1983, pp. 97-139.

Wheeler, M., *Early India and Pakistan to Ashoka*, revd. edn. London, 1968.

——, *Civilization of the Indus Valley and Beyond*, London, 1966.

——, *Five Thousand years of Pakistan*, London, 1950.

——, *Charasada*, Oxford, 1962.

Wilson, H.H., *Notes on the Indika of Ctēsias*, OUP, Oxford, 1836.

——, *The Hindu History of Kashmir*, Calcutta, 1960.

——, *Ariana Antiqua: A Descriptive Account of the Antiquities and Coins of Afghanistan*, London, 1841, rept. Delhi, 1971.

## Journals and Periodicals

*Ancient India — Bulletin of the Archaeological Survey of India*, New Delhi.

*Annals of the Bhandarkar Oriental Research Institute*, Poona.

*Antiquity — A Quarterly Review of Archaeology*, Cambridge.

*Asiatic Researches.*

*Bulletin of the School of Oriental and African Studies*, London.

*The East and the West* (New Series), Calcutta.

*Epigraphia Indica*, Delhi.

*Geographical Journal*, London.

*Herald*, Delhi.

*Indian Archaeology — A Review*, Delhi.

*Indian Culture — Journal of the Indian Research Institute*, Calcutta.

*Indian Historical Quarterly,* Calcutta, new reprint, Delhi.

*Indian Historical Review,* Journal of the Indian Council of Historical Research, New Delhi.

*Indian Museum Bulletin*, Calcutta.

*Indian Antiquary*, Journal of Oriental Research, Bombay.

*Indian Studies*, Wien.

*Indian Studies: Past and Present*, Calcutta.

*Journal of the American Oriental Society.*

*Journal of the Asiatic Society* (New Series), Calcutta.

*Journal of the Asiatic Society of Bengal*, Calcutta.

*Journal of the Asiatic Society of Bombay* (New Series), Bombay.

*Journal Asiatique,* Paris.

*Journal of the Bhāratīya Itihāsa Adhyayan Saṁsthān*, Allahabad.

*Journal of the Bihar and Orissa Research Society*, Patna.

*Journal of the Bombay Branch of the Royal Asiatic Society*, Bombay.

*Journal of the Economic and Social History of the Orient.*

*Journal of the Ganganath Jha Research Institute*, Allahabad.

*Journal of the Gujarat Research Society.*

*Journal of the Historical Research,* Jaipur.

*Journal of the Indian History,* Trivandrum.

*Journal of the Numismatic Society of India*, Vārāṇasī.

*Journal of the Pāli Text Society,* London.

*Journal and Proceedings of the Asiatic Society of Bengal*, Calcutta.

*Journal of the Royal Asiatic Society of Bengal*, Calcutta.

*Journal of the Royal Asiatic Society of Bengal* (Letters), Calcutta.

*Journal of the Royal Geographical Society,* London.

*Journal of the Royal Asiatic Society of Great Britain and Ireland,* London.

*Journal of the UP Historical Society,* Lucknow.

*Memoirs of the Archaeological Survey of India*, Calcutta.

*Modern Review*, Calcutta.

*Purāṇa, Half Yearly Bulletin of the Purāṇa Department*, All India Kāśīrāj Trust, Rāmnagar, Vārāṇasī.

*Purātattva*.

*Studies in History and Culture,* Journal of the Post-Graduate Deptt. of History, Berhampur University.

*Town Planning Review*, Liverpool.

## Proceedings and Reports

*Archaeological Survey of India, Annual Reports.*

*Archaeological Survey of Western India, Reports*

Cunningham's *Archaeological Survey of India, Reports.*

*Proceedings of the Asiatic Society of Bengal*, Calcutta.

*Proceedings of the Indian History Congress.*

*Proceedings of the Indian Oriental Conferences.*

*Proceedings of the International Oriental Congress.*

*Proceedings of North-East India History Association.*

## Dictionaries, Encyclopaedias and Gazetteers

*Abhidhāna-rājendra, Jain Prākṛit Encyclopaedia*, Ratlam, 1919.

*Bombay Gazetteers.*

*Dictionary of Pāli Proper Names*, by G.P. Malalasekera, 2 vols., London, 1937-38, rept. Delhi, 1983.

*Encyclopaedia Britannica.*

*Encyclopaedia of Indian Culture*, by R.N. Saletore, vol. I, Delhi, 1981.

*Geographical Dictionary of Ancient and Medieval India*, by N.L. Dey, 2nd edn. Calcutta and London, 1927, rept. 3rd edn. Delhi, 1971.

*The Imperial Gazetteer of India.*

*Sanskrit-English Dictionary,* by Monier Williams, Oxford, 1899, rept. 1951.

*The Students Sanskrit-English Dictionary*, by V.S. Apte, Vārāṇasī, 1968.

# Index